D0435553

Morton Gould

Morton Gould
1913–1996

Morton Gould

AMERICAN SALUTE

★ ★ ★ ★

by Peter W. Goodman

AMADEUS PRESS
Portland, Oregon

Frontispiece photo courtesy of the American Society of Composers, Authors and Publishers.

ISBN 1-57467-055-7

Printed in Hong Kong

Published in 2000 by
Amadeus Press (an imprint of Timber Press, Inc.)
The Haseltine Building
133 S.W. Second Avenue, Suite 450
Portland, Oregon 97204, U.S.A.

Library of Congress Cataloging-in-Publication Data

Goodman, Peter W.
Morton Gould : American salute / by Peter W. Goodman.
p. cm.
Includes discography, bibliographical references, and index.
ISBN 1-57467-055-7
1. Gould, Morton, 1913–1996. 2. Composers—United States—Biography.
I. Title.

ML410.G695 G66 2000
780'92—dc21
[B]

99-059948

For Debbie,
who made it happen

Contents

★ ★ ★ ★

Foreword

★ ★ ★ ★

PETER GOODMAN'S intrepid and engrossing biography of Morton Gould is a substantial contribution to our understanding of American cultural history.

After all, Gould seemed a living embodiment of "homegrown" music for more than half a century. He played piano in vaudeville houses; he led swing bands in programs over the radio; he won the Pulitzer Prize for composition. He starred in one movie (1945's *Delightfully Dangerous*) and wrote the scores for several others. He composed jingles, concertos, Broadway musicals, and symphonies. One of his last works was *The Jogger and the Dinosaur*, a 1992 concert piece for rap singer and orchestra; another late composition was a piece for President Clinton to play on the saxophone.

Arturo Toscanini and Leopold Stokowski led music by Morton Gould; decades later, so did Michael Tilson Thomas and Leonard Slatkin. As a conductor, Gould himself made more than one hundred recordings of everything from Rimsky-Korsakov to Charles Ives to George Gershwin to mambo. He was as comfortable in a theater pit as he was onstage at Carnegie Hall.

He was also a genuinely nice man—courteous, funny, interested, approachable, a terrific raconteur, a generous colleague. One recalls Will Rogers's famous comment about never having met a man he didn't like; for my part, I can safely say that I never met a man who didn't like Morton Gould.

"Composing is my life blood," Gould once wrote. "Although I

have done many things in my life—conducting, arranging, playing piano, and so on—what is fundamental is my being a composer, which has shaped everything else rather than the other way around."

Gould was a practicing musician for more than seventy years. Long before the advent of so-called classical jazz and fusion, he was already hard at work creating something similar with a zest, ease, and panache that later theorists could only envy.

His work ranges from the irrepressible exuberance of such early compositions as the *Latin American Symphonette* and *American Salute* through the more austere structures of the *Jekyll and Hyde Variations* and on through such sonic spectaculars as *Venice* and *Vivaldi Gallery*, with their divided orchestras and sumptuous scoring. There were half a dozen symphonies, concertos for piano, violin, viola, flute, for two pianos, for four guitars, and even—on one memorable occasion—for tap dancer. A valuable legacy, to be sure.

Of course, few of us knew the darker sides of Gould—about his long depressions, his nagging doubts, his persistent sense that somehow, despite everything, he had failed. Gallant to the end, Morton always seemed unflappable; he would never have let on to his periodic unhappiness, for fear of dragging somebody else into the middle of it.

Yet, now that he is gone, it is right that the full story be told and Peter Goodman—with his splendidly honed reportorial skills, his musical ear and open mind, and his ability to tell an epic story—is the perfect chronicler. Indeed, Gould himself, shortly before he died, selected Goodman as his biographer, and we may count ourselves fortunate that the two men were able to have so many long, candid, detailed, and wide-ranging discussions in the limited time they shared together. This is no hagiography, but rather an empathetic but unsparing portrait of a full man, with all the complexities and contradictions any such portrait ensures.

Shortly after Gould's death in 1996, I happened to pay a visit to Frances Richard, the director of symphonic and concert music at the American Society of Composers, Authors and Publishers in New York and a warm and tireless supporter of young musicians. Gould had served as the president of ASCAP from 1986 to 1994, and his photographic image now gazed benignly down on us throughout our conversation. "I want to keep him around," Fran offered as explanation, with a wistful smile.

So did we all—and Peter Goodman's biography helps summon back his spirit.

Tim Page
St. Louis
4 October 1999

Preface

★ ★ ★ ★

THIS BOOK was my wife's idea.

We had met Morton Gould and Claire Speciner at various events during the course of my work as a critic for *Newsday*, a suburban Long Island–based newspaper. I had reviewed his music, had written about him, had spoken with him about other composers and musical figures, and had even conducted an interview with him for the newspaper's short-lived cable television station.

And so it seemed natural, to her, that Gould, a native of New York City and longtime resident of Long Island, would be an appropriate subject for me, also a native New Yorker and longtime resident of Long Island. Eventually, I saw the light.

I did not approach Morton until the spring of 1993, at the Van Cliburn Competition in Fort Worth, Texas. His *Ghost Waltzes* was the competition's mandatory contemporary composition, and I was covering the event for *Newsday*. He was encouraging when I broached the subject of a biography over lunch; he did not tell me at the time that there had already been two such projects, neither of which had succeeded.

The work did not begin until late the next year, when Morton gave me copies of taped interviews made almost ten years before by Andrew Kazdin and Roy Hemming—the vestiges of the first of the previous attempts. I transcribed them and then attended the Kennedy Center Honors in Washington, D.C., in December 1994, to write about it for *Newsday*. Shortly thereafter I began interviewing Morton myself.

We talked on a weekly basis for several months, over the phone and in person. Morton was always gracious and generous with his time and assistance. We spent many hours in the living room of his home on Shoreward Drive in Great Neck, on the telephone, in the car; he also provided me with names, addresses, and phone numbers of sources. I then began interviewing Gould family members, friends, and colleagues. A complete list of these interviews, most of them taped, is included at the end of the book.

The unexpected and very sad climax of our work together took place in February 1996, during a visit to the Disney Institute in Orlando, Florida. Gould ran one rehearsal, attended one concert, and then collapsed and died the next morning. Once the shock had faded, *Newsday* granted me a three-month leave during which, with the remarkably candid and forthcoming cooperation of Morton's four children and his grandchildren, I spent day after day examining the extensive information in Morton's house. My family was sustained during those months by a gift from Sara Axel, who glorifies the title "mother-in-law."

This book would have been impossible without the unstinting cooperation of the Goulds: Morton himself; his brothers Walter and Stanley; his sisters-in-law Matty, Betty, and Zara; his children, Eric and his wife, Candy, David and his wife, Laurie, Abby Gould Burton and her husband, Stuart, and Deborah; and the grandchildren, Jessica, Jocelyn, and Benjamin Gould, Bryan and Connor Gould, and Jeremy and Eli Burton. Nor can I forget the openness and warmth of his beloved companion, Claire Speciner. They welcomed me into the family with open arms and the full-throated contentiousness that I came to recognize as the Gould family trademark. Eric was the sober-minded one, David the historian and philosopher, Abby the one whose tenacity and determination provided glimpses of their mother, and Deborah, with coffee and crullers at Shoreward Drive, the congenial hostess and, unfortunately, the one who suffered the terrible blow of being with her father when he died.

The Gould home contained the largest extant collection of information about his life. The basement was filled with file cabinets, boxes of published and unpublished scores, crates of recordings, and other information about a very long and eventful life in music. There were closets packed with records and notebooks, and drawers full of letters and other correspondence. From the letters I was able to reach many more of Morton's old friends and associates, dating back to his childhood in Richmond Hill, Queens.

Among the most important sources in the Gould household was a series of scrapbooks filled with clippings, dating from the earliest press notices concerning a young prodigy in Richmond Hill; these were kept initially by Morton's mother, Frances, and were eventually supplemented by various clipping services. There were also copies of virtually every one of his records, in 78, 33⅓, audiotape, and compact disc format, as well as tape recordings of airchecks, concert performances, and even gatherings of Gouldiana sent in by fans. When the house was sold in the fall of 1996, the archival information was sent to the Library of Congress, where it will eventually be cataloged. Each of the children also possessed gleaming nuggets, including photographs, programs, and other memorabilia.

Besides the printed information in the Gould household, there were three important sources of tape-recorded information. Two of them are straightforward: the Kazdin-Hemming tapes mentioned previously, made from August 1985 through March 1986, and my own interviews from December 1994 through the final flight to Florida, in February 1996. Both of these collections focus on the events of Morton's life (and it is remarkable how accurate his memory was compared with printed records when they were located). The Kazdin-Hemming tapes are valuable, among other things, for their concrete information about Morton's early life and because whenever Gould tried to gloss over an incident, Kazdin forced him to stick to the subject; often, when Morton's voice is heard in this book, it may be traced to these tapes.

In addition, there is a third set of tapes that I did not know existed until his daughter Abby described it after Morton's death: the reminiscences and notes he dictated into an Olympus Pearlcorder 200 microcassette player from October 1982 through January 1996. In this extraordinary diary he described daily doings and family life; related his dealings with both his wives and with other women; offered reflections on the people he worked with; and posted hour-by-hour listings of his work schedule. Occasionally he spoke directly to the supposed listener, and his discretion was so ingrained that he never mentioned the names of his women, nor the colleagues with whom he fought. Anticipating that his children would listen, he painstakingly mentioned every one, and the grandchildren too, at virtually every entry, being careful not to leave out a single name. The diary's greatest value is the picture it gives of a man deeply disappointed by life, even as he struggled to recognize that he had led a very good one.

This diary I also transcribed. It's an indication of how discreet and private this ostensibly candid man was that, although he made constant entries during the periods when others were interviewing him, Morton never mentioned the diary's existence, nor did he dwell on our work in his own entries.

All together, the tapes provided both an outline and a map: an outline of the events of Gould's life, and a map showing where other information might be found. The Gould family has the copies of the Kazdin-Hemming tapes and the diary. I have the tapes and notes of the dozens of interviews I made with the Goulds and others.

These were not the only taped records. In 1990 Gould and Agnes De Mille made an audiotape concerning their 1948 collaboration on *Fall River Legend*. Composer Ellen Taaffe Zwilich, who held the Carnegie Hall Composer's Chair at the time, conducted a videotaped interview on 10 November 1995 for the Carnegie Hall archives, which archivist Gino Francesconi let me view. David Gould also videotaped an oral history with his father in December 1991.

Among the most important outside sources were the archives of the New York Philharmonic, efficiently and agreeably attended by archivist Barbara Hawes, and the scrapbooks, microfilms, and correspondence files at the New York Public Library of the Performing Arts at Lincoln Center. Here were copies of reviews, program books, and the letters Morton wrote to Alexander Smallens. Information from the diary of Abby Whiteside was provided by Sophia Rosoff, president of the Abby Whiteside Foundation. Morton's letters to Whiteside are in the Gould collection. Information about Gould's recording career came from BMG, successor to RCA, provided by archivists Claudia Depkin and Mike Fitzell; and from Sony Classical, successor to Columbia, compiled by catalog manager Warren Wernick.

The history of Richmond Hill was obtained from files at the Richmond Hill branch of the Queensborough Public Library. Morton's report card from the Institute of Musical Art came from the Juilliard

School, through the kindness of chief publicist Janet Kessin; and his Richmond Hill High School report card was studied at the school in the office of principal Susan Feldman. Information about Woodstock was found in the Woodstock Library, particularly from *Byrdcliffe and the Maverick*, an unpublished 1960 Yale University master's thesis by Allen Staley; *Woodstock: History and Hearsay* by Anita M. Smith; and town historian Alf Evers's *Woodstock: History of an American Town*. Sophia Rosoff performed the invaluable service of extracting and typing the relevant entries from Abby Whiteside's diary. Sandy Fralin at the University of Louisville found and provided information about Gould's reception by the Louisville Symphony commissioning committee.

Finally, I must again thank my wife, Debbie, who endured the kvetching of a writer in the house, comforted me when I was down, and cheered me when I was up. And my sons, Leo and Stephen, who didn't complain very much at all.

CHAPTER 1

Starting Over

★ ★ ★ ★

ISIDOR GOLDFELD landed in the Port of New York on 30 May 1910. According to the passenger ship manifest, he was twenty-eight, stood five feet, seven inches tall, had the equivalent of $50 in his pocket, was a subject of the Austro-Hungarian Empire, and had been born and raised in the Bulgarian port city of Routscheck (now known as Ruse).

But this was America, where a man could start life over again, and it didn't take long for Isidor Goldfeld's identity to blur. Within seven years, he had padded his age by a year, found a new birthplace, and chosen a new name. For, when he signed his declaration of intention to seek American citizenship, Isidor Goldfeld had become an upper-middle-class native of Vienna, Austria, and the name he went by was James.

Dapper and charming, he wore spats, carried a cane, and loved to waltz and romance the ladies. He enjoyed reminiscing about life in the city of the Hapsburgs. He said he was the eldest son of a wealthy Jewish family that ran steamboats on the Danube; that he had been baptized Catholic to have an Army career; that he had served in the emperor's guard; that he had seduced someone's wife, fought a duel, and fled.

Had he really fought a duel? (Grandson Eric thought it strange that the scar was on his leg.) Was he indeed the black sheep of the family trying to eradicate his shame? How did he choose to become James Harry Gould? He would mumble and evade. "Who cares?" his eldest son, a true American, said to me in 1995. "What difference does it make? The only thing relevant is what is now." America was the place of hope, the land of new beginnings, the perfect spot for someone who depended on manner and bearing. The past was a husk to be either discarded or embellished. So he was originally Isidor Goldfeld of Routscheck, Bulgaria, not James Harry Gould of Vienna. So what? How many millions of immigrants took on new identities when they came to these shores? What counted was what he did starting in May 1910.

Goldfeld-Gould brought the man he had been along to this new place. Whatever the truth, the man he was and the man he had been had a powerful effect on his family. It was felt most strongly by Morton, his eldest son, who rose to become one of the most prominent of American composers but never quite became the man he thought *he* was supposed to have been.

James Gould's first years in his new world are draped in fog, glimpsed in the stories he told and the hints he dropped. When he landed in Hoboken, Gould had no connections in the United States. On board ship, he had met members of a German-Jewish family named Fischer, who owned some grocery stores, but he did not connect with them immediately on arrival.

Later he told of grinding poverty and good luck, how he lived on bananas for so long that later, according to one daughter-in-law, "he couldn't even look a banana in the face." A former Army buddy, now a waiter, recognized him in a restaurant and gave him a place to live. They would walk miles from Second Street in Manhattan to an apartment in the Bronx, to save the streetcar fare. He worked for a while as a violinist in the Yiddish theater.

And also, in the first of several health crises that had a lasting effect on his family, James Gould came down with pneumonia. He told Morton he was taken to Bellevue Hospital but "escaped."

During those first two years Gould made his first grab at the brass ring. This initial experience encapsulated James Gould's life as a businessman: brilliant ideas, terrible execution. James had brought from Austria an engraved wooden compact, useful as a holder for cigarettes or lipstick. He took it to the makers of Lucky Strike cigarettes. The company ordered thousands, for a Christmas premium—James's fortune was made! He wired gleefully to Austria. But these were handmade items. It would take years to fill the order. How could they possibly make enough for Christmas? And so the deal fell through.

A salesman never stops. James made an income somehow, for he never wound up in the seething tenements of lower Manhattan. He finally met up with the Fischers again and worked as a clerk in their Hoboken store before moving to Richmond Hill, where the families became close friends.

He got sick again and traveled to the Catskill Mountains to recover. "He met first my mother's brother, Louie, who was up there and introduced him to his sister," Morton told me on 4 February 1996. "And she lived in Jamaica, Queens." Within a couple of years James had married Louie's sister, the pretty Frances Arkin. Born on 25 April 1889, in Grodno, in the Polish part of the Russian Empire, she had come to the United States at the age of two; by the time she met James she was already a young career woman, working in Manhattan as a Dictaphone operator.

Frances Arkin left her job after marriage, but it wasn't the last time she had to work. Her feckless husband's reach continually exceeded his grasp. He had caviar tastes on a sardine budget, and it was often left to others to keep the roof over their heads and the food on their table.

The Goulds' first home was at 619 Stoothoff Avenue, half a block south of Jamaica Avenue in Richmond Hill, a rapidly urbanizing community in Queens County, New York, around the corner from a grocery store owned by Herman Fischer. The Goulds lived on the second floor of a two-story building of red-orange brick on the east side of the street. Their first three children were born here: Morton, on 10 December 1913; Alfred, on 23 June 1915; and Walter, on 12 April 1917.

Not every new American stopped in the Lower East Side or Hell's Kitchen or Little Italy. Hundreds of thousands of immigrants left New York as fast as they could, traveling to New England or the cities along the East Coast, or to the farms and factories of the Midwest. James Gould did not go that far. He found a place within New York's borders that offered rural pleasures, urbanity, and easy access to the city itself. Richmond Hill was one of the first suburbs, and it was just beginning to explode.

Richmond Hill had been founded in 1868 by Manhattan attorney Albon Platt Man and his artist friend Edward Richmond. They chose a wooded upland in south central Queens County, near the site of a Revolutionary War skirmish, bought about four hundred acres of farmland, and named the new village after either Richmond himself or the London neighborhood of the same name (the origin is not clear).

Queens County—not yet a part of the city of New York—was primarily gently rolling farm country that fed the growing colossus across the East River. Richmond Hill was crossed by thoroughfares that led from the eastern farmlands to the markets of Brooklyn and Manhattan; its primary avenue was the Brooklyn-Jamaica Plank Road, later Jamaica Avenue. The area grew steadily as the city prospered. The Mans donated land for the first church, school, and public library and eventually for the Richmond Hill Station of the Long Island Rail Road, at the corner of Myrtle Avenue and Lefferts Boulevard.

With its pleasant commercial avenues, broad, tree-shaded side-streets, and spacious homes with enclosed porches, Richmond Hill was a comfortable place to live. Stoothoff Avenue ran south of the Jamaica Plank Road; to the north it was called Elm Street. The civic activist Jacob Riis lived on 121st Street. In 1900 President Theodore Roosevelt, whose own home was not far away in Oyster Bay, took the railroad to Richmond Hill for the wedding of Riis's daughter Kate. The station was then one of the railroad's busiest commuter stops (finally drained of passengers by the nearby subway lines, it was closed down for lack of business in 1998).

There was still plenty of farmland; farmers' wagons were common on Jamaica Avenue, the horses plodding slowly to the East River, their owners asleep at the reins. But expansion was well under way by the time James and Frances Gould rented their first apartment. The Richmond Hill Public Library, a classic yellow-brick Carnegie library, had opened a few years before. There was a trolley line on Jamaica Avenue, and the first movie theater, the Owl, had opened in 1910 on the corner of Jamaica Avenue and 113th Street (within a few years, there were four theaters in a three-block stretch).

The Brooklyn Rapid Transit Company announced plans in 1913 to build nearby, so the merchants of Jamaica Avenue fought for an elevated line above their street, too. By 1917, the El had gotten to

111th Street; the next year, it was open to 168th Street—making it possible to travel by train from Richmond Hill across the Williamsburg Bridge right into Manhattan. Sewers were extended to the area in 1913. Jamaica Avenue was being paved, first with Belgian block cobblestones. Little Morton enjoyed watching as the pavement was gradually widened.

This was a community in transition (in 1897 Richmond Hill had merged with seven other incorporated villages and forty-eight municipalities to become the City of Greater New York). Immigrants—Germans, Irish, a few Italians, and fewer Jews—began moving in among the substantial residences of Albon Man's middle class. The schools were getting crowded. By 1916 Richmond Hill High School, which had opened only in 1899, was bursting with a student population of 1146.

It was always a struggle for James to maintain the trappings of middle-class life. In May 1995 Morton recalled how, when he was very young, their piano was repossessed. His mother began to cry, and the mover chided her, "Young girl, don't cry about this. You have a healthy child, that's more important than a piano." That instrument was soon replaced, for James was a hustler. But the pattern pressed itself deeply into the mind of the firstborn child: economic insecurity, coupled with worries about his father's health.

Stoothoff Avenue ran south to Atlantic Avenue, on the railroad's main line. During World War I American doughboys frequently marched down the roadway to and from an armory on Atlantic. Morton's friends told him they were German troops and warned him that if he ever saw them turn his way, he'd "better get ready to leave." Morton remembered himself as a timorous child, the troops marching past while a gullible toddler watched from a crowd of teasing six- and seven-year-olds. The home front had a powerful effect on him, from the games they played, wearing soldiers' and nurses' uniforms, in child-sized trenches, to the parading and the frequent sound of military and American Legion bands in the air.

Gould's earliest memories were a vivid mix of patriotism and music. There was even a charming prescience at his birth, when a neighboring family named Duncan brought the newborn a present: a ceramic bowl on which was painted a boy conducting a tiny orchestra. Gould kept it in his studio until he died.

Music was not their life, but it was an important part of the Gould household. James had wooed Frances with his violin, and there was that player piano, complete with rolls of popular light classics: Franz von Suppé's *Light Cavalry Overture* and *Poet and Peasant Overture*, Rachmaninoff's Prelude in C sharp minor, Sousa marches, Chopin polonaises, Strauss waltzes—and Christian Sinding's *The Rustle of Spring*. In 1995 Gould told composer Ellen Taaffe Zwilich, "If I dig deep, that is the favorite piece. To me, it's the best thing ever done."

Morton responded from the beginning. "Even as a baby in the high chair, I would listen to the rolls and react," he told Andrew Kazdin and Roy Hemming in 1985. One day, when he was four or five, Frances heard the piano in the living room. When she investigated, she found little Morton playing away, imitating what he had heard.

That's the story Morton Gould himself told. But while James was managing Morton's career, the old man made himself the center. According to a piece by T. R. Kennedy (*The New York Times*, 20 May 1945), James said that it was he who returned from work to hear "a distorted rendition" of "The Stars and Stripes Forever" coming from the living room. He walked in only to discover "that the music came from the piano but the youngster's chubby fingers were making it, not the roll." James Gould also claimed he found a scrap of paper on which young Morton "had scribbled marks like notes on a musical staff," a melody his son was able to play for him.

Here, as elsewhere, the father may have tried to insinuate himself where he hadn't actually been. Morton told a different story to another reporter. In an article that ran in the Forest Hills–Kew Gardens *Post* (12 December 1941), he recalled a night late in 1918 when it was rumored that World War I had ended. The city exploded: whistles, cheers, bands playing, all sorts of tumult. "I sat down and did some things I'll never forget," he said. "Something quite apart from myself just made exultant sounds come from that piano. I was only five, but I believe I remember to this day the exact form which the musical pattern suggested by those screaming whistles had in my mind."

In Frances Gould's version (*Long Island Daily Press*, 17 December 1938), James did play a role. Morton was five and James was away on business: "Morton was heartbroken," she said. "He told me he was lonesome and then went over to the piano and played a melody. 'That's how I feel,' he said."

The family seized on his talent immediately. By 1919 Morton had begun taking lessons from Ferdinand Greenwald, a local piano teacher. He was a handsome man and a good musician who, however, did not teach his young pupil how to read music. "Whenever I would play," Gould said during a trip through the old neighborhood on 7 May 1995, "I would have music, and people would turn the pages for me." The trick worked until his first encounter with a genuine, Vienna-trained pedagogue at the Institute of Musical Art a few years later.

Greenwald was involved in Morton's first acknowledged composition, the title page of which reads "Just Six, Valse Viennese, by Morton Gould, age six years." The cover includes a photograph of the boy at the piano, hair neatly slicked down and parted on the left, in homemade shorts and sailor shirt, with a frown on his face. Greenwald was the publisher and owned the copyright.

Morton refused to be proud of that childish composition—"It was pretty awful," he said. But it is a simple, sweet little waltz, with just a touch of schmaltz, nothing to be ashamed of. Perhaps Morton didn't write it at all. He was so short he couldn't reach the pedals without a special extension. Maybe he banged out a tune that his father or Greenwald wrote down, harmonized, and advertised as the first product of this budding genius.

By 1921 the Goulds, forced to move from Stoothoff Avenue, were living at 4839 Jamaica Avenue, a corner apartment on the second floor, upstairs from a shoe store and right next to the elevated tracks—a clear step downward. Besides Morton and his two brothers, the household also included Frances's mother and an unmarried sister, Alice, who worked as a milliner. The crowded apartment rattled and shook from the trains. "When the elevated went by," Morton said wryly in 1995, "you couldn't hear yourself sleep or think." A marvelous photograph from the period shows the three older brothers in identical jumpsuits, striding merrily along a street in Richmond Hill. Morton, distinguished by the careful cut of his hair, flashes a beautiful smile. It was during this period that he wrote something entitled "The Jolly Three."

Though things weren't easy, James Gould set out to make a name for his boy. On 10 January 1921, the *New York Globe* held a "prodigy night" at the home of Mr. and Mrs. William Cowen, 65 Central Park West, Manhattan, featuring performances by, among others, pianist Louise Talma, then sixteen; violinist Josef Gingold, then eleven and in the United States for less than a year; and Morton Gould, just turned seven. On 12 January a public recital was held at Stuyvesant High School on East Fifteenth Street. Then, on 14 February, the *New York Evening Journal* ran a photograph, heavily retouched, of Morton at the piano with the special pedals, in a velvet Fauntleroy suit lovingly made for him by his mother. "Boy of Six Composes Popular Waltz," reads the headline.

An unusual talent was developing in Richmond Hill. The following spring, on 17 March 1922, Greenwald's students gave a recital at the Brooklyn Academy of Music, during which Morton and fellow-student Abbie Bertolacci played the overture to *The Marriage of Figaro*. "I assumed that this was a race," he told Zwilich in 1995. "But they told me not to finish before she did." Greenwald had to come out onstage twice to slow him down.

Morton now began to perform in hotels and department stores, which provided some of the earliest anecdotes with which he regaled family and colleagues, such as the "bear concert" incident recounted by daughter Abby.

> Daddy was doing a recital in one of his little velvet suits, and all of a sudden the lights went out. There was this whole auditorium of people listening to him—and he kept playing. He didn't stop, he kept playing, and it kept people calm as a result—he played till the lights were fixed. Afterward people came up and said how wonderful it was that he did this, he kept the audience so calm, and he was such a little kid. They asked, "What made [you] decide to do this?" He said he had to prove to everybody that he wasn't scared of the bears that come out in the dark!

Gould gave his first radio broadcast in 1922, from Bamberger's department store in Newark, New Jersey.

But while Morton was presented by his father as a child prodigy, he also lived a relatively normal life in Richmond Hill. The Goulds spent about four years alongside the El. Then James Gould's own career took a turn for the better, because they moved to 123-17 Hillside Avenue, between 123rd and 124th Streets, only a few blocks away, but definitely a step up. Now they were literally across the tracks, north of both the elevated and the Long Island Rail Road.

It was a two-story house with basement, attic, and backyard, away from the bustle of Jamaica and Atlantic Avenues, on the border between Richmond Hill and the more affluent community of Kew Gardens. The household continued to grow; a fourth brother, Stanley, was born on 9 July 1922. The brothers slept two to a bed in one room—"I believe I slept with Alfred," said Walter. "I don't know whether Morton had his own bed, and I don't remember where we put Stanley." That might be because Walter didn't want to remember. According to Stanley, "The poor bastard who had to sleep with me got soaking wet all the time—and not because I was sweating too much. My brother Walter, I believe, was the biggest victim."

The family knew someone who owned a bakery, and on Saturday nights Walter and Alfred would pick up leftover pastries, a great attraction in the neighborhood. "The kids used to go back," Walter said, "and tell their parents, 'It's great to go over to their house—there's so much cake around that house.' Little did they know!"

"I remember it as a happy family, despite the fact that we never had anything," Walter continued. "I only think of that house, with all the problems we had, as being a very warm house."

"My mother's greatest pride," said Stanley, "was not Morton's talent but that we all got along so well."

Alice Coltman Mayer, born one day after Morton, met him when her family moved to Hillside Avenue while she was in the second grade. "It was a nice neighborhood," she said. "We played on 123rd Street a lot, going up and down with our scooters. We were in and out of each other's houses all the time. His parents were very nice—they liked me and my brother, my parents liked the Gould family. We spent a lot of time together." Mayer may even have been the precocious boy's first girlfriend: decades later, when she heard the choral piece *Quotations*, including a number called "The Lass of Richmond Hill," she said, "I may have been the first one, though I'm sure I wasn't the last."

Morton was always the musical star of the neighborhood. He would practice for hours, before and after school, while everyone in the house had to be quiet. Julia Heuman, a teenage neighbor, would come running at the sound of the piano—only to be met by James, with finger sternly at his lips. Later, Morton would sit in the backyard and compose. The family had one crucial rule: utter silence when Morton was at work. "We were told," Walter said, "that we had to allow him 'x' numbers of hours to practice and [he was] not to be disturbed. We could not be running around the house and making noise if he was practicing."

"All you had to do was whistle," Stanley said, "and someone would call out, 'For Christ sake will you shut up!' So we learned not to whistle, or sing."

Morton's music-making delighted the girls, though. "We would be playing with the scooters," his friend Dorothea Spreckles said, "and when we would get tired, we would go to one of the houses. Because almost everybody had a piano, we would say, 'Morton, play Alice.' And he would sit down and compose a little piece about her. He would do that about anybody."

Neighborhood children attended P.S. 54, on 127th Street and Hillside Avenue. In the early 1920s, P.S. 54 was an old, gaslit wooden building with three-holer latrines. The school was already so crowded that a temporary annex was erected in the back while a new four-story brick school was built (the new structure is still in use). Mayer and Spreckles have sweet memories of Morton playing as the students marched, two by two, in and out of school. But Gould remembered a tough neighborhood full of first-generation Germans, Irish, and Italians. "I think it was an Italian kid, used to come in the window," he remembered. "His mother was always being called up—she was furious, she would fight with the teachers. But he was a danger, because when he got mad at a teacher he would take flower pots and throw them at her."

When Morton was in fourth grade he became a stair monitor, to make sure the other students "didn't skip a stair." And some of them were big—teenagers who'd been left back. "I lasted one day, as I recall," Gould said. "These were kids twice my size. They were shaving, they were waiting to get their working papers and get the hell out of school. I remember saying, 'You skipped a step.' They said, 'So what?' I said, 'Go back down.' They said, 'Make me!' That ended that. The teachers realized literally I was endangering my life."

All his publicity didn't help. One newspaper reported not only that he was a prodigy, but his teacher called him the smartest boy in the class, and his fingers were said to be insured for a million dollars. A group of boys heard about it and lay in wait outside school. "They were standing there with a pair of pliers," he recalled. "And they said, 'Is this you?' I said, 'Yeah'—You never lied, it didn't do you any good." The cop on the corner finally chased the boys away—but only because he saw they had pliers. "They used to beat the crap out of me. Because I was a prodigy, because I played the piano, I was being a sissy," Morton told me on 7 May 1995. "To this day I don't carry a briefcase where you can see I am carrying music in it. I don't take music out in public."

Morton remembered his childhood as one of struggle and humiliation. He found little satisfaction in his own prodigiousness, as if it belonged to others—his father, or his family. Outsiders were unaware of this stream of unhappiness. Sol Katz, son of another Jewish family and a friend of Morton's brother Alfred, knew him as the neighborhood prodigy who was not allowed to play ball. "We played punchball, stickball, basketball, some roller-skate hockey," Katz said. Morton never engaged in any of that: "They worried about his hands." Nevertheless, the boy was not considered a sissy. "No, no, nothing like that," Katz recalled.

Certain important Jewish rituals were observed, such as the elaborate ceremonial dinners called seders during the holiday of Passover, a social occasion as much as a religious event. "I do remember helping my mother during Passover go down to the basement and bring up the Passover dishes," Stanley said. "We had some great seders. My aunts and uncles from Brooklyn would come over. To this day, I remember Uncle Sam sitting on a matzoh and not breaking it."

Typically, Morton's primary memory of his Judaism was of comic humiliation. Once, he told me on that same drive in May 1995, he was surrounded by the usual tormenters: "They wanted to beat me up because I lied. What did I lie about? 'You said that you were Jewish.' I said, 'I am.' They said, 'No you're not.' 'But I am.' 'No you're not! Don't tell us you're Jewish—you lied and we ought to beat the crap out of you for lying to us.' I said, 'Why did I lie?' 'Because Jews wear caps and have beards!'"

But the primary tension was between Catholics and Protestants, including anti-Catholic demonstrations by the Ku Klux Klan during which boys threw eggs at the marchers, and a local priest who warned his parishioners against patronizing Protestant-owned shops. Once, when Morton was pretending he was the Santa Fe's "Super Chief" in his little red wagon, Julia Heuman's father accosted him. "He asked me, how would I like it if the pope came to live in my house," Gould said. "I didn't know what he was talking about, I didn't know who the pope was. All I remember is his saying he would take a machine gun and shoot every Catholic."

CHAPTER 2

The Willful Prodigy

★ ★ ★ ★

NOTHING FURTHER was to be gained from Ferdinand Greenwald, and on 6 January 1923, a month after his ninth birthday, Morton's parents took him to the Institute of Musical Art on Claremont Avenue in upper Manhattan.

The institute had been founded eighteen years before by Frank Damrosch of the pioneering Damrosch family, whose members had founded, directed, or conducted the New York Symphony, the New York Oratorio Society, the Metropolitan Opera, and countless other musical organizations in the city. In 1926, the institute would merge with the Juilliard Graduate School to become the Juilliard School of Music. Admission to the institute was the first step into the musical society of New York.

Morton was examined by Frank Damrosch himself, because the school did not ordinarily accept fourth-graders. Gould related the first of his many memories concerning the institute in 1985: "[Damrosch] came in with a briefcase, he turned the pages for me, he was impressed." The institute's terse report of the audition? "Very talented. Very promising."

The institute, with its distinguished faculty and Teutonic methods, offered entry to the worlds of Brahms, Wagner, and Beethoven. Morton won a scholarship and was assigned to teacher Elizabeth Strauss. It seemed an auspicious beginning, but what should have been an exciting time became a nightmare.

Elizabeth Strauss, on the faculty from 1908 until 1932, had studied in Vienna with the Polish pianist and pedagogue Theodor Leschetizky. "She was," according to a biographical note prepared by Damrosch for a faculty listing, "a woman of strong convictions and conscientious adherence to what she conceived to be the highest ideals of good technique and artistic interpretation."

But Morton had a mind of his own, bathed as he was in the grand ideas of his father and supported by his doting mother. Gould and Strauss were not a comfortable blend. He had weekly half-hour lessons for two and a half years, from 13 January 1923 to 2 June 1925. For the period covering 13 January to 1 June 1923, the school entry reads: "Very gifted. Has a splendid ear and fine sense of rhythm. Progress very satisfactory." From 11 October 1923 to 30 May 1924: "Uneven. Improvement very satisfactory last two months. Is growing in seriousness and ambition." Finally, from 9 October 1924 to 2 June 1925: "Progress very satisfactory early part of year, but unsteady the later part. Too many lapses in application."

Gould considered his time at the Institute of Musical Art a stint in hell. There was the trip itself: to get to the Upper West Side of Manhattan from Richmond Hill required three trains—the Jamaica Avenue Elevated from Richmond Hill over the Williamsburg Bridge to Canal Street; from Canal Street to Broadway; then up Broadway to Morningside Heights, an hour and a half each way. It could not have been easy for an unaccompanied, self-conscious boy. To the end of his life, he refused voluntarily to identify his teacher "because it wouldn't reflect too well on her"—and when the name of Elizabeth Strauss was located, Gould claimed to have forgotten it. "This woman," he said, "was not equipped to deal with a nine-year-old."

It is also possible that this nine-year-old (and ten- and eleven-) was not about to accept a position as just one of many talented youngsters in a tautly disciplined academy. For one thing, he still couldn't read music. Morton had been able to fool observers, including the august Frank Damrosch. But when Strauss found out that he couldn't read or count, "there was hell to pay," as Gould put it. "I had probably one of the most miserable times of my life. [The school was] like a Marine boot camp. . . . At the age of nine I was suicidal. I used to stand on the subway platform and think of throwing myself under the train. I was trapped."

He couldn't learn to count, he said, because if someone cut an apple in half and then in half again, each portion "was still a half." He wanted to compose and improvise, but Strauss wouldn't allow it. She said, "What are you playing? Who do you think you are, Beethoven? If I ever catch you improvising again, you will lose your scholarship. How dare you!" He proudly showed her a new watch. She said, "If you are in such a hurry, go home!" When he got new music on his own, she would rip it up.

The child fought the teacher to a standstill. She wrote notes home; he didn't deliver them—finally she complained that his parents didn't even reply to her messages. Strauss recommended that Morton be tested at the Neurological Clinic, predecessor of the Neurological Institute now associated with Columbia Presbyterian Hospital. Gould suspected Strauss thought there was something wrong with him, but she might just have wanted to learn more about this gifted, difficult boy.

Morton was examined in the spring of 1925 by a team led by Norman Tallman, a doctor who specialized in neuroendocrinology, genetics, and early growth. "They twirled me in a chair, and they gave me blocks," Gould said in 1985. "Then they said they'd like to see the teacher. My parents told her, and the teacher said, 'No. He's crazy, I'm not!'"

"My parents pulled me out of the Institute of Musical Art."

This was the end of Morton Gould's academic musical training, and the start of a lifelong disdain for Juilliard itself. He blamed the lack of formal training, of any depth of schooling, for the insecurity he felt throughout his life. "I was always impressed by people who quote poetry, and all the literature," he said. "I know some of them are idiots. But I envy those who have read everything, who have experienced so many things in the field of knowledge and of culture." Yet he also disliked formal education, whether in the school system or the Institute: "I was a very impatient student, going to public school. I couldn't bear it."

Morton blamed Strauss for the fact that he no longer enjoyed playing the piano. Strauss had assured him that when he was finished, "[he]'d be able to put [his] hands on a plate of glass and break the plate of glass." But Morton hated the "pain is good" approach. "What that had to do with music, I don't know," he said. "I was a really good pianist. I would eat up music: I could memorize a Scriabin sonata in a day."

Gould's parents took him to Rubin Goldmark, an American-born, European-educated pedagogue and composer who headed the composition department at the newly created Juilliard Graduate School. The deeply conservative Goldmark had already taught Aaron Copland and George Gershwin, who found him unsympathetic.

Morton's visit was not fruitful. He was belligerent, he told Zwilich during their 1995 interview, intolerant of whatever was not "modern." "I played him Chopin, and then I played him some Gould. . . . I hit big tone clusters, which about knocked him out of his chair. He said, 'You are probably very gifted. I am an old man, you are a young man, I am happy the way I am, you are happy the way you are. Why don't we leave it at that?'"

Gould was brash and arrogant; he required special handling. His next teacher, however, was a good step forward: Joseph Kardos, a cultured Hungarian who lived on the Upper West Side, whom Morton quickly grew to admire and respect. Kardos was "a wonderful person," Gould said. "We played all the Beethoven symphonies, piano four-hands. He showed me art and literature." (Morton had always been adept at drawing, and there was a time when the boy was not sure which artistic path he would follow.) Kardos provided thrilling intellectual stimulation, exposing Morton, briefly, to the cultural world outside music.

But he continued to compose. And he continued to feel humiliated, as on the February afternoon in 1926 when, returning from a lesson, Gould was accosted by toughs from Hell's Kitchen who stole his money and his train ticket home. "There were four or five of them, and they took off, but they left one kid to guard," Gould told me in 1995. "Then I suddenly got mad, and I hit him, and he yelled, and they came back and then of course they wiped the floor with me." Bruised, bloody, shaken, and crying, Morton found a policeman, who let him onto the subway without paying and sent him on his way.

All along, Morton was performing anywhere James could find. The boy did not relish this activity, and in later years described it in funny, bitter anecdotes. He remembered childishness, not accomplishment—fearfulness and being found ridiculous. There is a parallel here with the experiences of the young Wolfgang Mozart, a prodigy taken by his father to earn money and fame. The comparison was made by Morton's friends and mocked by his enemies.

At some level it may even be warranted. Morton Gould was extraordinarily gifted, and James Gould was an ambitious father. But the paths of the young Morton and the young Wolfgang sheered apart quickly. James Gould had nothing like Leopold Mozart's depth of education and cultural understanding. Leopold had real accomplishment as a composer, performer, and teacher. James Gould had nothing but his son.

The Goulds were not very religious. James, who sloughed off his enforced Catholicism, was essentially an atheist who attended synagogue to please his wife. The younger boys went to religious school, though rarely to Friday or Saturday services. Morton stayed away and always disliked organized religion. But he did participate in one significant ceremony. On 25 December 1926, just after his thirteenth birthday, Morton was "confirmed," a religious ceremony similar to the bar mitzvah, when thirteen-year-old Jewish boys are allowed for the first time to read from the Torah, the first five books of the Bible. He learned the text phonetically and had no idea what it meant. "I remember seeing people crying. That was typical," he said sardonically in 1985.

The years must have darkened Gould's memory, for just after the occasion, he wrote a touching and earnest note to his parents, one that James Gould kept all his life. The letter reveals essential things about Morton's character:

> No words are beautiful enough, no pen delicate enough, no paper fine enough for the words of gratitude that are in my soul. . . . As I go through life, I hope that I will hold you for my example, and that my ideals shall be what yours are, and that your commandments and God's commandments shall be my finished character on the foundation you have already built. . . . My confirmation made me a youth. But, Mother and Daddy dear, my wish is, that to the world, may I be and act like a man, but to you, may I be the same, meek, loving, obedient, son that I was when I depended upon your hands to feed me, and your judgement to guide me.

Meek. Loving. Obedient. These characteristics made him the pillar upon which his parents' family and his own rested. They were also the qualities that may have prevented him from reaching the artistic pinnacles he sought.

Meek. Though he had a fierce temper, in public Gould was shy, modest, and unassuming, a meekness that finally became crippling. Gould lacked the personality that rivals used to drive their own careers.

Loving. Morton's loyalty to and support for his family was an enduring strength. He provided generous help, frequently financial but often emotional as well, to those around him. Cutting tensions arose within the family over who would control that support—his father or his wives. And from the onset of puberty, "love" would have another dimension for Gould. He loved women, and they loved him back. Morton was a champion of sex.

Obedient. Here was the canker that gnawed at his soul. Throughout his long, often distinguished, but in the end unsatisfied life, Gould could not throw off the traces. He never told his father to find another job; he never told his wife to fend for herself; he never locked himself away to commune with the muse.

The pressures that kept him home exerted themselves in the years after his thirteenth birthday, when James Gould's health began to fail once more. Morton had been studying assiduously at P.S. 54 and with Kardos, composing and giving occasional recitals. Upon graduation from P.S. 54 on 27 January 1927, he was one of eleven honor-roll students in a class of thirty-eight. He played his own transcription of Strauss's "Blue Danube" waltz during the ceremony. And he wrote the words and music to the Class Song, a grim warning rather than the heady optimism one might expect from a child of the Roaring Twenties:

> We've been used to the frolics and not to the woes,
> Past thoughts of yesterdays.
> We've climbed the past path without heartbreaking toil.
> The new path is centered on strife.
> We'll be carried and pushed with the worldly swirl,
> For we've entered the path of Life.

One can imagine the youth who wrote this sucking a breath between thin lips, bowing his head, and forging steadily, if not happily, onward.

Morton entered Richmond Hill High School, an overcrowded building with offsite annexes at both P.S. 56 and P.S. 99. A new high school was being built on what is now 114th Street, a block south of the Goulds' first apartment. The cornerstone was laid in 1927, the year Morton graduated from P.S. 54; he left the new building just two years later at the end of his formal schooling.

Morton made some of his deepest friendships at Richmond Hill. Here he met Joseph Prostakoff, a Russian-born bull of a fellow who became Morton's soulmate and intellectual companion. Here he also met David and Sol Berkowitz, musicians who became lifelong colleagues and allies, and Shirley Uzin, who became his first wife.

David's kid brother Sol—he was eight years younger—was known to have perfect pitch, but Morton's own ears were astounding. David asked Sol, "You want to hear perfect, perfect pitch?"—and brought him to Morton's house.

"We each played down a whole armful of notes," Sol said in 1996, "and Morton called out every one. I don't think there's a musician alive who can do that. He had the most incredible ears of any musician I've met, bar none."

Morton and David, who played the violin, formed a small orchestra, which Morton conducted. "They would meet at our house because we had a fairly long living room," Sol Berkowitz said. "They would push all the furniture aside. My brother David and Morton used to go down to Carl Fischer and buy two or three scores on Saturday, and then play them through the next Friday at the house." The repertoire was strictly classical—Haydn symphonies and other fairly simple scores. The rehearsals (which, Walter Gould recalled, also took place occasionally at the Gould residence) continued for a year or two. It was the only baton training Morton had.

James Gould was still working—Morton could not support them all yet—and the siblings told stories of his schemes. He sold batteries and spark plugs to garages, and then to department stores. He tried to persuade a local radio manufacturer to offer sets on the installment plan. "[His] motto was, 'There should be a radio in every home in America!'" said Walter Gould. "They laughed at him—radio was a rich man's thing."

James became involved in a plan to buy and manage the Dixie Hotel in Manhattan; the family would live there. That fell through.

Later he thought he had closed a big real estate deal, but just as they celebrated with a big box of chocolates, James got word that his partner had pulled out. According to an article in *The American Banker* (4 May 1928), he tried to put together a syndicated program about banking, "to spread among a majority of the population of the United States a knowledge of the correct principles of banking and economics." That never came about, either. Did any of James Gould's deals ever work? "Unfortunately," said Walter, "I have to say maybe none he actually did himself, or had on his own. That's why Morton had to start playing."

The whole family pitched in. Aunt Alice's earnings as a milliner went into the household till. Frances Gould sold corsets door to door, and later pots and pans. When he was ten, Walter sold furniture polish door to door; later he became a newsboy. All the money went to Frances, because James tended to spend it too fast. The Goulds were getting by.

The real threat was the matter of James's health. Walter recalled the day the family doctor walked him around the block to explain that his father was being sent to the Valeria Home, a sanitarium in Oscwana, New York, and that he might never come home again. To hear such news would be terrifying enough. But what remained in Morton's soul was even more disturbing.

James Gould had a violent temper that he took out on his wife and children. To Morton, the worst part of these rages was how they would sometimes end, as he recalled in 1985. "He'd get himself into a fit and start to hemorrhage. He'd be on the floor spitting blood and have to go to the hospital, or be put into bed with bloodsoaked towels." Morton was always afraid that one day his father would collapse for good. Where would the family be then?

Just a few years later, in the early 1930s, when Morton was earning a lot of money on radio, he thought of leaving home, but the specter of his father's death held him back. "There were periods I walked away from him," he said, "and didn't talk to him. They could be days, weeks—months, a few times. . . . But I didn't have TB, I didn't have all the things wrong with me that he did. At a certain point in a confrontation he could start to hemorrhage, et cetera, and of course my mother would be left with the patient."

Yet even this obedience haunted Morton, and his self-assessment by 1985 was harsh. He continued, "Had I had a strong enough drive—to break out of this box, to get away from my father completely, to get away from commercial radio, to become a symphony conductor—I would have done it—regardless of whether my father was hemorrhaging, and my mother would collapse over it, because unfortunately that's the way things are done."

Morton paid a heavy price, which showed itself in his constant resentment of the things he was required to do. It may have prevented him from composing his very best works and from getting much pleasure from performance.

"I was always embarrassed to play. I had to be coaxed. And to this day," Gould confessed on 21 August 1985, "I can remember when I resented the fact that my father would want me to play for somebody, would want me to play something. I resented it. I didn't want to do it. And to this day, retrospectively, I resent it."

But he did it. What if his father died, right there, spitting blood on the spot?

CHAPTER 3

A Teacher at Last!

THE MIDDLE TEENS are the years during which adult outlines begin to appear, sketches gaining contour, sculpture emerging from the stone. So with Morton Gould the period from 1927 to 1932 set the course for his life. He met his first love, found his teacher, made his first real trips from home, took the first hard knocks, and started to shoulder fully the family burden.

The Tuesday Morning Musical Club of Douglaston, a group of women from a wealthy suburb on the North Shore of Queens County, had already awarded Morton their first scholarship and offered him recitals. When Morton was around thirteen, the ladies introduced him to Vincent Jones of the School of Education at New York University. The music education department had become a four-year undergraduate program, and Jones had a newly minted Harvard doctorate in the history of music theory. The department, although primarily for teacher training, had a strong performance component. Besides theory, history, and pedagogy, the students also studied with professional musicians. "The faculty," said Gerald Ross, who succeeded Jones as chairman, "was basically adjuncts . . . drawn from top-flight professionals in the city." Jones himself gravitated toward instruction on the highest plane. "He was really a teacher of teachers and professors," Ross said. He also enjoyed improvisation, one of Morton's great skills.

It was from Jones that Morton got the bulk of his education in theory and composition, a fact in which the teacher took great pride.

"He always said, 'I was Morton Gould's first teacher,'" Ross said. "He said that Morton was a genius."

Morton's first love was always composing, and his home was the orchestra. The manuscript of his Rondo Op. 1, from January 1928, bears this inscription: "First composition under the tutorship of Dr. Vincent Jones in Theory and Harmony." The short score for the Suite No. 1, for orchestra, piano, and solo instruments, is marked November 1928, No. 1, Op. 8; it indicates, among other things, that the fourteen-year-old knew about Henry Cowell: it calls for a series of tone clusters, marked "to be played with whole hand across keyboard," "black keys," "all white keys," "hand and arm," and so forth. The score of Nocturne, No. 1, Op. 4, written in late 1928 and early 1929, was presented "to Dr. Jones April 17, 1929."

Although press clippings were full of hyperbole about Morton's studies ("youngest graduate in the history of New York University"), Gould's experience was very modest. He audited a few courses, gave some recitals, and worked privately with Jones. His connection with New York University lasted less than two years.

But there was an incongruity in Gould's experience at NYU, a small, significant flaw: his affiliation was in the school of education, not the liberal arts college. The college music department also had some important new faculty members, Marion Bauer and Martin Bernstein. Bauer, who had studied in Paris under the nearly ubiquitous Nadia Boulanger and others, was an ardent champion of contemporary American music. She was a co-founder of the American Music Guild, sat on the board of the League of Composers, was New York editor of the journal *Musical Leader*, and lectured on issues confronting native musicians. Bauer eventually became chairman of the department. Bernstein too was an important figure in the development of American music and an early supporter of the work of Arnold Schoenberg. But Bauer and Bernstein were musicologists, in the school of arts and sciences—and had virtually no contact with the practical performers in the education school.

In late 1928, Jones introduced Morton to the woman who had been his own teacher, a westerner named Abby Whiteside. Thus began the single most important musical relationship of Gould's life.

Whiteside was born in 1881 in Vermillion, South Dakota. She attended public school there, graduated with highest honors from the University of South Dakota, and taught at the University of Oregon. In 1908 Whiteside went to Germany to study with Rudolph Ganz. When she returned to the United States, she settled in Portland, Oregon. She might have stayed in that city forever, had she not experienced an epiphany in the mid-1920s. According to composer and pianist Robert Helps, who studied with Whiteside for a year in the early 1940s, "She woke up one morning, when she was about forty-five, and realized that her students played or they didn't play and she had really nothing to do with it," Helps said in 1995. "And she gave up her whole class and moved here to New York."

Whiteside began to develop a theory derived from watching what performers actually did. "She just went to concert after concert of people she really thought played very well," Helps said. "She got tickets down in the front row as much as possible and tried to just watch them play, to see if she could figure out physically what they were doing that made them play like that."

Whiteside wrote about the method she evolved in *Mastering the Chopin Etudes and Other Essays*, *Indispensables of Piano Playing*, and *The Pianist's Mechanism*. She was still developing the system when she began working with Morton. It had two key elements. First was a physical emphasis on the large muscles of the back and upper arms *down* to the fingers, rather than *from* the fingers on up. Her students would throw their hands on the keyboard, which she called "splashing" the notes. Second was a psychological component: Whiteside concentrated on helping her students find the emotional or basic rhythm of the music, without which no performance could be truly satisfying.

When Morton began, she was focusing on the upper arm, torso, and shoulder joint. As she wrote in the foreword to *Mastering the Chopin Etudes*, it was the torso that "initiated and implemented" in each pianist a basic rhythm, which was his or her own response to the music; if the upper arms did their job, the wrist, hand, and fingers would take care of themselves. She modified the theory so often that she quickly considered this first book completely out of date.

She also focused on the ear, rather than the eye, stressing that the importance of learning to read music at an early age was faulty and counterproductive. And finally, Whiteside was convinced of the value of improvisation, which she used with two goals in mind: involving the ear and creating a basic rhythm in the student.

How marvelous this must have seemed to Morton—a teacher who did not care when her students learned to read, and who loved improvisation! He clung to her. "Abby Whiteside was a born teacher," he said in 1985. "She knew how the body was built and shaped. . . . She did not believe in practicing five-finger exercises. She thought that was a waste of time—you started making music immediately. She used the Chopin etudes, which have technical problems, but have to be musically put together."

Whiteside wrote class newsletters for her students and kept a diary. Within a month of their meeting, Gould's relationship with Whiteside was established; her first entry about her new fifteen-year-old student is dated 3 January 1929: "I sent a letter to Mr. [Ernest] Hutcheson concerning Morton." (Hutcheson, an Australian pianist and teacher, had been dean of the Juilliard School since 1927.) There is also a trove of Morton's letters to her from the spring of 1929 until 1956, the year she died. Other than high school friend Joseph Prostakoff, Whiteside was probably Gould's closest confidant.

Stanley Baron, who studied with Whiteside before giving up the piano to go to college, described his teacher vividly.

> [She was] not a heavy sort of macho sort of woman, but she had pince nez, a very forceful voice, a very attractive voice. She was completely articulate. She could always say exactly what she wanted to say. . . . She was an outsider in every way. She disapproved of the way most people were taught; she disapproved of the way most people played. There were very few professional pianists she had a lot of time for. She liked people like [Walter] Gieseking and [Artur] Schnabel. She loved [Guiomar] Novaes. She thought a good deal of the Englishwoman Myra Hess. She was against people who played with their fingers, as she called it. . . . She was against the whole idea of learning by finger action, the whole technique of small muscle action.

Indeed, Whiteside didn't like much of what she saw and heard and didn't have access to the inner circles. Her unorthodox method and outspoken dislike of the academy prevented her from offering her pupils the entrée that better-connected teachers had. "She had every quality of a teacher—except the ability to place a pianist," Baron said.

Helps, who turned to Whiteside after he became disenchanted

with Juilliard, said that by the mid-1940s she was viewed as "this crackpot piano teacher that lived catty-corner to Carnegie Hall" (she then lived in the Osborne Apartments on West Fifty-seventh Street and Seventh Avenue). Because her theories were considered incendiary and absurd, "she had trouble putting her hands on really blazing talents," Helps said. "It's too bad."

Thus Abby Whiteside, the teacher and musician with whom Morton felt most comfortable, was, in Helps's words, "absolutely isolated" in New York—not a person who could help her most promising student significantly in advancing his career.

On 5 January 1929, Whiteside wrote in her diary: "Went to visit with Vincent [Jones] about Morton. I have a new bee in my bonnet—that of keeping Morton." Keep him she did. In few words, Whiteside sketches the picture of a turbulent adolescent; on 22 February, she wrote, "Had Morton in the morning. He was screaming about school and said, 'I've had five terms of English and see how I talk.'" On 2 March she recorded, "Morton told me that he heard in Toscanini all the things I had been talking about. I shall never have a nicer compliment than that." March 9: "Morton was discouraged today. It is too hard for him not to be able to do the things he wants. Today I asked him why he did not play his Nocturne better. He said, 'Well, I concentrate on this, the others I just play.'"

But while Morton was soaking up composition, theory, and harmony, he was still living with the erratic support of his father. Just how erratic was underscored when his piano was repossessed—again. "I came home from high school one day and it was the same story: I had a small grand, but I found an outline on the floor where it had been. It was gone," he related laconically in 1985. "My instrument. It must have made some effect on me. I don't know how long I was without it." Eventually, Morton got a used Steinway on the installment plan. The Steinway company let him keep the instrument no matter what problems he had paying, which earned his lifelong gratitude.

Morton—with his fledgling experience of the world, his journeys into Manhattan, his quick mind and bravado—was tiring of the routine and mediocrity of high school. He detailed his difficulties in his first letter to Whiteside, dated 19 June 1929, sent to her summer home in Glendale, California. It is full of his dry wit.

> Dear Miss Whiteside, about four weeks ago, I decided that I would write to you. And every day since then I made the same decision. Today, however, I left out the deciding act and instead sat down and wrote. I haven't much time to concoct a genuine excuse, so please accept the following one temporarily—"You'll have to excuse my not writing you so soon because I couldn't find an envelope." (period) Now to get down to "capitalist" talk. This is the first week of vacation, and the first week that I have done any real practicing since you left! (Keep calm) In a few weeks all the work that I was able to do for Dr. Jones was only two fugues! (Hold on tight!) You can guess the reason for this. (I love my dear school) I was also told that next term I will have to make up the subjects that I dropped this term, and I was forced to fill out my option card that way. Knowing that you are doing all that you can about this matter, I did my share, also. I'm so desperate about this that I went down to Union Square to the Anarchist headquarters, and I have arranged that in case I must attend high school next term, they will make it so that there won't be any High School for me to attend. (I'm paying for the dynamite.) . . . My music "teacher," Mr. Wood, asked me before the whole class if I ever took up "keyboard harmony." Upon my answering in the negative, he said, "You ought to, it would do you good. I know it helped me." Laugh that off. I would write more, but a few minutes ago I lost my pen, and I can't find it, so I'll have to stop. Sincerely—Morton
> P.S. Don't forget to get me out of school next term.
> P.S. Don't forget to read the first P.S. and act accordingly.
> (Curtain)

Then Gould included a detailed, probably tongue-in-cheek, six-day-a-week summer schedule, from 8:20 in the morning to 3:30 in the afternoon, with Bach, Schumann, Chopin etudes, concerto practice, score-reading, composing, and so forth, plus a half hour to copy manuscripts. The schedule was marked "subject to change without notice."

He may very well have studied this way whenever he could. But those interruptions—Morton wrote Whiteside again on 31 July 1929, but this time not from Hillside Avenue:

> Should I go back and register when school opens? or stay out? Personally I'd rather do the latter, but whatever you say . . . . I suppose you are surprised at seeing this come from Woodstock, New York, but that's where I am! Some of my "communist" friends came up to this village in the Catskills and invited me to come up and share expenses with them.

Music was not the only thing on Morton's mind as the summer began. New York was in a political ferment; Communists, Socialists, anarchists, radicals of many hues flourished. Even at Richmond Hill High School, he had been surrounded by earnest debaters. Leonard Boudin, later a famous lawyer for progressive causes, was a childhood acquaintance. Both Shirley Uzin and Joseph Prostakoff eventually became members of the Communist Party. Gould's own feelings about ideology were always tempered. He agreed with many left-wing positions and took part in rallies, concerts, and fund-raisers, but he never joined any party.

His love for the visual arts also continued strong, and he went to Woodstock thinking first of art, not music. Among Morton's friends were Leo Fischer, son of Herman Fischer the grocer, and his pal and fellow artist Arnold Goldberg, both a few years older and already living a bohemian life. They teased the youth about his dependence, Gould told me in 1996: "Here you are . . . still living with your bourgeois parents!" To a fifteen-year-old aching to quit school, the offer was irresistible. They "rented the side of a barn" and invited him up.

"This was opening the door for my getting away from my bourgeois environment. I thought that . . . I'd be able to meet artists—Eugene Speicher, John Nichols, Yasuo Kuniyoshi, maybe Georgia O'Keeffe." But Morton found far more—a freewheeling, free-living lifestyle that was a teenage boy's dream. Long before 1969's "three days of love and peace" (which didn't actually take place in Woodstock, anyway), the hamlet on the slopes of Overlook Mountain had been a haunt of artists, musicians, writers, and esthetes. In the summer of 1929, Woodstock was about to experience its last wild season.

Woodstock is situated in the folds of the Catskill Mountains, about forty miles north of New York City, in a long-settled area where centuries of farming had cleared most of the forest, leaving long, magnificent vistas. The first artists' colony was founded in 1902 by a utopian Englishman named Ralph Radcliffe Whitehead and his partners, Hervey White, a Kansas socialist, and Bolton Brown, a Stanford University art professor. They built a community, according to Allen Staley in his 1960 Yale master's thesis, with the aim "of realizing the idea of simple country life for associated though independent artists and craftsmen."

It failed quickly, but gradually Woodstock and a nearby community, The Maverick, attracted a stimulating crowd. Besides the many artists (painter George Bellows prominent in the group), figures such as attorney Clarence Darrow and sociologist Thorstein Veblen visited. Musicians included Leon Barzin, principal violist of the New York Philharmonic and later principal conductor and music director of the National Orchestral Association; flutist Georges Barrère; and Clara and David Mannes, founders of the Mannes College of Music. Singer Paul Robeson and dancers Ruth St. Denis, Ted Shawn, and Charles Weidman all performed there.

A sleepy village had become a volatile artistic and political community, with the added element of ethnic and religious contrast: Woodstock and other predominantly Protestant Catskill communities began to attract vacationing Jews from New York City. Aspiring artists rented corners in barns and haymows, at rates ranging from twenty-five cents a week to five dollars a month. One very popular social establishment, The Nook, was located in farmer Irving Riseley's barn, beside the Tannery Brook Bridge. In his book about Woodstock, town historian Alf Evers described its fare of soft drinks, sandwiches, and ice cream and noted that one of its walls was "covered with hasty little landscapes and flower paintings run up by colony artists for the tourist trade."

Morton loved the place instantly. "Dear Mom and Pop," he wrote on 29 July 1929, "This is the life! No social etiquette out here! Here was our menu yesterday—Breakfast: Corn flakes, two bananas, crackers. Dinner: Bread and a plateful of spaghetti, tea. Supper: String beans and onions (sweet & sour) 2 Baloney sandwiches, crackers, canteloupe. So, you see we're not starving out here."

Within the first week, he told Whiteside in the letter of 31 July 1929, he gave a recital "of modern music" and earned enough to stay through August. "The atmosphere, the scenery, the people, the quaint peasant costumes are beyond imagination," Morton wrote her. He was ready for his own summer of peace, love, and art. Everyone drank applejack, and he could have sat around all day, talking and flirting, or he could work. There was a small problem: he couldn't find a piano, so there went the schedule he'd so carefully described: "I cannot do much if any of your work on piano up here." But he made what he considered an extremely important friendship with a man they'd met at The Nook: choreographer Don Oscar Becque—"who, in case you don't know, is one of the *most famous ballet dancers in the country*! We started a conversation and I found out he was also a musician and pianist, and an ultra-modernist like myself."

Becque drove the boys through a summer storm (Arnold Goldberg and Bruno Fischer, Leo's brother, "half drowned" in the rumble seat) to the Villetta, a library and auditorium from the days of the first community. He told them it was his own house. After Morton played for him, Becque offered him work as accompanist for his dance classes and wove tales about bringing him along on tour.

Becque proposed that Gould give concerts in the Villetta at seventy-five cents admission. He also asked the boy to write the music for his recitals in New York that season. "Can you imagine what that would mean for me?" Gould wrote Whiteside. "The critics would give me regular write-ups. Don Oscar will devote an entire page of the program about me. . . . P.S. You should have seen him when I told him I wasn't twenty but fifteen."

At the time Becque, having spent a year with the Denishawn troupe, was indeed one of the more promising of the new wave of American dancers, an Oklahoman who knew Isadora Duncan and had studied classical ballet in Europe and New York. (He reached his peak in 1935 and 1936, when he was in charge of the Federal Dance Project in New York. Soon his own dancers and choreographers, including Doris Humphrey, Charles Weidman, and Helen Tamaris, rebelled, accusing him of incompetence and forcing him to resign.)

Morton was awestruck. Besides recitals in New York and Philadelphia, they might tour Europe and Russia, he wrote Whiteside. "You see, Don can get an invitation to Russia any time he wants to. He knows intimately such men as Stokowski, Diaghilev, Varese, Copland, Antheil, John Alden Carpenter, Prokofieff, John Dos Passos, Mike Gold, John Dewey, et cetera."

But Becque couldn't even get Morton a decent piano, and as the summer passed, Gould noticed another major flaw: he never got paid. When the boy demanded an accounting, Becque gave him a raise—but still didn't pay. Nevertheless, though his friends soon returned to New York, Gould made enough money from lessons and recitals to stay into the fall, composing. He was on his own for the first time.

There was another detail. The dancer was homosexual, and Morton did not know how to deal with that. "This was my first encounter with the world of homosexuals," Gould told me in October 1993. "I had thought I would meet women, but when I went to my first parties, I didn't understand what was going on." The wives and girlfriends stayed in the house, while the men disappeared outside. Becque invited Morton to stay with him; once there, the boy found there was only one bed. "If I went up there, nobody would comment," Gould said. "There might have been more comment if I didn't go." So he took a pickax handle from a nearby woodshed and kept it under the bed. "Whenever the guy turned toward me, I would grab the pickax handle—I didn't know what I would do."

Gould did find women that summer. He enjoyed telling about the time his lover's boyfriend returned unexpectedly. Leaving his sweater behind, Morton jumped through the screen window, which scratched him up. He spent the night wandering the woods. Finally he came out on the Kingston Road, where he was picked up by a milk-truck driver. His mother had knitted that lost sweater, and for years Frances wondered what happened to it.

George Kimball Plochmann, known as Kim, was a boy about Morton's age who was vacationing in Woodstock with his aunt. They met in Becque's dance class. Plochmann described his new friend: "High cheekbones, a long, rather somber face, very earnest eyes. He was thin as anything and had huge hands. I think he could stretch an eleventh on the keyboard." Gould struck Plochmann as shy, with a sense of humor that showed itself in the odd turns of his music. Plochmann also saw Gould was barely surviving. "He had zero money. He wore very plain clothes. I don't think he had any money to his name."

Kim's Aunt Elsa decided to present Morton in a private recital. They borrowed the chairs from the local funeral director and filled the music room. Plochmann said Gould played Mozart, Bach, and perhaps Brahms.

> And then [Morton] said, very casually, "There's a Beethoven sonata I would like to play, which is not numbered with the usual thirty-two." He said it was in four movements, and he sat down to play it. Everybody listened very carefully. It was a good sonata, very much Beethoven. When he came to the scherzo, he said, "It goes right into the finale." At the end, everybody liked it, but nobody seemed to have known it, until somebody said, "I don't think that's a Beethoven sonata at all. I think he improvised it!" Which he did. He didn't have any music, he let on he had memorized it, but actually he was composing it as he went along! If you didn't think he had any talent, you had to think so afterward. People were startled.

Undoubtedly.

Woodstock gave Morton an early lesson in the difference between the artist and the dilettante. "I found out very quickly," Gould said, "that the people I was with sat around and discussed art. The real artists . . . were doing it. It enabled me to bypass the period of theorizing about things and not doing it."

Gould's papers include a set of handpainted posters advertising two concerts. The program for the first included extracts from Stravinsky's *L'oiseau de feu*, piano pieces by Bartók, excerpts from Hindemith's *The Demon*, Gould's own Suite No. 1, and then "improvisations on a given theme." The second handbill describes a performance at the Maverick Concert Hall on 12 August 1929, with Stravinsky's *Apollo and the Muses*, two scenes from Prokofiev's ballet *Chout*, Schoenberg's Piano Piece No. 1, and, again, Gould's Suite No. 1 and improvisations. This was a program of exceptional boldness for any pianist in 1929. For a boy of fifteen to offer it, on his own, in such an environment, shows unusual daring. He was certainly not aiming for the pops crowd.

The major composition on which Gould worked at Woodstock was *Manhattan Rhapsody*. He wanted to do for Manhattan what Gershwin had done for Paris the year before in *An American in Paris*. In a postcard to his parents dated 14 September 1929, he said, "As things are going, my Rhapsody ought to be finished this week. I haven't played it [as a piano reduction] for any of the people here without having to repeat it." The next day he wrote them again: "My

Rhapsody will be finished in a few days. It's something! It is about 18 pages long!"

Classes back home had already started but he was still in Woodstock. He never returned to Richmond Hill High School. His school record ends thus: "Discharged 11 October 1929 to home instruction." He had been carrying a 79.5 average; his grades ranged from 60 in second-year English (he failed and had to repeat the term) to, not surprisingly, 100 in advanced music.

The score of *Manhattan Rhapsody* indicates that the piece was "composed September, 1929 in Woodstock, N.Y., orchestrated and scored October–December, 1929." A brief description follows.

> Manhattan—dynamic skyscrapers—moving masses—whirling wheels—subways—leap from darkness—elevateds—roar down—blackness—Times Square—music shows—Union Square—communist speeches—stinking tenements—Park Avenue—masses moving—masses of people—moving—a great machine—forever moving.

Detailed instructions are included as well: "Celeste and xylophone sound as written. Bass clarinet sounds a second below horns in bass clef a fourth below." A large flat sign or a large sharp sign indicated that all the notes following were flatted or sharped, respectively; this was cancelled by a large natural sign. A natural sign at top combined with a flat below, or a natural sign above combined with a sharp below indicated that "the lower voice or voices are flatted or sharped and the upper voices atonal"—or vice versa if the signs were reversed; these too were cancelled by a large natural sign. Gould had the boundless vision of youth.

He played a piano reduction of *Manhattan Rhapsody* at Kim Plochmann's Manhattan apartment that fall. But the dreams about working with Becque came to very little. They never toured Europe, and there was only one recital, featuring what should have been a twenty-minute ballet, performed late in 1929 at the Roerick Museum in Manhattan. "Don was very nervous and jittery," Gould told me in 1993. "One minute into the ballet, he made the [closing cue], the curtain came down, and that was the end of the ballet."

CHAPTER 4

Ugh, Vaudeville

★ ★ ★ ★

MORTON OBSERVED a great deal about art, people, and himself that summer of 1929. Aside from letters and postcards, Gould tried to express the effects of his Woodstock experience in a trio of brief typewritten prose sketches, entitled *Woodstock Characters and Episodes*, that appear to have been written the following winter. They reflect cynicism, acute self-consciousness, dislike for public display, and the powerful tug of sexual desire—all lifelong characteristics.

The first, entitled "My Actress," describes a recital for a "gathering of Woodstock's 'musical clique,'" in which for the first time his playing and compositions are "received in utter silence." After playing, he sits alone in a corner, "a seething furnace," eyes stinging from cigarette smoke. "A reckless attacker was suddenly defenseless—alone—in its place was a youth away from home." The women nervously watch as their men flirt and disappear. The only male "inclined to stay at least in the house," he is approached by an "extremely beautiful actress." He is attracted, but frightened. Later he and his friends walk in their pajamas through the silent woods. As they smirk, he bursts out, "God damn it—no lousy fairies and unsatisfied wives can do this to me." He is tempted, torn, frightened. While he dithers, the actress is seduced by someone else. "It probably wasn't the first time she had been seduced," he concludes bitterly. The brilliant youngster, having exposed himself in his music and his playing, is furious—at what? At the attention or the lack of it? He is disturbed by the homoerotic energy about him and the sexual drama within himself. He rages at the heavens.

The next piece, "Portrait of a Composer," is a description of his response to another post-performance gathering, a newspaper interview, and a frustrated sexual encounter. Most intriguing are two brief but electrifying connections between sex and composition that open and close the story, his only references to music itself. The first is a striking description of a concert and its immediate effect: "The orchestra was vomiting forth sounds. Hard, brittle sounds—a volcano spitting fire. A terrific culminating eruption. It is over." The audience is confused. Patrons in the boxes are bewildered, and from the balconies, boos are mixed with cheers. The composer appears onstage, frail, clumsy, and self-conscious. After an awkward bow he runs out "trembling—sick with fear."

At the post-concert party, the blushing composer imagines everyone looking him over: "Seems human. Head—necktie—crease in pants—shoes—front—back." When he refuses a drunken guest's request to play, "Mr. Witney the Wall Street Magnate" rebukes him: "'My dear young fellow I hope last night's concert hasn't—er—spoiled you—After all—you are not—er—in a position—to—Here have a drink and be a sport.' His master was speaking. After all he might hurt his feelings. He went to the piano."

Humiliated and furious, the composer vows revenge during an interview set for the next day: "And I bent before that lousy capitalist—let that correspondent try and see me." But the interview, too, goes badly. The composer snaps at the writer but describes a typical day, and then hates himself afterward: "What a damn fool I was, humbling myself before a lousy newspaper reporter. The next one that comes, I'll kick him out."

The final part describes another failed sexual encounter, in which the woman is willing but the boy is weak: "I could have her—forget music—everything—just her—forever—just once—most temptation—I must have her—must—all alone." He shifts toward her; her eyes look into his. "He wanted—to take her around—just—take her around." But she asks a silly question and "something inside him collapses." The woman leaves. "He closed the door after her. She was gone. He curled up. A beaten cur. In the place where she had sat. He didn't sleep that night. He was proclaiming himself—hurling blasphemies—tearing down—hurling up—passionately—loving without resistance. He was composing."

Gould was not a natural showman like George Gershwin, who never saw a piano he didn't like, or a self-dramatizing bon vivant like Leonard Bernstein, who loved to show himself and became uncomfortable if other brilliancies were around.

Gould loved the act of composition, yet he needed the affirmation that came with performance. He had a sharp tongue but usually bit it. He had a strong sense of his own worth, but a great fear of being revealed as unworthy. He turned his fury upon himself. He "bent before that lousy capitalist" and "humbled himself before a lousy newspaper reporter." Only when he was alone could he proclaim himself, blaspheme, tear down, build up, "love without resistance."

The stock market crashed in October 1929, the month Gould finished *Manhattan Rhapsody*. Fortunes disappeared and paper millionaires became paupers. Civil Service jobs with security and pensions became more valuable than seats on the exchange. One of James Gould's friends, a millionaire everyone envied, blew his brains out, Morton remembered. Any work was better than no work. The Great Depression had begun.

This was the time Morton chose to set out into the field. But which field: that of the concert pianist and composer pursuing high artistic goals? Or that of his father, to become rich, famous, and popular? Gould was continually stretched between economic demand and artistic desire. He had set out on two tracks at once. Inevitably, they began to separate, and he tried to dance between them. But for a year, from the fall of 1929 through the fall of 1930, they seemed to be parallel.

The home instruction to which Morton was discharged from high school, arranged by Whiteside, was NYU professor Max Cushing, "a very learned man" (as he remembered him in 1985) with whom the earnest composer read everything from Shakespeare to Wilder. Gould's experiences with Cushing marked the end of his academic training. Later he would deeply regret his lack of education, but now, in the darkness following the Crash of 1929, Morton had to support his family. So he hit the vaudeville circuit with Bert Shefter.

The older Shefter had studied at the Curtis Institute of Music in Philadelphia with both David Saperton and famed pianist Josef Hofmann. He was a conscientious musician who practiced a lot—something Morton rarely did, to Bert's disgust. Jacques Frey and Mario Braggioti, Phil Ohman and Victor Arden, Vera Lawrence and Harold Triggs—"The woods were full of two-piano teams," as Gould put it to Kazdin and Hemming in August 1985. Pop Gould may have brought the pair together; Whiteside, who had Philadelphia connections, might also have been involved. Their repertoire included arrangements by both pianists, though gradually more were Gould's; the programs ran from Chopin's *Fantaisie impromptu* to the Original Dixieland Jazz Band's "Tiger Rag."

If Morton had disliked department stores and hotels, he hated vaudeville. By the late 1920s, the variety show was dying. The great theater circuits were turning their auditoriums over to the movies, and Gould and Shefter did not often get to the remaining first-run houses. Gould recalled those days in 1985:

> We played the tail end of programs. There were some horrible houses. They didn't have decent toilet facilities. We had to use the sink to take off our makeup. The room would be filthy, the sink green with urine. I remember getting violently ill and my father having to come and take me out of there. There'd be a five-piece orchestra. The conductor would play the piano and smoke a cigar, and conduct from there. . . . I thought I'd be a concert pianist and a composer of so-called serious music. Then I had to play in places like that.

Shefter fought to maintain his dignity, Morton recalled.

> We'd get into a theater that had banged-up pianos, and he would say to the stagehands, "These pianos are out of tune." And the stagehands would say, "That's too fuckin' bad, what are you gonna do?" Bert would say, "They have to be tuned!" They'd say, "Too bad. You don't like 'em? Don't play 'em." Bert would say, "I'm a Josef Hofmann pupil, I came here—" And they said, "Great, why don't you go back there?"

Occasionally, Gould worked on his own. He spent a week as music director and accompanist for the ballerina Tamara Geva, George Balanchine's first wife. They rehearsed mornings in the frigid theater—a half-dozen bored musicians and their conductor in the pit, the classically trained dancer onstage, and the ingenuous youth as go-between. "Leave out the first two bars," Morton'd tell the conductor. "I will do a cadenza, you play eight bars of this, and twelve bars of that." The conductor would give the downbeat and off they'd go—too fast or too slow, and Geva would stalk off. "I went to see the conductor after the first show," Gould said in 1985. "The whole thing was a shambles, but the conductor couldn't care less."

The audiences were just as tough. Once Gould and Shefter were booked into a rundown house in the Bronx, to accompany Tony and Renee DeMarco, a well-known ballroom dance team who, it turned out, were not known well enough in that neighborhood. When the curtain went up, neither the audience not the performers liked what they saw. Onstage were two pianists in tails. Watching them, expecting something completely different, was a crowd typified by men in undershirts, feet on the seats, children careening through the aisles, women chattering, the crackle of popcorn, and the smell of peanuts. The audience groaned and booed. When the dancers came out, the crowd cursed at DeMarco, who passed his wife onstage and told her to keep going and not come back. The pianists were left to face the wrath of the Bronx.

Shefter told Gould to go right into the *Fantaisie impromptu*, which didn't help. The audience was yelling, but Shefter wouldn't stop. The crowd pelted them with refuse—Gould particularly remembered a can of mustard. The kid stopped, but his partner wouldn't. The curtain came down and the band started to play, but Shefter kept going until, Gould claimed, the stagehands had to carry him off.

Their work came in fits and starts. Gould lived with his family (they moved during this time, down the block, to 123-03 Hillside Avenue) and traveled by subway or trolley, often arriving home after one o'clock in the morning. It was all hard, especially because Morton hoped to become a concert artist, a great composer, or both. Yet here he was, eating in greasy spoons; you could get a full meal for a quarter, but the food was awful. Shefter ate fried clams from pushcarts ("He had a stomach made of iron"), while Gould had pastrami sandwiches. "My mother warned me about that," he recalled in 1985. "I ate terrible."

But Morton was getting nourishment elsewhere. There were

other opportunities for this quick, ambitious, talented young man. He was gobbling up the world.

During his first winter on the road, Morton approached the conductor Alexander Smallens, music director of the Philadelphia Civic Opera and assistant conductor of the Philadelphia Orchestra, whose mother lived near the Goulds. In a letter to Smallens dated 12 February 1930, he introduced himself by saying that Smallens's mother knew him, as did Esther and Leo Fischer, "but I've decided to go on my own initiative, and therefore bring about the result much sooner."

> [I am] a young pianist and composer. A composer primarily.... My compositions have progressed from waltzes at the age of six thru to preludes, academic rondos, part-song forms up to "ultra-modern" (for use of a better word) orchestral compositions. I will admit to you that I am only sixteen years of age. Please don't allow that fact to bias you as it has done others. . . . My idiom is ultra-modern not because of an adolescent sophistication, but because my physiological makeup is that way. I am a product of 1930—of skyscrapers, dynamic masses of steel and not of an era of hoop-skirts and horse carriages. . . . My compositions are so modern, the people who could do something with them either are academicians or composers themselves who are too occupied with self-interests.

Gould appealed to Smallens to listen to some of his work. "I would gladly come to Philadelphia if you would give me an appointment. If you do, please give me specific directions as to the address, being that I am totally unfamiliar with Philadelphia." The defensiveness and insecurity were already beginning to show.

Morton met with Smallens in New York, not Philadelphia. The conductor suggested that he find someone with whom to study orchestration. Finally Gould begged for tickets to Smallens's performance of Stravinsky's *The Rite of Spring* and Schoenberg's *Die glückliche Hand*. He got a pair for the dress rehearsal on 22 April 1930 and took Whiteside, who noted in her diary that night, "A red letter day . . . the hand of Fate. Tremendous performance."

Morton was working at a remarkable clip. That winter and

spring he mastered the Bach G Minor Toccata, Schumann's *Symphonic Etudes*, and Scriabin's Sonata No. 5, began work on the Tchaikovsky First Concerto, and played through Copland's Piano Concerto with his teacher ("Morton was wonderful at it but I was no good," Whiteside noted in her diary). They went to the Roerick Museum to hear Emmanuel Bay and Isabelle Workman, and to Carnegie Hall for Rachmaninoff. Morton played at New York University's New Auditorium, offering Bach, Debussy, Scriabin, and five of his own pieces. "It was quite thrilling," wrote Whiteside. "Trouble with the piano made things difficult, but Morton played in spite of no sostenuto and sticking keys."

By the end of May 1930, Morton could play the entire Tchaikovsky First Concerto (he learned the final two movements in a mere two days—"one for last Friday and one for today," as he wrote Whiteside, who had gone to California for the summer). His appetite for work was enormous, and his fame was spreading. Gould reported to her that Nat Shilkret, composer, conductor, and music director of the Victor Talking Machine Company, was interested in *Manhattan Rhapsody*. (In 1929 Shilkret's Victor Salon Orchestra had given the first radio performance of *An American in Paris*; RCA released the recording on CD in 1998.)

In early June 1930 Shilkret said that if Gould would copy out the parts, he would try out *Manhattan Rhapsody*. On 16 June the Pathé film company made a short subject about Morton himself. The filming took place at the company's studio in Queens. The heat under the lights was so great that Gould's makeup kept melting, and his "face" had to be reapplied every five minutes; there was a minimum of two takes per shot, and a still photo session at home. He wrote Whiteside that they had asked him to write an essay on his "theories of music," and to sign a release for distribution "*in all countries of the world*. Not half bad." In "Pathé Audio Review No. 29," distributed to theaters around the country, Max Cushing read an introduction with a brief biography of Morton, and Gould played the March and Finale from his Suite No. 1 and a "Satirical Dance," parodying classical ballet.

An undated Queens newspaper clipping describes the film with such hyperbole that it must have been written, in large part, by James Gould. The story reported that the "local genius" is considered "a rich find" by Pathé executives, and that "hardened music critics reveal him as a rival in technique and form to Stravinsky, Ornstein, and Ravel." It spoke of his "musical evolution" from the winter of 1928, when he was "a very fine pianist-composer who played almost anything," to the Woodstock summer of 1929, when he was "famous . . . as a strict modernist." The emphasis is all on "high art": there is no mention of vaudeville or department stores.

Morton's repertoire expanded. On 17 June 1930 he offered Whiteside a selection for his "modern" recital programs, including Debussy, Ornstein, Bartók, and Szymanowski, and announced that he was going to learn Mussorgsky's *Pictures at an Exhibition* "no matter what."

In July 1930 Gould went to Cushing's home in Wilton, Connecticut, "the grandest place you ever saw, and ideal for working," he wrote Whiteside early that month. He spent the entire month there practicing and studying and gave frequent recitals in the area. He worked with characteristic vigor. "I have started to fulfil my obligation to piano literature. I eat my meals at a farmhouse, so that I have no worry of any kind—just get up and practice, and wash my ears every week."

On 6 July 1930 Gould complained to Whiteside in a letter that copying out the parts to *Manhattan Rhapsody* for Shilkret meant that he would not be able to compose for a while, that he would have to cut his practicing down to roughly three hours a day—and that he didn't even like the piece anymore. "It does anything but make me optimistic over my abilities as a composer. However, I can't let this opportunity slip by." Nothing apparently came of this particular opportunity. Gould did not mention it again, nothing indicates that *Manhattan Rhapsody* was ever performed, and it was never published.

Morton's musical appetite was gargantuan. He continued to study Chopin, and also began preparing Franck's *Prelude, Aria, and Finale*, Bach's Seventh Partita, and Beethoven's Sonata Op. 111. Not to mention the concerto for piano and chamber orchestra he had just begun, and his discovery of Balakirev's *Islamey* and Debussy's *La soirée dans Grenade*. On 16 July he wrote Whiteside that he had the three big works memorized and had begun Chopin's B Minor Sonata. The sixteen-year-old also made explicit the close connection he felt between music and sex.

> A curious change has come over me emotionally. I get violently excited about musical compositions that I like, and probably take on the appearance of a madman while doing so. Oftentimes while playing I feel like jumping up and conducting. When playing a thing like Stravinsky's *Petrouchka,* I get emotionally wrought up into a white heat, perhaps almost a frenzy of ecstasy —almost the same reactions that I have when momentarily in love (?) with some gorgeous and voluptuous woman that comes in sight. This all leaves me quite exhausted and panting for breath.
>
> I begin to throb with the vitality and life surge that goes with youth. Life and living seem as a precious thing to me, as it appears to all who have yet to taste of it. I have to admit my extreme desire of the female sex, and according to various incidents this desire could, I think, be easily gratified. However ~~one doesn't~~ I have not developed to that stage where I would take advantage of anything that wasn't particularly attractive to me, even tho' it be a willing woman. I want to live everything I do—at least as much as possible. From this vantage point my future seems envious. "To work and to love."

The hormones were raging, and Morton's response is all the more striking because the environment in which he found himself in Wilton was, even more than Woodstock, homosexual. "There were a lot of professors visiting there," he recalled in 1985, "all highly cultured, nice, civilized people. But they were all homosexuals." This would be a continuing factor in his own career. Especially after World War II, many prominent American composers themselves were gay, working in networks in which Gould never felt entirely comfortable.

He also ran into professional jealousy. Pianist Harry Cumpson attended one of his recitals in nearby Greenwich and "gave vent to some cheap, obvious remarks" about his performance, deriding his ability to improvise. Gould took up the challenge and got into "a silly verbal argument" with Cumpson. "Anyway," he wrote to Whiteside, "I proceeded to do it and of course they all 'flopped' for it and greeted it enthusiastically."

Gould was making more strides in show business. Whiteside, in her 15 November 1930 class newsletter, said he was winning "real recognition on Broadway." He had already appeared at the Brooklyn Paramount and for a week at the Roxy, "the largest picture house in the city," and he was scheduled for the New York Paramount. But he no longer had time to study with her regularly. "His family are in financial difficulties so he is doing all he can to earn. It does not seem that he wants to stay in this vaudeville racket. He hates it."

CHAPTER 5

Clipping the Wings

★ ★ ★ ★

MORTON GOULD'S two tracks—the commercial and the artistic—began to diverge in 1931. He was running harder than before and beginning to make an impression in both worlds—but financial straits were also making a very serious impression. And during that time he met the first great love of his life, an affair that started, as they often do, with great exhilaration.

In March and April 1931, the seventeen-year-old pianist gave recitals at Wanamaker's department store in Manhattan. There was little publicity for the 6 March performance, which had been arranged by Eastwood Lane of the store's music department. Department director Alexander Russell "was very skeptical about Morton being able to hold an audience with his own compositions," according to Whiteside, but following the performance, Russell immediately asked for another engagement. Morton "has never played so well," Whiteside wrote in her diary that March. "He loves doing it, has absolutely no nerves, and usually plays better for a crowd than at any other time. . . . He is far from the zenith of his powers emotionally as a player but he is mature beyond his years in composition, and technically right now he has a spectacular technique."

The next concert, an all-Gould program on 8 April, drew a good audience, and the first significant review of Gould's career. "The talents of 17-year-old Morton Gould made the little Wanamaker Auditorium hum with astonishment yesterday," wrote Louis Biancolli (*World Telegram*, 9 April 1931), eventually one of Gould's most consistent New York supporters.

> The young man appeared in the triple role of pianist, composer, and improvisor. It was in the last capacity that he excited the greatest wonder and enthusiasm. [He is a] sincere recruit to the ranks of the modernist malcontents and a vigorous champion of the rights of jazz. Strong originality marked his works, and no little technical skill. As pianist, he belongs by choice to the percussive, mechanistic school that is largely concerned with the making of industrial sound.

After an introduction by Felix Deyo of *Musical America*, Gould played on themes submitted by Walter Damrosch and Henry Hadley, improvising in the styles of composers suggested by the audience. "Undeniably," Biancolli wrote, "Mr. Gould conveyed in an obvious manner the governing characteristics of Bach, Mozart, Beethoven, Chopin, Brahms, Debussy, Stravinsky, and George Gershwin in his impromptu playing. If occasionally the theme was twisted beyond recognition, the dexterity was always little short of prodigious."

Deyo too wrote about Gould, in *Musical America*. The 19 May 1931 issue of a newspaper in Ithaca, New York, quoted him as describing Morton's "arresting technique, capable of running the keyboard's black and white length with a use of the left arm and outstretched palm, leaving in the air an accretion of overtones. This bizarre technique, be it understood, is not sensational trickery but rather a necessary and interesting phase of pianistic development."

Russell (who held the Frick Chair of Music at Princeton University) wrote a glowing letter of recommendation for Morton that June: "I realized that here was another genius of the first water, born with a spark of the divine fire. . . . In my public lecture courses at Princeton University . . . he raised audiences to a high pitch of enthusiasm. . . . I look forward to important things from this young man."

He was not the only one with great expectations. That same month, June 1931, the Baldwin piano company gave Morton a piano and offered to subsidize his performances in the coming season. G. Schirmer planned to publish a recent composition of his, *Three Conservative Sketches*, and two popular works, a novelty dance and a waltz—"a very languid and sentimental thing," Gould wrote to Whiteside, "to which all the college boys and girls will slobberingly dance with their heads draped over each others' shoulders."

Gould expected Leon Barzin to perform and broadcast the March from his Suite No. 1 in the fall. Meanwhile he was taking classes with Marion Bauer: "It surely is a great experience. By the time one is thru with the class you have gained a thorough and comprehensive analytical knowledge of the standard piano repertoire," he wrote to Whiteside that summer. And he still gave weekly recitals in Connecticut: "Between the two I am just drenched in music, which is a very good thing for me. I'm just sitting on all my creative impulses. Personally I feel that I'm at the stage where everything depends on myself. I need time to be able to just sit down and think." Bauer invited him to perform his piano sonata at a League of Composers concert.

There were two other developments that summer of 1931, one on each track. On the artistic side, he made an arrangement of Ravel's *Bolero* that, as he wrote Whiteside, "if I do say so myself is a knockout. . . . And the females!—they give vent to screams and are invariably unstrung nervously. It totally exhausts the listener. I term it 'Morton's gift to repressed women.'" Carl Engel, president of G. Schirmer and editor of *Musical Quarterly*, heard Morton's transcription of *Bolero* and was extremely impressed with it; he told Morton that his version and interpretation were closest to Toscanini's rendition. At Engel's recommendation, Gould contacted Ravel's publishers about publishing his *Bolero* arrangement.

On the other side, Gould dropped only a hint to Whiteside: "Something is developing with Erno Rapee—he is the music director at NBC and for Radio City. When they do *Petrouchka* on the air he is using me as solo pianist. Will also 'plug' my compositions."

This was a year and a half before the opening of the Radio City Music Hall, the cultural heart of the massive Rockefeller Center complex then under construction between Fifth and Sixth Avenues in midtown Manhattan. Rapee, a Hungarian-born conductor and composer, had been conductor of the Rialto Theater in 1917 when it became the first New York movie theater with a staff orchestra, and then moved on to the Rivoli and Capitol. In 1924 he compiled a collection of themes to accompany movies; in 1927 he became conductor at the brand-new Roxy Theater, and then spent a year or so in California as general music director for Warner Bros.

Morton's life was overflowing—the miseries of vaudeville

matched by the joy of composition and study, combined with the stresses of life with father, and the intense, confusing pleasures of romance. He spilled it all out in a letter to Whiteside, four and a half single-spaced typed pages dated 20 July 1931—a magnificent exhibit of the mind of the male adolescent at a peak of creativity and excitement.

There is a relatively brief description of his musical life during a summer that was "so sweltering as to annoy one, especially if among other things you have to learn a Brahms and Beethoven Violin Sonata to play at concert every week." Gould was going so hard that "even taking a day off would be analogous to derailing a 60 mile an hour express train."

Meanwhile, he had done a horrible thing:

> A few days ago I reeled off five popular compositions in one day, and have submitted them to Schirmer—artistic scruples be damned. I have to get as many popular compositions published as possible, so that regardless of how well they go over, the net accumulation will mean some sort of steady income to me. I don't intend to ever have to live thru another season like this because I'd never last it out. . . . I am changing from the placid person I used to be. . . . The mental strain of all the work that I have to do which includes creative outbursts that in themselves are enough to make one burst under the tension, this together with the strain and worry of home conditions seems at times almost unbearable.

And a new element had entered Morton's life: he had fallen in love, physically, intellectually, and every way he could conceive of, with a girl named Shirley Uzin, a fellow student at Richmond Hill High School just a few months younger than he, who lived not far away on 252 Crescent Street in Brooklyn. Shirley had been dating David Berkowitz, Morton's violinist friend. Morton and Shirley met at a party David threw not long after the Wanamaker concerts that spring. She wrote about it in her biography of Mike Quill, the fiery New York City Transit Union leader who was her fourth and final husband (*Mike Quill: Himself*, p. 147):

> Morton was not the macho man. He had a thin, sensitive, serious face, high forehead, dark hair, long, beautifully sculptured hands. Because he gave the appearance of being preoccupied, his wry sense of humor was a surprise. It was a fun evening. Morton played the piano, David, the violin; we laughed uproariously at mildly dirty jokes and drank hot chocolate. I was flattered when Morton asked for my phone number. Soon word got around that we were crazy about each other. We were.

Gould's own account in the letter to Whiteside is relatively straightforward, although much of it is filled with coy psychologizing (he wouldn't even use her name: he called her "X"). His description is touched with egotism and the paradoxical passivity with which he later viewed nearly all his relationships with women. At the end of the party, he writes, "She finally managed to maneuver me into a very passionate embrace with her, in which she nearly swooned. I was interested and started seeing her."

He found Shirley "extremely intelligent, well versed in all the cultural arts and especially so in music . . . my conversation with her never gives out." She also is very straightforward sexually and "does not resort to any of the ridiculous feminine inanities that most girls feel obligated to employ, and therefore she is regarded as abnormal, immoral, and God knows what."

What "X" lacks, Morton wrote condescendingly, "is sympathy from someone whom she looks up to and could lean upon. She cannot find that confidant in a woman, as that species is cruellest to its own sex, and how many males would be at all interested in that side of a girl?" Feeling confident and superior, Morton predicted her future (and his own) in a later passage: "X will grow into the sort of girl, very intense, who will give herself to the man she loves, and it will be more than one man."

Then he spent some time talking about himself. He saw himself as "a peculiar mixture of intellectual sensuality and immorality, and physical chastity and puritanism" and commented, wryly, that he was the mature figure in his circle: "At my young age I act as father confessor and adviser to friends of mine as old as 23." In sentences that described, almost literally, the nature of his relationships with women, Gould wrote, "Gross sensuality for some reason or other repulses me, altho' I must admit being fascinated with it mentally. If I were an author, I would write novels having to deal with all sorts of immoralities and at the same time be married and have a wife, kids, and breakfast nook."

Although Morton considered himself far more worldly and wise than "X" ("She was so inexperienced that I even had to teach her how to kiss properly, and she wasn't playing off either"), she had already won some ground. Gossip about his flirtatiousness unnerved her; she wanted an explanation. "She doubted my sincerity!!"

She wanted him to declare his feelings. "Finally I gave in and spoke." What exactly he said he did not make clear to Whiteside in that letter of 20 July, but "X" was mightily moved. "She merged in the blackness of the night, and in a voice throbbingly quiet with a new-found emotion said, 'Morton darling, I think more of you now than I thought I ever could, even in my highest expectations'—to add words to that would be futile." In the next few years, he and Shirley would go on a dizzying emotional adventure. "I might be the inexperienced sentimental blunderer being taken for a ride. If so my answer is that I am having a grand time while it lasts," he wrote, in conclusion, to Whiteside.

Music was something else. There was plenty of that going on—not just vaudeville, chamber concerts, and the negotiation with Erno Rapee, but also—Fritz Reiner. In the summer of 1931, Reiner was preparing to leave his post as music director of the Cincinnati Symphony to teach opera and conducting at the Curtis Institute. Years before he recruited Leonard Bernstein and Lukas Foss (who both studied with him in the late 1930s and early 1940s), Reiner invited Morton Gould to audition for his conducting class. Gould described the encounter many times, but one of the most detailed was given during a Kazdin-Hemming interview on 1 August 1985.

Even then Reiner was terrifying, and Gould was very nervous going to the conductor's apartment. The conductor opened the door picking his teeth. He had just finished breakfast and wandered around the apartment, opening mail and going to the bathroom (Gould heard the toilet flush), while the young man played Chopin.

After a while, Reiner asked why he wanted to conduct. Gould had no direct answer. "I can beat 5/4!" "Any pig can beat 5/4," retorted the maestro, and he placed an opera score on the piano. "Play this!" It was Strauss's *Elektra*, which Gould had never seen. The supplicant began to play feverishly. Every time he started to feel in control, Reiner flipped a few pages ahead. He asked Morton to sing; Gould said he couldn't. Reiner responded, "Give me the general idea."

Then Reiner pulled out *Salome* and repeated the process. "I did fairly well," Gould remembered, "but I must say he had me rattled; he was so dour, standing over me, flipping pages, saying 'Don't waste my time.'"

Finally Reiner said, "That's the mark of a conductor: to read a score, to see it, and to hear it." Morton must have done all right, because in August 1931 he was offered a place at Curtis: room, board, and tuition.

The two tracks, only slightly divergent, shone into the future, and he had his woman at his side for the start of the journey. But then the tracks split.

On 15 August 1931 he wrote Shirley about a performance of American music the night before at Lewisohn Stadium in Manhattan, where the New York Philharmonic gave free summer concerts. George Gershwin played *Rhapsody in Blue* and, according to Morton, "just mangled the piano part—altho' it was re-orchestrated and revised in some parts, so that the opening especially was the 'hottest' thing you ever heard. It even thrilled me." Despite his criticism of Gershwin's playing and his sense of the composition's "many defects," Gould liked the *Rhapsody* and thought it "a pioneer in the field of new music—Gershwin put spats on jazz . . . and dragged it within the sacred domains of 131st Street and Amsterdam Ave."

At the concert he encountered Leon Barzin, now music director of the National Orchestral Association, who was still planning to conduct the March from Gould's Suite No. 1, with Morton on piano. "Altho' I wrote it when I was fourteen years of age, and it really is 'conservative' now, yet it will probably stir up much controversy and criticism, both adverse and otherwise," he wrote Shirley.

Meanwhile, he was still working on the concerto for piano and chamber orchestra, begun the summer before, for Bauer and was about to begin *South Legend* for orchestra, as well as "a Toccata or Chorale and Fugue for piano and symphony orchestra." He was still "copying out the parts to my orchestral compositions" and had sketched a viola sonata, two more piano sonatas, another chorale-prelude "on a Bach chorale," a theme and variations (to be orchestrated), and a revision of the March for Barzin.

None of which is to mention the popular compositions, which were always intended solely to bring in money for the family: "Art never flourished on a bread-line." But this mercenary approach made him defensive, so he cited authority to Shirley:

> Beethoven used to gyp his publisher, Haydn got money for every Symphony he wrote, Wagner borrowed money from Liszt, never paid him back, and then stole Liszt's musical ideas —so Morton writes for Tin Pan Alley. Landlords can't read orchestral scores you know. I can imagine how disappointing I must be to girls who picture me as an unfaltering and unswerving idealist, et cetera. . . . So I trust to luck and go my way—astounding everybody with my compositions and the way I play them, interpreting Schumann lousily, improvising like the biggest egotist in the world—and yawning. Am I hot air?

He misses Shirley, he wrote her, "the walk to Crescent Street and back," and signs his letter—no doubt referring to the conversation he'd mentioned to Whiteside—"Sincerely [underlined twice]—Morton Gould."

The next letter to Shirley, begun on Tuesday, 19 August 1931, included for the first time a real outburst of complaint and self-pity. He had spent the previous Sunday practicing Mozart and Brahms for a performance that night in Connecticut, "with the result that I was so exhausted as to hardly be able to get home." Monday morning, up early to work on his popular compositions—finished a dozen that day. He'd spent most of that day, Tuesday, putting them in shape for publication. Then he finds that he is to perform again the next Sunday—the last straw! "Really, Shirley, so much is expected of me . . . that attainment would make me more perfect than God himself, and the work would entitle me to laying claim to super-human physical and mental capacity." He only wants the money to get time to rest.

> As soon as I'm able, I'll say "to hell" with everything, including my Town Hall appearance. If I feel like concertizing I will, if I don't I won't. The primary thing I'm interested in is composing

> seriously and playing and conducting my compositions. C'est la! Just think, I'm expected and supposed to become a first-rate pianist, a great composer, a "high and mighty" musician with standing, a public "idol," a reputable conductor, an established improvisor, a successful "popular" composer—and at the same time acquire culture and education and attend to all the small menial tasks of ordinary living—and to be top-notch in so many diverse and antagonistic fields.

But he can't play the piano well enough and doesn't have the knack for popular songs. How can he study scores if he's to read the important books, and vice versa? All this work is running him down.

But then comes the excited postscript, "late Wednesday AM," announcing a 5 September booking at the Palace. "If I go over big, that means endless prominence and endless money. That will give me the opportunity to mature myself in my serious piano playing and come out only when I am absolutely 'finished,' thus leaving no loophole for criticism. Meanwhile I will be in a position to freely compose and afford to have photostat copies of my scores sent to conductors and await developments."

Barely a week later, Gould's cheerfulness was shattered: the Palace booking was postponed and the family was broke! On 4 September 1931, he wrote Shirley, "I spent the most miserable week while this whole business was being transacted, and my father and I have been sitting in Broadway offices for as long as five or six hours at a stretch." He rants and complains about how hard he's had to work, how "exhausted and disgusted with everything human" he is, but the tone is high and exhilarated, the language self-consciously romantic. Gould seems almost to revel in his bitterness: "Oh Powers that Be! Give me strength not to realize and not to understand!—For I am young, and I want to be happy."

The Palace postponement was very serious. Barely three months before his eighteenth birthday, Morton was already the economic mainstay of the household. While James Gould polished the car (one of his favorite activities) or smoked his pipe, Morton scrambled to keep the family afloat. As Shirley wrote in her book (*Mike Quill: Himself*, p. 147), "At seventeen Morton faced the raw reality of supporting mother, father, aunt, grandmother, and three younger brothers."

He revealed his desperation to Whiteside in California, in a letter written on 3 September 1931, the day before the one to Shirley. "This letter will probably be as unpleasant to you as it is to me to write it. However the situation is so extreme that I am throwing discretion to the winds. In plain words—would you be able to loan me or procure for me somehow some money—say one hundred dollars. . . . My father's condition physically being so precarious and Walter being sick with Scarlet Fever all adds to the general debilitated condition." He outlines the Palace postponement; he expects to go on the following week, "but nothing is definite yet, and we have to live until I do go on. Needless to say that I will make quite a lot of money in this vaudeville racket, but we are desperately trying to hold on until then." When Whiteside saw him again, on 22 September, he was pale and thin. She wasn't able to give him any money until 7 October.

Gould did play the Palace, in October 1931. Opening night was a disaster. According to Walter, Morton's appearance was a last-minute thing. Jack Benny, the emcee, had just introduced an act involving a Chinese comedian described as "the strongest man in the world." When the strongman walked onstage, two men ran past and the wind of their passage knocked him over. The audience howled with laughter. Then Benny, reading from a sheet of paper, introduced "Morton Gould, pianist." The audience was primed for comedy, so Benny tried to assure them that this was serious. Gould came out onstage—thin, pale, dour, as uncomfortable as always—and began his *Bolero*. The opening bars were slow, quiet, and repetitive—very minimalist. The audience assumed this was all part of the joke, and cracked up again. "Poor Morton, on his so-called big break," Walter Gould said.

That fall of 1931, Gould turned down Reiner's scholarship because he had to support his family. Never again would Gould get the chance to soak up the history of music, learning from the masters. From now on, he was outside trying to force his way in. It was something he ultimately managed with remarkable success—not even George Gershwin blurred the boundary between "art" and "entertainment" as consistently, and Leonard Bernstein, the only other contender, was never an outsider, with his Boston Latin–Harvard–Curtis–Tanglewood connections.

Years later, when Reiner, already mortally ill, had left the Chicago Symphony, the conductor and his wife, Carlota, showed Morton the letter in which he turned down the offer. Morton recalled the moment in 1985.

> When I got through reading it, Carlota had tears in her eyes, Fritz also was teary eyed. I didn't feel teary eyed. If I had seen it in a movie, I would have felt more touched. In one second I realized the whole thing. Suppose I'd been able to take advantage? How great, to study with Reiner and learn all the techniques, instead of the way I did, sort of bludgeoning my way. I would have been a much better conductor than I have been. Who knows what would have happened to me, even as a composer, if I'd gone to Curtis and been exposed to that atmosphere?

Instead, Gould was exposed to something very different—exciting, intoxicating, but sharpened by desperation, dampened with vulgarity, and haunted by the fear of missing that check. During an interview late in 1994, he described this period. His father was now working solely as his manager; Morton himself was earning between $65 and $75 a week in vaudeville, a very good income. Rather than mingling with Reiner, Hofmann, and their colleagues, Gould mingled with society. He and Shefter played at parties, hosted by Elsa Maxwell or jewelry executive Jules Glaenzer, attended by the Gershwins, Jerome Kern, Noel Coward, Cole Porter, Harold Arlen: "You might call it the Great Gatsby social orbit."

But Gould and Shefter were hired help. Unlike Gershwin, who would play all night at the drop of a note, Gould had to be coaxed into it. He met scores of members of the musical and entertainment worlds—by playing for them, not playing with them. Many important people, among them Bobby Short and Michael Feinstein, have made their way by such a blend of performance and personality. But Morton Gould, who had written that disconsolate essay about the miseries of working a party, would always rather not.

As 1931 drew to a close, Gould continued the familiar pattern: studying when he could, getting engagements where he could, with occasional big shows—the Roxy in October and December, the Brooklyn Paramount in November. He attended performances with Whiteside; they heard Rachmaninoff in concert on 7 November. On

6 December, Gould appeared in a Jewish benefit managed by Samuel Lionel "Roxy" Rothafel, who was already interested in his career.

On 18 December 1931 Morton gave what those around him considered his recital debut, at the concert hall of the Barbizon-Plaza Hotel on West Fifty-eighth Street. (He had already given four shows at the Roxy earlier that day, performing a novelty number of his, *Vienna 1931* for piano and orchestra, beginning another week of appearances.) Whiteside considered this recital her own coming out as well. "In a way, this is the biggest milestone of my professional career," she wrote in her diary. If Morton were a success, he would draw students. Yet she already knew that her star pupil was not cut out to be a great pianist. She compared him to the much younger Stanley Baron: "Stanley has real feeling for the piano. It is his medium of expression. It never has been Morton's. Morton thinks always in terms of the orchestra."

The recital was a big event in the eighteen-year-old's professional career as a "Wonder Composer-Pianist," as the program put it. He played Bach, Scriabin, and his own work: the theme and six variations from *Theme, Variations and Fugue in the Romantic Manner*, the Chant and Fugue movements from his piano sonata, *Three Conservative Sketches*, *Bolero*, and finally, the improvisations.

Louis Biancolli (*World Telegram*, 19 December 1931) recorded the astonishment of the audience, though he himself was a little jaded.

> Apparently Ravel's epochal *Bolero* has not yet shot its last bolt. Last night in the Barbizon-Plaza concert hall an incredulous audience sat with eyes, ears, and mouths wide open while Morton Gould, a young local meteor of the piano, literally catapulted as unorthodox and unabashed a conception of it as has stormed our concert halls.
>
> The writer already was acquainted with Mr. Gould's bombshell, having heard him expound it in the little Wanamaker Auditorium and in the more vast Roxy Theater, so last evening it was more or less of a dud. Not so with the audience, however. Mr. Gould's vigorous elbowing, pummeling, cuffing, and palming virtually unseated his listeners and unloosed a volley of "Bravos." . . . Under his arms (not fingers) the piano becomes an orchestra, a dynamo, an embodied growl.

Gould explained himself in the February 1932 issue of *Musical Advance*. Under the heading "Random Notes," the page-long journal article reads like the report of a bright, curious, but still unformed young man—one with a thick streak of skepticism about abstractions, but a strong interest in technology. Gould's account of western musical history focused on changes in technique and materials available to succeeding generations, from Bach through the Theremin.

He concentrates on mechanical rather than theoretical matters, showing no interest in the challenge to traditional harmony posed by Schoenberg. He discusses new ways of making sound, using tone clusters "played with the arm," "overtone effects, plucking the strings." He speaks of a double-keyboard piano "which practically eliminates octave playing"—there is even a piano with amplifiers instead of a soundboard. This is the voice of the practical composer, not a philosopher on the esthetics of music but someone who wants to know how to make the greatest variety of sounds.

Gould reserves his strongest statements for an assessment of jazz—in 1932 a very controversial subject:

> Jazz has its place and fundamentally is perfectly legitimate. The minuet was the dance of Mozart's time—today the college co-ed and her boy friend hop around to the rhythm symphony being written with a prelude substituted for the minuet, a "blues" for the slow movement, and a rushing turbulent rhythmic last movement—and the orchestra to consist of Theremins, saxophones, brass, percussion, xylophones, vibraphones, and double-keyboard pianos! Incredible? Wait and see!

CHAPTER 6

An End to Apprenticeship

★ ★ ★ ★

GOULD WAS BEING PUSHED further from the concert hall. He worked with Whiteside whenever he could, but most of his time during 1932 was spent elsewhere. Early in the year, he played a pair of Brahms intermezzos for her, "with the insight of a great artist," as she noted in her diary. Shortly afterward they went to hear Walter Gieseking. Gould's own work was also being played; Nat Shilkret broadcast the novelty number "Marionettes in Motley" in June. During the summer, Gould recorded his *Bolero* on a piano roll for the Ampico company ("They have sent out 27,000 advertising circulars about me and with my picture to their subscription list," he wrote Whiteside on 19 August).

At the same time he wrote *Cantata U.S.* for chorus and small orchestra, using texts by Carl Sandberg and Macnight Black. Among its eleven movements were "Prairie," "Machine," "Adolescent Love Song" (during which the tenor was to "croon" through a megaphone, to typify "the romantic naivete so prevalent in present-day life"), "Skyscrapers," and "Harlem." Gould was determined to be completely up to date: "The composer prefers that the performers on the clarinet and saxophone, trumpet, trombone, solo violin and percussion be 'hot' players, preferably jazz players"; the clarinetist and saxophonist should be capable of performing portamentos and breaks "with ease." The orchestra included a banjo, ukelele, and Hawaiian steel guitar. Presciently, Gould wrote, "It has been the composer's aim to absorb the jazz idiom rather than use it as an end in itself."

Income was sporadic. One month, he complained to Whiteside in that August letter, there was a nightclub date for which he earned a mere five dollars, and "wasn't even allowed to sit in the comfortable seats in the lobby." Several times he got sick from overwork, and his father's health had deteriorated once again.

If they could last through the fall, there was hope: Erno Rapee had promised Morton a job at Radio City Music Hall, which was scheduled to open 31 December 1932. There at last might be a way out of this stressful cycle. The young Gould had made connections, largely through his father, with some powerful people in popular entertainment. Roxy Rothafel had his eye on the boy, and Rapee worked for Rothafel.

By late 1932 Morton's relationship with Shirley had changed. Gone was the wise boy patronizing his inexperienced girlfriend. They were experienced, all right. He was in Philadelphia that fall with Shefter performing with Arthur Tracy, "the Street Singer"; he wrote to Shirley from there on 22 October.

> Last night I slept with the Bible realistically on one side and you imaginatively on the other. . . .Why did you have to look so gorgeous on Thursday night? You don't realize how much you upset me. I think of you every minute of my "P.P." existence (Puritanical Philadelphia). If I could only crush you to me and feel your warm lips and skin for one minute! I am impatient to see you already.

As the stint continued, his desire increased. On 25 October he wrote again: "I'm continually visualizing you and imagining your caresses. I would go on and on, but I only get myself perturbed." Morton was deeply in love—or at least in lust, which to teenagers is the same thing—and being kept away from his love by the cruel force of the real world.

The real world was brutally frank during the week in Philly. The theater manager cursed them out for playing a duet, and later, while Morton watched, dumbfounded, handed a gun to one of his cronies for a job. Morton and Bert had to literally fight with another lodger to get a bed one night. Finally, they were stopped and searched by the police on their way back to New York.

Gould had reached the end of his tether. Radio City would be a godsend. As he described it in 1985, vaudeville was "a depressing way of life. It was really tawdry. Some people think of things gone by, that it becomes nostalgic. But it was just horrible, a brutal kind of existence. And it was meaningless. If you are doing something with great discomfort but it involves a social gain or an artistic gain, that's one thing—but this was nothing."

Still, everything Morton did drew attention. He sold some music to the publisher Jack Robbins. Besides the Ampico piano roll, there was a Victor recording of *Bolero* and "Satirical Dance." Of the *Bolero*, one reviewer wrote in an undated notice, "It is indeed something of a *tour de force*, and while by the very nature of the work it cannot sound very characteristic or effective in the black and white coloring of the piano, Gould wrestles with it valiantly and elicits a surprising welter of sound. The arrangement is an ingenious and obviously exceedingly difficult one." As Whiteside wrote in her diary on 15 November 1932, "At last, he is getting in the inner circles."

On 10 December 1932, Morton Gould turned nineteen. He had all the formal training he would get. He continued to find support and encouragement from Abby Whiteside, and he developed many musical friendships and contacts. But once he began working at Radio City, Gould was on his own. Already defensive about his lack of education, he spent the rest of his life regretting the background he did not have and the networks from which he was excluded. But more than training or connections, what differentiated Gould from his colleagues was internal.

George Gershwin's life and experience, especially in breaching the barrier between "art" and "pop," was perhaps the closest to Gould's. Aaron Copland, like Gould and Gershwin, was a New York son of Jewish immigrants, but he specifically chose not to attend college to concentrate on becoming a composer and was single-minded in pursuit of that goal. Virgil Thomson, too, decided to become a composer relatively late in his youth. He received a Harvard education and, like Copland, was one of the first to study in Paris with Nadia Boulanger, with active support from family and educational institutions. Roy Harris, George Antheil, Marc Blitzstein, Roger Sessions, Walter Piston, William Schuman—all had extensive academic training and college educations, and all either were permitted or freed themselves to work as composers, often from the security of academic positions.

But most important is this: what they did with their creative lives was their own choice. None felt pressured for mere survival, whereas Gould accepted the burden of supporting his family. The image of his father on the floor, coughing blood, never left him; one of James Gould's lungs was now gone, the other failing, and everyone looked to Morton—the genius, the prodigy—to keep them going.

Morton did have a powerful ego. Although he came to admire Gershwin, that was not his original position. In August 1932 Gould had attended an all-Gershwin concert at Lewisohn Stadium and came away "sorely disappointed," as he wrote Whiteside. "I have always championed Gershwin, but a whole program of his works is terribly boring and shows up his deficiencies in a glaring manner." His comments are doubly ironic, since eventually Gould's own work was criticized for many of the same reasons. The program included Gershwin's "serious works" and excerpts from the musicals: "The latter was absolutely scandalous. Imagine the staid old German players performing 'hot' jazz, which has no place other than the jazz bands for which it was written." The music itself? Gould panned everything but *Rhapsody in Blue*:

> [It] makes use of banal motives and effects that have been worked to death. In the large forms his melodic invention is sterile, his developments decidedly amateurish. He has some striking moments and novel effects, but they are not followed up. His final cadences are exactly the same, a crescendo on a sustained chord with "blue" figuration. . . . His orchestration is always the same—an exceedingly limited use of color effects. Finally, Gershwin is primarily a Tin Pan Alley composer, and it is the height of absurdity for the Philharmonic to do an all-Gershwin program.

Morton found his career exhilarating but frightening. He felt he had no option: he was the breadwinner and that was that. "Many years later it suddenly occurred to me: who elected me? I don't remember any discussion of it," Gould said in 1985. "Did my parents spoil me in any way? Yeah, they let me work, go out and support everybody. The normal thing would have been to have kept me on ice, let me study, maybe go to Europe, and everybody else go to work, even if it meant giving up school—it never occurred to me, until the last couple of years, that there could have been another way of doing it."

He made no serious efforts to escape. Gould knew his place: it was to make music to make money to keep the family going.

CHAPTER 7

From Radio City to Radio

★ ★ ★ ★

RADIO CITY MUSIC HALL was to be the greatest theater in the greatest city run by the greatest impresario of the age—Samuel Lionel Rothafel. There were bigger names involved—Rockefeller Center itself was the gamble of John D. Rockefeller Jr., and the main tenant was David Sarnoff's RCA Corporation, with its associated National Broadcasting Company and RKO studio and theater chain. But the first building begun and the first building open would be under the management and direction of Rothafel himself.

Born in Stillwater, Minnesota, Roxy had been rising from triumph to triumph ever since he staged his first show in a tavern in Forest City, Pennsylvania. (Roxy earned his nickname playing semipro baseball in Pennsylvania after leaving the Marine Corps in 1907.) Producer Benjamin J. Keith hired Roxy to spiff his own theaters. In a short time, he was brought from the Midwest to New York, where he leapfrogged from house to house, using his acute blend of showmanship, efficiency, and innovation.

In 1922 he gave a pioneering broadcast from the Capitol and soon began to offer the first radio variety program. He left the Capitol and "Roxy's Gang" in 1925 to run what was then the largest theater in the world, the Roxy (the radio program went to his former boss, "Major" Edward J. Bowes, and—as *Major Bowes' Original Amateur Hour*—became one of the most popular shows on the air). In 1932 Rothafel left the establishment that bore his name to become head of an even more magnificent venture: he would direct the two theatrical foundation stones for the daring new Rockefeller Center complex in midtown Manhattan.

The Music Hall and the RKO Roxy were across Sixth Avenue from one another, the larger on the northeast corner of Fiftieth Street, the smaller on the west side of the avenue and down the block at Forty-ninth. Radio City's interior, designed by Donald Deskey, was a Bauhaus masterwork of sweeping lines, massive statuary, and immense open spaces. The auditorium was huge; its curved walls and eighty-three-foot-high ceiling overarched sixty-two hundred seats—the largest indoor theater in the United States.

Opening night, 27 December 1932, was an elephantine affair. It was cold and rainy; the Sixth Avenue Elevated that cramped the street made crowd control more difficult. Thousands of onlookers crammed against police barricades to watch the glittering arrivals. There were stars of every sort: the Rockefellers, including twenty-four-year-old Nelson; former governor and presidential candidate Al Smith; industrialists such as Walter P. Chrysler; media moguls Sarnoff, Condé Nast, and William Randolph Hearst; former heavyweight champion Gene Tunney; pioneer aviator Amelia Earhart; Charlie Chaplin; Clark Gable; Noel Coward; Irving Berlin—the list was blinding.

And Morton Gould, just turned nineteen, was at the piano in the pit along with Bert Shefter. It was his first steady job. The orchestra, numbering more than a hundred, was a mix of seasoned musicians and youngsters such as Gould and some recent Juilliard graduates. The arrangers and conductors under Rapee included Charles Previn, who succeeded Rapee upon his death, and Alexander Smallens.

If Rapee liked you, you were hired. He knew the Goulds from the Roxy and elsewhere. Musicians he didn't know got makeshift auditions: Harvey Shapiro, then a twenty-one-year-old Juilliard-trained cellist, tried out in the back of a restaurant. Rehearsals had begun three weeks before opening. The backstage facilities, complete with showers, were a far cry from the urine-soaked washstands of vaudeville. But the work was rigorous: seven days a week, from early morning to well past dark.

"Everybody was happy to have a job," recalled Shapiro. Morton and Harvey were the youngest players, and everybody took them for ushers in their beautiful velvet jackets. For Shapiro, fresh out of conservatory, this was a great adventure. The starting pay was $140 a week, including radio broadcasts—an immense sum when $25 was a solid wage and millions of people had no work at all. "I didn't have a penny, what did I know? For a dollar you could eat a good meal; for fifty cents I got the best Havana cigars," Shapiro said in 1995.

Rapee was a first-rate conductor with a broad knowledge of music and an understanding of Roxy's mix of high art and popular fare. But Roxy had made a mistake. He thought you could still draw crowds with stage shows. Opening night was an overstuffed fiasco: nineteen acts, from the Flying Wallendas to the Radio City Music Hall Ballet to the Tuskegee Institute Choir to "Ray Bolger, Outstanding Young American Dancing Comedian" to excerpts from *Carmen* to Martha Graham to De Wolfe Hopper reading "Casey at the Bat"—and on and on and on. The show started half an hour late and ran so long that Brooks Atkinson of *The New York Times* and other critics had to leave before it was over.

Roxy had aimed too high and worked too hard. He collapsed after the finale, was rushed to a hospital, and did not return for months. His high-low entertainment policy was a failure. "It wasn't real vaudeville," said Shapiro. "It was too fancy. . . . Once I remember they had Chinese playing tennis onstage. There were six thousand seats to fill. Who the hell is going to watch that?"

Radio City bled money. While Roxy was hospitalized, the board changed direction. Instead of two big stage shows a day, a one-hour stage show and a movie would be presented four times a day—five a day on Saturdays and Sundays, with, of course, no days off. Salaries were trimmed across the board. Roxy's own pay was cut in half, to $1000 a week. He even lost his name: the management of the original Roxy forced Radio City to change the name of its RKO Roxy to the Center Theater.

Players' wages went down to $90 a week. "They had to do it," Shapiro said. "Business was terrible. They said they were going to close up the place." The orchestra shrank, too. It started out with ten cellos, for example, and by the end of the year there were only four: "I was the last of the young kids left," Shapiro said.

Shapiro couldn't stand the Music Hall. He hung on for five years, before moving to Toscanini's NBC Symphony, and never went back. Morton's stomach got tied in knots every time he walked by the building. And Gould and Shapiro were among the lucky ones. The old guys, the cynical immigrants, were fired left and right.

The money was good, but the times were scary. Shy, diffident Morton, his family depending on him, did not have the cocky reserves of someone like Harvey Shapiro. "We were always on two weeks' notice," Gould said in 1985. "And even with the two weeks' notice, we had notice. There was not one second we felt secure." Rehearsals were sometimes scheduled after the last show, starting around eleven o'clock at night, followed by quick meals—with the next rehearsal at six the next morning. Morton often stayed in a midtown hotel.

As a keyboard player, Gould sometimes performed onstage, occasionally in costume. Nearly half a century later, he described the 1933 celebration of Washington's birthday, when he appeared in the Center Theater's birthday pageant for an entire week, wearing colonial garb: powdered wig, cutaway jacket, ruffled shirt, white stockings, and shoes with buckles—"which, by the way, kept falling off all the time. Clank." He played the spinet for a party that was interrupted by the arrival of a patriot shouting, "Stop! Washington has crossed the Delaware!" Unfortunately, at the first performance Morton didn't wait for the courier to make his entrance or announcement. He spotted him in the wings and stopped playing immediately (and inexplicably, to the audience), throwing up his arms in surprise. "Apparently I threw the whole thing off."

Rehearsals for the pageant were tough, too. It was so cold in the theater that the players in the pit wore hats and overcoats "with smoke coming out of their nostrils," while Morton sat onstage in wig and waistcoat, desperately cold. Suddenly, as they shivered, the orchestra contractor roared down the aisle, cursing furiously. Leaning into the pit, he yelled, "Two weeks'notice!" And he pointed at Morton: "You too, Mozart!"

"It's funny now," Morton said in 1985. "Nobody laughed then."

Gould's memories of his brief time at Radio City almost always concerned calamity and hardship. The pianists had more to do than the others; they rehearsed the ballet and singers, and occasionally gave solos. During one show Gould began with the orchestra in the pit, which rose to stage level and then started down. Meanwhile, he jumped off the stage, hurried into a hussar's uniform, plopped himself at the piano, and rose into view playing Liszt's *Hungarian Rhapsody* No. 2. Once he found himself running down Sixth Avenue from one theater to the other in full uniform!

Just being on stage could be frightening. During the summer of 1933, Gould and Shefter sat back-to-back at two concert grands at the front of the second of the three sections of stage, with the first section deep in the pit. The two sections rose together until the first was at stage level and the second, now covered by a curtain, was at the top of the proscenium "as if suspended from a cliff" and the pianists had to scramble down. Morton was in constant fear of falling —in which case, he wrote Shirley in July 1933, "My suit would have to be dry cleaned and you would be repressed all over again."

In his quest for the latest equipment, Roxy installed some Bechstein electric pianos, unreliable monsters whose tubes were always blowing: "In the middle of a solo, nothing would come out—'Two weeks' notice!'" Once Shefter was in an alcove playing the Bechstein when a tube blew. He crawled under the instrument to replace it and missed a cue—so when the spotlight shone, there was the silent piano and the pianist's rear poking up. The audience thought it was a gag, but Shefter almost lost his job.

"We worked without stop in a very depressing atmosphere, although it was a nice enough place physically," Gould said in 1985. During breaks, the men played cards, but Morton would go off and write, trying to ignore the cynics who warned him he'd never get out of the pit.

Morton did find time for other things, including recitals, individual broadcasts, and even a vacation. At nine in the morning on 13 February 1933, he played at Columbia University's Milbank Chapel, a performance an anonymous college reviewer considered "thoroughly satisfying, and from the technical point of view almost miraculous," with intensity and ease that "stamps [Gould] with the brand of genius." In May 1933 he gave a lecture-demonstration at Princeton.

Life was hard but fruitful. There was the discipline of work, while Gould learned about arranging, orchestration, what worked and what didn't, what an audience responded to. Sometimes Rapee twitted him about his ambition, demanding suddenly that he transpose something and teasing him, "What's the matter? You're a composer who's too good to read music?"

Rapee respected Gould's ability—there were dozens of pianists he might have hired, but he chose this one. "I wasn't exactly the best, but I was a good sight reader, and I could handle what I had to handle," Gould said. Rapee was an excellent conductor—he earned the Bruckner Society's Mahler Medal of Honor for the first radio broadcast of the Symphony No. 8 in 1942—and Morton absorbed understanding from him. But he also acquired Rapee's prejudice against Eugene Ormandy.

They were countrymen, and Rapee had hired the violinist for the Capitol orchestra in 1921. Ormandy eventually became concertmaster and then assistant conductor; in 1931 he was named music director of the Minneapolis Symphony Orchestra. By the time Radio City Music Hall opened, Ormandy had already led the Philadelphia Orchestra in lighter fare and substituted for Toscanini.

"Rapee hated him," said Shapiro. "He was always pissed off that Ormandy got Minneapolis, and then he got Philadelphia. Rapee was more talented. Ormandy was a very fine fiddler and a marvelous accompanist. Rapee was mad because he always wanted to conduct."

"We used to make disparaging remarks about Ormandy," Gould said in 1985. "'Look who's conducting a symphony orchestra!' It killed Rapee, because this is what Rapee wanted to do."

Morton didn't stay at Radio City long, for during the summer of 1933 he and Shefter were approached by the National Broadcasting Company. Although Gould later recounted mostly the travails of his time at Radio City, by then he was being treated fairly well. He had, he wrote Shirley that July, a "large and beautiful dressing room, with chairs and tables, even unto a bridge table, and a bathroom so large that if you were only here you could stay there all the time, and between shows I'd make love to you."

He also acknowledged some elements of personality that would severely undercut his chances of becoming a star. He recounted their routine thus: "We have to sit on the stage and play continuously for one hour and thirty-eight minutes—with everyone from Roxy down trying to make me smile—which I do before the curtain goes up and after it comes down."

In the years to come, Gould's inability and unwillingness to focus attention on himself became a significant handicap. Until the end of his days, he rarely smiled in public. Here he was, at center stage of the biggest, most elaborate concert hall in New York, with a place in the limelight, yet Morton could not shine.

Fortunately the performing world he was about to enter didn't require that sort of personality. By late July 1933, Gould and Shefter were staff pianists for NBC. "I don't have to depend on Radio City any more!" he wrote Shirley. "It looks as if my pit days are over."

When Gould and Shefter joined the National Broadcasting Company, radio broadcasting itself was little more than ten years old. In 1922, when James Gould took his son to play over WOR at the Bamberger's in Newark, the station had just been born. In the decade since, radio had exploded like a nova over American culture. The 1919–1921 edition of the *Readers' Guide to Periodical Literature* had no entries about wireless broadcasting; the next edition (1922–1924) had ten full pages.

The federal Department of Commerce began issuing broadcast licenses in 1921: five from January to November. In December 1921, they issued twenty-three. Then came 1922: eight licenses in January; twenty-four in February (including, on 20 February 1922, WOR); seventy-seven in March; seventy-six in April; ninety-seven in May. By the spring of 1922, the department had run out of three-letter call signs and began to create four-letter stations.

WEAF (ancestor of WRCA and then WNBC) began operations in August 1922, from the Western Electric Building in lower Manhattan. On 28 August 1922, it gave the first commercially sponsored broadcast (to sell apartments in Jackson Heights, Queens, not far from Richmond Hill). WEAF offered Roxy's variety shows, football games, and organ recitals from the City College of New York. None of the performers were paid—merely being heard over the air was enough.

The year 1922 also brought the first skirmish of a war still being fought when Morton Gould became one of the generals. Somebody was making money from the broadcast of copyrighted music, so the American Society of Composers, Authors and Publishers began demanding fees for its members—they wrote the songs, after all.

The broadcasters were incredulous and appalled—such demands profaned the purity of their enterprise—but ASCAP had the law on its side. In early 1923 WEAF paid $500 for a one-year license to use ASCAP music; in August, ASCAP won a case against WOR.

Then the stations themselves created the National Association of Broadcasters and tried to persuade songwriters to give them the work for nothing. In 1925 ASCAP's biggest guns, Victor Herbert and John Philip Sousa, lobbied in Congress against a bill to exempt radio from copyright, and it died in committee.

Radio music was at first mostly classical or semi-classical, performed by conservatory students and teachers. There was no folk or what became known as country music, and barely a trace of jazz—which, with its African-American roots and sensuality was denounced in local newspapers as "unhealthy" and an "abomination." Even the instruments were suspect; some stations banned saxophones as "immoral."

A peculiar mix of idealism and capitalism permeated the airwaves. Most broadcasters considered paid advertising bad form. But the potential for profit was vast, and the forces jockeying for position were behemoths. In 1926 the National Broadcasting Company was formed, its ownership split among RCA, AT&T, and Westinghouse. AT&T sold WEAF to NBC for $1 million, and the new station, WNBC, debuted on 15 November 1926, with a gala broadcast from the Grand Ballroom of New York's Waldorf-Astoria Hotel. The program included the New York Symphony under Walter Damrosch, soprano Mary Garden from Chicago, Will Rogers from Kansas City, a handful of dance bands, and the comedy team of Weber and Fields. Everyone donated their services, but from then on commercial sponsors were going to pay for the biggest shows.

By the next year, NBC had created two nationwide networks: the Red, fed primarily by WEAF, which evolved into the more popular and powerful grouping; and the Blue, fed by WJZ. (The terms "red" and "blue" sprang from colored pencils used to delineate the stations on a map).

The foundations for the Golden Age of radio were being laid, and so was the competition. After concert manager Arthur Judson was rebuffed by David Sarnoff in an attempt to link up with NBC, he joined George A. Coats and sportscaster J. Andrew White to form the rival United Independent Broadcasters, with WOR as its base. Then the Columbia Phonograph Record Co. signed on to create the Columbia Phonograph Broadcasting System. (At about the same time, RCA bought the Victor Talking Machine Co., forming RCA Victor).

Howard Barlow became Columbia's music director, with a twenty-three-piece orchestra; Donald Voorhees led a dance combo. The new network's first show, on 18 September 1927, featured Barlow's orchestra; the second, Voorhees's band. Then came a performance of *The King's Henchman*, an opera by Deems Taylor and Edna St. Vincent Millay, using singers from the Metropolitan Opera. Soon after Barlow hired an assistant, a young Russian named André Kostelanetz.

But this network did not have NBC's resources, and Columbia Phonograph pulled out. In September 1928, the operation was renamed the Columbia Broadcasting System, and twenty-six-year-old William S. Paley became president. The central players of radio were now in place.

A third network, the Mutual Broadcasting System, formed in 1934. It included WOR, which was now owned by the R. H. Macy department store. This became Gould's home, but it was always a distant third.

There were two basic formulas. First was the noncommercial "sustaining" program provided by the networks and paid for by the stations; here were the lecture series, much of the classical music, the early radio dramas, and other high-minded offerings. Second were the sponsored programs, produced for the most part by advertising agencies rather than their clients or the networks. They took up less of the day—in 1931, less than 34 percent of NBC's and less than 22 percent of CBS's output—but they supported the rest. Not surprisingly, differences in attitude developed between sustaining and commercial shows.

By the mid-1930s (as Erik Barnouw put it in the second volume of *A History of Broadcasting in the United States*) the sustaining people were to the commercial directors like "dependent relatives living on marginal pay," and the sustaining people, on the other hand, considered their commercial fellows "not free souls." Before that, though, October 1929 had hit radio as hard as the rest of the nation. RCA, for one, had been a spectacular performer before Black Friday: by midsummer 1929, when Morton was in Woodstock, company stock had passed $500 a share and split five to one—each share of which, by September, had risen to almost $115. In late November 1929, RCA stock was worth less than $30 a share.

But radio thrived. Its effect on American life was profound, greater even than the eventual impact of television. Nothing like this had ever happened before. Movie theaters, even those with talking pictures, began closing; library circulation decreased. The growth of the networks killed off small-town radio bands and ensembles, but there was lots of opportunity in New York City. The primary stations needed musicians for bands and orchestras, to provide continuity between programs, and for emergency service on the frequent occasions that something went wrong—when wires broke, or performers failed to appear, or someone's show was suddenly canceled.

Gould and Shefter had already played occasionally on the NBC Red network out of WEAF. Sometimes they did half an hour, sometimes fifteen minutes; sometimes they were by themselves, or accompanied a tenor, or joined an orchestra—always filling time in sustaining rather than commercial programs.

In July 1933 Gould and Shefter started work at NBC's original studios at 711 Fifth Avenue, the world's most advanced facilities when built just six years before. By 1933 NBC had built new studios in Radio City, impressive quarters with sliding panels to shrink or expand the space, glass walls for tourists to watch the broadcasts, everything elegant and up to date. Still, for Gould, it was far from perfect. Once again he put in long hours, often just hanging around and waiting for something to go wrong.

The staff pianists were used as accompanists, for rehearsals, and for anything else that needed a keyboard. The hour-long programs were preceded by one-hour rehearsals. Working for both the Red and Blue networks, he accompanied singers and quartets, or small orchestras, and stood by just in case.

"We would sit in little rooms on the upper floors of the RCA Building, little white rooms that looked like operating rooms," Gould said in 1985. "The engineer sat in his glass booth, and you sat by the piano, with an announcer. And nothing happened. But if a [transmission] line broke, the announcer got up and said, 'And now Morton Gould will play Liszt's Etudes' or whatever it was I was going to play. I would play until they fixed the lines. Sometimes it would be an hour. Sometimes they never fixed the fucking line, and you played until the end of the broadcast time."

He'd sit there until one or two in the morning after a full day's work, practicing if he had the energy, chatting with the announcer or the engineer, but feeling trapped because he didn't dare leave the room: "That's when the line would break." Gould didn't spend all his time in a standby studio. Occasionally a network headliner, Jack Benny or Bob Hope, performed in Washington, D.C., and the orchestra traveled by train for the show. He told me, during a conversation in February 1996, "I was the youngest guy, so I always had the upper berth. Then you would get washed and shave in the men's room in the morning." For a man who remembered playing Super Chief down Hillside Avenue on his little wooden wagon, this was close to heaven—but still not good enough.

Gould was prospering. In late 1933, with finances sufficiently secure, the family had moved from Hillside Avenue to a luxurious three-bedroom apartment at 115-25 Metropolitan Avenue, on the corner of Park Lane South, in Kew Gardens, Queens. In February 1934 Gould wrote Shirley that the Carl Fischer firm had commissioned him to arrange a violin solo for two pianos—and to look over the catalog to find other compositions suitable for similar work. ("Success!" he commented wryly. "From Cantatas I'm gradually working my way up to arrangements.")

But Gould stayed at NBC only through the spring of 1935, barely two years. Ironically, after all the worrying over "two weeks' notice" at Radio City, he was fired by the network instead. "I was never given any reason," he said in 1985. "I think they wanted to bring in somebody else, or somebody came back who had left—whatever the reason, I was given notice. I was devastated. This was a job and I needed it. I was supporting a family."

But there was work nonetheless, for besides working at NBC Gould had continued to make arrangements, perform with Shefter, and play his own recitals. Sometime during Gould's years as a party pianist, for example, he had finally met Gershwin. Gould remembered that once at a party Gershwin pulled him aside and whispered, "Do you like ice cream, kid?" George brought him into a quiet room; they sat down before a big bowl and ate the whole thing. Gershwin explained, while he ate, that he was so crazy about the stuff that his family tried to keep him away from it.

Gould orchestrated *Alma Mater*, a "football ballet" by Kay Swift, Gershwin's love at the time, for the School of American Ballet, which had just been founded by Lincoln Kirstein, Edward M. Warburg, and George Balanchine. A performance was held at the Adelphi Theater in March 1935; the company appeared again on 12 August at Lewisohn Stadium. It was, according to Henriette Weber (*New York Evening Journal*), a "most amusing show," a "very frankly modern and youthful . . . take-off on college life and the adoration of the football hero," marked by Swift's "tuneful" music, Gould's "effective" arrangement, and John Held Jr.'s "clever costumes."

Gould was fifteen years younger than Gershwin, and he never came close to being a member of the elder man's inner circle. But Gershwin was sufficiently impressed with Gould's talent to invite him to his apartment on Riverside Drive to read sketches for *Porgy and Bess*—and to demonstrate his own skill. Once, Gould recalled in December 1994, Gershwin said, "Listen, Morton, I want you to listen to this." With typical self-deprecation, Gould went on with the story: "And he got a fugue going, a three-voice fugue. He played for me—and he also told it to the elevator operator." Gershwin then assembled a cast and orchestra for a runthrough of the show, which would open in New York that October 1935; Gould, on piano, remembered that some members of the composer's family cried on hearing the music. But the score did not make a deep impression on him: "Don't forget, I was busy reading notes. I remember I thought, 'Hey, those songs, they sound pretty good from where I sit.'"

That was the extent of Gould's contact with the Gershwins, except for a letter from George to the mezzo-soprano Eva Gauthier written 16 March 1937, four months before his death. Gauthier, a famous performer of contemporary songs, was losing the services of Celius Dougherty, her longtime accompanist, and had asked for recommendations. "If you are still desirous of doing some American popular songs there are many boys in New York who would be excellent as accompanists," Gershwin wrote. "There's a very clever youngster named Morton Gould who is a conductor and pianist on the Mutual Broadcast Company out of New York. You might contact him."

Gould never did work with Gauthier, but a copy of Gershwin's letter remained one of his most valued possessions.

CHAPTER 8

Between Two Fires

★ ★ ★ ★

IN AUGUST 1935, when the twenty-one-year-old Gould made his first radio broadcast over WOR as the music director, composer, and conductor of *Music Today*, it was the start of an exhilarating, busy decade during which he accomplished something that only Gershwin and Bernstein ever surpassed—and only Gershwin did it Gould's way.

Gould successfully and consistently crossed the hitherto inviolable boundary between American popular and European art music; his work was played both by dance bands and by the greatest orchestras in the nation. His name was known to the average radio listener as well as to concert hall audiences, and he created music as deeply American in its substance and its attitude as anything written during the twentieth century. And—unique among American musical figures—he was a "radio composer." Gould built his career over the airwaves during the years when radio was the nation's most important and ubiquitous means of communication.

Not surprisingly, Gould's ascension aroused the envy of many powerful figures, particularly among composers of the European tradition and their supporters. His personal weaknesses, his insecurities, his family dynamics, his politics, his musical background, and even his blatant heterosexuality worked against him. The grand struggle that Morton began so enthusiastically wore him down and changed him from a young lion eager to battle the forces of musical reaction to a cautious, discreet, almost marginal figure.

The move to WOR had been engineered by his father. James Gould contacted a WOR executive named Jules Seebach, who had just hired the American-born Alfred Wallenstein to conduct the staff orchestra. Seebach and Wallenstein wanted a music department to equal those at NBC and CBS. Seebach also wanted to follow the path blazed by Kostelanetz at CBS the year before, with *André Kostelanetz Presents*: he would take a bright young composer-conductor with a classical background and a knowledge of popular music, give him an orchestra and a time slot, and see what happened.

On 6 April 1935 Morton got an on-air audition; in late August Wallenstein and Seebach hired him for what began as a half-hour weekly evening sustaining broadcast. His assignment was to conduct orchestral arrangements of popular songs, show tunes, and semi-classical melodies—eight a week. The starting pay was about $50 a week, of which he paid 20 percent to his copyist (later arranger), Philip J. Lang, and 15 percent to WOR's management agency, as a commission to retain the rights to the music himself.

This was Gould's show; he was no longer afraid of "two weeks' notice," and he felt more comfortable with the players. As he explained it in 1985, "They were used to doing programs from the classical repertoire with Wally, who was very demanding, but they knew the music, they had played it many times. . . . Suddenly they had to read all new music. If there were eight arrangements on the program, that was eight new pieces getting their first performance, and many of the arrangements were very complicated, very heavy." Gould was in an extraordinary position for a composer: he was being paid to write, play, and broadcast whatever he wanted—within limits, of course, though Gould did stretch them on several memorable occasions. "Obviously, I was not going to do a League of Composers New Music Festival, but nobody bothered me. I was responsible, even at that time."

Gould's taste was strictly middle-of-the-road. "I would do 'Night and Day' because a lot of people knew it, but I also liked it. How I did it was my taste. My music was colorful, but not commercial because it was too complicated. The big thing against me was that I was not commercial." His arrangements were significantly different from those of other popular musicians, including Kostelanetz. Light music was supposed to be predictable and easy on the ears, with no key changes, steady tempos, and no surprises. But Gould thought in other terms:

> One thing that my arrangements reflect is that they sound as if they were written for an orchestra. They have a symphonic texture, when other arrangements were more perfunctory, less imaginative, and less creative. My approach to arranging was as a composer, not an arranger. I could not write an orthodox, commercial kind of arrangement to save my life. I couldn't go two bars without doing something that would be musically interesting. And this is where the producer, if he were going for a commercial arrangement, would say, "Morton, that's nice, but that's going to throw the listener, he won't know where the hell you're going with that. You've got to stay with the melody." Did I listen? No.

Although he was a very original composer, Gould was just as effective building on someone else's foundation. "Night and Day," for example, or "Beyond the Blue Horizon," or, most famously, "When Johnny Comes Marching Home" would be the springboard for his imagination. "I used someone else's tune, a common denominator. It was the equivalent of using an everyday sentence and expanding on it, turning it into a poem or a piece of extended prose."

This willingness to join his own creativity to another's melody became a Gould hallmark, both a strength and a weakness. It may have derived from the internal rebellion against James Gould. Morton didn't get his interest in or knowledge of popular music from the family. Rather, as a member of the first radio generation, he got his music over the air. Gould, who had a musical reaction to almost any sound, could turn whatever he heard into something else. "What apparently happened is, I would be listening to a couple of arrangements of 'Night and Day,' and I felt my musical adrenaline going. I would be thinking, 'Jesus, there's more than doing two choruses with nothing flat around them'—once I tasted it, it was like blood, and I was off to the races."

That bloodthirstiness applied almost entirely to music, however. By all accounts, Morton was quiet and shy. The pianist Milton Kaye, who was at WOR, remembered Gould's arrival at the station. "He had this great reputation as a pianist and an improvisor," Kaye said in 1995. Kaye, born and raised in Brooklyn, was a Juilliard graduate who accompanied the violinists Jascha Heifetz and Erica Morini, and the bass Cesare Siepi, among others. He credited Wallenstein's "wonderful sense of interesting musicians" for hiring Gould, giving him the orchestra, and telling him to write for it.

Gould's arrangements of show tunes, Kaye said, were magnificent: "So bright and fresh. He had a good orchestra, which could move in the popular idiom a little bit, too, so it didn't sound too stilted. And then he put in an occasional original piece of his own. And he was just brilliant."

Harold Diner, a trombonist who dropped out of Juilliard when combining school and work got to be too much, joined the WOR orchestra in 1937 at the age of seventeen, after Gould had been there for a couple of years. Contrary to Gould's own appraisal, Diner considered his arrangements to be "highbrow commercial," on a slightly higher plane than the ordinary run of radio music. "You could tell by the writing that it was done by a musician who wrote just a little better than some of the commercial writers. It was not really symphonic and not really dance. It was just very musical," Diner said. And again contradicting Gould, Diner said that, although the players genuinely liked the music, it was not terribly hard—largely because the composer, even then, knew how to write comfortably for an orchestra.

The WOR staff orchestra had between six and nine violins, two violas, two cellos, four woodwinds, four saxophones that doubled on woodwinds, two horns, two or three trumpets, two or three trombones, a keyboard, a harp, and a percussionist—not far different, in size or makeup (except, of course, for those devilish saxes), from Joseph Haydn's Esterhazy orchestra or the general run of eighteenth-century European court ensembles.

By and large, Gould was a respected conductor despite his youth. "For the most part," he said in 1985, "I found the players very sympathetic and responsive, and they would be very excited. I would bring in an arrangement, they would read it down the first time, and they would be very enthusiastic, they would say, 'That's great.' They would applaud."

The WOR staff orchestra played for everything the station broadcast, so Diner and his colleagues knew all the leaders' quirks. Gould was known to be quiet and serious, not someone with a demonstrative or assertive personality. "I never remember him raising his voice or getting upset," Diner said. "Never. He was strictly business. He had a fine orchestra to work with. His arrangements were . . . musical enough that he didn't overdo his writing and run into trouble, like some composers who write so difficult that you can't conduct it. He was very quiet, very businesslike, and that was it. I don't remember ever any humor."

As Gould's program grew in popularity, and his skill with it, the orchestra expanded to nearly forty members. Initially, *Music Today* was broadcast from the station's studio at 1440 Broadway, which had room for no more than twenty-five or so people. In the late 1930s a few programs, including Gould's, were moved to the New Amsterdam Theater on Forty-second Street just west of Times Square, which had a capacity of twelve hundred.

He was working as hard as ever, yet to an important extent he was still not in charge of his life. James Gould was. "I remember his father, Jimmy, would always come in there with a pipe just clenched in his teeth," pianist Kaye said. "He'd come and sit through most of the rehearsals and performances, and usually he would go home with Morton."

"He used to walk around and say hello to the fellows in the hallway," Diner said. "I don't think he used to go into the booth." True, James had no involvement in the musical aspect of the work. But he was Morton's agent, manager, adviser—he had his son's power of attorney, he collected Morton's paychecks, he handled the finances. He tended to speak of "My son Mo't'n Gould" in one quick phrase and enjoyed giving the impression that he himself was the source of Morton's success.

Although radio provided Gould with a good, steady income, the work there was never first in his heart. Frequently Whiteside would arrive at her apartment to find Morton working, eating, or just waiting for her. Sometimes he encountered Arthur (Buck) Whittemore, a Vermillion native and Whiteside student, and later member of the duo-piano team of Whittemore and Lowe. Often, Morton and Stanley Baron played together—on 26 June 1936, Whiteside recorded in her diary, the two of them played Schumann's Piano Concerto. "Such boys," she wrote proudly. "They would be hard to beat."

Gould was ever more strongly her champion. On 13 December 1936 he wrote her a letter: "When I make money I am going to advertise you in all the papers so everybody will go to the Jesus Christ of piano playing. Come here to get your wounds healed that were inflicted by Juilliard." No wonder she loved him.

All along, he had been making headway with his serious composition. On 20 September 1935, less than a month after Morton started on WOR, Leopold Stokowski announced that he intended to perform Gould's *Chorale and Fugue in Jazz* that season with the Philadelphia Orchestra! (The same *Times* piece mentioned that John Corigliano, father of the composer John Corigliano, had been appointed the Philharmonic's assistant concertmaster.) Gould had written the piece, for full orchestra and two pianos, two years previously at NBC (one section of the score is marked "presto—à la Shirley"). It was to have been performed by the NBC orchestra under Frank Black. Those plans were scotched when Morton was fired, and the score languished until Ruth O'Neil, an associate of Arthur Judson and a friend of Whiteside, sent it to Stokowski.

The conductor himself wrote Gould on 2 November 1935. He was taking "a great deal of musical pleasure" in conducting Gould's *Chorale and Fugue* in rehearsals and "would like to play this soon in concert" if Gould were willing. Stokowski considered it a "remarkable work." He had a few suggestions, mostly to shorten it, and concluded, "I am very enthusiastic about this work and want to make it sound as well as I possibly can when we play it." He signed the letter "Sincerely your colleague, Leopold Stokowski." How thrilling: to be called "colleague" by Leopold Stokowski!

Although Gould did not attend the rehearsals, he met with Stokowski in the conductor's New York apartment. "He had a big red pencil," Gould said in 1985. "He was most gracious and correct. We read through the score, just turned the pages. That was it. I think he hardly said anything."

In program notes for the concerts, held in Philadelphia in January 1936, Gould explained what he was about. He wrote about the strength and sophistication of American popular music, themes that he would expand on aggressively during the next decade. "I have attempted to co-ordinate the characteristic of jazz with the classical form of a Choral and Fugue—done in a free style because of the material." Knowing that the Philadelphia audience was already disturbed by Stokowski's programming of new work, he argued for the subtlety of contemporary popular culture. The "legitimate" musician's conception of popular music—"sequences of syncopated fourths and a rigid rhythmic bass"—is wrong ("the commercial jargon for this defect is 'corny'"), and "any arranger who treated a dance tune thus would not get very far."

Chorale and Fugue in Jazz opens with a cinematic blare of trumpets and upper strings, after which the theme of the Chorale—which Gould described as "a 'blues' type of melody"—is presented by the saxophones and pianos, with flute ornamentation. The orchestration and mood, slow and lush, owe obvious debts to Stokowski's Bach. But the Fugue is something else. The subject—quick, catchy, syncopated, and swinging—is presented by the first violins, then taken up by the seconds and the high and low brass in four-part succession. The orchestra begins to sound very like a dance band, with bent notes, raucous trumpets, and slap basses, "simulating the effect of a band when it 'rides'—the effect of imperceptibly hurrying the intervals between beats, due to a collective stimulation and anticipation of the rhythmic pattern," as the composer put it.

Gould sets the theme of the Fugue in the horns and the Chorale in the violins, and the music builds to an excited climax culminating in a sudden, falling glissando from the solo clarinet—a quick, inverted homage to *Rhapsody in Blue*. There are traces of Gershwin throughout, including reminiscences of *An American in Paris* and Concerto in F.

The overall result could be clumsy and off-balance. There are clever touches, but Gould was still learning to orchestrate. The Chorale theme has little weight, though the Fugue is jaunty. One can easily imagine that neither Stokowski nor the Philadelphia musicians would have been able to give it the appropriate bounce. A recording made in 1941, by Leon Barzin and the National Orchestral Association, is awkward and not well coordinated, but enough comes through to indicate that the composer was moving in a very promising direction.

The performances themselves were extraordinary events. The first, on 2 January 1936, was part of a Stokowski aural experiment: for *The Rite of Spring*, he placed the orchestra behind the shell and miked it, leaving the dancers in unobstructed view. Morton went to Philadelphia alone to hear it (when he dropped in on Whiteside at 1:30 the next morning, she observed in her diary that he looked worn and "not very pleased or happy"). Stokowski programmed the piece again in a subscription concert on 9 January. This time the concert was an affair for extended family. Morton's parents went, as did Shefter, Whiteside, Baron, and Uzin; they all had dinner together before the performance. Whiteside described the experience in her class newsletter of 27 January:

> There we sat in a box, father, mother, sweetheart, teacher, and composer. He had three recalls, which is a lot for Philadelphia for anything written later than 1850, I am told. The criticisms were for and against but all of the papers gave him excellent space and Stokowski said to Morton, "We will play it until they like it." Then he told Ruth O'Neil who is a personal friend of his, "Let me see everything that boy writes. I want to keep in touch with him."

Needless to say, Gould remembered his own shortcomings, not the exhilaration. His behavior could be chalked up to youthful inexperience. When the concert was over, the young composer left the Academy of Music with the rest of the audience, in confused exuberance. Then he realized he should return to thank Stokowski, but he couldn't find his ticket stub and had to talk his way back inside. Once backstage, he was self-conscious and embarrassed, while the conductor, who considered that the audience that night was not responding properly, debated whether to go back out and give them a speech. "He was known," Gould said in 1995, "for really chewing out an audience."

In a letter dated 11 January 1936, Stokowski asked for more scores "because I am deeply interested in your work." Furthermore, the maestro wrote, "I am sorry the public did not understand your Chorale and Fugue, all I can say is I, personally, enjoyed it immensely."

It's not clear why Stokowski thought the listeners didn't like it. The local critics took the score seriously, and newspaper reviews of the first performance noted that the audiences cheered and called Gould back for curtain call after curtain call. After the 2 January performance, Edwin H. Schloss (*The Philadelphia Record*) called it "clever music ingeniously developed [sounding] most divertingly like a collaboration between Sebastian Bach and George Gershwin with a Stokowski performance"; Linton Martin (*The Philadelphia Inquirer*) said it "displays a sound sense of instrumental scoring, is spontaneous in expression, and is felicitous in fugal effect." He declared it "a pronounced hit" with the first-night audience, which applauded Gould "to the echo, or at least to the chandelier."

Only Samuel Laciar (*Evening Ledger*, 8 January 1936) was skeptical. He felt the score demonstrated that "strict preclassic numbers and jazz will not mix despite the cleverness of the composer's orchestration and the added fact that he knows how to write contrapuntally—up to a certain point." He acknowledged Gould's "excellent talent" but believed "Mr. Gould has simply fallen between two fires."

On 1 February, Frank Black led a performance on a nationwide NBC broadcast. Stokowski wrote again on 16 June, asking to see any of Gould's works "either published or in manuscript" for the 1936–37 Philadelphia season. He later took a close look at a symphony Morton was writing and marked up the score. But the conductor himself was on his way out. He had already resigned as music director and spent the next three years as co-conductor with Eugene Ormandy. Stokowski often played Gould, but *Chorale and Fugue in Jazz* was his only world premiere of a Gould composition.

Still, here was Morton Gould, already heard weekly on radio with his own orchestra, being performed by the magnificent Philadelphia Orchestra under the charismatic Stokowski. And he was only twenty-two.

On 28 May 1936, Gould became a member of ASCAP. His application (filled out by James Gould) listed seventeen published works, beginning with *Three Conservative Sketches* (published by Schirmer in 1932) and including "Marionettes in Motley," "Rumbalero" (a two-piano work published in 1934 by Carl Fischer Inc.), *Americana Suite* (also published by Fischer), and several two-piano transcriptions, such as "Bolero Moderne" (based on "Ay Ay Ay" and published by E. B. Marks Publishing Co.) and "Schon Rosmarin"(published by Fischer). There were no orchestral works, because none had yet been published—and because ASCAP did not collect fees for symphonic compositions. "It was the only performing rights society there was, and radio in those days was like television today—that was where the money was," Gould said in 1995.

The year 1936 was memorable not only for WOR and performances by Stokowski: Gould married that year, on 3 September. But what seemed to be a great step forward turned out to be barbed. When they met in 1931, Shirley Uzin was a beautiful girl, with olive skin, dark hair and eyes, and a brilliant smile. She was quick, smart, bold, rebellious, sensuous, and volatile. Many of these were things that Morton was not. He was shy and withdrawn, sallow, serious, obedient. But he had a tart, mordant sense of humor, and when a sly grin broke across his narrow face it melted hearts. It certainly melted Shirley's. But her parents expected Shirley to become a good wife, married to a doctor or a lawyer, with a house in the respectable Flatbush section of Brooklyn. Neither her affair with a struggling musician nor her involvement with radical politics appealed to them.

Upon graduation from Richmond Hill High School, Shirley entered Brooklyn College as a music major, but she quickly realized that she'd never be more than an appreciative listener and switched to drama to become an actress—a political actress, performing Clifford Odets's *Waiting for Lefty* all over the city with an agitprop company. She traveled everywhere to see Morton perform, to her parents' disapproval. The couple would neck on the subway or stroll in the dark between Crescent Street and Hillside Avenue. Sometimes she would sneak away from home to see him, telling her mother that she was going to the library.

When they were apart, Morton poured out his soul to her in fervent letters, sometimes more than one a day, and she responded in kind, if less frequently. His writing was full of dreams and wit, as well as explicit descriptions of what he intended to do with her when next they met. Her letters were just as impetuous, though more consistently and graphically erotic. The intensity of their feeling still heats the paper. (Shirley returned the letters to Morton in 1989.)

On 10 June 1932, apparently after Shirley had a fight with her parents, Morton wrote a long, pedantic letter to soothe her, entitled "Parental Homicide Justified." It reveals how he himself responded to slights and frustrations: "By striking out you open yourself to attack. By remaining shut up, the aggressor has no gauge by which to measure his attack—you have taken away his toehold—and I assure you his satisfaction is very much lessened when met by an immobile wall." Gould himself swallowed a great deal.

By summer's end, writing from the posh town of East Hampton, New York, Gould congratulated her on switching to theater, and explained hyperbolically that he was jealous of the stage for having stolen his sweetheart:

> You shall be making passionate love to someone else on the stage, and I shall be playing my *Tristan* to a thousand women in the audience whom I don't even know . . . Oh Art! So personal—perhaps meant for only one other—torn out of the heart and flung to the four corners of the earth! Just think . . . our love music—how many countless lovers may listen to [it] in the future . . . and never even think of us.

He wrote constantly, describing his work and his exhaustion. Frustration over cuts and changes others made in his music filled him with disgust, "but that's the game."

The next summer, on 7 July 1933, Morton wrote, "You were marvelous last night. You have such an innocent looking expression and manner about you after making love that I could eat you up—without seasoning." It was never a smooth ride, though. Morton, taking the cue from his ladies' man of a father, thought nothing of flirting and making passes at any woman who was around (though he insisted later that he remained faithful during his relationship with Shirley). But Shirley was as sexually adventurous as he, and there were bitter quarrels over her infidelities even before their marriage.

She had a fling early in 1934, in the winter, while visiting Morton's mother at the Valeria Home, the sanitarium James Gould had been sent to years earlier (the letters Shirley returned to Morton years later included a note from this lover, signature illegible, giving his Manhattan address and demanding that she visit him there). Gould found out; his response was lengthy, furious, anguished, and poignant.

His letter, undated but clearly from that time, begins obliquely, recounting a missive from Arnold Schoenberg shown to him by colleague Bela Rosza, which describes the German composer's penniless misery: "It is the most tragic letter I have seen. It is typewritten in broken English and is the groan of a great man being mutilated and being crushed."

Then Morton goes on for eight handwritten pages, describing how one of Shirley's nights on the town with this rival had shattered him (he had seen her parked in a car on Forty-ninth Street, the lover's hand thrust up her thigh). He threw everything at her:

> I awoke this morning with a parched throat and a parched soul. For one, I took water, for the other—? The most marvelous thing in the world that I coveted—that fed my art, my music while it lay dormant and stifled had suddenly struck me and stunned me—and wounded. You are guilty not only of the personal hurt you inflicted, but of the artistic blow. . . . I was going to write something vital and strong, tender and bare . . . . Now I'm derailed . . . . Everything has shattered beneath me.

Shirley has fallen for "an oriental blouse and mystic claptrap along with a rapish attitude." And the cad doesn't even have to give her a meal, though he offered her supper money:

> If he thought anything of you as a person, he would have spent part of the evening with you and taken you to dinner. This way all it meant was cramming in a piece of tail between appointments. . . . It is too bad you didn't accept the money—you would have made at least something out of it.

He expects to have a "terrific crack-up"—in private:

> I'll manage to be by myself when this happens—and save the feelings of those around me . . . . Well done, all my friends. The Prix de Rome is yours and the prize—a twenty-year-old soul, with creative urge, but with too much to say. He is choking . . . . I still love you—madly—why did you do this to me?

Yet he wavers even while writing: "If you want to, call me up—come to see me—I'll always welcome you." And under the signature is a line of score—blank.

They reconciled, and Morton continued to send graphic and impassioned letters. Her letters to him, especially during the summer of 1934, were equally passionate and also apologetic:

> Morton my dear one . . . I cannot help but think of your pale tired face when I left Sunday morning. My heart was melting and if you had said one word I shouldn't have left. Silly of course but I can't forget for a moment how nobly you treated [me] when I behaved like a cheap whore—few will ever know that your magnificent humanity has reached such heights, but for me it has endeared you to me to a degree beyond any verbal description . . . . But always before me is your sad humane face. How I want to press it against my breasts. Then I feel I can conquer the world. Oh my sweet, am I right in feeling that we are not two but one—more strongly than ever? Can it be that I can still feed your soul and help you in the labor pains of your creation? O make me feel that what I consider my most important function in life has not been destroyed by my blockheaded stupidity.

But there were now notes of caution and regret. On 3 September 1934 he wrote:

> The "black" incident is still in my mind too. Every now and then it grips me with surprising intensity. Whenever I get off the bus, in front of the Montclair, and walk down 49th Street, I must confess to feeling almost the way I did that night when we were seemingly in the last act of our little drama.

Perhaps in response to his own graphic writing, Shirley began devoting the bulk of her letters to explicit descriptions of lovemaking. Only once did she describe her political activities, though they were a frequent source of conflict not only with her own family, but with James and Morton.

Whatever the reason he fled Austria, James Gould remained a patriotic pan-German, a militarist and an autocrat. In the United States he became a staunch Republican who often battled with Morton over American gunboat diplomacy. He had little patience for communism or socialism—and not only did Shirley threaten control over his Number One Son, she was a Red besides.

Morton defended his father's behavior, if not his politics. While he himself might be progressive, he could not be a totalitarian and could never forget the humanity of those opposed to him. To Gould, the Hegelian dialectic of thesis, antithesis, and synthesis, and the Marxist argument for the inevitable historical progression from capitalism to communism, did not outweigh his sense that the lives of individuals would always be precious. And he could never forget the apparent fragility of his father's life.

Even while they fought over sexual fidelity, Morton made clear to Shirley the strength of his sympathy and support for his parents. A raging argument on 10 December 1934, his twenty-first birthday, drove Morton to tears. The next day he sent Shirley "a sentimental explanation for my sentimental breakdown." He defended his parents, especially his father, trapped, as he saw it, in the old ways:

> You see, honey, our sense of values exists in spite of a system—theirs because of it. If this were not so they would actively fight in the subtle struggle against this sickening force . . . . Then, you must realize, here are people as sincere, to themselves, as you think yourself to be. Human beings, in a body-wracking and soul-wracking fight against subtle unrelaxing odds. Loving me as fiercely and as selfishly as you do and for more than twice that many years. . . . Can't you see, can't you hear these people, with all their faults and loathesome qualities, crying out, groaning, twisting like worms in this neverending inquisition—life? . . . When one is sensitive enough to sacrifice for a cause—they must realize that the *reason* is the human beings involved.

Then Morton revealed the frightful image at the core of his sense of obligation:

> Just think, a man grows up vain, pompous, domineering, with all these impossible qualities. And at the same time, his lungs decay, he spits blood, human beings close to him die, starve, struggle, everything collapses—until he is solemnly lowered into the muck—and forgotten. These people want to cry too, honey, as you and I do at times. Don't hurt them more—they are like whipped animals.

If that's how he saw his father, how could Morton possibly break away?

Finally, he allowed himself a touch of self-pity: "It wasn't what was said, but what was recalled. Of getting up enough optimism to spend a nickel for a sheet of manuscript paper. Of long nights of desperate hopelessness and futility."

With wrenching force, he repeated her importance to him, mixed with a political sentiment that now seems sad and even slightly comic.

> Having you is to drink from a bottomless well. I pour myself into you—and someday I will flood the world with you—with sounds that will wreck decaying systems—and send people out to live, and fight anything that interferes. Our love is the most revolutionary thing there is. It is strong and sincere and sentimental and tender—and tied together by that white heat that solders our bodies together and scorches thru our insides until our burning liquid soothes the fire in us and leaves it glowing until it flames up anew.

This is an exceptionally moving document, romantic and sentimental yet also clear-eyed in its judgment of the emotions, both personal and political, swirling around and through these intelligent and passionately engaged young people. It explains, as little else does, why Morton was never able to break free of his father.

But Shirley continued to have affairs, which caused Morton great misery; as he wrote in one undated letter, "In the Shirley vs. Morton's father tussle, you have lost any support you did have." She also grew ever more active in Communist Party activities—getting arrested at demonstrations and almost winning a trip to the Soviet Union as the top money-raiser for a Young Worker fund drive. Her political involvement was much deeper than his, and it brought them to the brink of separation many times. Morton begged Shirley to devote more time to him. She accused him of selling out for money and of assaulting her sexually. "Frankly, my love for you is greater than it has ever been," he responded in another undated letter.

> Is it selling out to ask of the woman who loves me, that she help me, and come with me, and for her to show me the consideration

> without which love is merely a means of effective copulation? I am not a worker—neither was Beethoven. But in my music, that which you are fighting for marched when I was fourteen years old—and still is growing, and *will* grow until someday you and millions of others will be shaken by my symphonies, and march to my songs. What I am, it seems, can only be realized by two things—Miss Whiteside and a Soviet America.

So in the summer of 1936, they were still together, and Morton felt secure enough to think of marriage. At the beginning of July, he became a music director, making commercial recordings for the Kelvinator company (the contract included a car for his father). This would give him the wherewithal to marry Shirley and the time to compose.

"It sounds like a fairy tale come true," he wrote her on 2 July 1936. "Just think, honey, time and peace of mind to compose, rest, and do all the things I haven't been able to do during these past years. I am still dazed, and can't realize yet that my worries are comparatively over." He offered to repay all her loans to him, and went on, ecstatically, "And now, my gorgeous woman, you are *mine*! . . . Tuesday was truly the last time we left each other to go to our separate homes . . . . Being able to compose, conduct and have you are the things I've wanted most. And I *have* them!"

Whiteside too expressed her happiness for him in her diary: "It is the kind of a fairy tale that should happen to him and I am so delighted I can hardly be articulate."

Shirley's response, from the New Hampshire summer camp where she was working, was equally avid: "Dearest beloved, I am still so dazed so breathless that all these wonderful events will really come to pass I have to pinch myself to make sure this is the world of reality. Yesterday I couldn't work. I didn't hear when people spoke to me and I dropped things when I was serving the brats."

There followed a flood of letters to Camp Kear-Sarge, in Elkins, New Hampshire, sometimes as many as three a day, as Morton continued his broadcasts, made recordings for Kelvinator, worked on a symphony for Stokowski, went on family outings in the new car, attended Communist Party meetings (though he never joined), and looked forward ever more passionately to a trip to New England.

Their letters display not only the fervor of young love (on 14 July he writes, "Oscar [his name for his penis] still gives the fascist salute —but of course he is unaware of economic problems") but also the signs of trouble—Shirley's politics, freewheeling sexuality, and growing independence—so visible in hindsight. Morton assumed that his wife's role was to be completely supportive of the artist, to cook dinner while he worked, to be available for him night and day, to follow where he led; on 8 August he declared, "I'm afraid in love I'm a Fascist."

The demands of work were incessant, for Morton's own wishes were always subordinated to the need to make money: "Just think," he boasted on 20 July, "I'm one of the few conductors in captivity who has trouble getting off the air instead of on it."

They spent a week together in New Hampshire in August—though Morton brought along his parents, Shirley's eldest sister, Harriet, and his arranger, Phil Lang. Afterward the letters continued, both from Kew Gardens and from a boarding house in Yulan, a tiny community on the Delaware River on the edge of the Catskill Mountains of New York. His thoughts were of love and music: "When I lay in bed at night your ravishing body—breasts, thighs—mingle confusingly with themes from my Symphony," he wrote on 21 August.

On 3 September 1936, Morton and Shirley were married in a civil ceremony in New York City's Municipal Building and moved, temporarily, into Whiteside's apartment while she was in California. After the excitement of the summer, Morton made the wedding itself sound almost incidental. In a letter to Whiteside on 10 September, he wrote, "Last Wednesday night after the broadcast we stayed over at your place. I decided we'd have to legalize our sin immediately—so we got married Thursday morning."

CHAPTER 9

Radio Days

★ ★ ★ ★

MARRIED TO HIS TRUE LOVE. His star rising. Links with powerful musicians. Financial security. By the end of 1936 Gould was in a wonderful position for any composer at any time. From 1936 until 1945, he was on the air at least once a week, presenting a remarkable variety of music and performers coast to coast.

Except for Gershwin, no composer of the period—not Copland, Harris, Thomson, Barber, or others in art music, nor Kern, Berlin, Rodgers, Lerner—had Gould's reach across genres. It was a grand time for radio musicians, who knew they were involved in something new and unusual. There was a strong sense of camaraderie; the top players were in demand and took every job they could get—with Gould, with Kostelanetz, with Mark Warnow at CBS or Frank Black at NBC. The New York Philharmonic and the Metropolitan Opera could not compete with radio for wages.

When Gershwin died in the summer of 1937, *Down Beat*, in a full-page article by Carl Cons, prominently nominated Gould his successor. This motion was seconded late in 1938 by Jerald Mannin in the magazine *Radio Stars*; Mannin offered Gould as one of four heirs to the throne (the others were composer Ferde Grofe, Gershwin's arranger; Gould's friend Raymond Scott; and Duke Ellington). No one but Gould matched Gershwin until Bernstein came along.

These were golden days for Gould. His work was heard in the concert hall, and he wrote popular hits such as "Pavanne" and *American Salute*, satirical pieces he called "caricatones," and endless arrangements. Specifically for radio, there were four symphonettes, the Piano Concerto, and *American Concertette* (which Jerome Robbins choreographed as *Interplay*). Beyond that were two full symphonies, concertos for violin and for viola, *Concerto for Orchestra, Foster Gallery*, and the tone poem *Spirituals for String Choir and Orchestra*; and for concert band (an agglomeration Max Dreyfus suggested in 1939), *Cowboy Rhapsody* and *Jericho Rhapsody*.

WOR broadcast from 1440 Broadway or the New Amsterdam Theater. NBC was not far away, at Rockefeller Center, and neither was CBS. "Radio was full of people dashing to another studio and another program," Gould said in 1985. Every segment of every show was timed to the second, but there were always a few minutes between the last notes of one show and the downbeat of the next. So Morton would allow his first trumpet, say, to slide out of the chair, scramble into a waiting car, and rush over to the next studio just in time—or maybe not, in which case a standby was waiting.

Mark Warnow and his brother, Harry, were two of Gould's good friends. To avoid confusion, Harry Warnow changed his name to Raymond Scott, and gained notoriety with a six-piece band known as the Raymond Scott Quintette. Scott grew famous for numbers used repeatedly in Warner Bros. cartoons, and there were similarities of spirit between his jaunty sound and Morton's. Gould was among friends—and yet considered himself something special.

"I was much younger than the others involved, so I was sort of a fair-haired boy, the new boy on the block, which they all listened to with great admiration," he said. "Don't forget, I was doing things that in terms of commercial radio at that time were very advanced, symphonic in concept, texture, and approach. I was a Young Turk."

Gould was looking forward, not back. He drew excited responses. MGM executive Georg Bassman wrote on 18 January 1937, after one of Gould's nationwide broadcasts, "I caught your program yesterday from New York and truly . . . it was swell! For a moment we thought it was Kostelanetz . . . that is, until your name was announced. . . . And WHY don't you get a commercial [sponsor]????? The hour merits it, believe me."

Publisher J. J. Robbins of Robbins Music Corp. added compliments in a letter dated 16 February 1937, from his offices on Sunset Boulevard in Hollywood. "I've heard from many people that you are in the class with Whiteman and Kostelanetz and nobody is happier over this than I." Whiteside, too, compared him with Kostelanetz, who, she noted, had more rehearsals and depended on others for arrangements. A note in the magazine *Metronome* (January 1940) observed that an average Gould orchestration ran about fifty pages and took about eight hours to complete: since there were usually seven numbers in a show, that came to fifty-six hours of work for each half-hour program, most of it done at home but with the finishing touches penciled in on the subway. There is some exaggeration here: Morton did not do all or even most of the copying, and as his repertoire developed he repeated previous numbers. Nevertheless, the effort involved in mounting just one broadcast remains impressive.

Gould also had more than the radio programs to sustain his optimism. On 9 June 1937 he signed a one-year contract with Mills Music Inc., whose publishing catalog included Ellington, Hoagy Carmichael, and Cab Calloway, among others. For $50 a week (an advance on royalties, not a salary), Gould would write a minimum of six original compositions—piano solos, duets, suites or symphonic works—and six transcriptions of piano or orchestral works by others. The deal, arranged by James Gould, seemed just perfect but was flawed: neither father nor son realized that they had given Mills the rights to his music.

For Gould to sign with Mills was unusual for a composer with concert-hall aspirations. "The publisher one went to was not Mills Music, but G. Schirmer or Carl Fischer . . . You didn't go with Mills Music, it was a popular house. . . . They started their standard and educational catalog with me," he said.

When concert composers such as Copland, Barber, or Howard Hanson supported themselves teaching, scrabbling for engagements, or depending on wealthy patrons; when orchestras paid nothing or next to nothing for contemporary compositions; when ASCAP didn't even collect for concert music—Gould's arrangement was extraordinary.

But Morton was a solid investment. He knew what he was expected to write, he knew how and what he wanted to do and—endlessly prodded by his father—he learned how to mesh both expectations: "I was not coming in with a twelve-tone piece." He was aware of radio's restrictions in time and audience. "You could not do transcriptions of Beethoven's last quartets," as he said in 1985, and whatever he wrote had to fit within half an hour or possibly forty-five minutes, complete with announcements and sometimes commercials. "Within those confinements, I had what to me were certain standards I would not go below, and I wanted to be inventive, to have a certain amount of creative flair."

Mitch Miller, who went on to television fame in the 1950s with his "singalong" programs, worked in the 1930s as an oboist with the CBS orchestra and with Kostelanetz. He also freelanced like everyone else, and played with Gould. "Morton, he was the true genius," Miller said, "because his arranging came like you and I write letters. He sat down and did it, even during the recording sessions."

Gould, still dreaming of leading his *Tristan* with the Philharmonic in Carnegie Hall, was of several minds about radio. It was wonderful to be so busy, to be paid well, and to have money for his family. But serious composers weren't supposed to have weekly radio programs and be heard coast to coast. "I was always a little allergic to being successful in those days," he said in 1985. "My friends wouldn't like it." He tried to keep a balance between the commercial and the complex: "There was always—not pressure, but comments to simplify the numbers, they were too complicated, they should be shorter, and simpler, 'Put a beat on so people can dance.' I would say, 'I don't want them to dance.'" In later years he also tried to avoid popular devices, at least partly in response to friends such as Joseph Prostakoff. "I thought maybe they'd consider me more seriously if it wasn't too on target. I think that was partly in my mind, an attempt to avoid success."

Long before that, though, he was getting more concert attention. Twice in 1938, in April and September, he led all-Gould broadcasts on WOR. The music included several caricatones, sections of his *Americana Suite*, and the first and third of his three *American Symphonette*s. On 1 May 1938, on the CBS *Ford Sunday Evening Hour*, Fritz Reiner led the Detroit Symphony in "Pavanne," the second movement of his *American Symphonette* No. 2. The title "symphonette" was a clever attempt to Americanize and modernize the term "sinfonietta," linking it with such up-to-the-minute concepts as kitchenette and dinette. Although Gould came to regret using what became a dated, kitschy word, it is both accurate and effective, describing a short three- or four-movement work with relatively orthodox classical structure.

On 16 June 1938 Gould presented his Piano Concerto (featuring elbow- and arm-pounding tone clusters) over WOR, with himself at the keyboard, Wallenstein conducting, and dedicated, to her surprise, to Whiteside. The next day, syndicated radio writer Ben Gross led his column with a brief rave: "It proved to be a thrilling work, colorful and dynamic, a ★★★★ item. The performance, both of soloist and orchestra, was first rate."

That summer Gould twice led the New York Philharmonic in the orchestra's free, outdoor summer concerts at Lewisohn Stadium in upper Manhattan (although in neither case was he the sole conductor). Following the 31 July 1938 performance, which included his *American Symphonette* No. 2 in its New York premiere, the Mutual network ran full-page advertisements for "Conductor-Composer-Arranger Morton Gould." "New York Critics Unanimously Hail America's Outstanding Composer-Conductor with Unprecedented Tribute," ran the headline. The ad cited reviews from five newspapers, touted his weekly show of "Original American Music in the Jazz Idiom," and noted that he had been invited back to the stadium the next week.

Gould was making his way through American music during an era bubbling with creativity. At the same time, there were warning signs, even in the reviews displayed so proudly after the 31 July stadium concert. The critics condescended: "Mr. Gould conducted—as he composed—in a manner to indicate that he knew precisely what he wanted and how to get it" (*The Sun*); "he has been successful to a large degree in fulfilling his avowed purpose" (*New York Herald Tribune*); "he made it evident in the three movements of the short symphonic creation that he was far more technically proficient at this sort of thing than the majority of those who have tried their hand at it" (*The New York Times*).

The *Times* did allow that the *American Symphonette*'s "second division, a 'pavane' employing a constantly present ostinato, was especially engaging" and acknowledged that the music, with its "vitality and rhythmic urge," was "logically and cleverly put together, and displayed an intelligence and sureness that also was reflected in his handling of the stick." This was qualified praise, but still strong stuff for a young man learning on the job.

Gould was not afraid to take some licks at the musical culture he was invading. In a piece in the *The New York Post* (13 July 1938), Gould said, "I'll probably be hanged for saying it, but a lot of the boys in the dance bands are better and more courageous musicians than some of the symphonic artists who look down on them." And he was also an advocate for the medium of radio, as in his article "Radio Is Saving American Music" (*Down Beat*, August 1938):

> Radio, once considered the fire eating consumer of music, is today becoming the salvation of American music by affording a vast auditorium that is not only helping to bring recognition to our contemporary composers but the increased interest in serious music has put a premium on capable musicians, as witness the recent pirating and hi-jacking of instrumentalists from symphonic groups for radio orchestrations.

Radio, he pointed out, gave musicians work and composers exposure. Radio audiences were larger than anything possible in a concert hall, and listeners were more open-minded, not, in Gould's words, "die-hard classicists." The sheer size of the radio audience guaranteed that appreciation for new music, especially American music, could be found somewhere in the throng. And there was so much time to be filled that there would always be work for composers and performers. The classics were music of the past, a monotonous diet. He continued:

> Whether music introduced recently through the medium of the microphone is mediocre or of no lasting value is incidental; at least composers are being heard and given a chance to take their efforts to the people. Just as the music of Brahms, Wagner, Mozart et al. was financed by royalty and other musical enterprises in the Romantic period, American music will be developed through radio sponsorship and assignments.

It is easy now to snicker at such utopian vision. History demonstrates that quantity is no guarantor of quality (though time has its way of separating surprising amounts of wheat from what appeared at first to be mountains of chaff).

Morton did not slow his pace. On 31 October 1938, Max Pollikoff, concertmaster of Gould's WOR orchestra, played his Violin Concerto at Carnegie Hall, accompanied by pianist Jascha Zayde. Whiteside was not impressed: "The concert was a bore," she told her diary that night. Gould did not care much for the piece and never orchestrated it.

At the very end of 1938 Gould achieved another triumph. Reiner offered *American Symphonette* No. 2 on a pair of subscription concerts with his own Pittsburgh Symphony, in the Syria Mosque that was its home. Gould's program note described the composition as having been written "for the better type of radio program."

> [It] falls into a peculiar idiom in the sense that it has appealed to the average listener as something quite advanced—yet within his ken and in some respects close to his everyday popular music, and at the same time has appealed to musicians and more developed audiences as something light—but consistent in its idiom. This is entertainment—but American in feeling and conception. It utilizes the elements of swing in the classical form and structure, because the composer feels that the better elements of our popular music and the conciseness of the classical forms have a clarity and compatibility in common.

Ralph Lewando (*Pittsburgh Press*) enjoyed the "stirring provocative 2nd Symphonietta," "a rousing experience" that he found "truly entertaining, yet it possesses real musical values, form and variety, which cannot be said of jazz in its crude state as we hear it dispensed all over the land." Donald S. Steinfirst (*Pittsburgh Post-Gazette*) made it clear that, enjoyable as Gould's music might be, it was nevertheless startling to hear on an orchestral program. "If any of the Wagnerian Gods lingered in the neighborhood of Syria Mosque after last week's performance," he wrote, "we are convinced that by now they have wended their weary way back to Valhalla shaking their collective heads at the goin's on at the Mosque last night."

Reiner became Gould's primary champion. Morton did not travel to Pittsburgh to hear the performance, he recalled in 1985. Reiner rebuked him, saying, "I had a triumph that night. I thought you'd be there. I would have brought you up onstage for a bow. Why weren't you there?" Gould answered that it was only a short piece, to which the conductor responded, "It might have been only nine minutes, but *Reiner* did it!"

In his youth, Gould was not a composer of sweetness and light. Easy listening was neither his method nor his goal. His friends and associates worried that he was "selling out," and much of what he wrote was suitable for a large, unsophisticated radio audience. But Gould's intent was as serious as that of any concert composer, and the result was often dense, if not intellectually thorny, and anything but complacent.

Most of the two-piano music, for example, was based on familiar compositions: Ernesto Lecuona's "Malagueña," conflations of Chopin nocturnes and etudes, boleros with original melodies, variations on "Tiger Rag" or "The Stars and Stripes Forever," or such originals as his own *Americana Suite* or "Marionettes in Motley." The playing was often poorly coordinated, frequently awkward. Gould accelerated during crescendos, and he sounded frenetic and rushed. He had exceptionally large hands, able to reach eleven or even twelve notes at a stretch, and he liked to hit them in great bunches. The arrangements surge with energy; even the most peaceful moments are but eddies of a swirling current. The soul of Gould's youthful music was anxious.

In the two-piano "Tiger Rag," Gould offers a clotted introduction with no clue to the familiar tune. When the melody appears, it quickly blows away into ever more complex variations, including the beginnings of a four-part fugue. "Malagueña" is restless, driving, flashy, and filled with filigree, trills, broken arpeggios, interpolated notes, and headlong rushes. It is neither sensuous nor romantic, but impatient and even angry—Jazz Age with an edge.

The Gould-Shefter collaboration is sometimes bumptious, sometimes brilliant, and always strongly rhythmical—but never relaxed and comfortable. Often the music feels clumsy, tied too closely to the bar lines. It's as if the players were competing, neither able to let the other gain an upper hand. One can imagine listeners being excited, but also exhausted. It's not a surprise, then, to hear that Shefter eventually moved to California, where he became a successful composer and arranger of B movie scores. He and Gould did not stay in touch and rarely spoke of each other.

Gould's popular scores, from arrangements to caricatones to the somewhat more serious folk suites, are clever, showy, very musical, and often fun to hear and play. His sources were the folk music then being mined extensively by Copland, Thomson, and the "Americana" movement; conventional parlor music from Chopin to Rachmaninoff to Johann Strauss; and jazz and ragtime. Much of what he wrote was playful. In one caricatone, "The Prima Donna," he imitates the trills and vocalese of a warmup; in "The Ballerina," a thumping bass line conveys a not-quite-perfect pirouette; "The Child Prodigy" presents a student dutifully going through his exercises but, tired and rebellious, beginning to pound away discordantly. On the other hand, there is little evidence of deep thought. Gould was not interested, here, in plumbing any depths. He was writing living-room music, not meant to challenge listener or performer.

The symphonettes and Piano Concerto go further. They were earnest attempts to create substantial work from American sources and European structure, within the intellectual and temporal strictures of a popular radio program. The First and Second Symphonettes are each three movements and nine minutes long. The Third Symphonette has four movements and runs twelve minutes, and the Piano Concerto is a full twenty minutes—an extraordinary length of uninterrupted broadcast time, and an indication of just how much freedom Gould had.

The Second Symphonette (*American Symphonette* No. 2) is a genuine masterpiece, virtually sui generis. It is no wonder that this score became wildly popular, taken over by dance bands and arranged for all sorts of combinations. It deserved its place in the concert hall, not condescension and sniping.

The first movement, marked "moderately fast, with vigor and bounce," bangs the main theme off the bat with a bold big-band sound immediately familiar to its listeners. The theme is repeated, now with accents from a high-hat cymbal. Violins present a second theme, the trumpets respond, and it's off to the races—in condensed sonata form. Theme fragments rebound in a manner Beethoven would have recognized, though the timbres and ideas would have been novel. Everything is quick, bright, rhythmic, and infectious, and brought to a sudden, almost comically solemn conclusion. (Gould loved musical jokes, sometimes vulgar and obvious, but often witty and endearing.)

What follows became Gould's single most popular original composition, "Pavanne," a movement that the Mills brothers and everyone around him immediately knew was a hit. He spelled it "pavanne," perhaps as a joke, perhaps to differentiate it from the stately French court dance that the music in no way resembles. He meant the score to be played slowly, at barely half the speed at which it is usually performed, but it took on a tempo of its own.

Over a rhythmic pizzicato arpeggio in the lower strings, a muted solo trumpet plays a jolly, syncopated tune, with the flute following. After one repetition, the violins introduce a breathy fragment of a phrase, and the flute offers a reflective countermelody for the trio, expanded upon by the full orchestra. The theme returns, followed by a tiny coda. Always there is a sense of urgency under the deceptive sweetness.

About the finale, marked "fast and racy," Gould once remarked that it contains a "slight takeoff" on the prelude from Bach's E Major Partita for unaccompanied violin. But Bach is essentially unrecognizable in this collection of riffs, segues, and scraps of band orchestration transmuted into a raucous conclusion. The overall effect is remarkable: absolutely uncompromised, urban, mid-1930s America draped convincingly on a European framework. It starts fast, says everything it means to say, and stops. This is an American original, indebted to Gershwin but more sophisticated in orchestration and structure.

The Third Symphonette is too obviously a sequel. The first movement, also marked "moderately fast," is a collection of dance band licks, full of bent notes and syncopations. It's quick, the development is fragmented, but the overall effect is not as brash and is more dominated by strings. The second movement, "Intermezzo," is blues-based; there are hints of popular tunes—a touch of "A Woman Is a Sometime Thing"—and traces of tension, but the result is heavy and charmless. The third movement, "Gavotte," is a try for another "Pavanne." The form and orchestration are almost identical, with rhythmic underpinning; brief, syncopated melody played on muted trumpet; and equally brief second subject, followed by some development and orchestral interplay of the two melodic fragments. It's catchy and pleasant, but clearly derivative. And the finale is little more than a melange of herky-jerky dance band and movie music fragments, thrown together with no apparent structure. It's a disappointment, but not surprising in light of the speed with which Gould was working.

The Piano Concerto is an altogether more substantial work, in three movements marked "moderately fast with drive and gusto," "chant," and "fast—with gusto." It opens with a forearm tone cluster from the piano, the thick chord repeated by the orchestra, and then the main theme presented as a long, wandering melody in the right hand, while the left hand and the orchestra offer a running accompaniment. Eventually the violins carry the melody while the piano accompanies them. There is a meditative middle section for the orchestra harking to the opening theme, with the piano mildly melancholy. The theme returns abruptly in the full orchestra, the piano pounding at top speed. The first movement alternates between crushing motion and keyboard meditation, until its stark, abrupt conclusion.

Although the second movement is marked "chant," it is more of a contemplation. The piano continues its meditation while the horns and violins take turns with melodic fragments. The somber atmosphere is shattered by the finale, a four-part fugue presented in order by the right hand, clarinet, left hand, and finally, full orchestra, which race after one another playfully. The soloist is just a member of the gang. There is a quiet segment during which the piano at first is silent. It then offers fragments of the fugue, as if asking to start again. The orchestra ignores the piano until it erupts into a rollicking figure; the brass begin to follow and then the game starts anew until, with a final rush, everything comes to a brilliant conclusion.

The most surprising thing about this piece is how little display the piano actually gets. Aside from a few outbursts, the ostensible soloist either accompanies, punctuates, or comments upon what the orchestra is doing. Randall Hodgkinson, who played the concerto at Gould's eightieth birthday concert and on the later recording with the Albany Symphony, complained, "It has to have a little bit more for the piano. . . . Being a greedy pianist, and wanting notes, this is not what I think of as a concerto." Hodgkinson found the score "full of vitality, very skillfully written, and fun to play," although the music "sounds more difficult than it is." He considers the first movement to be the best constructed, the second, sketchy, and the finale, with its contrapuntal energy, excellent.

Gould's Piano Concerto is a successful piece that would be at home either in a pops concert or an evening of light classics. It is immature, showing problems in coordination between piano and orchestra, but is full of ideas and promise.

The peak of 1938 came when Fritz Reiner suggested that Gould write a major work based on the music of Stephen Foster. Gould chose thirteen pieces, from "Jeannie With the Light Brown Hair" and "My Old Kentucky Home" to obscure waltzes, quadrilles, and hymns. The organizing structure is a set of variations on "Camptown Races" that opens the piece and recurs throughout, like the promenade in Mussorgsky's *Pictures at an Exhibition*. Gould composed and orchestrated the score from September to November 1939. It was his most significant work to date.

Foster Gallery ("thirteen episodes for orchestra based on melodies by Stephen Foster") was premiered by the Pittsburgh Symphony on 12 January 1940. *Foster Gallery* was big; it was tough; it was Gould's first chance to let himself go all out; it was also the first chance of the critics—especially in New York—to assess him at full strength. The result was an explosion that marked him for the rest of his career.

He expected the audience to be uncomfortable; during a rehearsal break on the day of the premiere, he told the *Pittsburgh Post-Gazette*, "The audience will probably sigh in discomfort. . . . Lots of things might sound surprising tonight." He was right. J. Fred Lisselt (*Sun-Telegraph*) remarked that, after the performance, he was "assailed on all sides, as if I were to blame." All the same, Lisselt was moderately impressed: "There are tedious moments, but there is realism and the hurly burly of an American fairground that will compel me to return for a second hearing."

Other Pittsburgh critics were split. Ralph Lewando (*Pittsburgh Press*) "marveled at the amazing command of orchestration and [Gould's] complete knowledge of the fullest resources of the various instruments." He acknowledged that the treatment of familiar tunes "may shock the conservatives" but found the variations "exciting," "tender," "expressive," "admirable," and "ingenious."

Donald S. Steinfirst (*Pittsburgh Post-Gazette*) respected but did not enjoy it. Gould, he wrote, "isn't the first modern composer to founder on the shoals of Swanee River or stumble over the Camptown obstacle Races. . . . One is not likely to soon forget the spectacle of 'Swanee River' played in broken rhythm by five disassociated solo instruments."

Arthur Fiedler soon after recorded an abbreviated version for RCA, and the work itself arrived in New York on 8 and 9 March 1941, with John Barbirolli leading the Philharmonic.

Perhaps anticipating the reception *Foster Gallery* would receive in his hometown, Gould gave a defensive interview to William G. King (*The Sun*, 1 March 1941). "I seem to be something of a problem to a lot of people, because I've been tagged as a radio composer. I believe there is a tendency to overemphasize the commercial aspects of composing for radio," which after all had the practical virtue of helping to keep him alive and in close touch with popular music, jazz, swing, jive, and folk songs. "Some of our 'serious' composers seem to be holding themselves apart from this. But what's the use of trying to function as an isolated waterlily, writing stuff that only you and your mother like, and she only because she's prejudiced in your favor?"

None of the works—the program included Bernard Wagenaar's Symphony No. 3 and Roy Harris's *Three Pieces for Orchestra*—drew a positive critical response. *The Brooklyn Eagle* found the entire performance "a trifle depressing."

But *Foster Gallery* was lambasted.

The first, and heaviest, to weigh in was Virgil Thomson in the *Herald Tribune* (9 March 1941). Thomson was respectful of Wagenaar, a Belgian who had become an American citizen in the 1920s. He dismissed most of the Harris as "routine"—though it's intriguing to notice, considering Thomson's own Francophilia, that he wished the score and its performance had been more French.

But, in writing about *Foster Gallery*, Thomson focused on what would become the unexpected albatross around Gould's neck: his skill at writing for orchestra.

> [The composition] is rather overblown both musically and orchestrally. He orchestrates well enough, far too well, in fact. He knows more sonorous groupings of instrumental timbres than he has serious usage for. The music he writes, therefore, is likely to be less interesting than the sound it makes. It is not wholly uninteresting . . . and he has a certain musical wit . . . .

> The work is extra long, the orchestra extra large for the amount of musical matter exposed.

And Thomson makes no secret that it is the composer he is attacking: "I am not denigrating the beautiful Stephen Foster melodies that were its inspiration. I am complaining a little that these were concealed rather than exposed, obfuscated rather than developed."

Everyone else got in their licks the next day: The *Brooklyn Eagle* spoke of Gould's "smartly overorchestrated work"; Edward O'Gorman (*The New York Post*) called *Foster Gallery* "the least serious" of the American works on the program, though "the most cleverly contrived and successful of the three"; Robert Hagar (*The New York World-Telegram*) called Gould "Musical Ironist No. 1" for his "cheeky questioning"; *The New York Sun* called it "frequently strident and generally unsympathetic"; Robert Simon (*PM*) called it "as clever a piece of smart-aleckry as Carnegie Hall has heard all winter," complete with "an isn't-this-funny arrangement of 'Swanee River' for flute, trumpet, trombone, and banjo with a sour violin obbligato. Jeannie's light brown hair went to a barber shop, where it was torn out in fistfuls by a drunken barber."

This was devastating, Thomson's condescending commentary most of all—for there one of the most experienced and prominent of American composers, already known for Americanist work including the film score for *The Plow That Broke the Plains*, took Morton's greatest strengths and threw them in his face. He knew the orchestra too well! The wit was heavy handed! Nothing wrong with the Foster melodies—it was Gould!

Roy Harris could have been more French, but Morton Gould didn't have a chance.

Gould hadn't learned diplomacy yet; he still thought he was going to be one of the great composers; and he was not worried about offending powerful American musicians. His response was not long in coming, and he chose a significant rostrum for the counterattack. On 23 April 1941, Gould was the featured speaker at a luncheon sponsored by the New York Philharmonic-Symphony Society. As reported by Mark Schubart the next day in *PM*, the twenty-seven-year-old composer spoke out for American music "with some statements that made the classic assembly wince."

> "The trouble is," said he, "that there are too many *fifth-culturists* in music who are not only unwilling to let their hair down, but refuse to take off their wigs. We ought to have more native American music in concert halls, and get rid of our ingrown culture. New York is a dead-spot culturally. The rest of the country listens to native music and likes it. I for one know I get a bigger kick out of 'Frankie and Johnny' than I do out of *Tristan and Isolde*. It's a better love story. If you think it isn't culture remember that *Tristan* isn't so pure either." (Shocked titters.)
>
> After that, Mr. Gould demonstrated his skill at improvisation by turning "Lady Be Good" into a Bachian prelude and fugue; a Mozartian minuet; a Chopinish waltz; and a Stravinskian composition.

Not only were New Yorkers narrow-minded snobs, they were musical fascists—no one at the time could have missed the reference to Francisco Franco's notorious "fifth column," Fascist sympathizers working within besieged cities to support the four columns of troops outside. Secure in his radio fame, consulted by the grandest names on the podium, probably better known than any "serious" American composer except Gershwin, Gould had no reason to fear the blue-haired ladies of the Symphony Society and those snarling critics—some surely motivated by envy. In the months to come, he repeated his attacks on the hometown listeners.

In July 1941, when he was substituting for the ailing "Major" Edward Bowes, Gould expanded on the theme. New Yorkers had no grounds for their condescension about music in the provinces, he told Henry Beckett of *The New York Post*. "I've been amazed to find, all over the country, people who can read and write and make music and talk about it with a discrimination that is rare in New York."

Beyond that, he was determined to be a "practical" composer, not locked in a garret starving for his muse:

> Good art is always practical, and the significant artist is practical, too. Not showy or phony, but real, vital, eager to succeed with his product. Beethoven wrote on commission and would be called a chiseler today. His business letters read like Tin Pan Alley. When a symphony was requested he would come back

> with an offer to the publisher promising, for a higher price, to throw in four songs, sure to be hits, and eight easy pieces for piano.
>
> Radio will take us out of the decadent post-romantic period. Art has become like an ingrown toenail and something must be done about it. Another point about radio is that it forces a composer to be terse, to say what he has to say and then quit. Time is valuable on the air.

A bit later that summer, Schubart recounted in *PM* some of the ongoing combat: Gould was being called charlatan, faker, and phony as well as wunderkind, fine musician, and genius.

> One of the opinions that has earned him hard names is that most American composers who write what they call "American" music aren't doing that at all, but are just rehashing the old forms they learned from European masters and endowing them with a dash of Americanism by using a few native themes. . . . Mr. Gould, of course, did not study with European masters. . . . He never learned composition and orchestration formally, but picked up everything he knew from studying scores and listening.

No need any longer to boast of those nonexistent armfuls of diplomas and certificates. Now Morton criticized what by the end of the century would be called the "Eurocentrism" of his colleagues.

Gould was willing to slug it out. *Foster Gallery* was his first magnum opus, it was getting a lot of play, and he was not afraid to defend himself. But what about *Foster Gallery*? It was popular in the 1940s but has since virtually disappeared. Was Thomson right? Not entirely. Thomson's observation was acute; he heard what was in the music. But he, partisan of a cool, detached school that valued clarity and simplicity, could not have tolerated this florid, torrid, inelegant, raucous score.

Foster Gallery is Gould at his maddest and most indiscreet. The "Camptown Races" theme is wild and brassy, broken into fragments and chased around the orchestra. The music is shrill, feverish, and slightly off-kilter. There is a quiet interlude for "Come Where My

Love Lies Dreaming," with muted strings and woodwinds treating the theme canonically while a saxophone oozes along sleepily. In the "Canebrake Jig" that follows, the melody is split so thoroughly it is barely recognizable, and "Swanee River," with unorthodox instrumentation, is nobody's idea of traditional Stephen Foster.

Gould has a lot of fun blending "Old Black Joe" and "My Old Kentucky Home," breaking the melodies into the smallest possible phrases (a two-note call like a mournful train whistle is revealed as the refrain, "I'm coming, I'm coming"). The mood becomes ominous and painfully tense before fading away. Underlying all is a harsh, tough tone, a sense of barely contained anger. Gould is unwilling to let any melody come to a natural conclusion. He worries the old songs like a frenzied terrier with a rabbit. It's powerful, it's impressive, but you don't want to get too close until everything is over.

The paradox is that Gould was dismissed as a facile popularizer, when his most ambitious scores often were anything but charming and easy.

CHAPTER 10

Death of Young Love

★ ★ ★ ★

Morton Gould was not a handy man. He and his children enjoyed regaling friends and strangers with tales of their father's domestic failures. "I've never cooked, I don't bake. I can be sort of dangerous in the kitchen or with any kind of mechanical contrivance," he said, almost boastfully, in 1985.

He told a story about life with Shirley Uzin that says a lot about the disaster their marriage became. It occurred when the Goulds were living at 7734 Austin Street in Forest Hills, their second apartment after getting married. Neither was domestic. Morton was a klutz, and Shirley had no interest in domesticity. She was trying to bring the revolution home. One morning, she prepared rice for Morton's lunch in a square Pyrex container and told him how to heat it: "Take the rice, just the way it is, put it in the pan, and light it. After a short while it will be warm. Put it in a plate. Don't do anything to it."

When Gould got hungry, he went into the kitchen and followed directions: he put the dish into the pan ("I thought it was strange, trying to put a square dish in a round pan"), lit the stove, and wandered back to work. "Suddenly there was this horrible explosion, and I didn't know what happened. Of course the kitchen looked like a World War I battlefield. Did you ever see rice explode? It went right up to the ceiling. To this day, in an apartment in Forest Hills, there is probably someone sitting there, entertaining friends, and he's never been able to figure out what are those pock marks in the ceiling—how did that rice get there?"

It wasn't funny at the time. The marriage was probably doomed from the start. She was struggling to become a free woman in a conventional community and he was accustomed to being cossetted by an adoring family. Now that they were together for life, their differences became overwhelming.

When they were first married, in 1936, after a month or so in Whiteside's place, the Goulds moved to 8015 Grenfell Avenue, a few blocks from his parents. They lived there for about a year before moving to Austin Street, just north of the newly completed, limited access Interboro Parkway and near the end of a new subway line on Queens Boulevard. The Austin Street apartment was not much further from his family, but the parkway's physical barrier gave a slight psychological separation.

Even with that distance, Morton found it essentially impossible to complete the separation necessary for the growth of the mature adult—and even more so, perhaps, for the flowering of genius. Shirley, with the best will in the world, would have been hard put to replicate the household he grew up in. But she was not interested in building a cozy nest for her artist husband.

Frances Gould had made his clothes, cooked and baked and sewn, and with quiet dignity suffered the bluster and pretensions of her arrogant, impecunious husband. She kept the scrapbooks that documented her brilliant son's achievements, accepted the tumult of a male household, had occupied the place laid down in the American home for the wife. James, with his boasting, finagling, pride, and eye for the deal, had the personality that Morton did not. He did the negotiating, made the contacts and plans. James Gould gave the impression that *he* was the creative one; his son just set down the notes.

Alfred, a year and a half younger than Morton, was frail and slightly crippled by polio as an infant; sturdy Walter was two years younger than Alfred; and the athletic Stanley was five years younger than Walter. Alfred was the smart one; the family sent him to Brooklyn College. Industrious Walter sold newspapers and worked as a Tin Pan Alley song-plugger, while Stanley was still too young to strike out on his own. It was a contentious but close-knit family, each busy yet with much of their world focused on Morton.

Not Shirley.

She had her own life to live. If she broke from her own parents to set off with Morton, how long could she suppress herself to succor him, too? In her book (*Mike Quill: Himself*, p. 149), Shirley described how the relationship began to founder: "The predictable routine of our lives had leveled the peaks of passion. At twenty-one I was asking who I was, what I was, where I was going. Was an orderly three-room apartment the end-all, the meaning of my life? Was I Nora, trapped in a Forest Hills doll's house?"

Morton worked himself to exhaustion. But his wife did not take care of him—his parents and brothers did. Walter Gould recalled when Morton ran a high fever and needed constant care, but they could not afford a nurse. "Shirley could not spend the time with him," Walter said. "She was running off to her meetings. So we all took turns staying in the apartment so there would be somebody to take care of him. Not Shirley. That's the first thing that comes to my mind about her—her priorities were completely wrong for the time. Any time you are married to somebody, your priority has to be different."

"She had political things to do," recalled Matty Gould, Alfred's widow. "They were more important than Morton and her marriage. And the family resented that tremendously."

As she wrote in her book (*Mike Quill: Himself*, p. 149), Shirley clashed violently with the autocratic James:

> The arguments between us were frequent and acrimonious. He was relentless, often cruel, and each confrontation reduced me to a quivering pulp. I fought back. He couldn't push his daughter-in-law around. He responded with ill-concealed fury; none of his children had ever defied him. Irrationally, I believed this large family was united against me, a hostile phalanx ready to battle the outsider at a signal from the Generalissimo. I felt shut-out, taken for granted, ignored, useless, unimportant. Morton was locked into his own creative cocoon.

Besides the Goulds, there was also Abby Whiteside, no longer so happy with her star's wife. Whiteside terrified Shirley, who meekly attended the Sunday musicales, serving and washing and staying out of the way. "As long as I was contributing to Morton's well-being," wrote Shirley (*Mike Quill: Himself*, pp. 149–150), "the lady of steel was friendly and hospitable. When she knew our marriage was in trouble, her glacial albeit unspoken disapproval deepened my sense of isolation."

There were arguments and reconciliations. Morton was often out of the house and frequently spent time at a hotel in the Catskill Mountains called The Fieldstone. He told one son he occasionally found used condoms in the apartment; he told a later lover that during their marriage Shirley had an abortion after an affair. His letters began to sound unhappy and desperate. "Oh sweet," Morton wrote from The Fieldstone in August 1939, "there are only two things that I absolutely must have—you and music-paper." Shirley continued to attend Morton's performances and traveled to Pittsburgh for *Foster Gallery* in January 1940.

In March 1940 he sent a passionate little note from Ann Arbor, Michigan: "I love you, my darling woman—I'm hungry for you. Just wait till I get you on Saturday. Caress yourself for me." But by then the marriage was in dire shape. Since it was Shirley who didn't fit, she tried to accept responsibility. At one point, full of guilt, she went to a Marxist psychiatrist who convinced her she did not love Morton but needed him for financial security.

On 20 August 1940, Morton wrote in agony: "It's doubly bitter to realize that we are not separated only for these two weeks, or summer, but in all probability for life—and death. I cannot but be aware of the fact that we are losing not only each other, but part of ourselves—losing that rare thing that we had—and you threw away—our love." He tried to convince her that she could fulfill herself as his helpmate, the Cosima, perhaps, to his Richard Wagner:

> Is it so self-obliterating to be next to a man who will create out of the chaos, bitterness, happiness, sunlight and manure the song of you and me, and those around us? If you love me with the burning intensity that I love you, darling, you can contribute to and be part of and help me express this overwhelming thing in me that must hurl itself out to the people—our people—you and me—those fireballs inside of me that want to laugh and shout and cry and curse and please and crush and love—you! Are you betraying anything when you help the man, not to make enough for a smug self-contented fireplace—

> but to fulfill a rare destiny—fulfill it in a constant state of dynamic surge and projection?
>
> Darling, creating is like tearing out one's guts—it is both a devastating and exhilarating experience—but when one is continually crushed and thwarted, it implies a double battle. There is the contradiction of fanning a fire that always exists—or suppressing a fire that won't go out. I cannot trust myself to compose a large work of depth—I know that it would be too nerve-wracking at present—like allowing yourself to be caught in an undertow. I could be completely broken up personally—that is I would not be able to fulfil my everyday functions with people—and its completion would leave me in a deep state of morbidity, which might lead me to a fatal conclusion, rather than readjust myself to prosaic being again. . . . It is horrible to be a lonely human being—I never fully realized before, but I look on all these people about me—sitting with their own emptiness—attempting to be social—to fill, perhaps, another's void—and a new sympathy and understanding comes over me—for I realize that now I am one of them. Perhaps forever.

This argument was familiar to them both. What is more interesting is Gould's conviction that he could not follow his feelings artistically because that would destroy the lives of those around him and might even lead to "a fatal conclusion." Whether he meant to frighten Shirley or arouse her sympathy, throughout his life Gould suffered from deep, almost debilitating depressions. Even after he had risen to great heights and received high honors, the thought of killing himself was never far from the surface.

But he showed that face only to his family; outsiders saw something else. On the surface he was usually complaisant, compassionate, and gentlemanly, but buried resentments fed a dark reservoir of pessimism and cynicism that grew deeper the longer he lived. He knew there was a choice between following his art wherever it led, or repressing what was most difficult and threatening to his personal relationships.

Throughout creative history, the artist has been forced to decide—and the most successful put their inspiration first. Morton Gould came to that divide many times—and each time he opted for family.

The Goulds, (from left) James, Morton, Walter, Frances, and Alfred, in August 1919. Stanley was born three years later. (Photo by Alexander Katt, The Holler Studio, Brooklyn, courtesy of the Gould family)

The Jolly Three, (from left) Alfred, Walter, and Morton in identical homemade jumpsuits, Richmond Hill, circa 1920. (Courtesy of the Gould family)

Morton Gould at age six, late 1920. His mother noted on the back of the photo, "The *Journal* reporter wanted to see for himself whether Morton played like any normal child—therefore walked to the street and made him ride this bike." (Courtesy of the Gould family)

Morton in 1926 at age twelve, inscribed to Abby Whiteside ("whose teachings and friendship brought new inspiration into my life and work") shortly after they began working together in 1929. (Photo by E. White Studio, New York, courtesy of the Gould family)

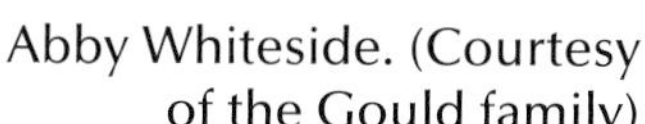

Abby Whiteside. (Courtesy of the Gould family)

Bert Shefter and Morton Gould at NBC. (Photo by William Haussler, NBC Studio, courtesy of the Gould family)

Morton with his father, pipe in hand, and publisher Jack Mills, late 1930s. (Courtesy of the Gould family)

The *Cresta Blanca Carnival* team, (from left) Jean Merrill, Brad Reynolds, Gould, and announcer Frank Gallop, 1942. (Courtesy of G. Schirmer, Inc.)

Preparing for the premiere of the Viola Concerto, (from left) Gould, NBC music director Frank Black, and soloist Milton Katims, 1943. (Courtesy of the Gould family)

Erich Leinsdorf (right) presents Gould with gold-plated record for *American Salute*, October 1943. (Courtesy of the Gould family)

Arrival in Hollywood for *Delightfully Dangerous*, (from left) Shirley Bank Gould, Morton Gould, and producer Charles Rogers, 1944. (Photo by Jack Albin, courtesy of the Gould family)

Morton Gould recording in 1945. (Courtesy of the Gould family)

Officials of the American-Soviet Music Society, (from left) guest baritone Mordecai Mauman, Gould, executive secretary Betty Randolph Bean, Serge Koussevitzky, Elie Siegmeister, Tanglewood executive Margaret Grant, Aaron Copland, and Marc Blitzstein, at a spring musicale, 1946. (Courtesy of G. Schirmer, Inc.)

Rehearsing for "American Serenade" tour, with soprano and soon-to-be sister-in-law Mimi Benzell and baritone Wilbur Evans, 1947. (Courtesy of the Gould family)

Frances Gould (left) and Jule Heuman, late 1940s. (Courtesy of the Gould family)

Shirley Uzin Quill. (Courtesy of the Transit Workers Union of America, AFL-CIO)

Morton and Shirley, with David, in high chair, and Eric, Forest Hills, 1948. (Courtesy of the Gould family)

With Benny Goodman at Goodman's home in Westchester, 1978. (Courtesy of the Gould family)

Presenting saxophone pieces to President Bill Clinton, at the dedication of the Thomas J. Dodd Research Center at the University of Connecticut, Storrs, 15 October 1995. (Photo by Peter Morenus/UConn, courtesy of the Gould family)

He was adamant about it: "I had friends who said, 'Oh, we artists.' I never related artistry to the way one lives. I think that's crap. That's a crock," he declared in 1985.

Shirley Uzin Gould moved out of Austin Street on New Year's Eve 1940. Morton was distraught and sought solace with another. "To this day," he said in 1995, "New Year's Day is very uncomfortable. It was a holiday where everybody was with people they loved, their family. I went to a New Year's party and there was a woman who was the wife of a friend of mine—and so on."

For a while he stayed at Whiteside's apartment ("I gave him a key because Shirley is living away from him at present," Whiteside noted on 15 January 1941), and then moved back to his parents. Shirley lived with friends around the city, and Morton wrote stiff letters far different in manner from before.

On 28 January he sent her a letter and some money "to help tide you a bit over this period." He was feverishly busy: in the next two months, besides the radio, he would conduct a Federal Youth Project orchestra in his own music, and the New York Philharmonic was to perform *Foster Gallery*. "Not bad, what? . . . Please take care of yourself, and try to adjust yourself intelligently to things as they happen. Don't hesitate to call on Ed [his friend Edward Morgenstern, a physician] should you get caught up with the colds or flu that are so prevalent. . . . All I can say is that I'm sorry that you tried everything, and every which way, except us."

Morton was devastated and did not tell his parents about the separation; in early February they begged Whiteside for information. Gould could not quite give up. In March he asked Shirley to visit him at The Fieldstone: "Please don't have any funny ideas about this—it is perfectly normal and natural—considering that we don't exactly hate each other." Whiteside documented his unhappiness. In April she wrote, "I feel so sorry for him and can do nothing about it." In May she recorded, "Morton is in the depths of misery over Shirley and I see no way out for him."

He even tried to join the Army, but the recruiters turned him down: in the oral history videotaped by son David in 1991, he recounted, "They said, 'Settle your personal affairs, get a divorce—then we'll sign you up.'" Morton continued to send Shirley money—for herself, for her dentist, as a gift—though she objected. They continued to quarrel; occasionally she refused to accept his letters, and he showed some anger. In July 1941 he wrote, "I am curious to know what makes you still use my name, instead of Uzin. I am positive that you told me that that was the name you would use for your home address. . . . In any case, you must change it, and *immediately*." (And he enclosed a check for her birthday.)

In public, Morton was disingenuous about the end of his marriage. The magazine *Radio World* (October 1941) conjectured that he wasn't married "because he's always been too busy to fall in love."

Finally, in the spring of 1943, Shirley flew to Reno, Nevada, for a divorce. Morton wrote her several times, impersonally, and with sparks of cynicism. By now he was nationally famous, leader of the *Cresta Blanca Carnival* on CBS. In April 1943 he wrote, "I feel like a smug son of a bitch every Wed. nite—and I'm afraid that Art is generally a phony proposition—compared to the reality of living and common people—and at best is a luxury to be afforded during more leisurely eras."

He tried to explain the end of their marriage in a long letter to Whiteside in September 1943. Shirley had accused him of being spoiled by success and called the acclaim and adulation "false glory." Since the divorce, Morton admitted, he'd been burying himself in work and seeing countless women to assuage his "restlessness." "With all the horrible defects and faults of our relationship together—Shirley and I had one thing—intensity and a peculiar sort of compatibility. . . . Love is the one thing that doesn't make sense."

Shirley's own analysis (*Mike Quill: Himself*, p. 150) seems reasonable:

> Morton had been strongly attracted to the volatile, restless, unconventional Shirley. What he needed, probably, was an undemanding, nurturing woman; what he had married was an insecure, angry, bewildered, passionate, immature girl who was creating shock waves around her as she groped and stumbled toward a realization of self that embodied a radically new concept—one not fully understood or accepted even today—the concept of a marriage as a shared partnership of equals.

CHAPTER 11

Morton at War

★ ★ ★ ★

ON FRIDAY, 27 June 1941, "Major" Edward Bowes had a heart attack in the bathroom of his apartment in the Waldorf Towers. Bowes (no more a military man than Colonel Sanders of Kentucky Fried Chicken) was the star of one of the most popular shows on radio, his weekly *Original Amateur Hour*, sponsored by the Chrysler Corporation on CBS and descended from Roxy Rothafel's old variety show.

While Bowes recovered, his staff huddled to find a temporary replacement. Fred Allen was considered and then someone mentioned Gould. Director Robert Reed snuck into WOR to listen. "It was just wonderful!" Reed exclaimed during a 1995 interview.

> I was overcome. I said, this is for me, who can I talk to?—it was Pop, his father. I had inquired around, and I could get Howard Barlow [CBS's music director] for five hundred a week. I told his father who I was representing, Chrysler and Bowes, and swore Pop to secrecy. I said, "What would you want?" He said, "One thousand dollars a show." That was funny—I was going to offer this kid a forty to fifty million audience, Pop should have been saying, "How much do you want *me* to pay?" But Bowes was clearing sixty-five thousand a week, and with income taxes at ninety-four percent, a thousand dollars would have cost him about a hundred dollars a week, which is a writeoff. It didn't make any difference to me, but the chutzpah of the guy!

James Gould wasn't such a bad manager after all: Morton got his thousand bucks a week, though he was, as usual, skeptical. In 1996 Gould remembered what he said to Phil Lang as they left the Bowes offices that day: "That Reed seems like a nice guy. But we're going to go in on Wednesday for rehearsal and he's going to be nowhere around. We'll tell the guys to take five, we'll go to the john, and guess who's going to be handing out the towels?"

But Reed really was running the show (which, when Morton conducted, was called *Shower of Stars*), and it was another step up for Gould. The press paid attention, the audiences stayed fairly high and he finally had a commercial show—even if it was only temporary. Morton wrote Whiteside on 9 July 1941, "So here I am, conducting a forty-two-piece orchestra in an hour's music, on the biggest commercial program there is. Somebody's crazy—but here I am working for Chrysler—and being featured just the way I envisaged—but had given up hope of ever getting."

One guest on the very first *Shower of Stars* was Frank Sinatra. Gould borrowed a Tommy Dorsey arrangement and added "a whole mob of strings," Reed recalled, something Sinatra had not experienced before. "They did the first chorus, then the bridge, and then the second chorus," Reed said. "[Frank] looked like he had been hit by a bat—he got pale. He said, 'That was the most beautiful thing I ever heard in my life!' He said, 'If I ever get a show of my own, I'll get covered up with fiddles.' It was so funny, so heartfelt." Gould's memory in 1985 was earthier: "[Sinatra] came out during the rehearsal, a skinny little guy. He looked around and said, 'Look at all those fucking strings!' He loved it."

Unfortunately, ASCAP was on strike, and Morton couldn't even play his own music. "I thought they were crazy. I was beside myself," Gould told me in 1996. "For months, I did arrangements of public domain music. I must have done 'Jeannie With the Light Brown Hair' backwards and forwards." The first week, Gould and Lang worked on arrangements until Wednesday, when there was a full rehearsal, another on Thursday—"eight hours straight," said Reed—and then the show. "There wasn't one blooper in the whole thing. I don't know how it was done," the director recalled. Morton always appeared deadly serious. "He had a beagle puss," Reed said. "We used to give him these hopped-up introductions: 'Here he is, the greatest conductor and arranger in the world!'—and he'd walk out onstage with that long, long face. I could never get him to smile. One night, he was walking out and he almost stumbled over a table someone had left there. He thought that was funny, so he smiled."

Gould's *Shower of Stars* was on for eleven weeks, through the summer of 1941. Which is not to say he was doing nothing else. The 1940s were Gould's golden age. In March 1940, for example, he had visited the University of Michigan at Ann Arbor to lead William Revelli's university band before an audience of four thousand in *Cowboy Rhapsody*, the first of three Gould wrote. Poet Louis Untermeyer (*Newsweek*, 8 April 1940) was effusive: "My god, I'm grappling for adjectives. It was brilliant—that's the word—and exciting, too. It had an element of surprise. You knew the tunes, but there was such a new presentation that it was dynamite. I was on the edge of my seat, or was it my saddle?"

Gould's pace increased in 1941, which, besides that New York premiere of *Foster Gallery*, saw the premieres of his Fourth Symphonette (*Latin American Symphonette*) and *Spirituals for String Choir and Orchestra*.

Spirituals, although a more substantial composition, got less attention, at least partly because the first performance, on 19 February 1941 during the New York City Festival of American Music, was caught up in a union squabble. Gould rehearsed with one orchestra, but a jurisdictional dispute meant another ensemble showed up for the concert. "It was the most disastrous performance you ever heard," Gould said in 1985.

But *Latin American Symphonette* was an immediate success. It got its first performance on 22 February 1941, by the National Youth Administration Orchestra under Fritz Mahler at the Brooklyn Academy of Music. The radio premiere, on 8 April, was carried coast to coast on the Mutual network and broadcast internationally on a shortwave hookup. (Other programs that night included *Fibber McGee and Molly*, opposite Gould on WEAF; Bob Hope and Jerry Colonna; Joe Louis's heavyweight defense against Tony Musto; and Vladimir Golschmann conducting the St. Louis Symphony.)

Fiedler picked up *Latin American Symphonette* for the Boston Pops on 11 May 1941. The *Boston Herald* critic was of two minds; he pronounced the second movement, "Tango," too long and thought the

"Conga" didn't need the forces of a full symphony orchestra: "A good noisy jazz band would have served." But he found "a real talent for orchestration" in the "Rhumba" and "Guaracha": "Here, at least, was a contemporary dance suite that did not lack vitality."

Stokowski chose the third movement of *Latin American Symphonette*, "Guaracha," for a nationwide tour of his All-American Youth Orchestra. Gould sent him *Spirituals*, and Stokowski responded enthusiastically: "I like the music immensely. We are playing your Guaracho and Rhumba and I think it is wonderful how you have caught the spirit of this music and yet expressed it through our kind of orchestra. I enjoy conducting this music immensely."

Morton himself was now in close contact with the people who ran New York's concert music. Early in May 1941, he had a lengthy interview with Arthur Judson, who ran both the Philharmonic and Columbia Artists, the nation's most powerful artistic management. Judson gave Gould the same advice he had given Ormandy: if Morton wanted a conducting career, he should spend time leading smaller ensembles outside the major cities. But Morton had no interest in becoming a music director, nor in giving up his lucrative, high-profile positions in radio and recording.

Judson liked Gould's music and sent a note on 13 May to John Barbirolli, then the Philharmonic's music director:

> The Latin American [Symphonette] will be the most effective work to perform. I think it is excellent. The one called "Spirituals" is a fine work with one movement perhaps a little reminiscent of Debussy's "Golliwog's Cakewalk." The "Lincoln Legend" rather impresses me reading it from score. Whether this essay into more serious music and classical form will be successful or not, I do not know. You will have to be the judge of that.

Barbirolli did not perform *Lincoln Legend*. Toscanini did. And Stokowski included "Guaracha" (which he insisted on calling "guaracho") in October 1941 with the Philharmonic, by which time *PM* was calling Gould the "bad boy" of American music.

By the beginning of August 1941, Morton had also written a concerto for the tap dancer Paul Draper, for a Carnegie Hall program in the fall. Draper never made the appearance and Gould misplaced the score; ten years later he wrote another *Tap Dance Concerto* for Danny Daniels.

On 17 August 1941, the day of the premiere of *A Song of Freedom*, Gould's ungainly and deservedly forgotten cantata, at Lewisohn Stadium, an essay by Gould entitled "Composing for School Groups" appeared in the *Times*. Condescending professionals were "sadly mistaken." He'd been mightily impressed in Michigan, and he recommended that, to make money, to stretch their talents and strengthen their positions, American composers should start writing for school and town bands:

> From personal experience I have found that the better school symphonic bands play with a quality, intonation, and spirit that one rarely finds among professional organizations, with the exception of a few top-notch symphonic orchestras under important leadership. . . . There are in the West small towns with populations of a few thousand that have school bands of two to three hundred young people. One has to go out of the big cities to discover the tremendous musical development taking place in this country. . . . The American composer, therefore, will find it well worth his while to explore personally one of the few outlets that will make him a practical functioning artisan and bring him into contact with the people of this country.

In other words, if you want to make a living instead of starving in a garret, go West.

Major Bowes returned to the air in the fall of 1941, but Gould's pace did not falter. Although the United States had not yet entered World War II, President Franklin D. Roosevelt and his advisers were trying to prepare the nation. One propaganda effort was *Keep 'Em Rolling*, produced by WOR and the federal Office of Emergency Management. Broadcast from Mutual's New Amsterdam roof studio, it was intended to present "what we are defending in America and the need for defending it," according to a network release.

The lineup was extraordinary: scripts by Lillian Hellman, Stephen Vincent Benet, William Saroyan; theme by Richard Rodgers and Lorenz Hart; guest stars including Ethel Merman, Burgess Meredith,

Lawrence Tibbett, Lily Pons, and Dinah Shore. Clifton Fadiman was emcee, and Morton Gould the music director. The half-hour show, which aired on Sunday nights at 10:30, premiered 9 November 1941.

A month later, the Japanese bombed Pearl Harbor—hours before *Keep 'Em Rolling* went on the air. Gould described what happened in the oral history videotaped by son David in 1991. He got a call from Washington to plan a special rehearsal—he had no idea why.

"Don't you listen to the radio?" asked the caller.

"No, I don't listen to the radio. Why?"

"Pearl Harbor."

"Pearl who?"

"We're at war!"

"With whom?"

"With the Japanese!"

"I had no feelings about it whatsoever," Gould said. "We had to change the Sunday plans. My only feeling was a cold professional feeling." Risë Stevens was the soloist; they threw out her arias and she sang "The Star-Spangled Banner." The playlet and music were rewritten "in a Japanese direction." A Defense Department spokesman flew in from Washington to speak, and there were announcements before and after each number: "Will all servicemen please leave immediately and report to their stations." That, said Gould, is when the reality of the war finally hit him.

Two of his brothers were already in the Army. Alfred, despite the weakness of his left arm, went into the tank corps and served out the war in the United States. Walter reached the rank of captain and served in Europe. Stanley enlisted in the Coast Guard. And Morton, dreaming of glory since Stoothoff Avenue, tried again to sign up. Although he was now the sole support of his parents, Gould nevertheless wrote to both the Army and the Navy, seeking to enlist. This time he failed the physical: he had a double hernia and a heart murmur. "They tested my groin and I almost collapsed—I really screamed out," he told his son. Gould was classified 4F and "deeply regretted" that he did not serve.

Nevertheless, he was continuously involved on the home front. *Keep 'Em Rolling* quickly became *This Is War*—a typical program, on 7 March 1942, included a sketch about the Army by Stephen Vincent Benet, narrated by Tyrone Power, and directed by Norman Corwin.

Early that year, Gould also wrote the soundtrack for the propaganda film *Ring of Steel*, narrated by Spencer Tracy.

Of course, what Morton remembered was mostly the things that went wrong, such as the naval episode concerning dreadnoughts and aircraft carriers, with "all kinds of eloquent pomposities." Gould wrote a symphonic arrangement of "Anchors Aweigh," and the next day he got so many comments he just knew there'd been a mistake. Finally someone said, "Did you hear the show?" Gould said, "How could I hear it? I was conducting it." "It was very funny," responded his friend. "When you did that salute to the aircraft carriers, why did you use those whistles?" The engineer, who was supposed to have used ships' horns, had hit ferryboat whistles instead. "So it seems," as Gould explained it in 1985, "that all through the program, when we were saying things about 'the great majesty of the sea,' there would be 'beep beep beep.'"

Gould also churned out patriotic numbers: "Buck Private" (after the war, renamed "Joe College"), "American Youth," "American Legion Forever," "March for Yanks," "March of the Leathernecks," "Bombs Away," "Paratrooper," and so forth, and for the Allies, "Marche Lorraine," "Red Cavalry," and "New China." They were all originally scored for orchestra and transcribed for band, primarily by Phil Lang.

Gould was also one of the composers asked in 1942 by Eugene Goossens, of the Cincinnati Symphony, to write fanfares for four horns, three trumpets, three trombones, tuba, timpani, and percussion. The composers included Bernstein, Piston, Harris, Hanson, and Creston, among others. The most famous result is Copland's *Fanfare for the Common Man* (which also became the foundation for the finale of his Symphony No. 3). Gould's contribution was *Fanfare for Freedom*.

His producer asked for a salute to the United States. The result—orchestral variations on "When Johnny Comes Marching Home," written overnight with copyists standing by—was *American Salute*, which has become a staple of the patriotic repertoire. ("It was years before I knew that it was a classic setting," he said in November 1985. "What amazes me now is that critics say it is a minor masterpiece, a gem. To me, it was just a setting. I was doing a million of those things.")

The pace of success accelerated. By the summer of 1942, Morton was working on a symphony for Reiner in Pittsburgh, and Arturo Toscanini was considering one of his works. In mid-August, Gould mailed the legendary conductor *Spirituals* and *Lincoln Legend*, a tone poem inspired by Carl Sandberg's biography. On 1 September 1942, Toscanini replied by hand, to "Mae.[stro] Gould":

> Have you any objection if I perform your Lincoln's Legend in my first concert at the N.B.C. in November the first? I don't know, nor I can't tell to you if the music is beautiful or good—clever or well written—I leave these things to the shrill critics, incapable of procreation but never doubting their wisdom! I only know, and I like to tell you, that at my first looking on your score I was much taken and fascinated with the incisive and penetrating musical strokes of your Lincoln's Legend. Isn't enough?

Enough? That wasn't all. For while his most ambitious works were being programmed by the major conductors of the era, Morton was also approaching the pinnacle of radio success: he was about to get another commercial show, his own this time. Gould explained it to a convalescing Whiteside in California: "Dear Miss Whiteside" —Gould almost never addressed her informally, despite their years of intimacy—"You can't do this to me. A grown-up person like you should have more self-control than to get dangerously ill. . . . So please be reasonable and get better quick and come home. Just think —without you I'll play piano like a Juilliard graduate—and probably behave like one."

Cresta Blanca Carnival, a forty-five-minute show sponsored by Cresta Blanca Wines, had its first broadcast on 14 October 1942, with singers Jean Merrill and Brad Reynolds and comedian Jack Pearl. Writing to his estranged wife on 28 October, Morton described the note from Toscanini ("How's that?") and his new show "with a large orchestra doing my stuff." On 1 November, Toscanini led the NBC Symphony in the world premiere of *Lincoln Legend*. On 11 November, Gould premiered *American Salute* on *Cresta Blanca Carnival*. On 12 and 13 November, Howard Barlow conducted the Philharmonic in *American Symphonette* No. 2. On 15 November, Stokowski (alternating with Toscanini at the NBC Symphony that season) conducted *Spirituals* in a broadcast. And starting on 18 November, Artur Rodzinski led the Philharmonic in a series of performances of *Spirituals*—including one on 7 December 1942, the celebration of the orchestra's own centennial and the first anniversary of Pearl Harbor, aboard a Navy training vessel at a Manhattan pier.

All this just before Morton's twenty-ninth birthday! It was a concentrated period of triumph such as few, if any, American composers have ever experienced.

CHAPTER 12

"Shirley Two"

★ ★ ★ ★

THE WAR YEARS roared by. Morton worked hard and long, and everything he did was successful.

From 1943 through 1946, Gould was the star of a weekly commercial radio show. His radio music was appropriated by everyone from jazz bands to choreographers. His concert works were performed nationwide. He was featured in a movie, and he wrote the score for a Broadway musical. He recorded regularly, and the results were best-sellers.

The Gould home in Forest Hills was a busy social center, while Morton kept a suite in the Warwick Hotel at Fifty-sixth Street and Sixth Avenue. Morton even married a Shirley again and started a family (somewhat to his surprise).

Gould was living his dream.

Cresta Blanca Carnival was the pinnacle of Gould's commercial career, produced by the William H. Weintraub Agency and directed by William Bernbach. When it went on the air in October 1942, Gould shared top billing with comedian Jack Pearl. But Morton wanted to be the unquestioned No. 1; as he said in 1985, "I wanted to do a strictly musical show, not a variety show. . . . I had a taste of blood, and now I wanted the whole bucket."

He got it. By 13 January 1943, *Cresta Blanca Carnival*, Wednesdays on WOR from 9:15 to 10:00 p.m., was all Gould's. And quite a show it was, until its run ended in May 1944. That first broadcast "without a funny man" (as Whiteside described it in her diary that day) was emceed by songwriter George S. Kaufman and witty pianist Oscar

Levant; it featured Brazilian singer Olga Coehlo and Benny Goodman with his sextet; there was even a short sketch by dramatist Norman Corwin entitled *2043*.

The first shows were similarly eclectic. Jarmila Novotná sang Verdi, the Golden Gate Quartet sang spirituals, Arch Oboler wrote sketches; guests included actress Maria Montez, soprano Eileen Farrell, actress Constance Bennett, and comedians Jimmy Durante and Zero Mostel. The music included a lot of Morton's work. And the theme became one of the decade's premier commercial jingles. A simple six-note ascending and descending figure that spelled out each letter of the wine company's name, it was inseparably associated with Cresta Blanca and was used into the 1950s.

The show was so successful that it was picked up by CBS as a purely musical half-hour over WABC. The emcee was Goddard Lieberson, just beginning his rise through the Columbia hierarchy. The producers went all out. On 14 April, the guests included violinist Mischa Elman; composer W. C. Handy (who gave a two-minute introduction to his "St. Louis Blues" before Gould and "two boogie-woogie pianists" played Morton's own arrangement); and singer Connie Boswell. Duke Ellington and soprano Vivian Della Chiesa appeared the next week; after that it was tenor Lauritz Melchior and blues singer Georgia Gibbs; singing actress Mary Martin and violinist Joseph Szigeti; soprano Risë Stevens; blues singer Ethel Waters; and, more and more frequently until he became a permanent member, blind English pianist Alec Templeton.

CBS promoted *Cresta Blanca* heavily and sent its affiliated stations elaborate press material: "Listen to the incredibly beautiful things he can do with his unusual arrangements, interpreted by his fifty-piece orchestra. And then, we think, you'll agree with music critics everywhere that a new star is burning brightly in the musical sky."

Gould's orchestra included colleagues from earlier shows, older string players, and up-and-coming freelancers. Max Pollikoff was concertmaster; there was Mitch Miller on oboe, flutist Julius Baker (later the longtime principal flute for the New York Philharmonic), and the composer David Diamond on violin or viola.

Diamond was in dire financial straits, and Gould gave him a lot of work: *Cresta Blanca*, recordings, film soundtracks, special engagements. "I was very impressed with Morton from the standpoint of stick technique," Diamond said. "It was very good, very clear, and very energetic—and he was extremely funny. He told wonderful stories."

Gould could be tough on the podium. His ears were exceptional, but he had a tendency to hear pitches wrong on the high notes—"like Heifetz," said violinist Milton Lomask, his contractor (the musician who hires the orchestra) and sometime concertmaster. "He'd say, 'Can't you hear that it's flat?' He would get quite angry." But the musicians held Gould in high regard. "Everybody knew what he was, that he was much too good for the *Cresta Blanca*," said Lomask.

During all this Gould completed his Symphony No. 1 and visited Pittsburgh to hear Reiner lead the world premiere on 5 March 1943. This was a full-fledged orchestral work in four movements, with no commercial or timing constraints. At first he intended calling it *A Victory Ode*, then *Symphonic Mural in Four Sections*, and finally, by February, simply Symphony No. 1. The dedication reads like this: "To my three brothers in the Armed Forces of the United States and their fellow-fighters." There is no mistaking the seriousness of purpose. Rather than an allegro-andante-scherzo-finale structure, its movements are entitled "Epitaph" (slow), "Dances" (scherzo), "Pastorale and Battle Music" (slow), and "Resolution" (also slow).

The mournful, keening opening movement is reminiscent of Shostakovich, particularly his Fifth and Sixth Symphonies, in harmony, line, and mood. There are also hints of Sibelius. Gould's own touch is evident in recurring snatches of "Taps." The second movement mixes barn dance, country fiddling, Hollywood effects, and dance and brass band. Few melodies are quoted, but the overall sensation is pure 1940s Americana. Yet even here, the music feels heavy rather than free.

"Pastorale and Battle Music" is striking. The woodwinds present a meandering, nocturnal melody, but the trembling strings convey barely noticeable tension. The rumbling fades, but things are on edge. Then Gould presents an extraordinary effect: a formation of bombers passes overhead, created by glissando and tonguing in the mid and lower brass. There's a single explosion from the bass drum, and then the bassoons (of all things) start a march that develops into a fugue.

The "battle" goes from there, with influences ranging from *Alex-*

ander Nevsky through to the *1812 Overture* and "The Bonnie Blue Flag." The orchestra grows very busy, but, paradoxically, the score never reaches a martial climax. Instead, the strings sing a long, poignant line, the oboes and clarinets hint again at "Taps," and the whole affair fades away. "Resolution" begins with a crash and fanfare, but the mood is ambivalent. Quiet musing in the cellos alternates with shrill upper strings and the fanfare. A broad theme in the violas and low brass is laden with sorrow. Eventually a piccolo-bright, Sousa-style march gets under way, but the ever-present "Taps" is a continual reminder of the death that brought the victory.

It is not notably successful music—the heavy influence of Shostakovich in the first movement is derived rather than digested, developments are episodic, the "airplane" sound is used only for effect, and ultimately Gould does not delve deeply enough into the glory or the gore of his subject. Nevertheless, it is certainly not the work of a lightweight, middlebrow vulgarian.

Donald S. Steinfirst (*Pittsburgh Post-Gazette*) recognized the score's worth: "The Symphony is a sincere, honest, in many places inspired, work. . . . Over all there is the impression of a vital work, of a composer with something to say, declaiming it musically and intelligently, using dissonance only as a means to an end."

On 14 March 1943, Stokowski programmed the "New China" and "Red Cavalry" marches with the NBC Symphony. Still, Gould would not be satisfied. In April 1943 he wrote to Shirley Uzin, in Reno, "I suppose there is something wrong in my not feeling happy in achieving things that most other people would give their right arms or libidos to get. . . . What the hell do I want anyway?"

Gould next sent Artur Rodzinski the symphony score and in a cover letter dated 26 May 1943 asked whether he would like something to open the next season—a symphony, a "cowboy rhapsody," or a concerto for orchestra, "a very virtuoso treatment of the orchestra in which, as example, the second movement might be a lyrical blues, and a third movement perhaps a wild and colorful boogie-woogie toccata."

"Dear Gould," Rodzinski replied, "I like your idea of concerto for orchestra very much . . . . Just heard NBC play your *Spirituals*. Gosh, what tempi! The last climax sounded like a funeral march. How about an effective concert suite of Victor Herbert? That might make a hit and be greatly demanded by every symphony orchestra."

Gould mounted the podium at Lewisohn Stadium on the Fourth of July weekend, his first performance there conducting the New York Philharmonic since 1938. This time he was the sole conductor and the primary composer for two wartime concerts: on Saturday a United Nations program, including works by Nikolai Miaskovsky, Oscar Lorenzo Fernandez, Frederick Delius, and his own *Folk Suite*. Then followed five marches leading off with *Fanfare for Freedom*; the concert concluded with an audience singalong in Shostakovich's *United Nations March*.

The Fourth itself, cold and rainy, was all-American: Schuman, Harris, Copland, two movements of *American Symphonette* No. 2, Gould's arrangement of W. C. Handy's "St. Louis Blues" (with the "white-haired Negro composer" present to take a bow, as *The New York Post* noted), string arrangements of Kern and Carmichael, and a repeat of the marches.

That Tuesday, Morton lunched with the pianist José Iturbi, who was to appear the next evening on *Cresta Blanca*. They wondered why more composers didn't use boogie-woogie in concert music. Gould said he'd write something for the upcoming show; Iturbi said he would love to play it, though there wasn't time between today and tomorrow to get it done.

Nevertheless, according to Harriet van Horne (*World-Telegram*, 4 August 1943), Gould called Iturbi with the music that night, and the next day they premiered *Boogie Woogie Etude*, for piano and orchestra. Arthur Fiedler picked it up the next week, and Iturbi took it to the Hollywood Bowl in a two-piano version for him and his sister, Anpero. By the fall, Iturbi had recorded the *Etude* and the "Blues" movement from the forthcoming *American Concertette* No. 1 for Victor.

The peak of the summer came with the premiere of the Viola Concerto on 29 July 1943 by Milton Katims with the NBC Symphony under Frank Black. Gould had been working on this full-scale, three-movement piece for months. In May he brought William Primrose to Whiteside's apartment for a runthrough, but Gould would not give the violist the two years' exclusive rights he requested. Philadelphia Orchestra violist Samuel Lifschey wrote in frustration on 31 July, after the broadcast, because his reception was disrupted by interference from construction work near his home. Nevertheless, Lifschey was impressed with the superb orchestration and the thematic material and idiom.

Gould even tried his hand as a columnist, writing a guest piece for Walter Winchell on 7 August. He offered a few wisecracks: "What note got mixed up with what chord the other night and was last seen disappearing in a violin run? What melody got lost in what arrangement and hasn't been heard from since? Musical notes next on the ration list. Composers will have to write slower music to conserve notes. What young American composer-conductor ought to stick to music instead?"

Then came the climax of this hectic summer: On 25 August 1943, the bulk of *Cresta Blanca Carnival* was devoted to the premiere of the *American Concertette* No. 1 for piano and orchestra, with Iturbi. Having written four symphonettes, Gould was trying something a little different (Iturbi, tired of playing *Rhapsody in Blue*, wanted a new American jazz concerto).

The *Concertette* struck an immediate chord. First, it brought about an offer from Jascha Heifetz, who wrote a letter dated 27 August 1943, from Newport Beach, California. He suggested that Gould write something similar for violin and orchestra, in one movement.

> I am particularly interested to have the mediums of this country used in the composition. I mean perhaps Negro Spirituals, Jazz, and anything that has an interesting rhythmical value. I am sure you understand there is nothing binding on either side. But if the work appealed to me at all, I would be most anxious to have something like that.

Gould turned Heifetz down. He was too busy; he didn't want to write on speculation, without at least the guarantee of a performance. Pop was furious: Morton would write a concerto for Max Pollikoff but not for Jascha Heifetz?

This rejection is consistent with another, also related to the *American Concertette*, that had greater ramifications. Not long after *American Concertette* aired, a dancer named Jerome Robbins visited Gould in Rockefeller Center. Robbins was twenty-five and had been with the Ballet Theatre, predecessor of American Ballet Theatre, for several years. He wanted to set the *Concertette*, but first he had a different proposal—about some sailors on leave. "It was very vague. It didn't sound enticing," Gould said.

Ballet Caravan, the company's touring unit, told Robbins that if he found a composer, and if they got it written, and if the company liked it, they might do it on the road, and if they liked it on the road they might perform it in New York. "I said, 'I am very busy. I cannot do things on speculation—I said I was terribly sorry," said Morton in 1985.

Morton offered them some alternatives: Alex North, "who was starving to death," Henry Brant, a few others.

> Amongst them I said there was a sort of new boy in town and I'd been told he was very gifted: Leonard Bernstein. I'm sure he would have known of Lenny, and Lenny would have known of Jerry, because the word was out, Lenny was a tremendous talent. Those are famous last words: the next thing I know, I was sitting at the Metropolitan Opera House, watching what turned out to be *Fancy Free*.

Robbins confirmed Gould's account in a letter of 15 May 1996: "I was looking for a composer and approached those I'd heard and whose music I liked; therefore Morton. I'm not sure about Ballet Caravan but I am sure about it being a possibility for him. All the other people he mentioned, except Bernstein, had the same reply—too busy, not certain enough, et cetera. Many people recommended Lenny."

The rest is history: Robbins's and Bernstein's historic first collaboration was *Fancy Free*, which became *On the Town*, and ultimately led to *West Side Story*. And on 14 November 1943, Leonard Bernstein, the clever youngster from Massachusetts, made his brilliant last-minute debut with the Philharmonic.

Gould made no claim for what he might have done instead. "Jerry and Lenny were the right combination at that time," he told Kazdin and Hemming in 1985. "Working with me might have turned up another kettle of fish—maybe a good ballet, maybe a bad ballet. The things that go to make *Fancy Free* the successful ballet it was and is, is Jerry and Lenny—I think that's very big of me, to have that attitude, don't you?"

But in 1944 Robbins did set *American Concertette*, for the high-level vaudeville *Concert Varieties*, produced by Billy Rose at the Seven Arts Theater. It became a free-form ballet for four pairs of dancers that he called *Interplay*—a name Gould much preferred, "a hell of a lot better than my cockamamie *American Concertette*."

Their memories diverged somewhat over the composer's involvement. Gould told me in 1996 that—just as he had not gone to hear Reiner perform *American Symphonette* No. 2 in Pittsburgh—he did not see the ballet until it had been playing for some time. "Somebody, I think Billy Rose, said to me, 'I can't believe it, you haven't seen it?' To me it was an old piece."

But Robbins said, in that May letter, "Morton must have known I was choreographing it because there was a rim-shot on a recording they made that I fell in love with but Morton said was a mistake and wanted to cut it out. He was very cooperative and left it in there. . . . I do *not* remember that he did not see it until after it played a while. I do not think that's true as I like to keep a good working relationship with the composer."

The result of these two episodes: Robbins created *Interplay* with little contribution from the composer. And there is not another Gould violin concerto, despite the flattering request from a famous virtuoso. These incidents fit the pattern: he was so busy and so consumed with making money that, out of arrogance and insecurity, he turned away what appeared to be golden opportunities. It was not as if they would never come again—after all, Morton Gould was not yet thirty.

Beyond the music, material glory also kept coming his way. Gould had luxurious facilities in Radio City, shared with a staff of six including Pop; Margaret Blackmar, his loyal secretary; arranger Phil Lang (the master orchestrator of Broadway for the next three decades); and Horace Grennell (later director of Westminster Records). On the walls of his thickly carpeted inner office were autographed photos of Stokowski and Reiner, with another of Toscanini on a side table. Sitting behind his "large, highly polished executive's desk," wrote Ron Eyer (*Musical America*, 25 December 1943), "sits a debonair young man with frank blue eyes, a shock of dark, lank hair and a well-fed look, who greets you with a boyish grin."

Eyer's profile is a fair description of the young man at the top of his game, including the self-deprecation and discomfort, as well as a confident belligerence. Morton Gould "detests everything about [his] chromium plated, businesslike setting" and spends two or three days a week there only for *Cresta Blanca*; the rest of the time he may be found in "his own creative sanctum, which he describes as an apartment within an apartment out on Long Island, where he lives with his Austrian-born father and Russian-born mother." What drove Gould most of all, Eyer wrote, was "an inner compulsion to write music . . . regardless of what the future may hold for him otherwise.

"Gould currently is a single man, although he has had one adventure in matrimony. He may try it again some day, but at the moment is too pre-occupied with stop-watches, copyists, and the goadings of the muse to give the matter much attention."

Well, not quite. For by his thirtieth birthday he had already begun dating the vivacious youngest child of a large, affluent Minneapolis family. Shirley Bank was born 4 May 1921, the last of the six children of Frank and Sophie Bank, first-generation Jewish immigrants from Eastern Europe—he from Lithuania, she from Russia. Bank became a commercial salvage agent, assessing the value of goods after a calamity and selling them. He died of heart disease in 1931, at the age of forty-nine. Shirley adored her father. "My grandfather Bank died when little girls still think their dads are knights in shining armor and have not yet been able to see them objectively as people," Abby Gould Burton asserted. "As a matter of fact, there was always a picture of him over her bed. And that's a ghost nobody could come close to being in life. . . . So he was always this amazing, wonderful human being. It was only talking to her brothers that you found he gambled, was a womanizer, and he never brought money in."

Which is not how Shirley's brother James Bank remembered it, though he acknowledged that the business was small while their father was alive. "Everybody was crazy about him," James Bank said. "He was good looking, everybody loved him. He was a hard worker. I don't remember any problem with the Depression. I don't remember being deprived of anything, or being told, 'Don't do this' or 'Don't do that.'" When their father died, eldest brother Marvin Bank, an ebullient man fifteen years older than Shirley and called "Red" for his strawberry-blond hair, made the business thrive.

If Frank Bank was outgoing and impecunious, his wife, Sophie, kept the household together. She was supportive of her sons but "had trouble with girls," Abby Gould Burton said. "My mother was raised in a household where women were not valued. . . . Bubby always thought boys were just the cat's meow, and my mother could never get off the dime."

That may have been the story Shirley told, but to brother Jimmy she was the darling of the family. "My sister and I—when she was sixteen, I think—she and I would go out dancing together. We were the greatest dancers there was." Supported by her brother Red, Shirley lived nicely in both Minnesota and New York. She attended the University of Minnesota with a double major in English and Spanish, graduated in three years, and went to New York to seek her fortune. Her fluency in Spanish landed her a job at the Pan American Institute, a foundation-supported organization devoted to promoting President Roosevelt's Good Neighbor Policy. "She was a very strong, independent girl and woman," James Bank said.

According to him and to Matty Gould, who became one of her sisters-in-law, Shirley Bank was having a wonderful time when she met Morton. Shirley's older sister, Rivel, already in New York, was a friend of William Weintraub, whose agency produced *Cresta Blanca*, and his wife, Anne. Through them, Shirley met Morton.

Gould usually held trysts in Manhattan and kept the bedroom in Queens for work and family. Most of his affairs were with older women; those with domestic arrangements in mind could be fended off by Forest Hills. "Living with my parents was sort of a protective thing for me," he mused in 1985.

Matty Gould was surprised that at one point during the war years, Frances Gould allowed one of Morton's women to stay at the apartment, though "she would permit almost anything in regard to Morton." That woman may have been Julia Heuman, the neighborhood girl nearly ten years older than Morton, whom he had known since childhood.

Jule, as she was known, had given Morton his first book of music ("a compendium of the most famous piano pieces of the world, five hundred of them," Gould reminisced in a 1984 diary entry). He had always been attracted to Jule, who was good friends with his mother. He remembered noticing her when he was eight: she would sit on the stoop in front of the house, in a short dress with rolled stockings, "and she really turned me on," he remarked in his diary shortly after she died in February 1984. Gould went on to explain what happened between them after the end of his first marriage: "Through a combination of circumstances, she and I got to know each other. We had a very fulfilling relationship." The physical aspect continued for years but eventually faded; nevertheless Morton and Jule stayed in touch until her death in a New York nursing home.

Always a frankly carnal person, Gould spent the period between his marriages in a state of work and sex. His friends worried that he would waste his talent in a frenzy of fornication. Sometimes he would hurry one companion through back stairs or freight elevators because someone else was waiting in the lobby. "If they didn't know each other it was not a problem: they could go in and out the same way," he explained in 1985.

He tried to keep his name out of the columns. At one point gossip columnist Leonard Lyons asked to see the letter from Toscanini. "I said 'No,' he said 'Why not?' I said, 'Because these are personal things for me, not for anybody else to see.' I was private. I did my thing in public when I conducted or broadcast." He considered the gossip columns tasteless and the wrong way to become known: "I wanted to be part of the serious world. But the fact that I had this much exposure immediately nailed me into a certain part of the artistic community, the pop part."

He had no interest in bedding glamor or fame, and he went on to assert, revealingly, "I don't react to a personality as such, to a name. . . . My reactions to women were as women, not as people. The moment I felt they were reacting to me because of who I was, that was finished. . . . To me the man-woman relationship is a sexual one. It's as basic as that."

He had many female friends whose relationships began sexually and deepened. "I have rarely been in love," he said in August 1985. "I've been in love only twice, and both of those were my wives. I've had great affection for a number of others, and in some cases deep affection. . . . My only problems have been with my two wives over the long pull."

This was the man whom the matchmakers Anne Weintraub and Rivel Bank introduced to Shirley Bank in 1943. "Anne liked me," Morton mused in 1985, "and I suppose, like a number of people, felt that I should meet somebody nice." The family had begun to feel it was time for him to find the legendary "nice Jewish girl"—and here she was.

Morton and Shirley Bank started off with a blind date early in 1943 (around the time Shirley Uzin was getting ready to go to Reno for a divorce, and while Morton was still telling Whiteside how important his estranged wife was to him). According to a family legend related by Matty, Morton told her he had written "Pavanne." "Sure," said Shirley Bank, "and I wrote 'The Star-Spangled Banner.'"

Gould felt uncomfortable at first, especially with acquaintances who knew Shirley Uzin. "We would keep running into people who would do a double-take, because all of a sudden here was this young girl, blonde, fair-skinned and blue-eyed, and the first Shirley was almost sort of an olive complexion, with brown eyes and dark hair—two completely different types," he recalled in 1985. "[Shirley Bank] was a beautiful, radiant young girl, very effervescent, very bubbly, very innocent. I remember her saying to me, 'You might not believe this, but there are people in Minneapolis, there are wives who sleep with other men and husbands who sleep with other women.' And I looked at her and thought, 'Oh my God, who am I going with?'"

Morton continued to see Shirley Bank, and not only because she was bright and fun: "I could be seen in public with her. . . . Here was a girl who was unattached and who fit the design."

Shirley Bank had no interest in music, but that was a point in her favor. "She was an absolute philistine in her reaction to the greater part of the musical literature," said Morton. "I would never think of looking at a woman and wondering if she liked music or not. . . . Had I married a wife who would love music and be backstage with me all the time, I think it would have driven me nuts." Shirley Bank was involved only with him, and that was wonderful. "We had great fun together. We laughed at the same things, and that is much more important than if she likes music or not."

Shirley's perspective can only be guessed. There was the story she told of her first meeting with the Goulds in Forest Hills, as related by Abby Gould Burton. When they got off the elevator at the apartment's floor, a GI waiting to descend nodded at them. "Hi, Al." "Hi, Morton." It was Alfred, whom Morton hadn't seen in months; the brothers were close but not effusive. Morton and Shirley entered the apartment. An older man was out cold on the floor, his wife hovering over him exclaiming, "James! James!" while a young man stood off to one side, rubbing his knuckles and saying, "He's not going to talk to her like that ever again. I won't permit it." At which point, Shirley told her daughter, "Your father then walked over your grandfather's body and said, 'Walter, this is Shirley Bank.' I should've gotten the hell out of there. I don't know why I didn't just turn around and walk out."

Shirley's account is probably a conflation and mild exaggeration of several incidents she witnessed or was told about, for in the fall and winter of 1943 Walter was with the First Army in England, preparing for the invasion of Normandy; and, in an interview in 1996, he denied having hit his father, though he remembered that once, right after the war, "Pop was giving Mother a rough time. I just took so much and finally I grabbed him by both arms and said 'Stop that!'" Nevertheless, Matty Gould said that both Walter and Alfred—though not Morton—did fight with their father over his treatment of their mother. All four sons tried to protect her; they fought with Pop in her defense and even, when they were teenagers, suggested that she divorce him. "She said no, she loves him," Walter Gould said.

So Shirley Bank moved in with Morton at the Warwick. He introduced her to Whiteside on 24 October 1943. Whiteside liked Shirley, but because the scars from Morton's first marriage were so fresh, she would not use that name. Abby called Shirley Bank "Pat."

Shirley did her best to win Abby over; over the next few months, Whiteside chronicles more time spent with "Pat," including a tête-à-tête on 15 February 1944, after which Whiteside wrote, "I can love her on her own account and feel that when Morton marries her their home will be a dear delight to me."

Morton relished Shirley Bank's competence and independence. As he explained in 1985, the last thing he wanted was someone who would want attention better focused on his work: "She never leaned on anybody. I never had the feeling she was a weaker person, or that I would have to give time and energy to do things that she couldn't do herself. She was always very independent, which was great for me—she took care of everything."

Shirley Uzin had been independent, too, but in the wrong way: she wanted a life of her own. Morton wanted someone who would take care of the quotidian and leave his hands free. Shirley Bank seemed to be that person.

She thought so too and set out to maneuver Morton, the once-burned bachelor, into matrimony. She did it by denying the goal, at least to him. "Shirley and I had never spoken about marriage. I had not thought of marriage." But Morton, who liked the Banks, felt guilty. "I thought, I can't do this to them, to be living with their little sister in sin," Gould said in 1985. "I remember saying to Shirley, 'You know, we are going to be with each other, we are living with each other. Why don't we get married?' "

Shirley set the hook: "She said, 'No, I wouldn't marry you, because you are not the marrying kind.'

"I said, 'Goddamn it, we will get married. Nobody is going to say to me you're not the marrying kind!' "

But Shirley had been planning on it for months. On 1 April 1944, she told Whiteside that she and Morton had looked at a house near Haverstraw, New York, that they might rent for the summer—"and if that happens they will be married very soon," Whiteside wrote that night. As during the first engagement, she was ecstatic: "It is all a fairy tale that he found this sweet girl. She is just right. Nothing could so enrich my life as their home together."

Fairy tales are spun of gossamer and myth, and this one had more than a little myth. The wedding itself was kept a surprise and a secret. Morton called Whiteside on 1 June to tell her "that he is going to marry Pat right away." James Gould then confirmed that the wedding would take place Saturday, 3 June 1944. The event was barely more elaborate than Morton's first. Whiteside (who recorded the event in her diary that day) and the Goulds lunched at the Russian Tea Room, went to her apartment across the street, and thence to the chambers of Judge Samuel Hull for "a sweet service with dignity and simplicity." They then traveled by car to Forest Hills for dinner. "The day was perfect. Pat was a sweet picture with her hair up. Morton was funny all day. He hates any kind of ritual."

This took the Banks by surprise. Rather than a wedding notice, on 4 June the Associated Press reported merely, "Morton Gould, 30, composer and orchestra conductor, and Shirley Bank, 23, of Minneapolis, obtained a marriage license at the city clerk's office." When reporters in St. Paul contacted the Banks, Sophie told them the couple had been married the month before, on 22 May, but were trying to keep the marriage a secret. This gave rise to speculation that

Shirley was pregnant. Their first child, Eric, was born 16 February 1945, eight and a half months after the wedding.

Matty Gould was convinced that Shirley was pregnant, and that was why she told her mother they had been married the month before. But early June may have been too soon for Shirley to realize her state. "Did Shirley manipulate Morton into marriage?" wondered Eric's wife, Candy. "Very possibly. A woman could fool him in a second, because she was a woman."

Jimmy Bank was scandalized: "Jesus Christ, the guy is divorced! It was like *The Scarlet Letter.*" But the rest of the family was moderately pleased: their darling had found a man she liked, "and he's Jewish—great!" They were concerned about his prospects, because he was just a radio bandleader. "My mother was worried," Jimmy Bank said. "How do you make a living as a composer? . . . He didn't have a regular job."

Morton gained from the wedding one of his grand, ambiguous anecdotes. The wedding weekend also marked the world premiere of his Symphony No. 2 (*Symphony on Marching Tunes*), broadcast Sunday, 4 June 1944, by the Philharmonic under Vladimir Golschmann. But the wedding caused him to miss the Saturday rehearsal, which astonished Golschmann. "He said, 'I'll see you at the rehearsal.' I said, "Volodya, I can't be there.' He said, 'You can't be there? We are doing your symphony!'" The discussion went back and forth, but Gould could not bring himself to tell Golschmann the reason for his absence.

The concert went forward—the only other work on the program was the Brahms Violin Concerto with Nathan Milstein—and afterward Gould and Golschmann went to the Russian Tea Room. Golschmann cautiously asked why Gould had missed the rehearsal. "I said, 'Well, I've got to be honest with you. Shirley is my wife. We just got married.' He said, 'When?' I said, 'Yesterday.' He said, 'Is that why you couldn't be there?' I said, 'Yeah.' He said, 'Why didn't you tell me?' He got hysterical. He fell out of his chair. He said, 'Morton, I am going to tell this story for years—what was all the mystery?—we must drink to you!'

"I have no idea why I was secretive," Gould admitted in 1985. Perhaps this free-living bachelor, who responded to women like a firehorse sniffing smoke, did not want to advertise his new status.

Perhaps he was aware that he had just been conned into a permanent relationship. Morton was deeply smitten with Shirley; he was, however, always frightened and contemptuous of public ceremony and ritual, especially when he was the focus. So it is in keeping that, when he could have gained publicity with a celebrity marriage, he shrank from the spotlight and even the congratulations of friends and colleagues.

Then, whatever attention Gould might have garnered was overwhelmed by the Allied invasion of Normandy just two days later, on 6 June. "I always kept mixing it up, because on the anniversary of D-Day I would say, 'Happy Anniversary!' to Shirley, and she would get flustered."

CHAPTER 13

Lenny, and Hollywood

★ ★ ★ ★

LEONARD BERNSTEIN knew of Morton Gould long before they met. Lenny had played Morton's music for years; "Rumbalero" (published in 1934, when Bernstein was sixteen) was one of his favorite two-piano pieces, according to biographer Meryle Secrest (*Leonard Bernstein: A Life*, p. 34).

But although his work was in the air frequently during Bernstein's music-saturated adolescence, Morton's name and compositions are all but absent from the Bernstein biographies and reminiscences. The omission appears innocent, unless one knows the nature of their relationship in the 1940s, when Gould was himself a star.

Composer Marc Blitzstein, a colleague of Gould's and a close friend of Bernstein's, introduced them during the 1942–43 season at Lindy's Restaurant in Manhattan. Morton was a radio veteran, a well-established member of the New York musical world. Bernstein, though struggling for a foothold in New York, had a solid foundation from Boston Latin and Harvard, winters with Fritz Reiner, Isabelle Vengerova, Randall Thompson, and Renee Longy Miquelle at the Curtis Institute, and summers with the Boston Symphony at the Tanglewood Music Center in Lenox, Massachusetts, as a protégé of Serge Koussevitzky.

It was his second attempt at New York. He had spent the summer of 1939 on East Ninth Street with Adolph Green, a friend since summer camp. Bernstein had no money; his father, Sam, still hoping to keep him out of music, refused to support him. So he eked out a living accompanying Green's little group, the Revuers (including Betty Comden and Judy Holliday), at gigs around town.

"[In 1943] I was already a name, I was on radio and everything," Gould said one December evening in 1994, after Bernstein had died. "He was the new boy from Boston. I remember Marc introducing me to Lenny, and Lenny talking about Koussy. Who was Koussy? Later I found out that Koussy was [Serge] Koussevitzky"—Bernstein loved to drop names and formalities. Gould and Bernstein began a professional acquaintance. "I had some interesting lunches and conversations with him, the way anybody had. He was a very talkative person," is how Gould put it.

But already Bernstein was harvesting the fruits of his many connections. He had worked for the Harms-Witmark publishing company making arrangements of Coleman Hawkins and Raymond Scott (Gould's friend Harry Warnow). He had completed and performed the Sonata for Clarinet and Piano, written for his friend David Oppenheim. Late in December 1942 he had frantically scored, and friends and family copied, his Symphony No. 1 (*Jeremiah*) to enter a competition sponsored by Koussevitzky. It did not win, but Harms wanted to publish it and Reiner told Bernstein he wanted Lenny to conduct it in the 1943–44 season.

Bernstein, as energetic as Gould and far more gregarious, rapidly expanded his connections. The Ivy League boy from Boston was making himself into the quintessential New Yorker; Ned Rorem, then an impressionable nineteen-year-old from Richmond, Indiana, met and immediately slept with Bernstein, whom he found (according to Joan Peyser, *Bernstein, A Biography*, p. 99) "very New Yorky, very glamorous." In September 1943 Bernstein became assistant conductor of the Philharmonic. He rented a studio in Carnegie Hall and, as soon as the season began, started promoting himself so assiduously that music director Artur Rodzinski banished him from the green room after concerts.

Then came the remarkable weekend of 13–14 November 1943. Bruno Walter was the guest conductor while Rodzinski took two weeks off in Massachusetts. Bernstein studied the program and attended rehearsals, but he also was preparing for the performance of his song cycle *I Hate Music*, part of Jennie Tourel's New York debut recital Saturday night at Town Hall.

Bernstein knew as the weekend began that Walter could not conduct the Sunday matinee on 14 November, that Rodzinski had declined to return, and that he was to make his debut before a national radio audience. The resonating success of that appearance—the youngest conductor ever to lead a Philharmonic subscription concert, one of the few Americans ever to do it, and a Jew at that—is well known. His friends and teachers, among them Copland, Lukas Foss, Reiner, Koussevitzky, Diamond, and Rorem, were thrilled. This brilliant young man, superficially humble but in fact supremely confident and well prepared, became an immediate star. By the end of the 1943–44 season, Bernstein had conducted the Philharmonic eleven times. He quickly became a popular guest conductor around the country.

And Morton Gould—who, despite his long apprenticeship and deep roots in New York's musical life, always considered himself on shaky ground—was a little puzzled about this newcomer. Gould, whose lifelong dream it still was to conduct the Philharmonic at Carnegie Hall, had just been passed by a glamorous younger man from out of town. Morton knew Lenny's talent, which was similar to his, but he didn't understand Lenny's attitude, his ruthlessness, or his breathtaking arrogance.

Bernstein told Gould the reason he was going to conduct the *Jeremiah* Symphony was that "Reiner would have a problem with it, with the time changes." Gould gave a gasping little laugh as he recounted the remark in 1994, as if even fifty years later he still couldn't believe the presumption: "He's talking about Fritz Reiner, who could put most conductors in his pocket in terms of technical prowess and musicianship. I thought to myself, 'Well, that's a very strange thing to say about a guy who's invited you to conduct, and now you're going to say you're better'—but this is Lenny. He had this drive."

Reiner also had offered to let Gould conduct the symphony and *Foster Gallery*, but Gould preferred that the great conductors perform his scores: "I want the Reiners and Rodzinskis and Stokowskis to conduct my work," he said.

Bernstein would brook no rivals, loved games and contests; he was a risk-taker who, through depression and setback, never doubted his own capabilities. He would stop at almost nothing to achieve his ends; his tongue could charm and sting. He reached out for constant embrace—but who could protect those who rejected him or threatened his dominance?

Certainly not Morton Gould, who hated the limelight, froze in front of a camera, would rather work than schmooze, who first met society as part of the hired help, who would rather swallow his tongue than defend himself, and who knew with ill-concealed resentment that he was just an ignoramus among those who, like Bernstein, were "truly educated." Gould, naively, wanted his music to sing for itself. He thought that if he worked hard his talent would be recognized as a matter of course. But Bernstein, more sophisticated, was eager to do his own speaking.

Already the musicians, the press, and even the public were beginning to see Bernstein's egotism. Oscar Levant joked, "I think a lot of Bernstein—but not as much as he does." Virgil Thomson complained that Bernstein was devoting his time to "sheer vainglory" (Secrest, *Leonard Bernstein: A Life*, pp. 142–143). Lenny was his own best press agent. "All he needed to win over hitherto bored music journalists was a conference room and a piano," wrote Humphrey Burton (*Leonard Bernstein*, p. 149).

Morton and Lenny had several more encounters, and each left the older man bruised. They attended each other's performances and rehearsals, and once, Gould recalled, he introduced Bernstein to the studio audience as "the Frank Sinatra of conductors, because he wore a bow tie, he was so thin like Frank was, and very young, of course." Gould immediately worried that he had offended Bernstein by comparing him with a pop star. "But then I realized that no, he loved it."

That little frisson was nothing compared with another encounter, this time not as host but as supplicant. Gould did not recall when it happened—he thought it might have been shortly before Bernstein became sole music director of the Philharmonic. It's more likely it took place while Bernstein was directing the City Symphony of New York in the mid-1940s, when their relationship was still fluid and open and Bernstein was already in a position to help Gould.

Gould brought along records and scores, but as he played, Lenny began to name influences—the composers whose music he heard in what Morton had written. "I listened. I heard. I was getting a little restless. And then he said 'Bernstein!' Well, it so happens I had written it about four or five years before the piece that Lenny thought.

And I think I said to him, 'You know, one of your gifts is that you can write history backwards,' or something like that. I closed the score and stopped the record. He said, 'What are you doing?' I said, 'Forget it.' And I told my publisher never to send him another score."

Gould didn't think Bernstein meant to insult him, but that "he had to dominate," and it gave Bernstein—frequently criticized for his own borrowings—a sense of superiority. "But it went through my mind: of all the composers to be criticizing another composer about being eclectic," Gould said in 1994. Indeed, for just two examples, there are clear resemblances between the "Conga" of Gould's *Latin American Symphonette* and the conga in *On the Town*, and portions of the dances in *West Side Story* are reminiscent of Gould's little-known *Prelude and Toccata* for piano, which both predate Bernstein's compositions.

Another, somewhat less damning, interpretation, is based on a precedent that is a staple anecdote for composition students, involving the American Roger Sessions and the Swiss-born Ernest Bloch. In 1919 Sessions sought out Bloch as a teacher. Bloch asked Sessions to play something of his own, and then, standing behind him, shouted the names of composers he heard in the work! Sessions was not defensive. He joined in and began to announce the influences first. Bloch accepted him, and they worked together for years.

It is likely that playful, competitive Lenny had heard this tale and was doing it himself, while defensive Morton could neither see the game nor join in.

David Diamond, a close friend of Bernstein's and a beneficiary of Gould's generosity, accepted the account. "That sounds like a true story," he said. Diamond knew Bernstein played such tricks frequently. "He did that with [Vincent] Persichetti, and he even did it with Copland once, but Aaron would just giggle. He knew how silly Lenny could be."

From 1943 onward, Morton was competing with a younger man better prepared than he in almost every way but raw talent. Even the work of those years was eerily and sometimes explicitly parallel.

There was *Fancy Free* and *Interplay*. Robbins and Bernstein sparked brilliantly and at once. Their ballet was original in concept, attitude, choreography, and music. It was an immediate hit. But *Interplay* is far more the success of the choreographer than of the composer; the dance is still in the New York City Ballet repertory, but the score is rarely heard alone.

Within months, *Fancy Free* became a full-fledged musical, *On the Town*, with what is now an almost legendary team of collaborators. When the show opened on 13 December 1944, in Boston, it had book and lyrics by Betty Comden and Adolph Green, score by Bernstein, choreography by Robbins, sets by Oliver Smith, and direction by George Abbott. It too was an immediate hit and ran for more than a year on Broadway.

But when the same group decided to work together on a second show—a clever, biting story about a gold digger who marries a billionaire on the day the market crashes—Bernstein, warned away from Broadway by Koussevitzky, would not join them. So they turned to Gould, who also had one foot in Carnegie Hall and the other in Tin Pan Alley. The result, *Billion Dollar Baby*, got mixed reviews and had only moderate success. It ran for about nine months and then disappeared.

The first symphonies of both Gould and Bernstein were premiered within a year of each other by the Pittsburgh Symphony. Morton's Symphony No. 1, patriotically dedicated to his brothers, was performed 5 March 1943, conducted by Reiner. It gained respectful reviews and was considered for the New York Music Critics' Circle Award. Then it too disappeared.

Lenny's Symphony No. 1 (*Jeremiah*), set to evoke the feelings aroused by the destruction of Jerusalem and inevitably provoking thoughts of the ongoing Holocaust in Europe, was first performed 28 January 1944, in Pittsburgh, with the composer on the podium. Three weeks later he led it with the Boston Symphony, and the month after that with the Philharmonic. The Music Critics' Circle voted it best new composition on the first ballot, and it got a coast-to-coast broadcast by the NBC Symphony under Frank Black. Bernstein's friend Paul Bowles wrote that *Jeremiah* "outranks every other symphonic product by any American composer of the younger generation."

Bernstein and Gould even made forays into the movies. Shirley and Morton (and James) spent the summer of 1944 in Hollywood while Morton wrote the music for, conducted, and appeared as himself in a B movie called *Delightfully Dangerous*. It was not very good. The next spring and summer, Bernstein was romanced by several studios and directors—he had a screen test for the director Hal Wallis and discussed filming *Fancy Free* with director Irving Rapper.

For those three years, Gould and Bernstein were head to head: young Jewish Americans who were composers of popular and concert music, ambitious conductors, and anxious to make their fortunes as fully *American* musicians—native-born, bred, and trained. Bernstein beat Gould just about every time—not necessarily because of the music, but for personality, background, political ability, clarity of focus—even, perhaps, because Gould was ferociously heterosexual and Bernstein belonged to the group of homosexual musicians just beginning to gain great power.

They remained cordial to one another, but Morton eventually recognized this unacknowledged rivalry. "My feeling," he told me late that evening in the winter of 1994, after much prodding, "is that Lenny felt that if there was anybody who could give him a run for his money—in certain areas, I'm not talking in the general, all over—" (and he paused for a long time) "accomplishments that Lenny had, it might have been me. Because we both—we both rummaged the same bins."

Gould tried to avoid speaking of outright competition, but he was hurt to have learned only posthumously that Bernstein played his music.

> Lenny knew a lot more about my music than he ever let on to me. He never said to me, in those lunches we had together, "Hey you know, one of the pieces I played together was your 'Rumbalero.'" . . . If I met somebody whose music I played, or whose performances I had an early record of or something like that, I would say at some point, "Hey you know, when I was sixteen or whatever, I remember sitting down and playing . . ." He never let on that I might have been an influence.

At the time it was happening, there were indications that the world and Morton himself knew he was being surpassed. In June 1945, when Morton went to Temple University in Philadelphia to lecture, on an invitation from his old teacher Vincent Jones, Jones spoke to a university interviewer about Gould as a genius—but made one telling comparison. As Gould recalled, Jones drew a parallel between him and Bernstein, saying they were both excellent pianists and conductors and had great talent for composition. But Jones did not call Bernstein a young Morton Gould. He said Morton Gould was like Leonard Bernstein.

Gould summed things up in an anecdote. He took Bernstein to a favorite restaurant where the maitre d' came bustling up to Morton, fawning over "the maestro." Gould introduced the still-unknown Bernstein. By the time they left, the waiters were calling Lenny "maestro." "Without hearing a note or anything," Morton mused, "I came in as the maestro and Lenny walked out as the maestro."

Whatever the portents, Bernstein's emergence was of no immediate concern in that busy 1943–44 season. After a Cleveland Orchestra concert in October 1943 that included *American Salute*, conductor Erich Leinsdorf gave Gould a facsimile of a gold record. In November, Gould joined the famed bass and actor Paul Robeson to perform at the second Soviet-American Conference, including a mass rally and concert 8 November at Madison Square Garden.

Early in 1944 both Vladimir Golschmann with the St. Louis and Dimitri Mitropoulos with his Minneapolis Symphony performed *Spirituals for String Choir and Orchestra*, and the violist Emanuel Vardi performed the sixth and, as it turned out, last of Gould's classical miniatures, the Concertette for viola and wind band, first in Washington, D.C., with the U.S. Navy Symphonic Band, and then at New York's Town Hall. (In a letter of 1 February 1944, Samuel Barber apologized to Gould for missing the broadcast but congratulated him for *Cresta Blanca*, which he heard on the radio: "It sounds very fine, with much color, vigor and vim, especially vim. Orchids to you.")

Percy Grainger scored a success with *American Concertette* with the National Symphony in Washington on 20 February 1944. Glenn Dillard Gunn (*Times-Herald*) declared that the piece "seems to justify the suggestion that Gould has taken the place George Gershwin created for himself in American music and has carried the jazz-swing-symphonic expression to loftier heights." Grainger himself wrote happily to Gould on 26 February: "A more delightful and grateful work to play (from the soloist's standpoint) cannot be imagined. The pithy and mind-engaging musical material is delicious to work at (at the piano) and the tonal relations between orchestra and piano are strangely satisfying—the balance of tone between the two being gauged with flawless precision."

Gould completed yet another *Cowboy Rhapsody* (the third), this time for orchestra, for the St. Louis Symphony. He conducted an all-Gould program on 18 March in that city's Kiel Auditorium. (Alfred and Matty stood all night on a troop train to get to the concert from Camp Campbell, Kentucky.) The performance was sold out—a testimony, one critic (*Globe Democrat*, 19 March 1944) noted, "to a youth which took its music just as seriously as those veterans of symphonic audiences." This critic was impressed by the brilliance of *American Salute* but found himself groping for words about Gould's Symphony No. 1: "It would be easy to say, as Beethoven's contemporaries did of Beethoven, as Bach's of Bach, that this was a strange and outlandish music . . . . But the strange part is that it did precisely conform to the tone-tints through which Gould sought to effect, by orchestration, a clear and concrete communication of his meaning."

The *Star-Times* was less charitable: "Only by somewhat dubious standards could the program of his own compositions and orchestrations be said to have included any 'serious' music."

Still Gould was also getting frequent congratulations and encouragement. There was a note dated 24 April 1944 from Jerome Kern, following a telegram sent to Larry Spier of the Crawford Music Co., thanking him for Gould's arrangement of "Long Ago and Far Away":

> Mr. Larry Spier, who is no slouch of a phrase-maker himself, couldn't possibly, with all his enthusiasm, convey to you a tenth part of my admiration and appreciation of your beautiful arrangement of "Long Ago" . . . . At the risk of being considered prodigal with adjectives, it must be set forth that the Kern household finds it simply entrancing.

After the St. Louis trip, Gould's next major musical activity was the Symphony No. 2, the *Symphony on Marching Songs*, commissioned for the centenary of the Young Men's Christian Association and premiered 4 June 1944, the day after the wedding. Robert Simon (*PM*) was frustrated: "The earnestness is apparent, and the skill, too, but I came away with an unsatisfied feeling—that a real musical talent has not yet found itself in spite of a serious effort." Even Louis Biancolli (*World-Telegram*) was defensive: "No doubt sections of the symphony lack depth, but then, the title takes care of the objection."

These sympathetic critics were expressing the difficulty that Thomson, in his more acerbic fashion, had with *Foster Gallery* a few years before. It is the mystery at the center of Gould's creative life. With all that talent, why did he not succeed more as a composer?

Two days after the premiere, the Western Allies invaded Normandy and finally opened the Second Front that Stalin had been begging for. Morton Gould went them one better: he opened *two* new fronts, one personal and one professional.

The newlyweds took time off to relax at a house in Westchester County found for them by Mitch Miller. On 9 July 1944, Whiteside noted ecstatically, "Pat just called me to tell me she is going to have a baby . . . . Morton talked his usual funny talk but he is happy about it. They go to Hollywood next Saturday. Some way I feel that this baby will be my real grandchild." About to become a father—and off to Hollywood, too!

The project was a B movie called *High Among the Stars*, a musical to be produced by Charles Rogers, directed by Arthur Lubin, and starring Susan Hayward and Jane Powell (fourteen going on fifteen and in only her second film). The cast included Ralph Bellamy and Arthur Treacher and featured Morton Gould. It had a ludicrous plot: spunky schoolgirl dreams about singing in Carnegie Hall with Morton Gould. But her sister pays for the girl's education by working as a stripper. Complications ensue.

Morton wrote the music and played himself. On 15 July 1944, he and Shirley left for California for two months of work, parties, and frustration. For one thing, James Gould went along. Both Matty and Zara Gould, Stanley's wife, said Shirley was furious: like Shirley Uzin, Shirley Bank was plunged immediately into battle over Morton.

That was only one part of the adventure. Morton was a star, and in Hollywood he was treated like one. Skitch Henderson, then a studio musician, was intimidated: "He was a superstar. We were always apprehensive about meeting people from New York."

The Goulds took an apartment on South Rodeo Drive. Morton also was assigned a bungalow at the studio—more luxurious than their apartment in Forest Hills—but spent little time there except to work. Shirley drove him to the studio and back (a New Yorker to the bone, Morton didn't drive, and his father wouldn't let him learn).

Shirley, in early pregnancy, was especially bubbly, excited to be in Hollywood and married to such a famous man. Morton called her his "golden girl," and wrote Whiteside on 1 August that he and Shirley were "very happy together." But he could not lie about the attractions all around. "There are a lot of decayed women out here whom I wouldn't mind consorting with for very short intervals of time."

Shirley also wrote to Whiteside, in a letter eerily reminiscent of a note Shirley Uzin sent when *she* first was married. This newlywed spoke of how she and Morton were falling more and more in love each day ("It hardly seems believable that I am now carrying our child. . . . Of course, Morton's reaction is that we are the only ones remarkable enough to have a child") and of how Abby would "of course be the Godmother." There's a discordant note which Shirley could not have heard: "He told me that only two people in his life have ever reached deep down into him—and they are you and I." Morton could not have forgotten what he once felt for Shirley Uzin.

Shirley enjoyed the Hollywood rounds more than Morton, who mostly remembered the music people: Stokowski, Joseph Szigeti, Risë Stevens, Jack Mills's brother Irving, who held lavish Sunday open houses with the traditional New York bagels and lox. There were plenty of former New Yorkers, especially among the composers: Franz Waxman, Miklos Rosza, Bernard Herrmann. "I hadn't seen Bennie since my adolescence," Gould reminisced in 1985. "He was a character, always acerbic, always disgruntled, a curmudgeon. I saw him having coffee. He picked up an argument we had had. He said, 'You're dead wrong about what you said about Vaughan Williams, you're crazy, I'm telling you.' And he went on. He never said hello. He was still mad."

Gould appreciated California's virtues. The studio bungalow was a well-appointed house with a fully stocked refrigerator, and he was impressed by Waxman's home overlooking the Pacific Ocean—"I swear you could see Japan, it was one of the most fabulous setups." But he was there to make a movie, and he hated everything to do with film production. There were the standard Hollywood changes. Susan Hayward was dropped and Constance Moore took her place. The title was switched from *High Among the Stars* to *Delightfully Dangerous*. There were the standard Hollywood creative decisions: at first, the movie was to take place in the Hollywood Bowl, but they didn't want to pay for it. Someone asked Gould for another musical location. He said, "Carnegie Hall" and they thought he was a genius. But when the studio saw photographs of the decrepit auditorium they decided to build their own. They called it Carnegie Hall, but it looked like the Hollywood Bowl.

The director couldn't hear the violins during the "Pizzicato Polka." Gould had the musicians pluck harder and harder. "Blood [was] coming out of their fingertips," but it didn't help. So he told them to play the "Pizzicato Polka" with their bows. "That's it!" exclaimed Lubin.

This was comic and incidental. What Gould disliked most was the filming itself, he recalled in 1985. "By seven in the morning I was walking around in tails and makeup, and the sun was hot, burning your skin," he said. "I was a leading man, I had people walking around after me to wipe up my sweat, to keep the makeup from running down, to apply new makeup. I'd take two steps in the sun, and they'd apply new makeup. So you walk around like a horse's ass."

Lubin wanted to open the movie with a closeup of Gould conducting. To get the proper element of artistic mystery, he wanted Gould to pretend he was conducting while lying on his back on a mattress, in the studio, with the camera hovering over him.

> You feel very silly at seven a.m. lying down on a mattress in a set of tails. [Lubin] kept saying "Cut!" Finally he said, "It doesn't look natural." I said, "For Christ sake, what do you mean, 'It doesn't look natural'? How could anyone conduct this way and look natural?" But that's the way they shot it. In the film I look like Bela Lugosi; it is one of the most hair-raising shots.

Even at fourteen, Jane Powell was sensitive enough to see that this famous man ("his was the first record I had, the first record I danced to," she recalled in 1996) was not having a good time.

> How he hated Hollywood! How he hated saying those lines. I thought he was very funny, even with his being that unhappy.

> He never smiled. He said he couldn't wait to get back home. He didn't want to talk. I think he was scared; he was uncomfortable. He had to say a couple of words and he was just petrified. He was a fish out of water, I guess; he just didn't want to be there.

Gould had no interest in being a film executive, although several studios offered positions. "I have no wish to sit behind a desk all day and talk about budgets with producers," he told reporter Eileen Creelman for a piece that ran on 8 June 1945, shortly after the movie was released. "Too many musicians go to Hollywood and disappear. They're making money, of course. But making lots of money doesn't particularly interest me. I live in New York, and I live simply so that I can even give up my commercial work entirely if necessary." (A disingenuous but essentially truthful comment. If making money wasn't his object, it certainly was for his father and, now, his wife.)

Morton was surprised to discover that the Hollywood composers were as self-conscious about their work as he was about radio; as he put it in 1985, "Some of these people said to me how they envied me, that I was cutting out and going back to Carnegie Hall, to New York, to Fifty-seventh Street. And I remember saying, 'You people, what do you mean? I'm going back to a small four-room apartment with one bathroom, two blocks from the subway—you are living like kings and queens.' . . . But I never thought of giving up Fifty-seventh Street or the four-room apartment."

He appreciated the music being written by the studio composers, despite the ignorance and philistinism of their bosses. "They weren't really prostituting themselves," Gould said. "They were doing very good and creative and important things—Erich Korngold, Waxman, Benny Herrmann."

As for *Delightfully Dangerous*, Laura Lee (*Philadelphia Bulletin*) wrote that it was "neither delightful nor dangerous but a naive little musical perhaps a notch above the average for small budget singles." She liked Moore, Bellamy, and Powell, but there was not a word about Gould.

He is awful, frozen in monotone, completely lacking in presence whether conducting or speaking. The only time he comes to life occurs after he introduces Powell to a group of executives and then says he has to leave. For a moment there's a desperate truthfulness in Gould's face. The music is eminently forgettable, kitschy pseudo-Viennese for the operetta within the movie and not terribly appealing elsewhere. One song, the ballad "Through Your Eyes to Your Heart," became fairly popular, but nothing else had staying power.

That was the last time anyone tried to make a Morton Gould movie.

He and Shirley were home by October 1944. Again Whiteside sensed trouble in Morton's marriage, though it's not clear of what kind. She saw them on 8 October and recorded that evening, "A very disturbing visit with the Goulds. It bodes no good for Morton. I can hardly bear the thought of it." The tumult and arguments at the Goulds had always been hard for her. Now she started avoiding his home, going only on special occasions, such as 19 December: "Went to the Goulds for dinner because Willy Kapell [pianist William Kapell, a good friend of Morton's] was going to be there and had a lovely time listening to Morton and him spar back and forth. They are very alike in their integrity." Whiteside's opinion of this Shirley too began to slip. On 27 January 1945, barely a month before the birth of their first child, Whiteside remarked, "Pat is very self-centered and of no calibre to really make life rich for Morton."

But the year 1944 came to a close much as it had begun, with a stream of activity, conducting and recording. In a column for *Musical America*, Gould made a prescient suggestion: communities above a certain size should tax their residents a dollar a year to support a local orchestra: "Music and the other arts should be as much the concern of our government as building bridges and railroads. [This tax] would eliminate the hysterical annual fund-raising drives and the feeling of insecurity that assails those who make our music and, in turn, affects their performance." It's a proposal that would still appeal to arts organizations.

On 22 November he recorded eight arrangements for Columbia Masterworks. Four days later, right after Thanksgiving, he led the Cincinnati Symphony in a pair of all-Gould programs. And shortly afterward, Gould received a compliment he cherished the rest of his life. Ernest Bloch, living at the time in Oregon, wrote to Boaz Piller, a Boston Symphony bassoonist, on 17 December 1944 after a broadcast of *Spirituals*:

> From the first notes I was enthralled—Here, *at last* (!) a *real* composer—American?—inspiration, sensibility, evocation, all the *spiritual* qualities of which most of the Others' lack, and, furthermore, *technique* of form, of orchestra, mastery of his thought—*Modern* without being "charlatanesque" or "Crazy," like, alas, so many other weak impotents! Yes, there for the *first time* in years that I have been satisfied and really conquered by an "American composer." I even find these *Spirituals* infinitely superior to *all* of Shostakovich which I know. . . . As I live *removed from everything* both time and the world—I know nothing of this "Mr. Gould"—is he young? What is his address? Has he already had things published? What are his works? Is this a first hearing?

Morton framed a copy of the letter and kept it above his desk, along with those from Gershwin and Toscanini.

CHAPTER 14

Broadway and Beyond

★ ★ ★ ★

IF 1944 WAS A GOOD YEAR, 1945 was better. The largest and most horrible war in the history of the world had come to an end, and Gould was now the center of a prosperous little enclave. James Gould (who, against all odds, yet lived) ran the business, managed the career, collected the checks, and paid the staff, rent, and expenses. Morton took what he needed, with no concern about the books. Gould estimated his annual income as anywhere between $30,000 and $100,000, but very little of this revenue was derived from concert music. ASCAP didn't even try to collect for performances, and the fees were insulting. "I remember my publisher in the early '40s asking for a twenty-five-dollar fee, and being told that for twenty-five dollars they could play a good European composer," Gould said in 1994.

Where concert composers such as Schuman and Hanson were supported by university positions, Gould depended on music alone. Only Copland, and now Bernstein, could do that, and Morton did not have their compunctions about how he got paid. "In those days, he would do anything to make a buck," said Bowes's director, Reed. Gould filled notebook after notebook with sketches and ideas, wherever and whenever they came—at dinner, at parties, on the subway. He didn't even date his scores. "When you're living it, you're not knowing it," he told Zwilich in 1995. "You only know it after."

February 1945 was particularly hectic. On 1 February Golschmann led the Cleveland Orchestra in the premiere of Gould's *Concerto for Orchestra*, commissioned at the instigation of Leinsdorf (who then went into the Army and couldn't conduct it). The Cleveland critics treated the concerto with respect and customary disdain. It is in three movements, just as Gould had envisioned it for Rodzinski in 1943: the first vigorous and assertive, the second lyrical and bluesy, the finale a virtuosic showpiece for the orchestra over "that dizzy, frenzied, and slightly moronic pattern-making known as 'boogie-woogie'" (Herbert Elwell, *The Plain Dealer*).

At the same time, Morton learned he would be returning to the air once again for the ailing Major Bowes, and on 8 February 1945, Gould began a reprise of *Shower of Stars* on CBS. Eight days later, on 16 February, the Goulds' first child was born. There was a disagreement about his name: Shirley wanted to call him Franklin, after her father and the late president, but Morton preferred Eric. After a short tussle (there were congratulatory notes for both Franklin and Eric), they settled on Eric Franklin. The musicians paid their respects. As director Reed recalled, "The boys in the band set something up. Gould gave the downbeat and nothing happened, except Max Pollikoff played 'Rockabye Baby.' Morton almost fell off the podium, and he blushed."

Whiteside, who visited the hospital two days after the baby was born, recorded in her diary that night, "Pat [Shirley] looked beautiful and as though nothing had happened." The infant resembled Morton.

Morton and Shirley had set up housekeeping in a four-room sixth-floor apartment not far from the 1939 World's Fair grounds, between Queens Boulevard and the Grand Central Parkway. James and Frances moved to the same complex. The younger Goulds' apartment had a foyer, a small kitchen with a fire escape outside the window, a living room, a bedroom, and another small room that Morton sometimes used as a studio (he also worked in the foyer). The couple slept on a pullout bed in the living room.

Shirley met a group of other young mothers in the courtyards and playgrounds of Forest Hills, among them Ruth Troob (whose husband, Lester, was in the music business) and Norma Perlman, whose husband, Eli, an allergist at Mount Sinai Hospital in Manhattan, loved music and became one of Morton's closest friends. Shirley Two ("everybody called her Shirley Two," Norma Perlman said) was "absolutely beautiful . . . and very anxious to have a big family—and she succeeded in doing so."

Morton said Shirley told him she wanted two boys and two girls

—and that's what they would eventually have. "It didn't come as a surprise to me," he said in 1985. "Shirley wanted children. She was very clear about that."

Norma and their friends saw that Shirley was smart and capable, perfectly able to maintain a growing household with an absent husband. "It was a standard joke in the family that whenever a child was born, or whenever Shirley needed him, he was on the road, somewhere else," Perlman said. "She was really self-reliant; she rarely called on friends to help out." Norma and Shirley would joke that in the wintertime, when the other fathers were out sledding with their children, Eli and Morton were never to be seen.

Yet Morton was a devoted father, in his own way. He lavished a warm, unquestioning love on his children, wrote frequently and individually from wherever he was, and laced the notes with funny drawings. "He cared so much," Perlman said. "He always called, he wrote the most beautiful letters, he would illustrate the letters."

The years in Forest Hills were happy. Although Morton brought in a lot more money than most of their neighbors, Shirley was not extravagant. "Shirley was very proud of the fact that she was very careful of where she shopped, and how she shopped," Matty Gould said. "I think this was something she took upon herself, not that Morton could not afford things."

She loved being Mrs. Morton Gould. "She was very incensed with the bank because she couldn't sign her checks Mrs. Morton Gould. She had to sign them Shirley Gould, and she really resented that," Matty recounted. "We got hysterical about that."

The bank wasn't the only institution to have a problem with "Mrs. Morton Gould." So did James. "Shirley would have liked to have run the family, but Pop got in the way a lot," reported Zara Gould, Stanley's wife. "Like she wanted Morton to learn to drive, but Pop said no way, his head would be in the clouds. She won: he learned to drive"—but not until they moved to Great Neck. It's not that Shirley thought Morton couldn't run his own life. Rather, she felt that if anyone was to be in charge, it should be she. "Shirley would have liked to have controlled everybody's life, including her children's," said Stanley Gould. "There was conflict all the time between her and Pop over Morton," said Zara.

The work didn't let up. Gould had recorded sporadically in the late 1930s and early 1940s, but the contract he had signed with Columbia (Goddard Lieberson's company) on 11 December 1941 finally gave him a long-term home. The first agreement, from 15 January 1942 through 14 January 1943, had called for a maximum orchestra of forty, and twelve selections with an option for four more. These first recordings, released as *A Morton Gould Concert*, were already familiar: "Pavanne," "Espana Cani," "Donkey Serenade," "Ay Ay Ay," "Dark Eyes," "Where or When."

In March 1945 Columbia Masterworks' Red, or popular, label released *After Dark*, the first work under the next contract, this time a two-year agreement dated 23 October 1943, which called for eighteen sides (nine discs at 78 rpm) per year. The packaging of *After Dark*, from title to album cover, was Lieberson's idea. (Gould said in 1985 that he thought the title was "too pop.") Its selection of eight numbers—ranging from "Besame Mucho" to "Dancing in the Dark," all arranged, orchestrated, and conducted by Morton Gould—was an immediate hit. After that the flow became steady: *South of the Border*, recorded 1 January 1945, released in November; *Interplay*, recorded 28 June 1946, released in July. This steady stream of "mood music," a mix of light classics, originals, and arrangements, continued into 1954, when Gould left Columbia for RCA. These records helped consolidate his position, for good and ill, as a major figure in American popular music.

Yet Morton noticed odd things during the Chrysler broadcasts that spring of 1945. "I was having a lot of trouble getting them to be supportive, to advertise my show," he said in 1985. "They were sabotaging me." Then he discovered why: CBS planned to give *Shower of Stars* to Kostelanetz and his wife, coloratura soprano Lily Pons. After his wartime service, Kostelanetz wanted to get back on the air. To Kostelanetz, Gould must have seemed a dangerous rival, but when they came face to face, Gould lost—and quit. "I just walked. I said I was leaving, I broke my contract . . . . I gave up six or eight weeks of the show, and everybody thought I was nuts. . . . I felt there was a principle involved." Kostelanetz mentions nothing of this in his memoir. He doesn't mention Gould at all.

On VE Day, 7 May, Gould was in Milwaukee conducting. He got back to New York in time to attend a gala luncheon 13 May at the Hotel Astor for a screening of Warner Bros.' Gershwin movie, *Rhap-*

sody in Blue. This was an important event, with famous guests including Paul Whiteman, Walter Damrosch, Richard Rodgers, and Benny Goodman. Mutual broadcast part of the luncheon.

And that was just the first half of this momentous year. The second half brought an even greater adventure: a Broadway musical in collaboration with one of the hottest teams in the business. *Billion Dollar Baby* had book and lyrics by Comden and Green, choreography by Robbins, sets by Oliver Smith, direction by Abbott, with Smith and Paul Feigey as producers—the same team that had unveiled the revolutionary *On the Town* less than a year before.

The news that they were beginning another show was so exciting that backers lined up for the chance. Bernstein had been warned off by Koussevitzky, but the team wanted someone like him, with a classical background and a popular touch. Gould fit the description. Comden and Green and the others "sort of knew him, but not very much," Comden said in 1995. She remembered with amusement how he introduced himself: "The phone rang, and someone said, 'Hello, this is Morton. You know, Morton Gould'—and he whistled the 'Pavanne,' as if I didn't know who he was. It was a very funny, self-satirical thing to do." It was also typical of Morton, who never did believe people knew who he was.

Fancy Free and *On the Town* were modern, with-it, jazzy shows, full of the cocky exuberance of muscular America, confident even in wartime, cheerful and charming. For *Billion Dollar Baby*, the creators attempted something riskier: a satirical look at the Roaring Twenties, that frantic, grasping era that had preceded their parents' screaming fall into the Depression.

The plot was simple and wicked. Maribelle Jones, the heroine, is a smart, cunning, money-hungry beauty from Staten Island. She dumps her sweetheart, a naive marathon dancer, and hooks up with a gangster, then a mob capo, and then the capo's lieutenant. The climax of Act I is a bloody murder in the middle of a Ziegfeld-style floor show. The climax of Act II finds our heroine marrying the billionaire—at the very moment of the Great Crash. She scatters jewels and money among the crowd while her husband scrambles to pick them off the floor. It was going to take a hell of a show to make a plot like that go over at the end of 1945, when nobody wanted to hear about greedy babes and suicidal plutocrats.

Rehearsals began in October 1945; there was a stream of interviews, photo spreads, and blind items about everyone involved, from Joan McCracken, fresh from *Oklahoma!* and now cast as Maribelle, to Comden and Green, to Gould. Morton was feisty. He fought with the writers about top billing; they won. He fought with Robbins and chased the choreographer around the theater. "Jerry was Jerry, and me was me," Gould said in 1985. "The first time he heard the orchestra play my ballet music, he was really elated." But later, after Gould had put together some ragtime-sounding music, the choreographer responded differently.

"He got mad," Gould recalled, "and said it should be a piano. That's all he had to say to me—I think I chased him up the aisle. No way you were going to tell me how to orchestrate!" Instead of following the Broadway custom in which the composer writes a short score while someone else orchestrates, Gould did virtually all his own orchestration, with some assistance from Phil Lang. Why? "Because I was stupid. I always wanted to control it. I did all the big things, the overture, the ballet music."

In the middle of rehearsals, Gould, Robbins, and Smith prepared and presented *Interplay* at the Metropolitan Opera House, with Gould himself conducting. The dance entered the repertoire on 17 October 1945, and the reviews were joyous. "This is one of those rare productions which are so bright, so un-fussy and presented with a sense of such easy competence that the air suddenly seems clearer and purer," wrote Edward O'Gorman (*The New York Post*). "With enlivening and refreshing music by Morton Gould, *Interplay* is a consummation devoutly to be wished by balletomanes," said Geena Bennett (*New York Evening Journal*). The piece, only Robbins's second work, was "a big step beyond *Fancy Free*," according to Edwin Denby (*Herald Tribune*).

Oh, and by the way, on 21 October Max Pollikoff gave the premiere of Gould's *Violin Suite*, with pianist Alice Rivkin.

Billion Dollar Baby opened on 15 November in New Haven, Connecticut. Smith's sets didn't fit and had to be cut down. Although the period represented was less than twenty years in the past, so much had been forgotten (or repressed) that an insert was added to the program explaining what was going on. The reviews weren't promising: *Variety* (21 November 1945) called it tawdry: "Local break-in indicated that birth of 'Baby' was premature. . . . Do not open."

"As we were checking out," Gould said in 1985, "there was literally a hayseed, a guy leaning against the building with a piece of straw in his mouth, who said, 'Better do better in Boston, bub.'"

In Boston there was more trouble: Abbott fell ill and Comden, Green, and Robbins took over. "They had a field day," Gould said. "That was the worst thing that happened to us," Comden recalled. Abbott missed the whole out-of-town tryout, she said. "We had no guidance. We couldn't do much work, we couldn't fix things. That was indeed a blow for the show."

They opened at the Shubert in Boston on 22 November, to packed houses. The reviews were thoughtful—with warning signs. Elinor Hughes (*Boston Herald*, 23 November 1945), recalling *Pal Joey* and *Of Thee I Sing*, wrote, "Satire in musical comedy is a tricky weapon, and must be so handled that people will laugh first and think afterward, for if they are made too uncomfortable, they will resent it." She thought *Billion Dollar Baby* was so good that it was "likely to startle . . . contemporaries as much as it frightens their elders, who suddenly find themselves confronted with vivid representations of an embarrassingly unlovely period. . . . The opening night laughter was not comfortable."

Yet Elliott Norton (*Boston Post*) found the show a "lush rolling pageant and, at the same time, a roaring, hilarious travesty on the era of gin, din, and jazz . . . a jeering, delirious, delightful show . . . mischievous rather than malicious." The music, he said, "mocks the songs and song styles of the period." It was "apt, though not especially tuneful."

Billion Dollar Baby opened in New York, at the Alvin, on 21 December 1945, to responses ranging from raves to bitter denunciations. The only element universally praised was Robbins's dances. John Chapman (*Daily News*) found it "even better" than *On the Town*, which was still running. And he cast an approving eye on Gould: "I have never cared for his syrupy, over-orchestrated arrangements for the radio, but in the case of *Billion Dollar Baby* I am on his side. He can be funny and he can be terse, as well as fruity, and his score suffices."

Gould knew what he had done: avoided prettiness and written subtle, knowing music that never let the listener relax—though at the end of his life he regretted his unwillingness to be simple. "I think I was always very conscious about not being too popular, and not doing something too obvious," he said in 1985 about his stage music in general. "I had all the quirks, all the extensions and the contractions, the bypassing of the obvious statement. I should have seasoned it with some of the obvious statements."

Some liked the edge to the show, and some didn't; as Comden acknowledged in a May 1946 interview with Helen Ormsbee (*Herald Tribune*), "Believe me, we had no nostalgia for the '20s. It was a dreadful decade." The most positive response to Gould's music came from Delos W. Lovelace (*The Sun*): "Now that Morton Gould has this *Billion Dollar Baby* on his hands . . . he comes still closer to looking like a modern Mozart. . . . You can say . . . that he is just a junior Kostelanetz. But the fact is that the boy is good."

Everyone acknowledged that the score was clever, sophisticated, and pointed—but not the sort that left one whistling the melodies. As Lewis Nichols (*Sunday New York Times*) commented, "Mr. Gould's tunes are all right, if not all headed for the juke boxes." Some of the writers sounded personally wounded, like the unnamed reviewer for the *San Francisco Chronicle*:

> To sum up *Billion Dollar Baby* . . . I'd say it must be described as a vicious satire on a most ungraceful passage in recent American history. . . . It hasn't a sympathetic character in its entire length. . . . It is a tough, unbending caricature of a glittering, cheap, repulsive, shallow, morally unkempt decade. . . . Morton Gould, who composed the music, has written tunes which lack any hint of simplicity of melodic line. The music's hypermodern avoidance of anything remotely approaching prettiness is constant and irritating; consequently there isn't a memorable song in the show.

But that appealed to Howard Barnes (*Sunday Herald Tribune*), who particularly enjoyed Gould's "savage melodic lampooning" of the Charleston.

Perhaps Comden and Green succeeded too well with their bleak look at the 1920s. *Time* magazine noted that Maribelle ("a predacious, flinthearted little heel") was both too harshly realized for the sort of jamboree presented and too poorly realized to rise above it, and that by evening's end, the incessant "thump and slambang" of the musical was "a little fatiguing." The most prescient commentary came from Irving Hoffman (*Hollywood Daily Reporter*, 24 December 1945): "Two decades hence, we'll look back and recall *On the Town* with fond memories. But *Baby* will be forgotten, unwed, unhonored—its score unsung."

"It was a flop," Gould said in 1985. "It only ran seven or eight months. Anything is a flop if it's not a success." In fact the show had a respectable run of 221 performances, and a brief, semi-staged revival in New York in 1998 revealed a cunning, witty show that, if anything, was far ahead of its time.

Gould was neither a junior Kostelanetz nor a modern-day Mozart, as he was being forcefully re-reminded. On radio Gould didn't swing the weight of a real Kostelanetz, yet his popularity was held against him in the concert hall—especially in Boston during the reign of Serge Koussevitzky. On 30 December 1945, barely a week after the opening of *Billion Dollar Baby*, Gould made his debut with the Boston Symphony. The program was all-American: Schuman, Robert Russell Bennett's "Symphonic Picture" from *Porgy and Bess*, and three works by Gould (*Cowboy Rhapsody*, *Concerto for Orchestra*, and *Harvest*, for harp, vibraphone, and strings, a gift for Shirley Bank Gould).

The program set the critics' teeth on edge and unnerved the musicians, who had real trouble with the music. Of the *Concerto for Orchestra*, Rudolph Elie Jr. (*Boston Herald*) wrote, "Its idiom is completely popular, and the Boston orchestra is just not able to perform this music without sounding corny. . . . It is just not fair to ask them to play this music—and I refer to *Porgy* and the *Cowboy Rhapsody* as well—because they always come out of it looking a little silly."

Warren Storey Smith (*Boston Post*) used Gould's skill in handling an ensemble against him. "As conductor and composer, Mr. Gould has little feeling for the symphony orchestra as we have known it. In his hands it sounds like a small team, or, in some cases, like a dance band blown up." He too considered that the Bostonians simply couldn't play the stuff: "Perhaps it means you can't mix oil and water."

L. A. Sloper (*Christian Science Monitor*), one hand to his nose, delivered the sharpest cut of all. He feared that the music was "not performed in the best rug-cutting tradition. For the Boston Symphony Orchestra, although it can play anything, was clearly dealing here with an unfamiliar idiom. It knows the language, none better; but its linguistic abilities are of small use when it visits the musical slums."

Morton Gould, boy from the slums. He was growing accustomed to this. But now, freed from the radio grind, with a bright, aggressively supportive young wife and a growing family, he began to look elsewhere. He expanded his guest-conducting and stepped up his recording. He also took the risky step of going on tour with an orchestra and soloists.

Gould was helped in this expanded career by brother Walter, who had been a decorated captain in General Courtney Hodges's First Army in Europe. Walter was the only other member of the family to make a career in music. Before the war he worked as a song-plugger; afterward he took a job with James Davidson, a manager from the William Morris Agency who was opening his own agency.

Shortly after Walter Gould began with Davidson, he took over a tour with the tenor Lauritz Melchior. Afterward Melchior asked that Walter be his manager, and Walter joined Davidson full time. Gradually, he developed into a personal manager, primarily with vocal clients, including Robert Shaw, later conductor of the Atlanta Symphony; Gregg Smith of the Gregg Smith Singers; and Robert De Cormier, founder of the New York Choral Society. Walter eventually took Morton's career away from their father.

"He didn't fully understand what Morton wanted out of his musical life," Walter said. "Pop was very concerned that Morton should make money. Morton was not concerned to make money. He felt he had paid his dues—now he wanted to do the things, musically speaking, that meant something to him: writing seriously for the symphonic field. I don't think Pop ever would agree with that. He would much rather he wrote a couple of songs that became No. 1 on the Hit Parade."

Walter was a florid, bluff man, a vigorous member of the victorious new generation, eager to provide music for a novelty-starved nation. He also saw that his idolized elder brother was tired of churning out arrangements and wanted to stretch himself, to think about writing the *Tristan* he had described to Shirley Uzin so many years before. It must have seemed inevitable that Walter would ease Pop away from active management. "I guess. I don't know," Walter told me in 1995. "I cannot tell you where one thing starts and another ends . . . . I was out, going around, contacting various offices, et cetera. And it was only natural that I would also try to sell Morton at the same time."

And Morton made two other important connections: the producer and engineer Howard Scott, whose first Columbia project in 1946 was a Gould recording; and Dimitri Mitropoulos, music director of the Minneapolis Symphony since 1937 but soon to mount the podium of the New York Philharmonic. Scott and Mitropoulos epitomized the polar attractions that pulled at Gould. The conductor was a brilliant, ascetic Greek whom Leonard Bernstein had once loved, to whom no music was foreign, and who strove for the pinnacles of art. The producer was an Eastman School of Music graduate who always felt that Gould's biggest mistake lay in trying to make serious music and avoiding what he did best: popular arrangements.

On 11 January 1946, less than two weeks after the Boston concert, Gould was in Minneapolis to hear Mitropoulos lead a program that included his *Concerto for Orchestra*. John K. Sherman (*Star Journal*) called it "a blatant and breathless exercise in modern American rhythms, a glib, entertaining piece of musical Americanese. . . . That engine of tone developed in the finale, with its boogie-woogie base, was a hair-raiser." Mitropoulos was enthusiastic. Later that year, on 24 October 1946, the conductor wrote the thirty-three-year-old composer: "I am very happy to see you grow up artistically in such a wonderful and generous manner, and I am happy that you make me believe in you." He had planned to play *Harvest* during the 1946–47 season, but the orchestra lacked a vibraphone, so he substituted *Minstrel Show*.

In the middle of February 1946 Morton led the Pittsburgh Symphony in an all-Gould program. By now Donald S. Steinfirst (*Pittsburgh Post-Gazette*) had been won over by his "immense gifts of orchestration" and with the "phenomenal display of his abilities as composer and arranger."

Gould's travels were interrupted in March, when one in a series of hernia operations kept him hospitalized for nearly two weeks. In June he went to Philadelphia to lead the Robin Hood Dell Orchestra in Gershwin and his own music, featuring the brilliant Oscar Levant on piano, in a performance that Columbia recorded and released the next month as *Interplay*.

"Big success—15,000 people," he wrote on 9 July 1946 to Whiteside, who was at the Ghost Ranch in Abiquiui, New Mexico. He loved the orchestra—"which, as you know, is the Philadelphia. It is a fantastic instrument to conduct—I would say the finest orchestra from every point of view. Stokowski must be a real top notcher to have built an organization that plays that way even without him." (The ensemble had been in the hands of Ormandy since 1938; Gould would not give him credit.)

Gould stayed home preparing something that would surely never make the Hit Parade: an a cappella setting of excerpts from Thomas Wolfe's *Of Time and the River*, commissioned by John Finley Williamson's Westminster Choir. Gould was anxious to hear it performed, he wrote Whiteside in the same letter, "because this is the first attempt in that medium. It is a good experience and discipline—because of the imposed vocal limitations, lack of percussion or other sound effects to help me out in place of inspiration."

Morton also confided, "Just between us for the time being—I think you will be a grandmother again. Yes—it seems that when I sublimate my desires, my mind reacts—but my body stays in bed and just goes on its carnal way—regardless."

The history of *Of Time and the River*, a five-movement, twenty-five-minute composition, is clouded. The Westminster Choir College in Princeton, New Jersey, possesses programs that indicate that the piece was given its premiere 8 October 1946 at the Auditorium of the Free Academy in Newburgh, New York. Later performances that season included only the first, fourth, and fifth movements; there are no indications that the choir did it again. Gould later denied he had ever heard it performed and quickly began downplaying its significance. Writing to Whiteside on 18 July 1951, he declared that he had forgotten the whole thing until she asked. "Williamson after initial enthusiasm got cold feet—and it was never done."

Gould made another significant move that summer of 1946. He left Mills Music and joined Chappell and Co. Inc., home of Romberg, Kern, Gershwin, Coward, Weill—the nation's leading publisher of show music. To avoid the situation at Mills, wherein the publisher owned the rights, Chappell created a joint company, known as G & C Music Corp., half owned by Gould and half by the publisher.

In late 1946 Gould started taking lessons with Whiteside again, and even began to practice. His musical standing never seemed higher. He was amazed to discover how many orchestras had his work in their repertoire. He was one of the most-performed American composers, according to surveys conducted by Robert Sabin for *Musical America*: in 1944, he was third after Gershwin and Copland; in 1947 and '48, fourth after Copland, Gershwin, and Barber (Gould's presence continued well into the 1950s). And he was deeply involved in a significant project: the Symphony No. 3, for the Dallas Symphony, which he completed in January 1947 and dedicated to his parents. In a letter to them he wrote, "I have never dedicated anything to you, tho' you are two of the most important people in my life. Therefore, I think it fitting to dedicate my new Third Symphony —which I think and hope is my best big work so far."

He led the first performance in Dallas, on 16 February 1947. On 2 March, David Gould was born. In mid-March the archivist and musical historian Nicolas Slonimsky included the Symphony No. 3 in his supplement to *Baker's Biographical Dictionary of Musicians*. Even then, Gould's musical track was confused. Slonimsky wrote asking Gould for "a long session" to straighten things out. How many symphonettes were there? Where did the First, the Swing Symphonette, belong? He begged Gould to date his scores, but the composer never did.

There was great interest in the new score; George Szell in Cleveland wrote Gould that he was "eagerly and impatiently awaiting its arrival"; similar requests arrived from Stokowski, Rodzinski, and Pierre Monteux in San Francisco. Gould played it for Toscanini, who (as he recalled in 1986) "liked it very much." Ultimately, Mitropoulos gave the Symphony No. 3 its next performances, with the Philharmonic in late 1948, after Gould revised and shortened the fourth-movement passacaglia at the conductor's suggestion.

Another significant project: in the fall of 1947, Gould would embark on his first (and only) orchestral tour with soloists, under the auspices of James Davidson and managed by Walter Gould, with tryout concerts in Rochester and Philadelphia beforehand. The program was all-American, with a heavy portion of Gould: Copland's

Rodeo, songs by John Alden Carpenter and Robert MacGimsey, Victor Herbert's *Fortuneteller*, *Interplay*, "Stardust," "Surrey with the Fringe on Top," and Cole Porter's "Begin the Beguine." It was the first time in years Morton had played in public, and the experience was exhilarating. He wrote excitedly to Whiteside in a revealing letter on 19 July 1947, after the Rochester concerts on 17 and 18 July. First he remarked that he had barely practiced: "Before I left for Rochester last week I did rent a Steinway Hall studio for five hours—but used it for two."

> You know, I can't figure myself out. I really should have been very nervous and concerned—don't you think? I expected to be—and predicted as much to Pat [to Whiteside, Morton called Shirley "Pat"]—yet I was as relaxed as if I really could play .... I'm afraid that I must blame you for this lack—because all I did was to set my meter in the Whiteside manner—and there I was playing and conducting violins in back of me—woodwinds to the left—celli to the right—brass off on the sides—a real three ring circus—and I couldn't even have the satisfaction of feeling strained or looking worn out when it was over.

Morton was greeted with respect, and the concerts were thrilling physically, intellectually, and emotionally. "I found my whole body much more alive—because all my muscles were in use in order to project to the orchestra. I have never felt so sensitive thruout my whole being." It was all a tonic. Still, feeling good made him feel bad. "I must admit that I can't get used to the idea—and it always surprises me pleasantly. Maybe I am more important than I think—but that is the discipline that I must never lose—I *must* be dissatisfied and *produce* and *work*—rather than contemplate my achievements and become smug and static."

Much to his surprise, Morton continued, he missed the family: "I've been away from home a week—and I'm so lonesome and miss Pat—and Ricky and David. I just can't wait to get back and have them climbing all over me and interfering with my work—but I love it. Really—to have Ricky climb up beside me and decide to help me by writing music on my paper is aggravating and wonderful at the same time."

Next Gould conducted and recorded (eighteen sides this go-around) a second time at Robin Hood Dell, after which he felt let down and moody. As he wrote Whiteside in a letter dated 1 August 1947, "I am in one of my 'in-between' periods in which I fuss and fume and smoke—but no fire. It is peculiar how I can go thru a relentless and grueling schedule of performances and all around productivity—and as soon as the deadlines are met—and I have open stretches of time—I fall apart."

The fall tour, billed as "Morton Gould: American Serenade," began 13 October 1947. It took a forty-piece orchestra, baritone Wilbur Evans, soprano Mimi Benzell, and him (as composer, conductor, and pianist) on a swing through the Midwest and South, with dates in Iowa, Oklahoma, Nebraska, Alabama, Georgia, and Tennessee. But Davidson did not know some basics of touring. He began with performances at Iowa State University in Ames—two days by bus from New York with no income, instead of concerts from New York through the Midwest to Iowa. "It was unbelievable to start there," Walter said. There were other, similarly uneconomical decisions: a jump from Omaha, Nebraska, to Birmingham, Alabama, in one day —which meant that the orchestra rushed to the station right after the performance while Walter held the train, then traveled all night and the next day.

Reviews were generally favorable, epitomized by Malcolm Miller (Knoxville, Tennessee, *Journal*, 6 November 1947): "The concert illustrated what a capable, well-conducted orchestra can do with so-called popular music. The program was altogether delightful, zestful, and refreshing. . . . Gould's conducting indicated splendid musicianship and unfettered originality in interpretation."

But Morton found the going rough. In his letter to Whiteside of 29 October 1947, written on the train from Joplin, Missouri, to Memphis, Tennessee (marked "enroute to nowhere"), he complained of the variation in instruments and the lack of time to try them out. "In one place—the stage tilted *downward* at a sharp angle—had to grip my feet to keep balance—and conduct at same time."

Davidson made no money because of the way he had laid out the travel; Gould did not like the strain of traveling and playing. Davidson offered to try again, but Morton wouldn't do it. "It was a shame," Walter said. "Had he been with one of the two big bureaus—Columbia Artists Management or National Concert Artists—he would have had any number of years of touring, if he had wanted it."

Walter himself found something more precious than money. During that long train ride from Nebraska to Alabama, he sat with Mimi Benzell. The captain and the coloratura chatted and grew close, and two years later, when Benzell decided, with his encouragement, to leave the Metropolitan Opera and make her move to Broadway—they married.

CHAPTER 15

Clouds Around a Peak

★ ★ ★ ★

GOULD CLIMBED two grand peaks during 1948. First came the premiere of *Fall River Legend*, the ballet by Agnes De Mille, a classic of the American dance repertoire and Gould's only completely successful collaboration in any form. The second was the Philharmonic premiere of his revised Symphony No. 3, the first major fruit of Mitropoulos's support. But that year also included the start of the postwar redbaiting that destroyed the lives of many Americans, put a crimp in Gould's career, and changed him permanently from an outspoken citizen to one who held back. Gould had begun his descent into the valley that darkened his life almost until its end.

De Mille was already one of the nation's foremost choreographers. *Rodeo* of 1942, with its Copland score, was becoming a staple (Gould took it on his tour, though some presenters objected to Copland as too advanced). The dances she created in 1943 for Richard Rodgers and Oscar Hammerstein II in *Oklahoma!* opened the way for modern dance on Broadway; *Carousel* and *Brigadoon* soon followed.

De Mille was fascinated by Lizzie Borden, the Fall River, Massachusetts, spinster tried and acquitted for the ax murder of her father and stepmother. In the fall of 1947, Ballet Theatre's Lucia Chase commissioned it for the coming spring, and the choreographer set out to find a composer. According to De Mille's account in *Lizzie Borden: A Dance of Death*, Gould's name was suggested by Ballet Theatre musical director Max Goberman, who had conducted *Billion Dollar Baby*. When Gould and De Mille reminisced in preparation for the first recording of the complete score, a conversation recorded in 1990, De Mille supported this effusively, recalling her initial conversation with Goberman: " 'But he does popular music!' 'No,' said Goberman, 'he has two strings to his bow. He can compose equally well with classic music, interpretive music, and popular music in all its forms.' Everyone I spoke to said, 'Oh, he will orchestrate it for you more beautifully than anything you can imagine. He's a master orchestrator.' " (One can imagine Gould, who despite his pride in craft hated being known primarily for orchestration, bridling at this.)

But in the late 1940s, Gould told Milton Lomask that De Mille said her colleagues had suggested David Diamond, Copland, Lukas Foss—everyone but Morton: "They never mentioned you."

In any case, De Mille and Gould made a natural team, at least partly because they both had experience with commercial theater. Gould even contributed an essential part of the libretto—Lizzie Borden's fate. De Mille, convinced that Lizzie was guilty, couldn't find a way to portray the acquittal. Gould solved the problem like Alexander with the Gordian Knot: "Hang her," he said.

"My eyes bugged out," said De Mille. " 'But that goes against history,' I said." Gould argued that it was acceptable poetic license, and besides, "I can write hanging music, but I can't write acquittal music." They got along famously. In 1990 De Mille called him "the most actively cooperative composer I have ever worked with."

At one point, her dancers had trouble keeping count because no two bars had the same time signature. "Must it be this hard?" she complained. "I don't think so. I was just trying to impress you," Gould responded, forthwith drew bar lines on the score, "and behold, we could count in regular fours for half a minute." He was willing to change, cut, alter, and improvise on the spot: "There was no thought on his part of music as sacrosanct or absolute," De Mille wrote. When she was not happy with what he wrote, he said, "Well, throw it on the floor. We'll do another." This was different from her experience with Copland, who handed her the *Rodeo* score and said, "Now this is it. I'm going to orchestrate this and nothing else. There will be no changes, additions or deletions." When she begged for eight additional bars, he simply said, "No." Gould, on the other hand, "was utterly without pretension or stubbornness and he helped in any way he could. . . . I had never before worked with a first-line composer of such generosity" (De Mille, *Lizzie Borden: A Dance of Death*, pp. 164–165).

In 1990 De Mille gave an example of teamwork remarkable as a description of the creative process, and equally as a corroboration of Gould's equation of composition and sex. The pair—each of whom was married—took the elevator in the Osborne to Whiteside's apartment. They were discussing a pivotal episode leading to the hanging.

"You got more and more excited," she said in 1990, "I got more and more excited. We actually ran down the hall." Once inside, Gould began throwing off his clothes—hat, overcoat, muffler. She went on:

> There was a trail of Gould garments all the way to the piano. You sat down, you put your hands on the piano and began banging out the most extraordinary climax I have ever heard in a ballet. And I was talking all the time, and dancing—"And then, and then, and then she faces them and they turn their backs." And you went right on playing without stopping. And at the end I threw myself upon your bosom, and you panted and I wept. And I said, "Morton, do you remember one note of what you did?" And you said, "I don't think so." I said, "Here's some paper and here's a pencil, and you start thinking." It was absolutely as if we'd both been caught in a whirlwind. It was done in five minutes.

This was far different from Gould's experiences with Robbins (they battled from start to finish) and from those he would have with Balanchine (whom he held in awe). Perhaps Gould and De Mille fit so easily because they were not only completely pragmatic, but male and female.

While De Mille prepared her ballet, Gould was his usual busy self. In the middle of March 1948, he led the Rochester Philharmonic in another "American Serenade" program, to the now-familiar condescension. Gould, said one critic (*Binghamton Sun*, 16 March 1948), was "awkward and often ludicrous" onstage, and the audience would be right to object because "they paid good money for the opportunity to listen to good music," which this program "did not present."

Back in New York, *Fall River Legend* opened on 22 April 1948, with Gould conducting (Goberman handled later performances). He got lost on his way from the pit to the stage for curtain calls, he recalled in 1985. "Finally I hear a voice calling, 'Where's the goddamn composer!' I had visions of arriving onstage in a dark house, with everyone gone home." When he did arrive, he was met with ovation after ovation, and for once the positive outweighed the negative in his mind. "John Martin, the *Times* critic, the leading dance critic, gave it a wonderful write-up; he loved the score, and said he thought the ballet was a masterpiece." Frances Herridge (*PM*) considered it De Mille's best work to date "and one of the finest ballets in the modern idiom."

De Mille (*Lizzie Borden: A Dance of Death*, p. 218) considered the reception "mixed" and focused on Miles Kastendieck (*Journal-American*), who found the choreography "conventional," not credible, "stagey and superficial," and the music "derivative, functional, and rather empty," with clever devices but "little originality." Irving Kolodin (*The Sun*) declared, "A separate piece could be written about Morton Gould's score, which was relevant and danceable without being in any sense original."

De Mille and Gould cut about fifteen minutes, and the work became a company staple, one that they took on a tour of the Soviet Union in 1966, along with *Billy the Kid*.

Is it derivative and unoriginal? It certainly follows the paths laid down by Copland and Thomson in their Americanist period—but where they frequently quote from folk music and hymn tunes, Gould's melodies are all his own and his handling of the themes is inventive and highly effective. There is even a touch of Elgar, but by and large it stands on its own. (Gould's commission was $750, plus performance royalties; De Mille collected $1500.)

Gould devoted much of the rest of 1948 to revising the Symphony No. 3. He took a long pause from the recording studio, producing almost nothing for Columbia until 1949. During the summer he steeled himself for the expected critical dismissals. "The new movement is a Passacaglia and Fugue and I am really quite proud of it," he wrote to Whiteside on 16 July 1948. The Philharmonic performance should be "an important milestone in my composing career—that is why I have exerted myself as never before to make this as foolproof as possible from an esthetic point of view. As I sweat over the notes, in the wee hours of the night, I can see the write-ups already saying 'glib,' 'slick,' etc. Maybe I should learn to orchestrate in a muddy way so that everything would sound chaotic and unclear and therefore have the aura of hidden messages."

Mitropoulos had not yet been named music director of the New York Philharmonic, but the announcement was expected shortly, and his programming for the first eight weeks of the 1948–49 season was adventurous and eclectic: Webern, Schoenberg, Mahler's Symphony No. 7 (for the first time in New York since 1923), Bartók, as well as the standard Brahms, Schumann, Mozart, and Beethoven. Gould's premiere was 28 October 1948, repeated the 29th and 30th. The night of the premiere, Whiteside wrote in her diary, "[It was] the first really good performance I have ever heard of one of Morton's compositions."

The symphony's four movements are marked "rhapsodic and intense"; "moderately slow and relaxed"; "moderately fast"; and "slowly moving—fast." Only the first of those markings adequately describes the music: the opening is powerful and driving, almost angry, with great weight and momentum. The second movement is lyrical and songlike; the third is a complex fugue with jazzy syncopation and whooping in the brass—a lot of fun; the finale is long and intricate. It is the most accomplished of Gould's orchestral works so far, full of intriguing ideas lavishly developed. For a listener without preconceptions, its depth and seriousness are immediately apparent. Gone are the obvious references to Shostakovich, Sibelius, and Stravinsky; there isn't a trace of folkloric Americanism; the third and fourth movements show their descent from swing and jazz, but in ways admirably integrated into the symphonic structure.

The result is not without flaws. The finale, despite its revisions, is long and ungainly; there are stretches where the composer seems to be having more fun trying out different ways to say the same thing than to maintain a lucid structure. Ungainly it may be, but this score deserves a place among the major American symphonies.

The critics in 1948 did not feel that way, but many were willing to listen with some openness. Howard Taubman (*The New York Times*) considered Gould's symphony "in places his most serious and substantial composition," though "not wholly successful. . . . The composer has eschewed the richly upholstered coloring and instrumentation that have marked some of his earlier and more glib scores." The symphony's weakness, he said, was "failure of melodic invention in the end movements," its strength the "dignity and sustained quality of the slow movement." Here he felt defensive for liking something by Morton Gould: "After all, when a composer can turn out a respectable slow movement, it is a sure sign that he is not to be dismissed lightly." Taubman heard something important in the third movement, the jazz scherzo, with its "irresistible momentum: It is as if Mr. Gould made the jazz medium, through the skill of his writing, accessible to the virtuosity of 100 highly trained symphonic players. . . . Any one who thinks that the conductor—and his men—have not heard and learned from the lads who play hot should have been around last night to listen to the third movement of Mr. Gould's symphony."

Gould himself was moderately pleased. In a lengthy analysis to Whiteside that November, he wrote, "I think the last movement (Passacaglia and Fugue) is a real achievement for me—the Passacaglia completely—and the Fugue almost—even though this movement received the least positive reaction on the part of listeners." He needed to discipline his writing better and was determined to go on from there: "It is so easy for creative people to repeat themselves—because it is always more comfortable to work with proven means—but I must avoid this. Not in the sense of just being different, but of never getting comfortable and smug—negating any real growth and maturity of expression."

Nevertheless, that was the end. No other conductors took it up, and Mitropoulos never played it again. From now on, Gould avoided standard symphonic structure, though he used the label for later works, including the masterly *West Point Symphony*, a band score he called his Symphony No. 4.

There is irony in the mere existence of a *West Point Symphony* by Morton Gould. By 1952, when he was invited to help celebrate the sesquicentennial of the United States Military Academy, Gould's broadcasting career was in tatters and he had been all but banished from the air as a result of hounding from right-wing witch-hunters.

The philosophies of socialism and communism reached their political peaks in America between the world wars. Gould, a child of the Depression, put his sympathies and voice on the side of the poor and the workers. "There were a lot of things to be liberal about," he said in 1985. "There was no security, no Social Security, no unemployment benefits, no pensions—you would have to be heartless not to see that there was something terribly wrong and terribly unjust."

Gould felt about the Communists he knew the way he felt about academics: he respected a few, such as Party chairman Earl Browder and Prostakoff, but considered others to be mediocrities, "people who need a dogma, like a father or mother." Nevertheless, he appeared at rallies, signed petitions, was the headliner at concerts and benefits. Folksinger Oscar Brand met him in 1940 at a concert for relief of refugees from the Spanish Civil War. "Morton was known for a couple of his songs," Brand said. "He was a celebrity. So any program that had him on was great."

Not to the investigators. Unfriendly eyes had been watching Gould's political activities for years. The House of Representatives' Special Committee on Un-American Activities, led by Rep. Martin Dies, noted that in November 1943 he had participated in the Second American-Soviet Conference, along with Paul Robeson, at Madison Square Garden. They noted in 1944 he had been listed as an affiliate or sponsor of such alleged Communist fronts as the Artists' Front to Win the War, the Coordinating Committee to Lift the Embargo, and the Reichstag Fire Trial Anniversary Committee. They knew he was involved with the Progressive Citizens of America, another alleged Communist front. They knew that, in October 1948, he was one of five thousand "leaders in the arts and sciences" who supported Henry Wallace, President Truman's former vice president, in his Progressive Party campaign for president. (The Communist Party had thrown its support behind Wallace.) And they didn't even know Gould was chairman of the Popular Music Committee of the American-Soviet Music Society, whose overall chairman was Koussevitzky, with vice chairmen Elie Siegmeister, Copland, and Bernstein.

They knew he'd been married to Shirley Uzin, and that they had been divorced—but the investigators thought they'd had a baby after the divorce, with no indication of remarriage. Yet the very next paragraph in the file showed that Gould had married Shirley Bank and had a son. (These files were not the most accurate way to keep track of and to tar thousands of Americans.)

According to Walter Gould, the first sign his brother was being hurt by his political activities occurred during the Wallace campaign, at the end of 1948, after Walter had negotiated a deal with Roland ("Chick") Martini of the Gardner advertising agency for Morton to appear in a program sponsored by the United States Air Force. Morton went to Denver, Colorado, to conduct at the outdoor Red Rocks amphitheater. "Chick called me," Walter said, "and said we've got the deal, hire the orchestra. I told Morton he had the deal. Morton came back from Denver.

"All of a sudden, Chick calls and says there's a terrible situation: someone in Congress said that Morton was in Philadelphia conducting at a Henry Wallace rally. And he gives me the date. I said it was impossible, because Morton was in Denver at the time." Nevertheless, the Goulds let Martini out of the arrangement.

That at least was something Morton knew about, but there were things happening below the surface. Decades later, Abram Chasins told Gould that early in the postwar period, when he was music director of radio station WQXR, owned by *The New York Times* and one of the nation's pre-eminent classical broadcasters, station executives advised him to cut down on the leftwingers Gould and Copland. Chasins told the *Times* critics, who said they would denounce the ban in their columns. So he held off.

The attacks kept mounting, those the Goulds were aware of and those that were not revealed until decades after the damage had been done.

The 1948 presidential election—famous for Harry S Truman's upset of Thomas E. Dewey—was also the high-water mark of the postwar leftist movements. Not only was Wallace defeated, his fourth-place finish (behind even Dixiecrat candidate Strom Thurmond) indicated the fundamental electoral weakness of the positions he represented, and with which Morton Gould had become identified. As the battle over communism in the United States grew more ferocious—from the notorious "Hollywood Ten" through the infamous Army-McCarthy hearings—Gould's political views were increasingly suspect.

In one highly publicized incident that hit very close, Copland's *A Lincoln Portrait* was dropped from Dwight D. Eisenhower's first inauguration, in 1952, two days beforehand, on a complaint from

Rep. Fred E. Busbey of Illinois. Gould's career was damaged accordingly, though the changes in his fortunes were also affected by the decline of radio, the musical move away from Americanism toward the "international school," the rise of the Second Viennese School of Schoenberg, Webern, and Berg—and by his own prickly nature.

Entering his late thirties, Gould was a familiar musical figure. The radio days were over, but he was recording nonstop and Broadway still beckoned. Gould was an active guest conductor and, encouraged by Mitropoulos, trying to expand his creative reach. Nevertheless, the blacklist had a serious effect on his livelihood. "There was no official announcement," he said in 1985. "You're busy and not aware, when certain conditions change, whether it's a normal transition to something else or whether things are changing because somebody has changed it for you by making certain outlets not available."

Television was getting started, and it seemed natural that Gould move to the new medium. TV, however, neither needed nor could afford radio's large-scale musical organizations. NBC's legendary orchestra limped into the 1950s, and the CBS orchestra lingered for a while, too. But the buzzing of musicians from job to job began to weaken as the broadcast ensembles disintegrated.

Nevertheless, Gould proposed a number of possibilities to James Davidson: "We very quickly got the message that I would not be acceptable." His name was included in the magazine *Counterattack* and then the book published in 1950 entitled *Red Channels: The Report of Communist Influence in Radio and Television*, a listing of Americans in the arts who had been connected with organizations considered Communist or Communist fronts.

Viewed at the end of the twentieth century, the book is an artistic Hall of Fame: harmonica player Larry Adler; actors John Garfield, José Ferrer, Howard Duff, Edward G. Robinson; historian William Shirer; commentator Howard K. Smith; novelist Irwin Shaw; poet Louis Untermeyer. *New York Times* music critic Olin Downes was there; so were Jerome Robbins, actress Ruth Gordon, folksingers Pete Seeger, Oscar Brand, Josh White. Among the composers were Copland, Blitzstein, Bernstein, and of course, Gould. But in its day, a place in *Red Channels* was devastating. "It was quite a thing to be in this book," said Oscar Brand ironically in 1996. "All the NBC and CBS executives had it," Gould said. The networks, which operated under federal license and were vulnerable to advertising boycotts, were particularly sensitive to pressure.

Gould's personality did not lend itself to public display, and now identification with issues such as civil rights and public housing had also become a liability. "My publisher would say, 'They took off your music on such and such a program. You'd better take it easy, don't get onto any more committees.' There was a quiz show I was supposed to be on. At the last minute they took me off. They called my brother Walter and said, 'Why are you trying to palm Morton off on us? He's blacklisted.' So I lost whatever possible transition might have occurred at that time," Gould said in 1985.

"I would get no further than mentioning his name," Walter said, "and they'd say, 'We can't use him.'"

But this was not immediately apparent. At the end of March 1949, Gould was prominently involved in the three-day Scientific and Cultural Conference for Peace, the so-called Waldorf Conference, in Manhattan, organized by the National Council of the Arts, Sciences and Professions (a designated Communist front). He chaired a panel and greeted the Soviet composer Dmitri Shostakovich, who was visiting the United States specifically for the meeting.

"Shostakovich said to me, 'It's hot in here,' Gould recalled in 1995. "That was it. We spoke very little. I was interested in talking music with him, but we had none of that, no conversation whatsoever."

The Waldorf Conference was interesting mostly for its political ramifications. It attracted a galaxy of notable Americans, among them Norman Mailer and Arthur Miller. But it was also a major effort of Soviet propaganda whose results were watched by both sides. Carlos Moseley, later chairman of the New York Philharmonic board, worked at the time for the United States State Department. (Moseley was trained as a pianist—he was the soloist when student conductor Leonard Bernstein led the Boston Symphony at Tanglewood in August 1941.) During the war Moseley was in the Office of War Information, and in the immediate postwar period dealt with matters of military government and the "reorientation branch." With his musical and military-political backgrounds, he was well qualified to watch the interaction of Soviet Communists and American intellectual and artistic figures. The State Department sent him to observe.

"All American composers would have been delighted to speak

with Shostakovich," Moseley said. Politically, he said, Gould "was not one of those I knew who was a much greater problem. I don't know that he was any problem." Nevertheless, the House Committee on Un-American Activities and *Counterattack* noted Gould's presence at the conference. The FBI asked him about it, and he told them about his exchange with Shostakovich. Meaningless, except for the perception of a musician involved with a hated and feared enemy.

Still, none of this was high in Gould's consciousness as he concentrated on his two latest Broadway projects.

The one which came to fruition was *Arms and the Girl*, based on a 1933 play by Lawrence Langner and Armina Marshall, *The Pursuit of Happiness*. The plot was old-fashioned even then: a young woman during the American Revolution tries to seduce a Hessian soldier into changing sides. *The Pursuit of Happiness* had been known as "the bundling play" because it highlighted an old Puritan custom in which a courting couple could spend the night together as long as they were wrapped in separate blankets—and there were a lot of jokes about that.

The Pursuit of Happiness was adapted by the brother and sister team of Herbert and Dorothy Fields, whose credits included Cole Porter's *Dubarry Was a Lady* (Herbert alone) and Irving Berlin's *Annie Get Your Gun* (Herbert and Dorothy together). The Fields approached the thirty-five-year-old Gould cautiously. "In their minds I represented a very serious concert composer," he said—and they hadn't liked *Billion Dollar Baby*. Dorothy told Morton that if they worked together, the score could not be like *Billion Dollar Baby*. The atmosphere was very different from the earlier musical, whose creators were young, rambunctious, and experimental. In 1949 Herbert was fifty-two and Dorothy forty-five years old, steeped in musical comedy tradition. "Dorothy and Herb had very set approaches," Gould said in 1985. "They were very concerned with me, that I would not be commercial enough, that I would write music that was too symphonic."

Arms and the Girl had an excellent creative team (the choreographer was Michael Kidd) and a talented cast including the French singing actor Georges Guetary in his Broadway debut, Nanette Fabray in her first starring role, and Pearl Bailey for a couple of showstoppers. But the production was bedeviled from the start. Fabray broke under director Rouben Mamoulian's tight discipline and had to leave the show for a week. Bailey was a diva who insisted on doing things her own way.

And the story itself never really worked. "There was no ending to the show," Gould said, "no resolution whatever." A lot of other things went wrong. They decided to bring in George Washington on a horse. "So in Boston, when we didn't have any ending to the show, or a second act, they were going down to the stables—everybody walked the plank on this."

Dorothy Fields became angry at Gould, he recalled in 1985. "She would get violent and accuse me, say that I'm 'destroying her lyrics,' my music is 'mainly for Carnegie Hall, it's not for the stage.'" Then they became convinced the problem was the orchestration, and brought in Robert Russell Bennett as a show doctor—so Gould sent his staff back to New York. "They got me mad, and I said, 'As far as I'm concerned you can take this show and shove it.' . . . In the field of orchestration, I'm the top of the heap. You don't bring in somebody to question my orchestration. . . . They were desperate; the show wasn't working."

The Boston critics were kind but knew the show had problems—most focused on the book. Elinor Hughes (*Sunday Herald*, 22 January 1950) even exhorted Gould to be more assertive: "If the Fields family and Mr. Mamoulian are hereby requested, most respectfully, to cut down on their contributions, so Morton Gould, the composer, is urged simultaneously to increase his. . . . Mr. Gould, by no means a self-assertive person, is also inclined to give more play to Dorothy Fields's excellent lyrics than to his own melodic vein."

Arms and the Girl opened in Manhattan on 2 February 1950 at the 46th Street Theatre, with Shirley, nine months pregnant, in attendance. As Whiteside recorded, "Pat came, which scared everybody to death for fear labor would start in the middle of the show. But it didn't." (The baby was born soon after the curtain fell. On 3 February Whiteside wrote, "A big day! Morton called me at 7:15 and said, 'You are the grandmother of a baby girl.'") Shirley wanted to call their daughter Nora, after Ibsen's heroine; Morton wanted to call her Abby. He prevailed, again.

Whiteside thought *Arms and the Girl* charming and was sure "it [would] have a run." But the critics disagreed. "Musical-Play Should

Have Been Better," read the headline in the *Herald Tribune*. Brooks Atkinson (*The New York Times*) observed that the show "never really triumphs over the meager humor of the skittish joke on which it is founded. . . . In craftsmanship and point of view it is closer to *The Student Prince* than they probably intended."

Gould's work got brief and unenthusiastic comment. The score, with such songs as "A Cow, a Plow and a Frau," sounds laughably dated, except for Bailey's two torchy numbers. The composer himself concluded in 1985 that he had given way to Dorothy Fields too easily. "I would start to write a tune, and she would say, 'No no no, that's not commercial, keep it simple.' . . . I should have given it a little more imagination."

Arms and the Girl closed after barely fifty performances. Dorothy Fields went on to write such hits as *Sweet Charity* with Cy Coleman. But this was the last time a Gould show made it to the Great White Way.

There was an intriguing notice, however, in the *Herald Tribune* on 20 February 1950: Jo Mielziner, Rodgers and Hammerstein's primary set designer, had turned to production. His first show "will be a musical version of Eugene O'Neill's drama, *Desire Under the Elms*. Morton Gould will do the score and Edward Eager is being sought as lyricist."

A man who buried his failures and moved on, Gould was extremely tight-lipped about *Desire*. But it was one of his most important projects, away from the froth of *Arms and the Girl* and the edge of *Billion Dollar Baby*. Written and premiered in 1924, *Desire* was considered a great American tragedy, a story of intense love, fear, hatred, desire, and frustration, complete with incest and infanticide. The main characters were Ephraim Cabot, the hard-bitten, virile, and domineering farmer, and Abbie, his much younger second wife, beautiful, greedy—and attracted to Cabot's son, Eben, who hated his father for working his mother to death and was desperate to win the land for himself. It is not hard to imagine how the play must have attracted Gould, for the psychological relationships must have resonated within him: the dominating father who overwhelmed a gentle mother, and the tormented son tangled in cables of love, hatred, and fear.

Mielziner, who had designed the set for O'Neill's *Strange Inter-*

lude in 1928, told the playwright of his wish to set the play to music at the end of 1948. O'Neill mentioned it in a letter of 3 December 1948 to the critic George Jean Nathan: "There is chance of musical version of *Desire Under the Elms*—not lighter stuff but serious play—opera so to speak. (Jo Mielziner had the idea and is handling it—but no contract yet. It may take one or two years.)"

Mielziner, Gould, and Eager plunged into the work enthusiastically. The novice producer quickly built a maquette of the staging, they created a libretto, and began casting. The first person chosen was Shannon Bolin, an ingenue from South Dakota who was a member of the Actors Studio and a trained singer about to appear in the NBC Opera production of Puccini's *Suor Angelica*.

Bolin said Mielziner told her, "It takes a real actress and it takes a good singer." She was accompanied at the audition by her husband, the pianist Milton Kaye, who knew Gould from WOR. "Morton came over to me," Kaye recalled, "and said, 'Who's that girl? Who's that girl?' I said, 'That's my wife.' He said, 'What?' So he said, 'She's it! That's my Abbie. That's it! Abbie in *Desire Under the Elms*.'"

Gould and Eager worked well together, Kaye observed, and James Gould was uncharacteristically quiet, "because of Mielziner." The show was scheduled for production twice, in 1950 and 1951, but fell through both times. The play itself was revived for a short run in 1952; O'Neill died in 1953. And the folk opera died too, with conflicting accounts of its demise.

It was suggested at the time that they could not cast the role of Eben; and it is possible that Mielziner wasn't able to raise the money. Both of these seem unlikely—there was no shortage of young talent after the war, and Mielziner, with his long theater history, should have been able to find plenty of backing. A darker possibility, mentioned by Kaye, Bolin, and Walter Gould, is that Richard Rodgers objected to "his" designer becoming a producer. Morton denied the possibility; he was reluctant to talk about the project at all. Kaye and Walter Gould said Rodgers let Mielziner know that if he went ahead with the production, he would never be given another Rodgers and Hammerstein show. "Jo felt he needed this—this was his livelihood. So that was the end of *Desire Under the Elms*," Walter said.

"It was a heartbreaking thing," Bolin said. "Morton was sick about it." Although she went on to a successful theatrical career

(*Damn Yankees*, among other things), she felt this would have been her greatest opportunity, and the music itself, she and Kaye agreed, was different from anything Gould had done before. "It would have pushed Morton to another level," Kaye said. In subject matter and approach it was closer in conception to *Fall River Legend* than to either of his Broadway shows. With the collapse of *Desire*, Gould did not consider a theater work again until the mid-1970s.

Whatever the reasons, however, by the beginning of the 1950s, after one bloop hit, one out, and a balk, Gould's career on Broadway was over. His place in broadcasting was being throttled by the blacklist. And the flood of European refugees, coupled with the rise of a new generation of internationally oriented American composers, combined to make Gould's overtly patriotic style not just old-hat, but downright reactionary.

But he had plenty of recording work, an important home-town champion in Mitropoulos, and a manager who worshiped him. Life was still full of possibilities.

CHAPTER 16

"Morton Gould and His Orchestra"

★ ★ ★ ★

IN 1947 HOWARD SCOTT was a twenty-seven-year-old ex-GI graduate of the Eastman School of Music and Juilliard, learning the record business as an apprentice to Goddard Lieberson, the newly named head of Columbia Masterworks.

Scott spent the summer of 1947 transferring 78 rpm recordings to the brand-new 33⅓ LP, and Gould was one of the first men he worked with: "Morton and Kosty were the classical pop guys; they had a green label; blue was for Masterworks, and red was for pops. Green was a crossover," Scott said.

Scott became one of Gould's primary producers and colleagues. "Morton was unique," he said. "Everyone else had rehearsals—even Kosty had rehearsals. Morton had no rehearsal time." Often, he hadn't even completed the arrangements when work began. Scott vividly recalled one session when he and the engineer were listening to a playback while Morton sat in a corner writing parts for the next arrangement: "So the musicians not only had never seen it, but Morton had never heard it except in his head. Now that's incredible!"

Scott enjoyed Gould and even got a kick out of Pop: "He thought he was a composer. He used to sit in the control room with me, with his cigar and his cane, and say, 'Well, I think I wrote a pretty good piece there. My son, I told him what to do.' He said, 'I gave George Gershwin the idea for *Rhapsody in Blue*.' "

Morton put on no airs. "Bruno Walter and Kostelanetz used to bring a suitcase and a valet," Scott said, "to change from their business suits to their recording outfits. But not Morton. He'd come in from the road in his business suit, strip off his jacket, open his tie and shirt, and then start to conduct. When he was finished, sweaty and everything, he'd button 'em up and leave."

Gould recorded for Columbia from 1942 to 1954, thirty-nine original LPs, including twenty-four on the twelve-inch Masterworks label, eight ten-inchers, and seven pops recordings. Here, however against his will, Gould cemented his reputation as a light composer. Besides the popular arrangements, his repertoire was in light classics: Victor Herbert, Albert Ketelbey, Ernesto Lecuona, Percy Grainger. Harking back to his teen years and *Manhattan Rhapsody*, he made a series of "rhapsodies" for piano and orchestra, arrangements of Gershwin, Weill, and Rodgers. He arranged Tchaikovsky's *The Months* Op. 37a for piano and orchestra, and so on.

Much of his work was well received. After hearing Gould's Grainger, the composer wrote ecstatically on 18 January 1955: "I cannot tell you how elated I am at your exquisite rendering. . . . Tempo, tone-color, feeling, everything is just perfect. . . . You are the first to ever record *Spoon River*—and WHAT a recording! . . . How lucky I am to have my music recorded by a composer-genius such as yourself, and not merely by a conductor."

Gould's arrangements were exquisite—fragrant and delicate in "Moonglow," muscular for "Beyond the Blue Horizon," sometimes even wildly inappropriate, as in a "Blues in the Night" that begins like the mule train in Grofe's *Grand Canyon Suite.*

"He was very highly respected," said flutist Julius Baker, a future Philharmonic principal flute who played in Gould's ensembles. "He was a very talented musician. . . . He had a talent for picking the right instrument for a part."

"He was capable of getting a little testy," said bassist Homer Mensch, another Philharmonic musician, "but it smoothed out after a while." Bassist David Walter, a Toscanini veteran, recalled him this way:

> He was a tough man to work for, but tough in a very nice sense. He just wanted you to do exactly what he wanted, no monkey

> business. He was not abusive, he was witty. But the wit in no way interfered with the job at hand. He was very serious and pragmatic in his conducting. . . . I never remember him—as I remember so many other conductors would—preening or asking for admiration or posturing. He looked like one of the musicians who happened to be playing the orchestra instead of an instrument.

Yet if you are received as one of the boys, you may be perceived as just one of the boys. Gould never had the glow known as "charisma," and it worked against him. He expected audiences to appreciate his brilliance on their own. He would not go out of his way to seek attention, as Bernstein and Kostelanetz would, nor did he have the sparkle that helped colleagues such as Mitch Miller and Skitch Henderson cross into television.

"I must tell you, as a conductor he had no charisma," said cellist Harvey Shapiro, who worked with him at Radio City, went on to the NBC Symphony, and wound up teaching at Juilliard. "He is a very honest musician, very funny, but cold. I played first cello with Toscanini, Reiner, Stokowski, Rodzinski, everybody. They had charisma. Even Kostelanetz had charisma."

"Morton had a delightful, sardonic sense of humor," Scott said. "But he was boring. He had as much charisma as a jellyfish." That was no problem on radio, where you can't hear a person smile. But in the visual age of television, it was a handicap. Gould also did not put as much preparation into his recordings as others did. His primary focus was always on composition.

David Oppenheim, who became Scott's superior at Columbia Masterworks, observed this difference between Gould and others. "André was much more careful about the recording process," Oppenheim said. "Morton wasn't. With André there would be meetings before the sessions; he brought in an outside producer, we had meetings in his home. Morton just came into the sessions, we turned the mikes on, and we did what we could."

By the time Oppenheim arrived, Gould was growing uncomfortable. He had already lost one battle with Kostelanetz, and now he feared that he would be placed with Epic, a secondary label. "When it came to being important to the label, it was Kostelanetz, not Morton," Oppenheim said, "and I think it disturbed him, as well it might. ... André got star treatment and big ads, and he didn't." Oppenheim saw Gould on the beginning of his long downward path and his displeasure was evident. "Morton I think had previously been used to a better shake than he was getting at the time I showed up. ... He would let you know he was dissatisfied and displeased, so it wasn't always very nice."

Gould did do some original work at Columbia—they recorded his *Tap Dance Concerto* with Danny Daniels and the Rochester Pops in 1953—but the strains continued. The denouement came with *Showpiece* for orchestra, commissioned to demonstrate a new high-fidelity speaker system, performed and recorded by Eugene Ormandy and the Philadelphia Orchestra—but, to Gould's enduring dismay, never released.

Gould felt an air of mystery about it from the beginning. First RCA called to discuss a secret project. The firm was about to move to stereo, and artists and repertoire director Alan Kayes and other executives wanted him to write a demonstration piece, to be conducted by Stokowski. Then Lieberson called with the same idea, though not for stereo. Morton was torn between RCA with Stokowski, and Columbia with Mitropoulos. Lieberson added a twist: the Columbia orchestra would not be Mitropoulos and the Philharmonic, but Ormandy and Philadelphia.

Gould and Ormandy had a long, cool history dating back to Rapee at Radio City and Stokowski at Philadelphia. "So I called Goddard," Gould recalled in 1986, "and said, 'I'm very sympathetic to this, but if Ormandy knows I am going to write it, he won't want to record it because he doesn't like me.'" Lieberson contacted Ormandy; he told Gould that when he proposed his name, Ormandy replied, "He is the logical choice, that is the man who should do that. But when you tell him I am going to conduct it, he might not want to write it because he doesn't like me."

Lieberson thought this was ridiculous, and Columbia was Gould's company, so the piece was written in early 1954, and he traveled to Philadelphia in May for rehearsals, performance, and recording. Conductor and composer were introduced to one another on the stage of the Academy of Music.

"He said, 'Mr. Gould, I want you to stand right next to me.' I said,

'Dr. Ormandy, call me Morton.' He said, 'I just met you.' Okay. He calls me Mr. Gould, I call him Mr. Ormandy."

Whatever else he thought of Ormandy, Gould knew he was a superb musician who had the orchestra in magnificent shape. "They start to play my piece down—they read it like a lot of other orchestras play it after they have rehearsed it. I was standing next to Ormandy wallowing in these wonderful things coming out. Ormandy was right on top of it, doing an absolutely first-rate interpretation of it."

The conductor asked the composer how it was going. "I said, 'It's wonderful! Great! What an orchestra!' "

A bit later, the horns complained that the score was impossible. "Ormandy says, 'Now gentlemen, if anybody else had done this, I would say perhaps you have reason to say this. But Mr. Gould is a master orchestrator—not only will you find it playable, but it will be most effective.' "

Each man had very politely slapped the other. Gould did not want to hear Ormandy call him a great orchestrator; Ormandy did not want Gould to compliment the orchestra rather than himself. "Some of the men afterwards told me they got such a kick out of this," Gould said in 1986, "because we were both being very friendly, and neither of us was doing this purposely, but we were saying both the wrong things!" He likened it to an encounter between streetwalkers turned socialites: "They each look down on the other because they came out of the same pot."

The premiere was on 7 May 1954; the next day the piece was recorded, along with a host of other music. Everything was released except *Showpiece*. "I just don't know what happened," Gould said. He speculated that Oppenheim did not like the piece. But Oppenheim was not the producer; Scott was. Both Scott and R. Peter Munves, another Columbia producer and engineer, said *Showpiece* was not released because it was recorded in monaural sound—just before stereo appeared. Columbia's high-fidelity project was a speaker called the 360 K, Scott said, and they wanted a demonstration record. The engineers did not even bring their two-track machine to Philadelphia. Then, suddenly, mono was obsolete.

Nevertheless, Mitropoulos fought for *Showpiece*; he programmed it with the Philharmonic and took it on tour in 1955. By then Gould was at RCA. He had signed a three-year contract for a minimum of three LPs a year, on 26 October 1954. Columbia Records president James B. Conkling responded graciously on 1 December: "I know that Goddard, and some of the rest of us, did not feel that our future planning was able to take sufficient advantage of your ability to be really fair to you." Gould's last Columbia recordings (with one important exception) were made in July 1954, with the all-star Columbia Concert Band, for an album entitled *And the Band Played On.*

RCA let Gould expand his repertoire and even advertised him as "Mr. Stereo." He recorded for the Red Seal label until 1969.

During the early 1950s, aside from the discs that paid the bills, Gould pushed himself beyond the standard symphonic forms. His major works turned in novel directions: in 1951 and 1952 he wrote *Tap Dance Concerto* and *West Point Symphony.* The next year came *Dance Variations* for two pianos and orchestra and *Inventions* for four pianos and orchestra, commissioned by the Steinway Corporation for its centennial. In 1954 there was *Showpiece.* The next year brought the film *Cinerama Holiday* and a piece for Benny Goodman, *Derivations* for clarinet and jazz combo. In each, Gould tried something new and unusual.

West Point Symphony was one of thirteen sesquicentennial commissions (others were Harris's *West Point Symphony for Band* and Milhaud's *West Point Suite*). Far from viewing him as a security risk, the Army invited Gould to spend a week on campus before the premiere, which took place on 13 April 1952.

The performance was broadcast and got some excited responses. Edwin Franko Goldman wrote, "I think that it is one of the finest band works that has ever been written, and we will use it frequently in the future." The score now is a West Point workhorse, performed as often as four times a season. But because it was a band work played outside New York, the score was ignored by critics and concert musicians. Even today, it is far better known among bandsmen than elsewhere.

The symphony, somber and funereal, is most unusual for a piece commemorating a school dedicated to war. The first movement, "Epitaphs," is marked by the use of "Taps" among its many themes, as well as the "Dies irae" buried among the trombones. The primary sensation is of death and mourning—appropriate but unexpected. The second and shorter movement, "Marches," is more upbeat and straightforwardly martial, full of fragments from familiar marches and battle songs. As it reaches its peak, the tramp of feet is reproduced by a "marching machine"—a wooden box with suspended pegs (Gould learned this from radio sound effects).

Tap Dance Concerto is more involved. Gould had written a similar work for Paul Draper during the early 1940s, but the piece was never performed, the composer lost track of the score, and Draper eventually fell to the Red hunters. One day in 1952, the dancer Danny Daniels (the jilted boyfriend in *Billion Dollar Baby*) visited Gould. Work was slow and Daniels was depressed, but he had an idea for a ballet and decided to ask Gould if he had any suitable music. The reaction Daniels got was very different from the one afforded Jerry Robbins nearly a decade earlier.

"I was talking to him and he was looking at me, and eventually I realized he wasn't even listening," Daniels said in 1996. "He said, 'How would you like to do a tap dance concerto with me?' I was bowled over. First of all, I didn't really know what the hell he was talking about. And then, what went through my mind is, 'I think he's saying he wants to write a piece of music and he wants me to dance to it.' So I said sure."

Gould wrote another score, making him the only composer of two tap dance concertos. He was the dominant partner. The soloist's part was fully notated, and Daniels worked on it in his basement in Whitestone, Queens. As usual, Gould was flexible. At one point, he asked Daniels about the third movement. "I said, 'I don't know, let me work on it,'" recalled Daniels. "So [Gould] said, 'Ah, we'll throw it out and do a new one.' So he wrote another piece. He just tossed it off."

"The rhythm was the thread of the piece," Daniels said, "and the orchestra was intricately involved in the rhythms of the tap dancer. It was an incredible experience to dance the piece, because sometimes the rhythm would be going contrapuntally to the orchestra, and sometimes we would be together. Once I started dancing it, I thought I had died and gone to heaven."

Gould and Daniels gave the premiere 16 November 1952, in Rochester, and Columbia recorded it there on 19 January 1953. To fill the other side of the disc, Gould wrote *Family Album*, a nostalgic little suite for orchestra.

Daniels considered the premiere one of his most thrilling experiences. "When Morton conducted, it was like I couldn't do anything that the orchestra wasn't right there with me." The Rochester newspapers applauded the work. Norman Nairn (*Rochester Democrat and Chronicle*) thought Daniels was "spectacular" and found Gould's music "attractive and imaginative."

John Martin (*Sunday New York Times*) was also appreciative: "What seems to make it unique is that the composer has actually written the dancer into the music exactly as if he were a violinist or a pianist." Daniels, with Walter Gould as his manager, performed the work some forty times throughout the United States and Europe before hanging up his dancing shoes.

The concerto's second hearings that year had their own significance. They marked the only times Leonard Bernstein conducted one of Gould's works—and also resulted in a stinging snub. The performances were 13 and 14 June 1953, in Waltham, Massachusetts, where Bernstein was directing the second annual Brandeis University Festival of the Creative Arts. The theme was "The Comic Spirit," and the concerts were to feature the American premiere of Francis Poulenc's opera *Les mamelles de Tiresias* and Darius Milhaud's ballet *Le boef sur le toit*. But Bernstein could not get the rights for the Milhaud and thought of the concerto.

By now Gould was willing and went to Massachusetts for the occasion. But at the end of the first performance, Bernstein—contrary to musical etiquette—did not call the composer for a bow. Backstage afterward, he apologized profusely to Gould: "Oh my dear Morton, I forgot to introduce you!"

Then he did it again the second night.

"That I was angry at, because I made the trip to come up to pay my respects to him—very honestly I wouldn't have gone up if I thought he was going to ignore me," Gould recalled in 1994. Daniels —whom Gould described as "livid" at the snub—did not recall the incident but remembered being unhappy with the conducting: "I felt I was in competition with Bernstein. . . . I thought Lenny danced it better than I did. . . . I'm dancing, and I glanced over at him, and I thought he was making a silly ass of himself the way he was conducting it."

The *Boston Post* dismissed the concerto: "In that the music is light, especially the Minuet, which bids fair to attain something of the popularity of the composer's Pavanne, the Concerto might be described as gay, rather than comic—unless you consider the title comic in itself."

That's correct: only if you thought the concept of a concerto for tap dancer amusing in itself would you consider the piece humorous. Gould was not trying to make jokes, but it was getting hard to find people who could hear his music as anything more than entertainment.

On 7 April 1953 the Rockefeller Foundation gave the Louisville Orchestra $400,000 to commission and record new symphonic and operatic music over the next four years. There were to be forty-six new works a year, one-half to two-thirds by Americans. Among the commissions that followed were Copland's *Orchestral Variations*, Carter's *Variations for Orchestra*, Schuman's *Judith*, and Mennin's Fifth and Sixth Symphonies. On 5 February 1954, less than a year after the program started, the Louisville Philharmonic Society Commission Recommendation Committee held its fourth meeting. According to the minutes, "Mr. Whitney offered the name of Morton Gould, but Mr. Anderson and Mr. Herz voted against him. Mr. Anderson stated that Morton Gould's music offended him."

Dwight Anderson was the music critic for the Louisville *Courier-Journal* and later dean of the University of Louisville's music school; Gerhard Herz was a musicologist on the faculty there. They did not think Gould was a serious composer. In 1996, Herz said he objected because Gould did radio and commercial work. "There were more important composers of serious music than Morton Gould was at the time," Herz said. "He did not seem to me at that time to be ready yet for the commission." Even Robert S. Whitney, who put Gould's name forward and voted for him, was not a strong supporter. Scott, Louisville's producer, said that when he himself suggested Gould, Whitney said, "He's not a serious composer."

It did not matter that Gould had written three symphonies, or that his ballet music was in the repertory of American Ballet Theatre, or that he had a catalog of other concert works. He was not ready for Louisville. Gould's only Louisville commission was *Flourishes and Galop*—for the opening, ironically, of the Robert S. Whitney Hall of the Kentucky Performing Arts Center in 1983.

He was constantly busy, but this lack of recognition indicates how he was perceived. "We got that all the time," Walter said. "In the years I used to be out trying to push him, I would talk to some of the orchestra managers. . . . To get them to think of Morton as a serious composer was almost impossible." But Gould's relationship with Mitropoulos deepened and his mastery of orchestral forms grew. *Dance Variations* is a case in point. Commissioned by Arthur Whittemore and Jack Lowe, the score was first performed on 24 October 1953, with Mitropoulos and the Philharmonic, in a program that included the premiere of Ernst Krenek's *Concerto for Two Pianos*. There could not be a greater contrast between the twelve-tone writing of the Krenek and the overtly virtuosic and brilliant Gould. The critics (except for Biancolli) heard nothing interesting in either piece, but at least they respected Krenek. Harold Schonberg (*The New York Times*) called the Gould "a slick, professional, jazzy pastiche." Jay Harrison (*Herald Tribune*) said it was "one of Mr. Gould's politer jokes."

It is hard to fault the reviewers, with their brief exposure to the music and over-familiarity with Gould's history, for underestimating the power of the score. The first or second time one tends to hear only a glittering surface. *Dance Variations* is in four movements, most of which fly by at breakneck speed. Gould's harmonic language and organization are tonal and conventional, yet the music is passionate and unsettling. The opening movement, "Chaconne," is not sweet and charming, but jagged and broken. The second movement, "Arabesques" ("Gavotte," "Pavane," "Polka," "Quadrille," "Minuet," "Waltz," "Can-Can"), is fragmented and torn—just as the ear begins to recognize something, it's gone; its "Can-Can" is pounding and raucous. And the concluding "Tarantella" is frighteningly angry. Far from being a simple-minded crowd-pleaser, *Dance Variations* is a score of depth and complexity, the work of a mind that is hiding in plain sight.

Gould considered *Dance Variations* among his most important pieces, but no one heard it that way. The members of the musical establishment could barely hear him at all. He was no longer promising, no longer the future of American music; he would no longer get even the benefit of the doubt. Among the few who tried to make something of the score was Agnes De Mille, who used it to choreograph *The Rib of Adam*, which appeared and disappeared during Ballet Theatre's 1956 season. The recording, at the end of 1955, was not by Mitropoulos on Columbia, but by Stokowski with the San Francisco Symphony, on RCA Victor.

An even more telling example of the hostility Gould endured was the treatment accorded *Showpiece*. Mitropoulos first played the score in a pair of subscription concerts on 19 and 20 February 1955. Harold Schonberg (*The New York Times*) was scornful: "The work . . . is slick, superficial, and has all the permanence of an ice cube in a glass of water." He added a deadly thrust: "The partiality that Mr. Mitropoulos has shown for Mr. Gould's music through the years is hard to explain."

The *Herald Tribune* remarked on its texture, "so laden with instrumentation for its own sake that the ear's reaction is to an aural thesaurus of orchestration rather than to music as such."

Determined to get a fair hearing, Mitropoulos offered it at another subscription pair, 7 and 8 April. But he did *Showpiece* no favor by making it the only work accompanying the first New York performance since 1947 of Mahler's Symphony No. 6. Perkins (*Herald Tribune*) and Taubman (*The New York Times*) complained about the Mahler's length. Everyone but Biancolli swiped at Gould. Taubman tarred Mahler by association, declaring that while the Austrian "was a deeply serious and greatly gifted man touched with genius and [the Gould] is a *pièce d'occasion* by a slick craftsman . . . both works qualify as music for a hi-fi age."

Harriett Johnson (*The New York Post*) thought that using *Showpiece* as a curtain raiser was "about tops in bad judgment. . . . The piece would best fit into a jaunty evening at the Lewisohn Stadium or as atmosphere for a high-tension movie." Only Biancolli enjoyed both works. He felt the Mahler was "powerful and exciting," while the Gould was "smart and animated, flashing with surprises and brisk with good cheer."

But Mitropoulos was still not through. He gave *Showpiece* seven performances on a coast-to-coast tour, and three more during the European tour that followed. Nothing helped. If ever a name was unfortunate, it was *Showpiece*. Gould meant the score as a concerto for orchestra, and such a neutral title might have deflected some of the artillery. The work itself, a massive set of variations following a glorious orchestral tune-up, is more than the sum of its parts, which are many, dazzling and difficult. Beyond mere instrumental effect, it challenges an orchestra to demonstrate power and skill. Like Gould himself, *Showpiece* is witty, sardonic, and complex.

But given the critical reception of his music and Mitropoulos's enthusiasm for it, it is not surprising to learn that at the end of the 1955–56 season, when Taubman, the brand-new chief critic for *The New York Times*, launched a devastating attack on Mitropoulos, Gould was one of the whips he used to flog the conductor. Nor is it surprising that, after Mitropoulos left the Philharmonic but as guest conductor programmed yet another Gould, he warned Morton about the future, as Gould recalled in 1994: "I said to him, 'Why, Dimitri, after what the critics have done to you, and said you shouldn't be playing too much of me, why do you want to do this?' And he said to me, 'No, my dear, I want to program it because I like your music. And, when I leave, you won't get performances here again.'" Which is essentially what happened.

But while the pressure against him rose in New York, and he suffered for his politics, Gould's grasp of form and orchestra grew, and he found other outlets. By now he was a major figure among school bandmasters; his ballads, sagas, rhapsodies, and marches were being programmed and performed in schools everywhere. His friendship with Benny Goodman, begun at *Cresta Blanca*, bore artistic fruit, and RCA put him to work immediately.

The record company, ahead of Columbia in new technology, introduced stereo in 1956; it wanted to take advantage of Gould's adventurousness. "We were at the cutting edge of stereo," recalled Alan Kayes, then chief of artists and repertoire. "Arthur Fiedler and the Boston Pops was our equivalent, if you will, of Kostelanetz, but nobody had the musical and technical savvy about stereo that Morton had, as a composer and as an arranger. He understood its values, and translated them technically into music."

Gould began recording for RCA on 14 October 1954, at the Manhattan Center studio: arrangements of Cole Porter and Harold Rome. Five sessions in December were devoted to suites from *Carousel* and *Oklahoma!*, and Gould's own suite from the upcoming film, *Cinerama Holiday*.

Between the sessions of 22 and 29 December, on 23 December 1954, Deborah Gould was born. By this time, the Goulds had moved to Great Neck on Long Island; a photograph of mother and daughter in the *Long Island Press* the next day proclaimed her the ten-thousandth patient at North Shore Hospital.

Gould did not put much stock in *Cinerama Holiday*, the second of a series of movies that used extra-wide-angle lenses and special sound equipment; he considered it "a glorified travelogue." The big project for his first year at RCA was a two-disc set called *The Serious Gershwin* (paired with *The Popular Gershwin*, which featured such pop figures as Eddie Fisher, Eartha Kitt, Hugo Winterhalter, and Dinah Shore). In nine sessions from 14 January through 6 April 1955, Gould recorded the Three Preludes, *An American in Paris*, *Rhapsody in Blue*, Concerto in F, the "Jazzbo Brown" piano solo cut from the opening of *Porgy and Bess*, and a Gould suite from the opera.

RCA's crack producers, Richard Mohr and John Pfeiffer, were in charge—men who, he told Whiteside in a letter written 10 July 1955, were "most sympathetic and intelligent and capable." (Several of the cuts were released by BMG in 1998, packaged with historic performances by Gershwin himself.) Gould was excited. Besides the Gershwin and other recordings, he was "'working up' a Symphony—and 'working out' my *Jekyll and Hyde Variations*, which I've been cooking for some time now. Also taking shape after a long period of gestation is a Piano Concerto and Violin Concerto." Once again he described his black depressions to Whiteside and the difficulty of pulling music out.

> The period of digging into one's self is always distressing—and the starting point is always nothing—and then discarding and rejecting—and one never knows whether you dredge up gold or muck. . . . The irony is that the one virtue—if it be that—that even unsympathetic people grant me—is a supposedly easy facility. Well—all I can say is that it is not an *easy* facility, and if it is—I would hate to function with any less!

Sure enough, when RCA released *The Serious Gershwin* in the fall of 1955, the Gould biographical note led off thus: "Morton Gould is one of the most facile of our present-day creative musical talents." He took to calling himself "Monsieur Facile."

The reviews were favorable, though neither Gould nor Gershwin was fully accepted. One critic (Toledo *Blade*, 28 November 1955) wrote, "Some of this music . . . is faintly preposterous, much of it is elemental and disturbing. . . . The performance savors of night club ostentation and the recording is not uniform."

Nevertheless, others put *The Serious Gershwin* among the best recordings of the year, although there was criticism of Gould's keyboard work. Irving Kolodin (*The Saturday Review*, 29 October 1955) found the orchestral works "persuasive," but admitted that, with Gould's tendency to accelerate toward climaxes, he was "not convinced he is the best pianist RCA could have found." The performances, as Kolodin indicated, are often driving and sometimes raucous—which is entirely appropriate; Gershwin's own renditions are even faster. Gould's solo work is deft and idiomatic, his sense of rhythm lively and acute, and the recording exceptionally clear. He'd been playing music just like it during Gershwin's lifetime and heard the composer at home, in concert, and at parties; this may be considered a "historically informed performance," if not fully "authentic."

RCA immediately allowed Gould to stretch further, with a recording of Rimsky-Korsakov's *Scheherazade* that took four sessions, starting in June 1955, while the Gershwin work was proceeding, and finishing in September. Gould then rerecorded many of his arrangements, including the Lecuona music collected under *Jungle Drums* and *More Jungle Drums*, and several sets of marches released as *Doubling in Brass* and *Brass and Percussion*. He would not stick with any one repertoire.

One of Gould's less known yet most successful compositions was written in 1955 for Benny Goodman: *Derivations* for clarinet and jazz combo. Goodman, a prickly and unpredictable man, was one of the few major musicians with whom Gould maintained a close friendship. Gould gave me a telling description of their first meeting: "I was not sure he would cotton to me, and he was not sure I would cotton to him . . . but we very quickly got the feeling that once we got past our respective outer facades, whatever protective devices we each used to keep ourselves invisible, we responded to each other."

Goodman had been the catalyst for one of the greatest American scores of the century, Copland's Clarinet Concerto, commissioned and written in 1947. But that was a standard work for orchestra. This time, the clarinetist wanted something for his band, and Gould responded with a fully notated piece that comes as close to sounding like improvised jazz as anything ever written.

The saxophonist Walter Levinsky, a member of Goodman's band, was struck by how easily composer and clarinetist worked together. "It was the first time I had run across a big-time composer who seemed to have no ego," Levinsky said. "He seemed to be open to suggestions for changes. There were times when Benny would say, 'Morton, I think we could do without those eight bars,' and Morton said, 'Fine, take it out.'"

The piece remained unavailable until April 1963, when Columbia called Gould back one last time. This was for an extraordinary disc called *Meeting at the Summit*, featuring Goodman in the Copland Concerto, Bernstein's *Prelude, Fugue and Riffs*, and Stravinsky's *Ebony Concerto*, both written for Woody Herman, and *Derivations*, with the composers conducting their own works.

Levinsky thought highly of the music. "Parts of it were jazz, more so than Milhaud's *Creation of the World* [*Creation du monde*], and definitely more jazzy than the Copland concerto. . . . *Derivations* had sections in it that sounded like Benny was playing ad lib, and it wasn't ad lib; it's a very good marriage of jazz and classic writing."

Thus, in the 1950s Gould was working around the disdain of the music world. The serialists were making their inroads into academia. The Americana school of Barber, Schuman, Harris, and Copland fell out of fashion, and so did concerns about writing music that an audience could assimilate without too much work. But Gould had his band music, guest-conducting (even if mostly at pops and patriotic programs), a home at RCA, and, until Bernstein took over, the consistent support of Mitropoulos.

CHAPTER 17

Great Neck, Long Island

★ ★ ★ ★

LATE IN 1952, Morton and Shirley Gould and their three children moved from Forest Hills to a large old brick house at 327 Melbourne Road in the Village of Russell Gardens, Great Neck. Barely five miles from Forest Hills, it was a change of incalculable significance. From the careful, almost penurious existence of a two-bedroom apartment in Queens, they had arrived in an affluent, thriving suburb.

The Great Neck peninsula, just east of the New York City line, is a patchwork of middle and upper-middle-class communities, with luxurious homes abutting the remains of Long Island's Gold Coast estates. (Kings Point, on the northern tip, was the model for F. Scott Fitzgerald's West Egg, home of Jay Gatsby's unattainable Daisy.)

The Goulds had been looking for a home for some time. Morton and James found a "gorgeous" house in Redding, Connecticut, Morton recalled in May 1995. "Shirley said to me, 'Oh no, you don't. You're not putting me up with the kids in Redding and I'm going to get a call from you every other night, "Honey, you know, it's too far for me to come home tonight, I'll have to stay over." You're not exiling me!' "

She had met Morton at the Warwick; she knew how he worked.

Eventually the couple focused on Long Island, near where he was born and felt most comfortable. Their criteria were education and community: "I wanted my kids to have the chance to meet all kinds of different religions, all kinds of different colors," he said. Gould also wanted a place with easy access to the city: "Although I was born and raised on Long Island, I was basically in attitude a New Yorker."

Morton was thirty-nine, and this was the farthest he had ever lived from his parents. He took a few steps into the community, attending village board meetings, going to Great Neck Symphony concerts, giving a talk at the library. "It was a nice feeling," he said. "But I've always had to be a little careful about how active I get. If you do things, you become vulnerable to every organization that comes around." The Goulds joined Temple Beth El, but they were not involved beyond sending their children to the Hebrew School to make sure they became bar-mitzvah.

This life was new to Morton, but it brought Shirley back to something resembling her native habitat, and she turned to homemaking with vigor and imagination. She redesigned and redecorated the house, knocked out walls, expanded rooms, and turned the third-floor attic into a composer's paradise, light and airy with large windows, plenty of shelves, and two large drafting tables for writing. Morton would no longer have to work in the foyer with children underfoot. They even got his Steinway into the studio, though not without trouble. The third-floor stairway was so narrow the instrument got stuck. Finally, with a lot of commotion, a window was widened and the piano hoisted in from outside.

The house was Shirley's domain; now she could wrest Morton from his father and begin to live the way Mrs. Morton Gould should. Shirley even got Morton to learn to drive. And there was no more worry about outshining the neighbors. In Great Neck, if you had it, you flaunted it, and if you didn't, you pretended you did. "In Forest Hills, she was being thrifty and showing what a good wife she was," said Matty Gould. "It was not 'til they moved to Great Neck that it changed. I think there she found people who were living in a style that was different from the way they were living. Morton's income was better, and she could do more."

Shirley wanted her children to live a comfortable life. She wanted summer camp, sports, music lessons, the best colleges, professional careers. Morton had no conception of this life. His mind had never left the Depression, and he watched every penny. Nor did it matter how his children did in school; he might envy others their educational backgrounds, but he also carried his childhood contempt for the classroom. So Shirley ran the house and raised the family. "She was a very devoted mother," said Norma Perlman, who moved to nearby Roslyn at the same time with her husband Eli.

Morton, with his reputation as a physical incompetent as well as his intense work schedule, had no objection. "When we moved to Great Neck," said Eric, who was nearly eight at the time, "she would be changing the storm windows—my father couldn't do anything. It was laughable." Morton was uninvolved in child-rearing. "He would just kind of sit there," Eric said. "The one thing we knew from my father was you knew you had his unconditional love. . . . All he was really concerned about is that we were happy."

That was not enough for Shirley. "My mother would push, push, push, push," explained Eric, who attended Columbia University and New York University Medical School. "[She] was a vivacious, energetic, pushy person. You had to do well; you were the best." "My mother was ambitious," agreed David, who went to Princeton and Harvard Law. "She knew what she wanted. My father, had I decided at the age of fourteen to become a ditch-digger, he would have been just as happy." Shirley took the children to museums and shows, opened their eyes, encouraged them to make something of themselves. "She was the one who expanded the horizons of the kids," said Perlman. "That was her job."

Shirley was also determined to help Morton. An excellent cook, she threw extravagant formal dinners attended by friends and colleagues ranging from Schuman, Goodman, Henderson, Miller, and Balanchine to Irene Selznick, financier Martin Segal, Bill Bernbach (of the Doyle Dane Bernbach advertising agency), Whitney Young (of the Urban League), and Bob Bernstein and Arthur Krim (of United Artists). "She made the dinner parties, and she had the people there," Eric said in 1995. "My father's concept of networking is nonexistent. He would be content to sit at home and just see his family."

Shirley and Morton were a loving couple. "I have fond memories of my early childhood," said Abby Gould Burton, "them being warm together, loving, holding hands, he putting his arms around her, she sitting on the couch next to him. It was not just him going to her, but she going to him, fixing his hair and shirt, making sure we all got in the car to the station to meet him when he came from the city. She loved being Mrs. Morton Gould, and used [the name] all the time."

Only Abby was interested in her father's music. Both boys took instrument lessons—Eric on clarinet, David on trumpet—but neither showed talent or interest. Abby climbed up to his studio with a coloring book and colored quietly or listened. "He would play a piece for me, and say, 'What do you think of this, Abs?' . . . We would play his new records, we would open up the boxes together to see his new album covers, and whenever he had people visiting him I would bring cake up to them."

"He had two drafting tables, face to face. The left side was his business side . . . and the right side is where he did his music. And whenever he would score a piece, he would say to me . . . 'Okay, I'm getting ready to orchestrate this. Do you want to look at this?' He would show me the blank paper—'See how big this is? How many instruments?' Then he would show me, two days later, 'This is what I've done; these are the trumpets.'"

The children learned to recognize his moods. There was the misery when he had just begun and the notes wouldn't come. Every time Gould started a project, he would say, "I can't write any more, I've hit a dead end, I'm finished." It was a standard thing, Eric recounted: "I know, dad, you're dried up, that's it!" It frightened Abby when she was young: "What's going to happen if he does dry up? Poor Daddy. How's he going to write?" But eventually, Gould's bleak moments became a source of grim humor. As Abby recalled, "When he said to me, 'I'm too old for this,' I would say, 'Excuse me, when I was five you were saying this, so if you think I take this seriously—." Even when Morton wasn't working, they knew that at any moment he might tune out entirely. His eyes would go distant, the notebook would come out of his pocket, and he would begin sketching.

Shirley was not interested in Morton's music. He asked her to travel with him, repeatedly, but she rarely did. She seemed more involved with being the wife of a famous man than in what he did. In the early years, their main source of friction was money. Morton was doing well financially, but Shirley had to fight for every penny. He was generous to his parents; they traveled to Florida every winter while his own family, as Shirley bitterly pointed out, never took vacations.

"As I was growing up," said Eric, "every dollar you would have to justify, every time. If I bought a model airplane for a dollar, he would say, 'Eric, are you sure you are going to build it, to use it, to love it?' Everything had to be blood to get anything from him. And he did that to my mother incessantly. For his parents he would let go a lot of money, but for her, everything was spit blood."

Initially Shirley used Morton's temper as a disciplining tool. "He would fume," Eric said. "He would start to scream and get red. His eyes would bulge and everything, he would scream and scream and scream and come face to face with you. But he never would hit you or anything like that. He had a terrible, terrible temper. We were a little afraid of him." But Morton cooled down quickly and begged for forgiveness. "So after a number of years of this, you'd realize these tempers were harmless, and you dealt with them."

The battles over the purse were different. Eric felt the tension all the time. "I didn't understand all the arguing," he said. "He was very tough on her, and I remember screaming at him to stop. . . . Every time she would spend money—the money issue would come up every day. He was a tyrant. . . . I definitely did not feel like my parents had a loving relationship growing up," he said. "But she was happy, she was genuinely happy."

Another factor was the political pressure, which reached its peak soon after their arrival in Great Neck. After years during which he was observed and chivvied by investigators from the House Committee on Un-American Activities, Gould finally became the subject of a probe by the Federal Bureau of Investigation, which opened a file on him in December 1954. The FBI found nothing: the field agents' request to interview him was denied, and on 5 June 1955, the investigation having "failed to indicate that Gould was ever a member of the CP" and having determined that he had not been active in "CP fronts" for the previous three years, the case was closed.

Gould had stood his ground—refusing, for example, to make an under-the-table payment to get his name removed from the blacklists and indicating that he would not be a cooperative witness if called before Congress. But he also had changed his public focus to support of the fledgling state of Israel. On 7 June 1952, he had led members of the Philharmonic and a cast including Benny Goodman, Robert Merrill, and Roberta Peters in a program of "Music Under the Stars" at Ebbetts Field to benefit the American Fund for Israel Institutions. Three years later, at Madison Square Garden 15 and 19 December 1955, he was featured in the fifth annual Chanukah Festival for Israel, along with Edward G. Robinson, Mischa Elman, Kim Hunter, Jarmila Novotná, Jan Peerce, and the Symphony of the Air.

The years of uncertainty left Gould permanently scarred. In the turbulent 1960s, when his children became activists, he was terrified lest they sign the wrong documents and get into permanent trouble. "The McCarthy thing had a huge impact on my father," Eric asserted. "He was a very fiery young guy. But after that I did not see him wanting to put himself out there."

"When I was in college, from 1968 to 1972 at the Rhode Island School of Design," said Abby, "my father was petrified I was going to sign something."

"I would always joke about how my dad wouldn't sign things," said David, who became involved in both Democratic and Republican politics. "I would say, 'Dad, this is my first-grade report card. I can't get into school unless you sign this. The Great Neck School Board is not a Communist front, I swear to God.' . . . He always felt guilty about it, as if he did something wrong. And he never would talk about it."

In the mid-1950s, though, the Goulds appeared to be not only normal but luckier than most, with a famous, well-to-do father, an aggressive, intelligent, concerned mother, and four bright children flourishing in their new suburban home.

"Went to Morton's to spend the night," wrote Whiteside on 17 April 1953. "There is not much furniture but there are good beds. The children are delightful. Abby is full of irresistible charm and the boys are wonderful. The house is lovely and Shirley has done a wonderful job with color. It is all lovely."

Things at home may have seemed fine, but the world of music was still changing, threatening Morton's position again. In 1956, Elvis Presley began recording for RCA. His first release, "Heartbreak Hotel," was a No. 1 hit, and then they just kept coming. It was the start of the rock'n'roll revolution: for singer-songwriters, for home-grown bands of guitar, sax, and drums, for music closer to its black roots than the deracinated forms of the previous decades. The musicians and composers of the 1930s and 1940s were about to become very old-fashioned indeed.

If Gould was accustomed to disdain in the concert hall, at least he'd been able to earn his bread with those rich orchestral arrangements. But although the Baby Boom had not yet been named, the forces it represented—postwar fearlessness, rebellion, and energy linked to lots of spending money in the pockets of teenagers—were cracking the smooth surface of pop. Gould was very prominently on that surface.

"Morton and I spent hours talking about it, wondering what we would do," Skitch Henderson recalled. "I envied him because he was a composer of significance and I was in the plastic music factory. He was worried because of what was happening to the music profession. Rock and roll had a devastating effect on all types of music."

But the full effect of this sea change in American popular music would not be felt for years. Meanwhile, Gould did his work, and the people around him continued trying to advance his concert music. In 1954 Virgil Thomson retired as chief critic of the *Herald Tribune*. He had been one of Gould's most powerful tormentors, but now he wanted to conduct. He surprised Gould by asking to use *Spirituals*.

Gould knew Thomson primarily by his writing and his reputation among musicians. "I was not too impressed with him as a conductor, and I had heard all sorts of stories from some of my colleagues, who can be very cruel, about his high-pitched voice and how he got mad at them and stamped his feet." The phone rang, and a voice said, "Morton? This is Virgil." Gould repeated, "Virgil?" "Yes, Virgil Thomson." ("I wasn't that close to him that when he said 'Virgil' I would know who he was," Gould explained in 1995.) Thomson explained his plans and asked for *Spirituals* as a closing piece. "I didn't react. He said, 'Did I say something wrong?' I said, 'No no no.' Because in one second what went through my mind were the bad reviews he gave my *Spirituals for Orchestra*. He said, 'You sound as if you don't like them.' My first impulse was to say, 'You son of a bitch, you want to do my *Spirituals for Orchestra* to close a program?'"

Thomson's conducting career was short and unhappy, and he did not conduct *Spirituals*; it's easy to believe that Morton's distaste for him was apparent. Gould communicated and miscommunicated. There were friends and alliances in music, and he was not part of many of them. Although he knew, worked with, and respected the many homosexuals in the field (Mitropoulos, his champion, was gay, as were Copland, Barber, Thomson, Diamond, Ned Rorem, and many others, including the bisexual Bernstein), he did not socialize with them. According to Anthony Tommasini in *Composer on the Aisle*, his thorough and well-balanced biography of Thomson, gay men were the most active networkers. An "active networker" was the last thing Morton Gould was—at least, not in New York.

On the other hand, he stayed in close touch with the secondary orchestras. Almost from its founding in the mid-1940s, Gould paid attention to the American Symphony Orchestra League, initially devoted to mid-level and regional ensembles. Roger Hall, in the late 1940s general manager of the orchestras of Fort Wayne, Indiana, and Erie, Pennsylvania, knew Gould as "a fixture" at ASOL gatherings. "Morton, who was very shrewd about things of that kind, attended those league conventions," Hall said. "There he was in the midst of hundreds of orchestras which might play his works." It paid off in performances among smaller orchestras—but not the ones he yearned for. "He made it his business to know the conductors and the managers of orchestras around the country, not only the majors," said Hall. But Gould did not campaign for himself. "He wanted to keep up with what was going on in the symphonic field," Hall said, "but he did not push his music in the sense of beating everyone to death to do his works."

"Morton wasn't aggressive," said Sophia Rosoff, a Manhattan piano teacher who studied with Whiteside and eventually headed the Abby Whiteside Foundation. "Morton wasn't a big party man. Lenny was all over the place—you couldn't not be aware of him. And Virgil Thomson was all over the place."

"He didn't pander," said Silas Edman, a one-time Philharmonic official who was later executive director of the Chicago Symphony. "He didn't go out and campaign. Copland did. But he didn't pay court to the Bernsteins or any of the other conductors who might have been playing his music. . . . Morton was who he was, and you took him or left him. He was an active participant—in small parties. He had that acerbic, kinky sense of humor, and was enormously entertaining. . . . But if you watched, there was a distinct difference in the way Morton would behave in a large group. He would head for a corner."

Often, his allies did not have the clout of others. In 1949, for instance, Norman Corwin produced a United Nations concert celebrating the signing of the Universal Declaration of Human Rights, with music to be performed by the Boston Symphony. Corwin recommended that Gould, with whom he'd worked on radio and who had sponsored his membership in ASCAP, write music to open the program, but Koussevitzky delegated the musical activities to Bernstein. Corwin told Gould, in a letter in July 1992, that "LB opted for his pal Copland, who wrote a fanfare [*Preamble for a Solemn Occasion*, premiered 10 December 1949]."

There was also the personal rivalry, especially from Bernstein, an increasingly important factor in the cultural life of New York and the nation. "I used to drive Bernstein nuts about playing *Spirituals*," David Diamond said. "He said, 'It's cheap.' I would say that Lenny could be very jealous about anybody who had great facility and was extremely popular with audiences. . . . With me, he would say he's a second-rater. He himself was not very sure about his own music, which would make him more severe about somebody who was having great success with audiences."

"Rightly or wrongly, Bernstein considered him a rival, and did not do any of his music," said Robert Sherman, of the classical music station WQXR and a man who grew up in New York music. Other composers agreed with Bernstein's estimation. "I was bewildered by Copland's reaction," Diamond said. "I would say, 'Morton has a lot of technique.' Copland would say, 'He knows nothing about counterpoint, he just makes arrangements.'" Even William Schuman, a friend, told Martin Segal that Gould was just a second-rater.

In an unwelcome way, Gould *was* an heir to Gershwin. "That's exactly what Gershwin ran into," said Sherman. "When he had a classical piece, everyone said, 'What kind of pretentiousness is this?' They didn't take him seriously, as a pop composer. The popular people wondered what the hell he was doing trying to write classical."

Even a man such as Sherman, the son of pianist and pedagogue Nadia Reisenberg and himself very well educated musically, had no sense of Gould in the 1950s as anything other than a composer of light music. "I thought of him as *American Salute*, a real Americana composer, the way you might think of John Williams today," Sherman said. "He was someone who wrote for the public taste. I did not know of the pieces not written for the public taste." Even at WQXR, Gould's music was filed under "pops and light classics."

Morton talked occasionally about music with Whiteside, though he apologized for how little he did say ("It is more and more difficult to 'discuss' my work—all my discussions and theories will be in whatever I actually compose," he wrote on 30 July 1950). On 13 January 1954 Gould sent her a lengthy discussion of his major works. "What I think is apparent is that, despite superficial deviations and transient influences, basically I've been following a very specific pattern right along, regardless of reactions critical or otherwise. . . . I feel a great deal of my problems have been those of functioning in a pattern particular to me—for good or for bad—but not being 'like' the accepted patterns or formulas." He had done his own listening and come to some conclusions:

> I would say that disconcerting as some of my trends might be to my friends at times, over a stretch of years I do have a consistency in approach and development. I was pleasantly surprised at some of the things I was able to express, and in complicated forms. . . . At its best I think my work has a kind of vital exuberance and "go"—and a lyrical quality. Its shortcomings are mainly in extended movements—and in the two extremes of being aware of what people like Joe [Prostakoff] will say—or his exact opposites.

As far as the general reaction to his music was concerned, Gould felt it was "obscured or beclouded by superficial considerations—or too close an association with some of my basic source materials, not to mention my 'practical' activities."

In August 1954, a depressed Gould wrote Whiteside again: "I find it so difficult to fulfill myself in a serious creative way. To be sure that every note is honest and necessary—to combine feeling and thinking—Fantasy and Discipline—lineal movement and harmonic warmth—these make for aggravating quicksands. It is as easy to compromise with a fugue as with a 'popular' melody."

Two summers later, Whiteside's health had deteriorated, and when she left for Menlo Park, California, friends who saw her off were worried. Gould wrote afterward: "You realize, of course—that your leaving New York is not recognized as an accomplished fact—even by those of us who saw you off at the train. . . . You have left a tremendous void."

In August 1956 he listed what he was working on (the popular recordings were never part of the conversation): "The *Jekyll and Hyde Variations* for Mitropoulos—the Full Evening Ballet with Balanchine—and a special musical-dramatic setting of the Declaration of Independence. This latter will be premiered at the inaugural concert in Washington, D.C., in January."

He finished the *Jekyll and Hyde Variations* for orchestra in early October: "This is a major effort and my most complex to date . . . I would not attempt to evaluate it—it either is or 'ain't'—but I do know that there is very little compromise in it—and so far I feel good and fulfilled over its completion."

Two months later, Whiteside had a heart attack and was hospitalized in Redwood City. Morton wrote immediately, in a letter postmarked 4 December 1956. The writing is crisp, the ink dark, as if he had been pressing down hard: "How upset we all are by your upset. And how I wish I could have hopped the next plane to be with you. . . . Of course, you must recover and get well immediately—for all our selfish sakes."

Abby Whiteside died on Morton's forty-third birthday, 10 December 1956, at the age of seventy-five. Gould was now without his artistic conscience, mentor, and guide. Except for the quiet support of his brother Walter and a few friends such as Joseph Prostakoff, Gould was on his own, trying to balance between art and commerce.

CHAPTER 18

Fading Out

★ ★ ★ ★

BY 1956 THE WORD must have been circulating that Morton Gould was no longer a danger to the republic (if he ever had been), because he was commissioned by NBC's Washington, D.C., stations, WRC and WRC-TV, to write a piece for President Dwight D. Eisenhower's second inauguration, to be performed by the National Symphony under Howard Mitchell at Constitution Hall on 20 January 1957.

There was no objection or complaint, as had been raised just four years before about Copland's *A Lincoln Portrait* at the first inaugural. Gould worked on the score during the summer and fall. The program for the concert was high middle-American: Lily Pons sang "Caro Nome," violinist Ivry Gitlis played Saint-Saëns's *Introduction and Rondo Capriccioso*, then came Gould's *Declaration*, with a spoken chorus by the Singing Sergeants of the United States Air Force. After intermission, there were appearances by Fred Waring and his Pennsylvanians, Ethel Merman, and Raymond Massey, and the evening ended with "The Battle Hymn of the Republic." If anything would set a cultural critic's teeth on edge, this blend of familiar classics and earnest schmaltz was it.

For *Declaration*, Gould concocted a weighty score that featured narration of events leading up to the Declaration of Independence and portions of the document itself. He extracted an interesting suite of the purely instrumental music, which Mitchell recorded in 1958 for RCA. It opens with "Liberty Bell," a prelude in the form of a passacaglia, full of bell-ringing and excitement yet using a harmonic structure that sounds Asian. "Midnight Ride" is a scherzo on Paul

Revere that takes its rhythmic cue from the "Battle on the Ice" of Prokofiev's *Alexander Nevsky*, with more delicacy, as befitting a still night. "Concord Bridge" is a memorial rather than battle music; "Summer '76" is lyrical and melancholy, a serenade for solo violin, viola, and cello against strings and woodwinds. The finale, "Celebration," is a loud, bell-ringing chorale and fugue to commemorate the creation of the new nation. There's little in the music to suggest that its composer specialized in clever orchestral arrangements of Broadway ballads and marches, nor a trace of the swinging Americana of the symphonettes.

On 2 February 1957, Gould received a letter from Vice President Richard Nixon (who had gotten his start as a postwar Red-baiter in California), saying how much he enjoyed *Declaration*. Obviously, Morton was cleared. But the piece did not go far. Mitchell played it at Carnegie Hall the next month; Skitch Henderson played it badly a few times with an orchestra he was trying to form: "I didn't have an orchestra that could play his music at that time."

But Gould was moving as firmly as he could away from the sound that made him famous. His next important score was the direct response to a challenge from Mitropoulos, who had told him one day over lunch in the early 1950s, "Enough laughing. No, you must be serious." Gould explained, in an interview on the subject in 1995: "My music was basically happy, and he felt that I should explore something more complex. We were talking about the different dogmas in music. This was a period where really, as I recall, unless you wrote serial music you were not taken seriously."

Gould said he responded to Mitropoulos's goading with *Jekyll and Hyde Variations*, exploring the contradictions within a personality. The simple-sounding theme reversed itself in the middle, so the second half was the first half played backward. "On the surface, I am a very peaceful person," Gould said, "but inside I am a very turbulent one. . . . I was also thinking about Mitropoulos, who in a way was a Jekyll and Hyde, part priest and part performer. He made no secret of his sexual orientation; he was trying to wrestle with his own erotic desires and yet maintain the discipline he needed."

Gould used a serial pattern and its modules "to express a conflict between the malignant and the benign," between love and murder. He used tone rows, but not in the purest sense—he was willing to repeat them, to create lyrical passages, "to take the edge off." The process was difficult: "There were particularly demanding problems. I could not just settle for an effect, it had to be in the context of this kind of discipline."

He worked on *Jekyll and Hyde* longer than almost anything other than *Desire Under the Elms* or the Balanchine ballet. He considered it one of his most important works, "in a way an autobiographical piece. If people say, 'What reflects Morton Gould the most?' they would pick the more obvious pieces, *American Salute* and so forth. Yet I think *this* expresses me," he said.

Mitropoulos was pleased with the result, and the New York Philharmonic played it twice, at Carnegie Hall, on 2 and 3 February 1957. "He gave it a wonderful performance," Gould said. "It was right up his alley, using not only a system he admired, that he had a tremendous affinity for, but the off-the-wall stuff was emotionally part of his chemistry." But Taubman's missile against Mitropoulos had exploded the previous spring, and since then the critics had kept up a steady barrage. In September 1956, Judson had been ousted, and in October the board announced that Bernstein would "share the direction of the orchestra" beginning in the 1957–58 season. It was expected that the Greek would soon give way to the American.

It was too late for Gould and Mitropoulos. The last thing the New York musical establishment wanted in 1957 was music exploring their personalities. Irving Kolodin (*The Saturday Review*, 12 February 1957) was condescending. He acknowledged that Gould "has made a serious effort to write a serious piece. . . . Presumably Gould would let us know that he is not incessantly brash and flippant, or always as light-hearted as his best-known pieces suggest . . . . Gould was undertaking a Jekyll and Hyde transformation of himself." He complained that the theme was "austere" and smirked that "one was not quite sure whether Gould, with his sleight of hand, was pulling a rabbit out of a hat, snatching a handkerchief from a sleeve, or making musical wine from tonal water." Morton could do no right; in his hands, even dodecaphonism was just a gimmick.

And that was almost the end. Mitropoulos never played it again. He stepped down on 19 November 1957, and Bernstein became sole music director. Mitropoulos was scheduled to conduct in 1960–61, including yet another new Gould, but his final appearance with the

Philharmonic was a stupendous performance of Mahler's Ninth Symphony on 24 January 1960. On 2 November, he collapsed and died of a heart attack while rehearsing Mahler's Third at La Scala.

The depth and complexity of *Jekyll and Hyde* continually surprised listeners. On 23 March 1961, Gould led it with the Atlanta Symphony, and Chappell White (*Journal-Constitution*) described it as "probably not the kind of music his reputation had led us to expect." He concluded that the piece was so complex, a single listening was not enough for "sure judgment."

At that time, almost no one heard Gould clearly. If they had, they might have realized that this was an unusual and worthy piece, not only for the composer but in the context of twentieth-century American music. Starting with the bitter theme, it is a portrait of roiling complexity. Not even the most tranquil moments are entirely free; pain and discomfort are just beneath the surface, which heaves like an oily sea and sometimes explodes with the force of repressed anxiety. No one saw fit to remark that a composer derided for the facility of his popular recordings had chosen here to write music that groaned with ugliness. Gould, trying to escape the gilded cage, had created something disturbing, and he couldn't find anyone to pay attention.

It seemed as if no one was hearing Gould at all. Carlos Moseley, with his long-standing Bernstein connection, joined the orchestra as press director in 1955, became associate managing director in 1959, managing director in 1961, and eventually president in 1970. He was at the Philharmonic during the last two years of Mitropoulos's time, yet he said of Gould, "I don't associate him and the Philharmonic—the question of performing his music never came up." Of *Jekyll and Hyde*, Moseley said, "I know the title."

Yet that was the period when Gould was making his most strenuous effort to break free of the curse of popularity. Producer Scott thought it was a mistake. "His greatest talent, his greatest achievements—in my opinion, not his—were his fantastic ability to arrange our great American heritage, Cole Porter, Richard Rodgers, Jerome Kern. . . . He gave that up because he didn't want to do that—he wanted to be a serious composer, a grim composer."

"I walked away from the whole pop idea," Gould said in 1986. "Blacklist or not, I had all kinds of offers from orchestras to do pops concerts. . . . I didn't want to keep that image. . . . I was ashamed, I was self-conscious about it, I was embarrassed about it." Gould was trying to get serious just when his champion left the Philharmonic in disgrace. From then on, as Mitropoulos predicted, Morton Gould slowly disappeared from the orchestra he thought he would be involved with for life.

Seven years after Mitropoulos's death, Harold Schonberg devoted only two paragraphs to him in *The Great Conductors*. When it came to Gould, the Philharmonic virtually forgot him. As Moseley put it, "Morton, whom I admired as a person, was a very skilled writer of lighter stuff. . . . Nobody ever turned down anything proposed by Morton Gould; it was just not proposed by whoever was going to be conducting."

The loss of his champion hurt Gould in just the place he wanted to be, a composer taken seriously by the New York Philharmonic, but his family did not realize this. Shirley's vision focused on fame and fortune, not on something as tenuous as artistic validity. She and the children were more like James Gould, who wanted to keep his son in the public eye, than Walter, who wanted to help him find his own way.

By the late 1950s, home life became more difficult. The dinner-guest lists changed as Shirley turned her attention from Morton's musical companions toward friends with power elsewhere. William and Frankie Schuman, who had been close friends (Bill and Morton shared the same sense of humor) were invited less frequently, and finally not at all. Shirley felt, the children said, that Schuman could have done more for Gould, and she was not going to socialize with someone who wouldn't advance his career. Mitch Miller too was no longer invited. Mitch and Shirley did not get along. "She was a ball-breaker," he said. "She was a compulsive housekeeper. When you'd get up, she'd start plumping the pillows."

By the early 1960s, when the signs of Gould's fall could not be ignored, the gatherings took on a business and political atmosphere. "It wasn't Daddy's musical people as much any more," Abby Gould Burton said. He wrote a substantial amount of concert music, but where once a new Gould would have been played by the orchestras of New York, Pittsburgh, Cleveland, and Chicago, his scores now were premiered by smaller, less important ensembles. After a while, Skitch Henderson realized, "Morton was not getting performances any more. He was rushing all over the country writing for every tin-town philharmonic to get played, when he used to get played in New York."

But Gould was still a mainstay of RCA's record clubs. He wrote another score for a *Cinerama* movie, *Windjammer*, and extracted a suite far more satisfactory than from *Cinerama Holiday*. In January 1959 he recorded Tchaikovsky's *1812 Overture* and Ravel's *Bolero* at RCA's Manhattan Center. That year, Stanley Adams persuaded Gould to join the board of ASCAP, of which he'd been a member since 1936. He had suffered with the rest of the industry when ASCAP went on strike against radio in the early 1940s. He knew it was a powerful, select organization comprising the most important composers for Broadway, Hollywood, and the Hit Parade. ASCAP was so powerful that the broadcasters had formed a rival organization, Broadcast Music International or BMI, and the federal government had taken ASCAP to court and forced it to accept regulatory measures, including loosening membership requirements.

Until 1959 most of the younger membership saw ASCAP as "a small, select society," with the atmosphere of a private club, Gould recalled in 1986. Adams was elected "as a sort of Young Turk; one of the things he wanted to do was to give the board a twentieth-century look, if that were possible." The board comprised twelve writers and twelve publishers, of which three each came from the concert field. This was out of proportion to revenue from classical music, but it was felt that concert music needed and deserved particular support.

Adams lived in Great Neck, and when Gould moved there Adams began urging him to run. "I hardly knew Stanley," Gould said. "The last thing on my mind . . . was to be on the board of ASCAP. . . . I didn't think of it, any more than I thought of being a surgeon or electrician." But Adams argued that he wanted to turn the society around. "Finally he said, 'At least let me put your name on the ballot—you probably won't be voted in, but at least it will be a good gesture.'"

Voting at ASCAP is not democratic; it's more like one dollar, one vote. The more writers earn, the more votes they have, so Berlin and Porter had far more power than new composers with their first hit. The top vote-getters often stay on the board for decades. "To my amazement and shock," Gould said in 1986, "I got a telegram congratulating me for having been elected to the board. And I've been on it ever since." For once, Gould's multiple careers stood him in good stead: "To these people I represented Carnegie Hall, although to Carnegie Hall I represented Tin Pan Alley. I always had enough crossover so that enough people knew me and liked me. One group looked at me as being long-hair, and the other saw me as short-hair. And I had not made enemies."

He joined the board in April 1959, and Adams immediately put him on the symphony concert committee (he soon became chairman, and remained there until elected president). Board members have included Copland, Creston, Thomson, Jacob Druckman, and other composers known in the concert world, but Gould was a constant, always the top classical vote-getter, and one of the top two or three overall. He understood the problems of writers, performers, and publishers as well as anyone else. And the personality that did not help in public was just the right blend of sapience and smoothness to make him a calming, effective presence.

But when Gould was on stages larger than ASCAP, he did not fare so well. For a few days in February 1958, he was in the center of a storm about the excesses of master builder Robert Moses, for decades one of New York's most powerful men. One of Moses's most cherished projects had been to harness the energy of Niagara Falls and the rapids of the St. Lawrence River for electricity. Immense structures were built at Niagara and Massena, on the Canadian border, for $600 million. Moses had a grand idea for the opening of the Robert Moses Power Dam at Massena on 5 September 1958: he commissioned paintings by Thomas Hart Benton and a score by Morton Gould (for $5000 plus expenses) to be performed atop the dam straddling the border. Gould told *The New York Post*, "I had never been under a dam, let alone on top of one. Finally, I decided the piece should be for a symphonic band, not an orchestra, because strings tend to get dissipated in the open."

The result was *Saint Lawrence Suite*, a ten-minute work in four movements that got its world premiere with the composer leading the Royal Canadian Ordnance Corps band. "I stood right on the boundary line," Gould told the *Herald Tribune*. "I had half the band in Canada, half in the United States. Two solo trumpets, one on either side of the border, played connecting interludes."

But these New York City newspapers didn't write about the occasion when it occurred. They got on the story five months later, in February 1959, after upstate legislators began attacking what they considered a waste of taxpayers' money. The suite had become a scandal. Moses himself wrote a blistering letter to the Albany, New York, *Knickerbocker News* in which he declared the criticism "too absurd for extended comment." He refused to apologize. "In all civilized countries," he said, "government, in one form or another, recognizes the arts. No doubt there will always be critics who will regard any recognition of the arts as extravagant."

It was a small skirmish in Moses's battles, and Gould was bemused—though he relished the commission. RCA released *Saint Lawrence Suite* in *Doubling in Brass*, along with some Sousa, and more Gould. The politics didn't hinge on the composer's own patriotism, which was never questioned.

On 7 February 1965, Alan Rich in *New York*, the new Sunday magazine of the *Herald Tribune*, wrote about serious and popular music, and musical snobbery. "Today's audiences," he said, "are terribly concerned with . . . keeping the musical repertory segregated on one side or the other. . . . There is nothing you can say that will kill a Broadway show faster than to call it an opera. You cannot break a serious composer's heart faster than by telling him that he is popular with the masses." Among contemporary composers, Rich focused on Gould:

> Mr. Gould, in case you think of him merely as a clever conductor and reorchestrator of popular ballads, has written a number of large-scale symphonic works which use a fairly popular and uncomplicated melodic style, and which are graciously and shrewdly aimed toward making their point and moving on. Current taste, however, tends to relegate Mr. Gould to a place on the far side of the wall, or at best to a sort of no-man's-land on top of the wall itself.

He concluded with a plea for its demolition, "to allow the kind of free crossfeeding between serious and popular music that went on before it was built." But Rich's was a lonely voice at the time, when the concert life of the city was dominated by Bernstein at the Philharmonic and Harold Schonberg at *The New York Times*.

For a few years at the beginning of the 1960s, Gould seemed to maintain his momentum. Even with Bernstein officially in charge, there was one last significant Gould during the Philharmonic's 1960–61 subscription season: *Dialogues* for piano and string orchestra, with the composer at the keyboard. Mitropoulos was to have presented it, but he died before he could return to New York, and *Dialogues* was conducted by Paul Paray on 12, 13, and 14 January 1961. It would be twenty years before a Gould composition was heard again on a Philharmonic subscription program.

He did not disappear immediately. Once the Philharmonic moved to its new home at Lincoln Center, the management looked for ways to keep busy in the summer. Kostelanetz was asked to create a series of programs modeled on the London Proms, with the aim of giving New York good "off-season" music. Kostelanetz led four of the first eight programs, in May and June 1963. There were two guest conductors: André Previn, just beginning his own long passage away from Hollywood, and Gould.

The opening program shows what was intended. It was "An American Gala," and Kostelanetz led everything from Copland's *A Lincoln Portrait*, narrated by Carl Sandberg, through Schuman's *New England Triptych* to a suite from Kern's *Show Boat*. Other Kostelanetz programs had themes such as "Vienna Night," with soprano Beverly Sills, and "Music of Tchaikovsky," narrated by Ogden Nash. Previn led two programs, including "A Previn Evening" of Prokofiev, Mendelssohn, and Copland, and a setting of *West Side Story* for jazz trio.

Gould closed out the first season with "Fiesta" (19–21 June 1963), Spanish and Hispanic music featuring the Ballet Español Ximenez-Vargas and including *Latin American Symphonette*; and "The Dance" (22–23 June 1963), a clever exploration of music for and about dance, beginning with Menotti's overture to *Amelia Goes to the Ball* and including Copland's *Dance Symphony* and Gould's *Tap Dance Concerto*.

Kostelanetz, in his memoirs, recalled the Proms fondly—especially that opening "American Gala"; he talked of the people involved, including Sills, producer Roger Englander, Nash, Previn, "and the two final concerts included dancers Danny Daniels and Royes Fernandez" (*Echoes: Memoirs of André Kostelanetz*, p. 222). Somehow, he forgot to mention that Gould conducted those two final concerts, or that he had written Daniels's piece. Gould's name appears nowhere in the story of Kostelanetz' life, neither as colleague nor rival. It's a striking omission, but understandable if Kostelanetz considered the younger man a rival and competitor—if he, too, like Bernstein, felt that he and Gould "hoed the same patch."

Previn, who understood from personal experience how difficult it is to earn respectability after the "taint" of commercialism, came to know, respect, and admire Gould. He had no firsthand knowledge of the Kostelanetz memoir, but when told of it during a 1995 interview immediately responded, "That's not an oversight."

There is an important difference among musicians between a person who makes his own arrangements, as Gould did, and one who hires others to do it for him, as Kostelanetz did, explained Previn:

> When someone says, "Here's the Kostelanetz arrangement of 'Tea for Two,'" you always wonder who of the following twelve people wrote the arrangement. And when they said, "Here's Morton Gould playing his arrangement," you knew he'd done it. And that's a major, major difference. Because if a guy says "This is my work," and it is but it isn't, that's never popular with the lead players.

But the Philharmonic was only one place and Gould looked elsewhere. He succeeded fairly well, developing a relationship with the Chicago Symphony that resulted in several important recordings and his only Grammy award. The television networks, more relaxed by the end of the Eisenhower years, offered him work for documentaries. In 1960, Gould wrote soundtracks for NBC's *The Secret of Freedom* and CBS's *The Turn of the Century*; and in 1963, there was *Verdun*, a part of the CBS documentary series *The Twentieth Century*, which was the forerunner of Gould's most extensive television writing. The biggest projects he engaged in at the time were series: *World War I* for CBS-TV and *The World of Music* for National Educational Television. The first was a long-term challenge he met successfully; the second was another attempt to go before the camera, which sank under the weight of his frown. Again, the fellow with the long face was a failure.

World War I, which ran weekly from 22 September 1964 to 23

March 1965, was the brainchild of Burton Benjamin and Isaac Kleinerman, producers of *The Twentieth Century*. They chose to use one writer for continuity, and turned to Gould, who worked every day until three or four in the morning, churned out forty pages of music a week, and extracted a significant suite, which he recorded on RCA. He considered it the best of his television and film scores. It drew much of its energy from childhood memories, of playing soldier in Richmond Hill, hearing the military bands and watching the marches and troop trains.

This product of memory and craftsmanship was a subdued and frequently melancholy body of music. The bittersweet flavor of Gould's *World War I* fits the often somber character of his other war music, going back to the Symphony No. 1. The music features deft evocations of the pomp and waltzes of prewar Vienna, gently cheerful portraits of peacetime America, and before, behind, and after everything, the doleful sound of a main theme that seems to recall all those ghastly dead.

It's in great contrast to the jingoistic, martial, and patriotic grandeur of Richard Rodgers's far more famous score of World War II, *Victory at Sea*. CBS News president Fred Friendly liked it enough that he intended, he wrote Gould on 8 April 1965, to use the theme as the "audio identifier" for his news programs.

Pop albums of the period include *Love Walked In* and *Sousa Forever* for RCA (the latter free to anyone who bought a new RCA stereo phonograph). In a footnote to the *Desire Under the Elms* debacle, Mielziner designed the AT&T pavilion at the 1964 World's Fair in New York and got Gould a $20,000 commission to write theme music, a sort of consolation prize. The designer wrote Gould: "I cannot let the opening of the Fair go by without saying, 'Thank God for Morton Gould's talent, his generosity, his loyalty, and his ability to swallow some bitter pills when the doctor insists on prescribing them!'" More significant scores of the time include *Festive Music*, commissioned by the Davenport, Iowa, Tri-Cities Symphony for its fiftieth anniversary, and *Formations*, a unique suite for the University of Florida's 'Gator marching band. And, at the request of Edwin Franko Goldman and William Revelli, who hoped to standardize the instrumentation for concert bands, he wrote *Prisms* for the American Bandmasters Association.

What was a "serious" musician to think when, at the time Gould was turning out this grand variety of popular and *Gebrauchsmusik*, he also was the host of an ambitious program about music itself, on public television? *The World of Music* ran from November 1964 through the spring of 1965. It was produced by Jerome Toobin, a close associate of Stokowski and manager of the Symphony of the Air, and among its writers were Joan Peyser (later editor of *Musical Quarterly* and biographer of Boulez, Bernstein, and Gershwin) and Robert Sherman.

The programs ranged from a discussion of folk music with singer Martha Schlamme to episodes on Charles Ives and Edgard Varese. Ruggiero Ricci demonstrated violins at the Forty-second Street store of Rembert Wurlitzer. Noah Greenberg and the New York Pro Musica presented some early stirrings of the "authentic performance" movement. This was a very serious affair.

That's how Gould treated *The World of Music*, to the dismay of the broadcasters. Uncomfortable as always before the camera, he clung to the script, and nobody knew how to draw him out. Sherman described Gould's presence by referring to a display of photographs, taken by his son Steve, at the radio station's offices: "There is Kathleen Battle graciously smiling, and Yo-Yo Ma laughing. And he has a picture of Morton Gould. Dour. That was the persona he projected. . . . He did not have sparkle, nor any kind of zest or enthusiasm." He seemed like the announcer at an old-fashioned classical concert. Gould read the script as if it were a sacred document, and everything about him was boring and dull.

His appearance could not have been more different from that master of television, Bernstein, whose Omnibus broadcasts were already classics and who was deep into his televised *Young People's Concerts*. Bernstein loved the camera and it loved him back. He was joyful, effervescent, outgoing, welcoming—all things that Gould was not. And, since *West Side Story*, he had a solid grip on that position between popular and high culture that had for a time been occupied by Gould. No matter the suspicion with which the mandarins of the concert hall viewed Bernstein: they knew him as a conductor of power and substance, an artist to be reckoned with. Not Gould.

Of course, Morton turned this set of television experiences into yet more absurd anecdotes. Stokowski agreed to appear on *The*

World of Music because of his relationship with Morton. They assembled before the cameras; it was a warm day and the aged conductor was impeccably dressed in a heavy suit. "Everybody else was perspiring, but he was not," Gould said in 1985. Morton asked the opening question, and Stokowski slyly responded, "Why must we talk about music? You and I had such fascinating conversations about women. Let's talk about women."

The sweat rolled down Gould's back. Stokowski refused to change the topic until the shooting had to stop. As someone buzzed in Morton's ear, "You and your fuckin' friends," Stokowski innocently asked, "What's the matter? Did I do something wrong?"

After this series, Morton never worked before the camera again, which Shirley could neither fathom nor accept. By now it was apparent that Morton was not making it the way they had expected and wanted. Disappointment may not have been Shirley's primary motivation—her husband's incessant infidelity must have been a factor—but now the signs of strain in their relationship became more visible. Fights over money grew in intensity and viciousness, and Shirley found other ways to batter him. One weapon derived from a tragic incident late in 1962, before Morton's forty-ninth birthday on 10 December.

Gould drove to Forest Hills to get his parents for a party, and Deborah, who would turn eight that 23 December, tagged along. Morton waited in the car while she trotted importantly to get her grandparents. Frances was frail and forgetful, perhaps in the early stages of what is now known as Alzheimer's Disease, and Morton told his youngest child to make sure they took the elevator. She faithfully relayed that message, but James would have none of it. He steered the little party to the stairs, where Frances tripped and fell down the whole flight.

She suffered a broken hip, was hospitalized, and could not return to the apartment (nor could James look after her). Few nursing homes would accept a person in her mental and physical state, and so Gould placed his beloved mother in the New York State mental institution at Creedmoor, in Queens. She lingered for almost a year, and on 23 December 1963, she died.

Frances's death, alone in a state hospital, gave Shirley a splendid club. Shirley began to insist the fall was Morton's fault (and ultimately, even Deborah's). "Shirley told me that Morton never should have sent in the seven-year-old to get her grandparents," recalled Candy Gould, Eric's wife. "And he's responsible for what happened to his mother." She also fumed at Morton for sending Frances to Creedmoor. Gould remained forever regretful about his mother's final days, and Shirley never let him forget it.

Abby became aware of the deteriorating relationship as a sixth-grader, in 1962; by the time she was in the seventh grade, she spent most of her time "trying to get them divorced. Pleading with them, begging with them, saying 'You're both good people, you're destroying each other. You can both lead happy lives.'"

Shirley attacked Morton for failing to be more prominent. "I started hearing things about 'Your father could be bigger than Lenny [Bernstein], but he won't do it,'" Abby said. "I heard a lot of yelling, Mom on the phone saying, 'Morton doesn't know shit about marketing himself, he doesn't know anything, Lenny has the right idea, Arthur Fiedler has the right idea, he's on Fruit of the Loom.' . . . He could be a lot better off, we could be a lot better off, we should be living in a bigger house, we should be living in Kings Point.'"

"I know she was really angry, and disgusted with the fact that he couldn't seem to get any higher up or more famous or more successful," Abby Gould Burton said. "She used to tell me that all the time."

Morton refused to do commercials the way Fiedler did. And every time Bernstein appeared on the screen, Shirley would fume, "That should be your father up there." But Morton had kept his musical and family lives separate, so no one in the family had a full understanding of his situation. Abby Gould Burton went to Philharmonic concerts and saw Bernstein greet her father effusively. "'Mortoneee!' he would say, rolling his rs, with that stupid scarf around his neck" (none of the Goulds liked Bernstein), "and give him a kiss on both cheeks," she said. She would ask her father why, if Bernstein liked him so much, he didn't play Gould's music: "And Daddy would take my head off, he would get so angry."

Shirley told Abby she wouldn't divorce Morton because he had threatened to kill himself if she did. When Abby relayed this to her father, he responded, "What kind of horseshit is she telling you?" By then, Eric and David were almost out of the house, and Abby was past the most impressionable age. Most of the pressure fell on Deborah, who considered herself awkward, gullible, and put-upon. Her knowledge of her father was expressed in a favorite family anecdote. In elementary school, the children were asked what their fathers did. This being Great Neck, the answers rang out: "He's a doctor!" "He's a lawyer!" Deborah's response: "My father walks the dog and takes out the garbage."

The girls began to fight about their parents: Deborah sided with Shirley, and Abby with Morton. When Deborah was young, she hated her father. "For a while I didn't care one way or the other. Then it turned into venom. I picked up my mother's cues," she said. She had no memory of her parents behaving affectionately toward one another; she knew they slept in separate beds and that Shirley would pretend to fall asleep before Morton came into the bedroom. "I knew she was angry at him, and I knew that she didn't want to have anything to do with him. I remember vividly the battles about money were constant. I didn't understand what the words meant, but I understood from the tone that these were the worst things any two human beings could say to each other."

These fierce matches during the early and mid-1960s terrified the girl, who would sit outside the kitchen and cry. She knew how Shirley tightened when Morton entered the room, and how she turned her head away when he went to kiss her. Eventually, Deborah responded the same way. "He would walk into the room and my whole body would tense. I'd get physically ill."

Little or none of this was visible outside the family. Writer Geraldine Friedman and others of their friends observed a couple who were, if not overtly demonstrative, civil and respectful. But the poison was building, even as Gould began his most strenuous attempt to gain serious recognition as a conductor.

CHAPTER 19

Chicago, and Balanchine

★ ★ ★ ★

FRITZ REINER, his health failing rapidly, retired from the Chicago Symphony in 1962. He was replaced by Jean Martinon, a fifty-three-year-old Frenchman who had conducted in America for the first time only six years before. Reiner, tyrannical and brilliant, had made the Chicago into one of the great orchestras of the world; his RCA recordings were prized. Martinon, whose primary experience was with second-tier European ensembles, had never held a position of such prominence. He was virtually unknown in the United States, which posed a problem for the orchestra and the record company, whose classical division was battling Columbia.

RCA had exclusive arrangements with the Boston Symphony under Leinsdorf and the Pops under Fiedler. Columbia's two main orchestras were the Philharmonic with Bernstein, and the phenomenally successful Philadelphia under Ormandy. With the departure of Reiner (he died 15 November 1963), Chicago was vulnerable. After a decade churning out records with one of the great conductors, it no longer had a contract.

"We had just finished what turned out to be a marvelous ten years with Fritz Reiner," recalled Adolph (Bud) Herseth, the orchestra's principal trumpet. "Martinon had his own strengths and weaknesses, but he was not a big-selling name."

"It was really a scandal," Gould said in 1985, "an orchestra like that with no recording contract." Meanwhile Gould wanted something reliable to play his expanded repertoire. "I would really need to have an orchestra rather than a pickup group, as great as this was," he said. "A symphony orchestra is rehearsed. You do the music at a concert, and then go in and record."

"Martinon was a superb musician and conductor," said Roger Hall, who in 1963 became chief of the RCA Red Seal division. "But he did not have the stature with the public that he should have had, and so I approached the Chicago Symphony with a proposition." Hall wanted to make Chicago RCA's "house orchestra": after a stipulated number of recordings with Martinon, usually three per year, RCA could use any conductor it chose. Chicago accepted, and during his tenure at RCA (through 1970), Hall recorded the Chicago with such men as Seiji Ozawa, André Previn, and Georges Prêtre.

And Morton Gould. "I couldn't wait to do some work with Morton in Chicago," Hall said. The timing was good: Gould's name was still prominent, he was on television with *The World of Music*, *World War I* was favorably in the public ear, and Morton was earning his keep at RCA.

Silas Edman became general manager of the Chicago Symphony in 1965. Like Hall, Edman respected and admired Gould, and knew that RCA was in trouble after Reiner. Edman, Hall, and the Goulds worked out an arrangement whereby Morton would guest-conduct the Chicago Symphony during its low-price Saturday night pops concerts and record afterward. Edman hoped to develop the concerts into a series devoted to American music, with Gould the key figure. This fit Gould's plans; he wasn't interested in the subscription series: "I was not out to go to Chicago to do all the Brahms symphonies. That was not my target." His target, as he explained it in 1985, was "oddball things."

The orchestra had played his music fairly often—usually *Spirituals* and *American Salute*. Gould had conducted at the Ravinia Festival in 1955 and led several performances in the *Great Music from Chicago* television series. His first appearance in the popular concerts series took place 6 February 1965, with a program intended for immediate recording: Sibelius's *Lemminkainen's Homeward Journey* and *Pohjola's Daughter*, Copland's *Dance Symphony*, and his own *Spirituals for String Choir and Orchestra* and *American Salute*.

Morton, as usual, kept his musical life separate and went to Chicago by himself. Walter knew how important the appearance was and flew to Chicago to surprise his brother. "When the concert was over," Walter said, "I came backstage. He was in shock: 'What are you doing here?' he said. I said, 'What do you mean? This is an important engagement!' Nobody else was there—his wife, his family—nobody."

Spirituals and *Dance Symphony* were recorded 8 February, in Orchestra Hall, and released in October. Gould's disc was only the Copland's second recording (the first was on CRI, by a Japanese orchestra), and it drew respectful reviews: "Gould's performance is extremely fine, and the orchestral execution is equally superb," according to *High Fidelity* (December 1965).

The next concert was even better and even more obscure: on 6 November 1965, Gould led excerpts from *Swan Lake*, followed by Ives's Symphony No. 1, Sibelius's *The Swan of Tuonela*, his own *Festive Music*, featuring Bud Herseth, and Rimsky-Korsakov's *Capriccio espagnol*. It was the Ives's professional premiere. The symphony was a student work written partly as a Yale assignment in 1898, and the performance was Gould's idea. The Ives boom was beginning: Bernstein was playing and recording the later work, Schuman had made his orchestral arrangement of Ives's *Variations on America* the previous year, and Ozawa was to perform the complex Symphony No. 4 with Chicago in the next. Looking for work at the edges, Gould discovered this.

The Chicago critics paid attention. Roger Dettmer (*Daily News*, 7 November 1965) found the work "absorbing," as it foreshadowed his later music, and thought Gould conducted "straightforwardly." Thomas Willis, replacing the cantankerous Claudia Cassidy at the *Tribune*, gave Gould credit for bringing the score to Chicago, though he was not impressed with his conducting. Donald Dierks (*Sun-Times*) said, "The Symphony No. 1 should establish that [Ives] is no American primitive." Gould, he observed, was "not a picture conductor . . . but he does get results and has a composer's concern with what another composer has indicated on a score."

The concert's program was recorded on 8 November in one two-and-a-half-hour session. Scott, who produced all Gould's Chicago discs, said RCA did not want to spend any extra money on the project. According to Scott, "Roger said, 'We haven't got the money.' I said, 'How much have you got?' He said, 'Seven thousand five hundred dollars.' I said, 'I'll take it.'" Gould recorded the full thirty-three minutes in a single afternoon session. (When principal flute Donald Peck checked his files, he exclaimed, "I can't imagine they did all of that in one session, but that's what it's listed as, from two to four-thirty!")

Morton returned to Chicago for a program on 29 January 1966 that included the Khachaturian Violin Concerto (soloist Samuel Magad), Ives's *The Unanswered Question* and *Variations on America*, Tchaikovsky's *Nutcracker Suite*, and Gould's suite from *Porgy and Bess* and *American Symphonette* No. 2. The orchestra went into the studio on 31 January to record the two Ives, and the recording was released that summer. It got exceptional reviews. Irving Kolodin (*The Saturday Review*) was almost effusive: "Gould brings a remarkable balance of enthusiasm and understanding to these performances. . . . The Chicago Symphony has rarely sounded so well or been better reproduced." Conductor and producer were rewarded with the only Grammy of Gould's career, so unexpected that neither of them was in the audience for the ceremony. "And they didn't want to let us record it!" exclaimed Scott.

Altogether, Morton made six Chicago recordings from 1965 to 1968. The four others were another Ives disc, of the radical *Orchestral Set* No. 2, the *Robert Browning Overture*, and "Putnam's Camp" from *Three Places in New England*; Carl Nielsen's Clarinet Concerto (with Benny Goodman) and Symphony No. 2 ("The Four Temperaments"); Rimsky-Korsakov's Symphony No. 2 ("Antar") and Miaskovsky's Symphony No. 21; and Tchaikovsky waltzes. They were the high points of his recording career: a set of consistent performances with a magnificent orchestra. "Chicago is such a great orchestra," Gould said in October 1985. "It had nothing to do with me. If you start off and just stay the hell out of their way, you can't get into too much trouble."

The musicians pretty much agreed. "He was just an absolutely delightful guy to work with," Herseth said. "Morton was very clear, and not pretentious at all, not temperamental . . . . I've played with any number of conductors, and they are going to impose their personality on you no matter what. Morton was not that way. He had a very nice idea of how he wanted the music to sound, but he was willing to accept whatever the orchestra was presenting to him in their musical concept. That's what every good conductor should do. Period."

After the Ives, probably his most exhilarating Chicago work came in June 1966, during the orchestra's first June Festival and just before Orchestra Hall closed for renovation. On the first two nights, 15 and 16 June, the soloist in Nielsen's Clarinet Concerto was Benny Goodman, a Chicago native making his first appearances with the hometown orchestra. The night before, Gould had written an encore for his friend, a clever arrangement of Fred Fischer's "Chicago" which opens very seriously, with orchestral chords that only later one realizes are in the familiar rhythm and harmony of the song's opening refrain. In principal flutist Donald Peck's words, "It starts out as the Weber Clarinet Concerto—very cute—and then angles into 'Chicago,' and the audience goes wild."

It's the sort of thing that should bring a smile to every face—but not to a critic in Orchestra Hall. Donal Henahan (*Daily News*) hated the whole concept: "If you are one who gets his kicks out of such mock-music events as Benny Goodman and the Chicago Symphony playing a Morton Gould orchestration of "Chicago," with Gould conducting—if, I say, you are one of those, you would have had a good time at Orchestra Hall on Wednesday night. For all others, the delights were fairly restricted." RCA recorded "Chicago" but never released it. The orchestra took it on tour to Europe, and it was included in special Chicago Symphony fund-raising compilations.

The renovation of Orchestra Hall was a disaster. The acoustics were so damaged it could not be used for recording. "That was a terrible blow," Gould admitted in 1985. "And I found myself at lunch meetings with board members, and the president, and they were asking my advice—if you put boxes on the stage, would it help the sound, and so forth. RCA even ran a test recording session there to see if it was usable, at great expense. But the verdict was no."

There was speculation that Gould himself was in line to become music director, a position he did not want. "Had I been gunning for a post, well," he said. "But I was not qualified, certainly not for a post like Chicago." Nevertheless, his relationship with the orchestra continued for two more years. One weekend in February 1968, he was called in when Martinon was ill. Sixten Ehrling took over but could not make the Monday runout in Milwaukee. The orchestra flew Gould in.

He did not know the program: Wagner's *Eine Faust Overture*,

Beethoven's Piano Concerto No. 1 with Gyorgy Sebok, and then some Ravel: *Alborada del gracioso*, *Ma mere l'oye*, and *Rapsodie espagnole*. Gould's friend Sol Berkowitz was in Great Neck the day Morton got the call. "We all had lunch, and then Morton sat in a corner and learned two major symphonic pieces. While the conversation was going on."

When Gould walked into the Pabst Theatre, the musicians were taken aback. "They said, 'What the hell are you doing here?' I said I was conducting." The players knew Martinon was out but had no idea who would lead them. Gould had never even seen pianist Sebok before.

Gould kept up his extramusical activities, including an episode involving a runout 29 January 1968 in the Bloomfield, Illinois, Township High School. At lunch the day before, Scott and Gould eyed two women nearby, who eyed them back. One of the women said she might drive to Bloomfield to hear the concert. "I'd be delighted if you'd come out there," said Morton. "And we left the table," Scott said, "saying, 'Oh boy, they're pretty nice. I'll take this one, you take that one.'"

The next night the woman Morton fancied appeared backstage, "much to our pleasure and surprise," Scott recalled with glee. "[Gould] said, 'It's so nice to see you,' and 'it's such a spiritual meeting,' and all that stuff—'you like me for my mind, of course'—and she was going for all kinds of this bullshit. He had a line with women that would knock your socks off."

Ultimately, Scott drove the woman's brand-new Pontiac back to Chicago while she accompanied Morton in his chauffeur-driven limousine "with a bar in the back seat." Gould commemorated the occasion years later when he inscribed the score of *Celebration '81*, "From Morton Gould to Howard Scott. What again? Do you still drive? As ever, Morton."

Gould led only one more concert in Chicago, on 9 March 1968. The climate there and at RCA was changing. Edman was ousted from the orchestra, Orchestra Hall's acoustics continued to be sadly lacking, recording rates began to climb again, and Scott was let go from RCA. One of Gould's most unusual discs came about as a result of the shift from the United States to Europe. He had been planning to perform and record two virtually unknown, previously unrecorded symphonies by Shostakovich, No. 2 ("To October") and No. 3 ("May Day"), both of which had choruses, a great added expense.

The recording was made in London, with the Royal Philharmonic Orchestra and Chorus, and released in August 1968. Kolodin (*The Saturday Review*) commended Gould's enterprise and declared he had "a strong feeling for the idiom." Kolodin also reviewed another Gould recording, a high-fidelity release on the Gallery label of several pieces for band, with the composer conducting the Knightsbridge Symphonic Band. "Were I a player in a college band, or in a professional organization," Kolodin wrote, "I would be grateful to Morton Gould for applying his talents for organization and his skill in tonal blendings to the enrichment of a literature which is more remarkable for quantity than quality." (Choreographer Eliot Feld set two of the band pieces, *Santa Fe Saga* and *Formations*, for his company, and they remain in the repertoire.)

Gould's time in Chicago was over. It won him a Grammy and respect, but he never again had as significant a relationship with an established orchestra. Meanwhile, the musical world was changing again. With the growth of the postwar generation only then becoming known as the Baby Boomers, the attraction of pops and semiclassical music faded as rock took a stronger grip and "pop" itself became a term of derision. Although only four years older than Bernstein, Gould had been active so long he seemed to be a member of an older, obsolescent generation.

He tried to accommodate, with two unusual discs. The first, recorded in October 1965, was *The Two Worlds of Kurt Weill*—Gould's arrangements of Weill songs from Berlin and Broadway. And finally, in December 1966, he made a futile attempt to "get with it" in *Morton Gould Makes the Scene*, featuring arrangements (not his own) of "Winchester Cathedral," "Georgy Girl," "Eleanor Rigby," and "Daydream," among others.

Both recordings were doomed, though for different reasons. The year 1966 was long before Weill had been canonized, although he had had a successful career on Broadway in the 1930s and 1940s, *The Threepenny Opera* had been performed Off-Broadway in the mid-1950s, and Bobby Darin had struck it rich with "Mack the Knife." But much of Weill's work with Bertolt Brecht in Germany was known more by rumor than hearing, and his concert music was known not at all. Gould selected half a dozen songs from each period and arranged them. "Mack the Knife" was heard twice: the first slow and funereal, using something close to Weill's own orchestration but without the bite. The New York arrangement was entirely uptempo (at one minute, fifty-seven seconds, it was almost exactly half the length of the Berlin setting) and not quite as vulgar as the Darrin. The Berlin arrangements are careful and respectful; the Broadway versions are more typical of Gould's lighter work, thoughtful and inventive.

But Weill did not need Gould for orchestrations. The disc gave Gould pleasure to create, but it had not much other reason for being. As for *Morton Gould Makes the Scene*, he had to be talked into doing it, took no pride in it, and never tried anything like that again. He was heartily ashamed of it.

After Chicago, Gould's RCA work tapered off. In 1969 there was *A Musical Christmas Tree*, carols and traditional tunes, half recorded in London and half in New York. He led the Royal Philharmonic in harmonica scores written for Larry Adler by Darius Milhaud, Arthur Benjamin, Ralph Vaughan Williams, and Malcolm Arnold. Then his contract lapsed. Sales were falling, he and Walter felt the marketing department was not pushing him, Roger Hall left RCA, and by 1970 Gould was without a recording contract for the first time in nearly thirty years.

At the age of fifty-seven Gould was entering limbo. He would spend the next decade and more always active, but fading nevertheless. Morton apparently had taken his best shots, and missed.

There was, however, one very important project that had already been going on for more than a decade, and in the mid-1960s looked as if it would finally come to fruition. George Balanchine had begun work on his full-length ballet in the early 1950s as a proposal by Louis Bromfield, once considered among the most important American writers of the century. But a career that had begun with great promise and a Pulitzer Prize had degenerated into mediocrity, and Bromfield was excoriated as an out-of-touch conservative.

The novelist was a balletomane, and when he approached Balanchine with his idea, the composer he mentioned was Gould. Bromfield suggested a work on Johnny Appleseed, the mystic wanderer who traveled the Midwest in the early nineteenth century planting apple trees and preaching. Balanchine and Gould knew one another

—Gould orchestrated Kaye Swift's *Alma Mater*, choreographed by Balanchine—though they were not friends. And the team began discussing the ballet.

"There were just a few of us," Gould said in 1985, "sitting in a very lovely townhouse, having a gourmet dinner and special wine, discussing this, and drinking to the idea. Everybody seemed very gung ho." Bromfield wrote a libretto, and Gould began sketching ideas in 1952 and 1953. The work progressed slowly—composer and choreographer were both busy, and the author's sketches were never satisfactory. Bromfield died in 1956, but the idea didn't.

After that, Balanchine changed the focus to another semi-mythical American. "One day George said to me he didn't like the Appleseed story, he wanted to make it Audubon, the legend of the Dauphin." This version of the life of John James Audubon held that he was the son of Louis XVI of France, escaped to America and become a backwoodsman. (Research has since shown that Audubon was the child of a Haitian woman and a French sea captain, entirely too prosaic.)

Johnny Appleseed became *Audubon*, a never-completed work that ultimately became legend within the ballet world as *Birds of America*. The writer Glenway Westcott, an acquaintance of Whiteside, wrote one libretto; Lincoln Kirstein tried another. The work, which involved life in the forest primeval, frontier warfare, birds and other woodland creatures, and the presentation of Indians at the French court, moved very slowly. "George was never happy with the scenario," Gould said. "Lincoln questioned him, I questioned him. It seemed as if it would never come off. But George would say, 'I don't care, we will do it.'"

Gould produced reams of music and sent sketches to Balanchine. "I was a little insecure about this," Gould said. "Here was this great genius—I felt maybe he had the wrong guy, that he had come to me by mistake." In 1955 Balanchine and his then-wife, the ballerina Tanaquil Leclercq, had dinner in Great Neck. Gould asked him how he perceived the ballet: "Should it be a revolutionary work, something radical?"

"He would sniff when he spoke; he had sort of a tic," Gould recalled. "He said, 'You know, we do a twelve-and-a-half-minute ballet, a fifteen-minute ballet—we experiment. A two-and-a-half-hour ballet—no experiment.' . . . He said, 'Curtain go up, audience must know what we do. If they don't know what we do, it no good.'"

If Balanchine didn't like a sketch, he would say, "That is very good concert music." When he liked it, he would say, "Good." ("That was like someone else getting euphoric," said Gould.)

The opening was to take place at dawn in a deep forest. Gould wrote "dawn music, 'Daphnis and Chloe.'" Balanchine did not react. Gould wrote more, and more. Finally, Balanchine said, "Don't choreograph. You write music and I choreograph." According to Gould, "George bounced off the music—he didn't want me to imagine anything but music."

Some time later, Gould wrote a concerto grosso for four violins and orchestra, "a virtuoso piece, a transformation of hoedown tunes." The soloists were to sound like sophisticated country fiddlers. "They play, in the first and last movements, like a bat out of hell." Stage designer Rouben Ter-Arutunian was now sitting in. Gould had barely played the first two measures when Balanchine grew excited. "He was euphoric. He says, 'Great opening!' I said, 'No, George, this is the second or third act.' He said, "Why? It's a great piece. We open with it.'

"I says, 'George, this is you opening on a black stage, there's dawn.' He says, 'Don't choreograph. This is dawn.'"

Ter-Arutunian interceded: "You know, he's crazy, but he's right. He's going to say crazy things to you, Morton, but he's right."

"And suddenly, the light turned on in my head. For one second I had Balanchine's genius up there. . . . He said to me, 'What are you saving it for? You write something else for the second act. The audience hear this, the audience stay. If they wait for second act to hear this, they go home.'"

On another occasion, Balanchine remarked, "Nobody writes waltzes any more. Apple waltzes. We write apple waltzes." Gould knew there was no such thing as an apple waltz: "But when he said it to me, I suddenly heard it. In fact—boom—I wrote more than seven. There was something about this man that triggered off whatever talents one might have around him. Every time I met with him, I would go home and write a new batch of music. I never knew where the hell it was going. He asked for a French march, I gave him three French marches. I wrote a cotillion, a quadrille, a polonaise."

In the mid-1960s it seemed as if the ballet would at last come about. In April 1965 City Ballet general manager Betty Cage confirmed the commission, and said the company hoped to schedule it in spring of the 1966–67 season.

That season passed with no *Birds of America*, but by the end of the decade, work had reached the point that Barbara Karinska, who had designed costumes for *The Nutcracker*, began making sketches. The Concerto Grosso was completed in October 1969, the *Apple Waltzes* the following month, and smaller numbers the next year. There were meetings to discuss the production. Jacques D'Amboise was to dance the role of Audubon.

But nothing happened. Barbara Horgan, Balanchine's secretary and now conservator of the Balanchine Archive, said, "In my opinion there was never a serious attempt to produce this. We could never seem to put the production together in any practical way, or to put money up for it. They would talk to one another all the time. I remember Morton Gould being a presence all the time I worked with Balanchine." Indeed, the first work Balanchine presented at the New York State Theater in the brand-new Lincoln Center was *Clarinade*, set to *Derivations*, with Benny Goodman the soloist.

Birds of America "would have been as big a thing as anything Mr. Balanchine and Mr. Kirstein had ever tried to do," Horgan said. "I was always going out and getting music copied from Morton and giving it to Mr. Balanchine." The problems, she asserted, had nothing to do with the music. "Mr. Balanchine was very admiring of the music that Morton brought to him. There was no question of ever looking for another composer—but the other parts didn't get put together."

Gould hoped for a production until Balanchine's death. It seemed feasible in the late 1970s, and the company penciled it in for the 1982–83 season. But all that remains are some costume sketches and the music, orchestrated and ready to be played. Morton mourned the loss all the rest of his life.

One can understand Gould's perplexity at the idea of using the Concerto as "dawn music." After a barn-dance tune-up, the solo violins twine about one another in rhythmic and harmonic complexity while the orchestra emphasizes, punctuates, and pushes the movement forward. There are traces of *Showpiece* and some of the concert scores. The second movement is plaintive, sweet, and lyrical, about as melancholy as the composer ever gets. This is music with a rich sensibility, derived almost entirely from American sources. Copland has been heard and assimilated; there is a harder edge than Barber, Harris, or Hanson, and none of the disingenuous simplicity of Thomson. It is an effective and evocative piece, worthy of far more consideration than it has gotten.

Apple Waltzes is in the same vein—it has the dance rhythm and a sense of forward motion, but also much hesitation and doubt. If Ravel's *La Valse* is a European's evocation of the grand dance gone mad, these waltzes have passed through several thicknesses of the American lens, looking at the old world with foreign eyes.

While Gould was endeavoring to create a great American ballet with George Balanchine, he also produced a series of major works examining the possibilities of orchestration, sonority and balance. He even, for the first time, followed a European trail. In less than six years in the mid-1960s, he wrote, heard performed, and recorded enough symphonic scores to make him the envy of contemporaries begging for one small commission. But these were for ensembles far from the centers of concert music and usually at the instigation of men who had worked with him for years.

Venice (an "audiograph for double orchestra and brass choirs") was commissioned in 1966 by his old radio friend Milton Katims, then music director of the Seattle Symphony. Using a federal education grant, Katims asked Gould to write a piece for two orchestras. "My first reaction was, 'Why don't you come to me when you have something for one orchestra?'" Gould said in 1985. He hit on a solution after a family trip to Europe that summer, which included a visit to Venice, "the home of multichoirs, of antiphonal music, of Gabrieli and Vivaldi." He thought of the Piazza San Marco, the pigeons, the bands competing on every corner, and the fireworks.

The score is programmatic music, with movements entitled "Morning Scene with Church Towers," "St. Mark's Square," "Cafe Music," and so forth. It calls for two full orchestras plus a pair of offstage brass choirs but can be performed also by one orchestra split in half, or with additional brass, wind, and percussion. The premiere, on 2 May 1967, involved the Seattle and Spokane symphonies under Katims, in Spokane. It is not a tone poem in the sense of those by

Respighi or Richard Strauss. Rather, Gould gathers impressions, bits and pieces of sound, and blends them in ways that are suggestive, not imitative.

The premiere was well received; the final movement, "Night Festa with Fireworks," when for the first time Gould brings all the forces together, was encored. Thomas Goldthwaite (*Spokesman-Review*) was pleased that there were "no overwhelming fugues, no interminable sequences tossed drunkenly about and not much musical tennis. . . . What impresses is the fragile nature of the composer's impressions and how wondrously they are expressed by the most economic means."

Gould conducted *Venice* numerous times over the next few years, and it was recorded by RCA with Katims and the Seattle Symphony dubbing both parts. For the other side of the disc, Gould tried a slightly different experiment: *Vivaldi Gallery* for string quartet and divided orchestra, which Katims premiered on 25 March 1968.

Once again, he used split ensembles: two string orchestras, with a quartet between them and the woodwinds, brass, and percussion providing the continuo. Gould appears to have been inspired by Lukas Foss's *Baroque Variations* of the previous year. Both composers use chunks of existing compositions as a foundation, but where Foss wipes the older music away like chalk, Gould assembles his fragments like a quilt. The sources are recognizable, but he turns what had been cheerful and propulsive music into something nostalgic and even melancholy.

The closest Gould could bring himself, however, to the prevalent abstractions was *Soundings*, commissioned by the Junior League of Atlanta for the Atlanta Symphony and Robert Shaw, his brother Walter's business partner. Composed in the summer of 1969, *Soundings* is in two movements, "Threnodies" (shades of Krzysztof Penderecki's 1961 *Threnody for the Victims of Hiroshima*) and "Paeans." While completing the score, Gould wrote to Shaw, in a letter of 10 August 1969, defensively explaining how he could not write in the modern style:

> Originally I "took off" in an abstract and experimental direction —but I admit finding it difficult to write in this vein, fashionable as it might be. . . . Regardless of merit—and tho I want to be

> loved by my peers—I am not that kind of a composer . . . and above all I must be myself—perhaps a dubious distinction but at least an honest one.

Shaw led the premiere of *Soundings* on 18 September 1969, accompanied by an editorial entitled "Gould and the Grant" in the *Atlanta Constitution,* which congratulated the orchestra for opening its season with a piece by "the most versatile conductor-composer on the American scene," and for winning a $250,000 grant—its first—from the National Endowment for the Arts.

Chappell White (*Journal-Constitution,* 19 September 1969) wrote, "Anyone expecting a light composition in the jazzy style that has made Gould's popular reputation must have been surprised, for *Soundings* is an intensely serious, deeply felt work"—though he could not refrain from mentioning that the composer "is a master orchestrator." Bob Rohrer (*Atlanta Constitution*) was even more pleased: "The composer uses tone clusters, fluttering effects in the strings, occasional veiled reference to jazz styles, and a number of other techniques, but all are molded into an original, convincing statement."

The next year, the Louisville Orchestra finally recorded some Gould, in the 108th release since the Rockefeller recording project. Robert Whitney had retired, and the new music director was Jorge Mester, though it was Gould who conducted *Soundings* and *Columbia: Broadsides for Orchestra.* The latter was another large orchestral commission, this one in 1967 from the National Symphony and his old colleague Howard Mitchell, and the Rouse Company, with a matching grant from the NEA. It was a set of sequences based on "Hail Columbia" and "Columbia, the Gem of the Ocean."

Then, in 1972, the young American composer Barbara Kolb won plaudits for her own work, *Soundings* for eleven instruments and electronic tape. In late 1973 she learned that Gould was going to lead the American Symphony in a performance of his *Soundings.* Kolb had known of Gould since childhood—her father was a jazz musician and music director of WTIC in Hartford, Connecticut. But she knew only of his band work, and as a composer she focused on atonal composition. Kolb wrote Gould on 23 October 1973: "I would hope that you may consider changing your title since my work has been given a considerable amount of publicity. Also, I would imagine that you may not want to retain a title which was acquired by another in so recent a period."

In response, Gould complimented Kolb on her own piece ("Strangely, I must confess that I understand the music, but not the liner notes") and extended an invitation to meet. No titles were changed. What a strange feeling it must have been, for a composer who was working with Balanchine and whose music had been performed by every major orchestra in the nation, to have been brought up short by a colleague barely into her thirties. When they met, Gould laughed at the coincidence; they became friends who spoke on the phone and occasionally met for drinks or concerts. They rarely spoke about music.

CHAPTER 20

War at Home

★ ★ ★ ★

THE LATE 1960S were a very fertile period. Gould conducted around the country and around the world. He had some television success and gained recognition as a conductor and explorer of the repertoire. But he had been exiled from the orchestra and the city he considered part of his birthright. And his marriage was now a sham.

Besides the fights over money, Shirley decided to begin a career; the first wave of the women's movement attracted liberal, educated wives such as herself who realized they had given up something very important when they followed convention and stayed home to raise their families. Now her sons were at college, Abby was about to leave, and only Deborah remained at home.

Pearl Berkowitz, a psychologist and New York City school administrator and the wife of Morton's friend Sol, suggested that if Shirley got a degree, she would get her a job. Shirley jumped at the idea. In 1965 she enrolled at St. John's University, in Queens, to study speech therapy. Morton hated it. Now she was angry at him, and he was angry at her, for moving off the established path. "I was a chauvinist pig," he often said.

"He was horrible, horrible," said Deborah. "I remember vividly how my father went off the wall when she said she was going to go back to school."

"She said, 'I want to do things, I want to go to school, to have a career,'" said Norma Perlman. "He did not like the idea of her going back, he did not encourage her going to find out what her true potential was. He didn't help her."

Candy Feldman, a well-bred girl from straitlaced New England and a Barnard College freshman, began dating Eric Gould, a senior at Columbia, in 1965 and married him a year later. Before she met the family, Eric warned her about them because, as Candy explained, "the last girl he brought to dinner had left in tears." She continued: "In my family, nobody cursed, nobody spoke out of turn, certainly nobody spoke up to my parents, nobody ever made a remark against anything they said." So she sat nervously while chaos raged. "The conversations in that family! Everybody was very sharp, very witty, and all very self-deprecating. Because they knew if they dished it out, they would have to take it too. 'Oh yeah, Ma? Well, fuck you!'"

After Candy and Eric became engaged, Shirley opened up to Candy in a way that startled the young coed. "I started going antiquing with Shirley, and really spending time with her, and it became very apparent that she was very angry with him. . . . She wanted to do this and that with the house, she wanted to buy this and that; he always made it very difficult. I'm eighteen years old, and I'm listening to her vent about how horrible he is and how difficult he was, and Morton this and that. So I just kept my mouth shut." She wondered why Shirley didn't leave, but Shirley was of a generation that stayed married. She was not the type of woman who left her husband, she told Candy.

Yet Shirley continued arranging those magnificent dinner parties, for she, too, was torn. "On the one hand, she hated him. On the other hand, she was mad at him because he didn't do enough to promote himself," Candy said. "Obviously, if she had hated him, she wouldn't have cared. There was always, I thought, that ambivalence."

Born in Jodhpur, India, Kanti Rai was a twenty-six-year-old physician and chief resident at North Shore Hospital in Manhasset, Long Island, when he met Morton and Shirley Gould at the home of the Perlmans. It was a gathering of old friends, including Alfred Florman, North Shore's chief of pediatrics and one of Rai's teachers. The young doctor was flattered. "Morton and Shirley took to me right away," he said, "and whenever Shirley had a slot at her dinner table, I was invited. I loved it. At six o'clock in the evening, I would get a call. I'd say, 'I'm coming!' and I'd have a great time." Although Morton held his own with quick, dry wit and understated intelligence, Shirley was the catalyst. "She was sharp, very well read," Rai said.

Often she would set Morton off, launching him into a convoluted, hilarious anecdote.

Shirley also loved to argue and had a range of deeply held, powerfully expressed opinions on the full spectrum of the day's liberal issues. "She had a certain monopoly on what liberal thought was, what minorities were, what civil rights and justice were," Rai said, "and if people did not absolutely accept her definitions and wanted to have their own definitions, it was not your right with her. . . . She would not give a point in argument, and that sometimes led the discussion to very unpleasant levels."

Morton would shrug and say, "There's Shirley being Shirley." But everyone knew, as Rai put it, "if you were on Shirley's shit list, you would never hear the end of her badmouthing." Over the years, Matty Gould and even Norma Perlman found themselves on the outside looking in. But Rai, eventually chief of oncology at Long Island Jewish Medical Center and the physician who treated Shirley during her last illness, was never on the shit list. He became part of what may have been Shirley's proudest moment: she arranged his marriage.

In late 1966 she invited him to a dinner that included Martin Segal and his wife, Edith, who had known the Goulds since the early 1950s. Afterward, she told them, "That's the man I've picked for your daughter Susan."

"I had no idea that Shirley had plans for Susan and me to get married," Rai said. "And Susan had no great interest in an Indian; she certainly had never dated an Indian. The idea never crossed her mind." But the pair began dating and found that they were made for one another. They were married in New Delhi, in November 1967. "And we came back and were told by everyone that Shirley, in October of 1966, had this plan in mind. And she never said boo to either Susan or me." So let other people speak adversely of Shirley Bank Gould: "In our family," said Segal, "everybody says you can't say that, because Shirley is the one who introduced Susan and Kanti."

By 1968 Shirley had begun the career to which she devoted herself until her painful death in 1992. Pearl Berkowitz, principal of a school for emotionally disturbed children with units in several large hospitals, hired her to teach high school English at the New York Psychiatric Institute, in Columbia Presbyterian Hospital in upper Manhattan. Shirley blossomed. Although it was a New York City public school, the facility was very selective. Its patients were brilliant and well educated, the children of professionals and high government and corporate officials. Shirley was a wonderful teacher. "It was like going to the theater," Berkowitz said, "She was on all the time. She loved the students. She was enthusiastic."

This was not something Morton wanted to hear. He took his cues about relationships from his father, who made sure that the woman kept house and raised the children. Shirley accepted that in the 1950s, when Morton's star was still high, but by the late 1960s, with Morton's light waning and her own ambition growing, she had lost much of her tolerance. When Abby left to attend the Rhode Island School of Design, Shirley moved into her bedroom and the split, as far as the children were concerned, was official.

The children's attempts to understand and mollify their parents went beyond divorce. In 1968, while Shirley was in the kitchen, Eric, David, Abby, and Candy discussed Gould's extramarital affairs with him in the living room. "We said, 'Listen, we know that you and Shirley do not have much of a romantic relationship,'" Candy said. "'And we understand. That you see other women.' And he got this sort of bemused look on his face. He almost smiled, like 'Thanks, kiddies, but I don't need your permission.'"

At the Psychiatric Institute, and later at the much more dangerous Bellevue Hospital, Shirley was known as a gifted, courageous teacher. Richard Glavine was a psychiatrist who had breakfast with her and other staff members before school. "She was an extraordinary person," Glavine said. "She was earthy, and yet she was dignified. She was totally honest—brutally honest at times. I never heard her say something that was sugar-coated or wanting to please somebody. . . . And the fact that she liked me and seemed to pick me out of this group to be this special friend—it was very flattering."

Shirley developed her own friends, including a group of homosexuals such as Glavine, his partner, Norman Mellk, a decorator, and Daniel Berger, who worked at the Metropolitan Museum of Art. She struck them all with her intense loyalty and generosity—she once lent Glavine and Mellk her air-conditioned car for a vacation and later gave them a color television. They knew of the fixity of her opinions, and her disputatiousness, but Shirley also used that ferocity for her students. "She was furious if the kids were labeled in some way. . . .

She would go on the grand rounds and argue with the doctors if she saw any injustice in the way they were being treated," Glavine said.

For the first time, Shirley Bank Gould had her own life. Morton had provided neither money nor support, and her children had not been enthusiastic. Now when Shirley wanted to go out, she went with Glavine, Berger, or others. Shirley and Morton rarely socialized together outside of their dinners. When he visited friends on Long Island, she refused to go, nor was he invited on her jaunts. She was the star, the woman with famous friends and backstage connections. Yet her children observed with some amusement that, however much she despised him, Shirley had no hesitation calling the New York City Ballet or American Ballet Theatre and announcing, "This is Mrs. Morton Gould—I would like some tickets for tonight."

If Shirley could not control her husband, she tried to control everyone else. In Forest Hills, Shirley and Matty Gould had a very close friendship; Matty adored Shirley. But over the years she would be frozen out for one slight or another. When Morton's brother Alfred was in his final illness, he stayed with his own physician rather than one Shirley recommended—"and she didn't speak to us for a year," Matty said. Neither did "Pat" have a hold on Whiteside, and the affection in their early correspondence did not last. According to Candy Gould, Shirley resented the fact that her first daughter was named after Morton's beloved teacher. After Whiteside's death Shirley made no secret of her feelings. "My mother hated her," Deborah stated. "I don't know why. . . . She just hated her."

Having arranged one marriage, Shirley tried to prevent another. Mimi Benzell, Walter's wife, died in 1970, and when Walter began courting Betty Isquith, Shirley campaigned against it. "She said to me, 'Good bye,'" Betty said. "Because she hadn't selected me. . . . But her oldest brother, Red, told me her approach to his second wife had been the same. He said to me, 'Don't let her worry you, she does the same to me.' She didn't pick me out; I didn't come and ask her." Nevertheless, even Betty Gould recognized Shirley's strength and determination. "I admired Shirley, I truly did," she said. "To the very end she continued to work—she was a real feminist."

Shirley also had more and more trouble with her ambivalence about Morton. Shirley's hectoring and pushing could not make him someone he was not, and the person he was no longer satisfied her.

More than anything else, thought Daniel Berger, Shirley was frustrated and angry because she considered Morton boring and cheap. "I think he was kind of a moon, rather than a sun," Berger said. "I think she felt she wanted to be married to a sun—I think she thought he cheated her. And she might have been angry at herself, really. Maybe . . . she thought this would be the person who would be forever interesting and exciting for her, and in the end, maybe she was angry because she didn't read him properly."

And of course there was sex. Shirley must have been aware of Morton's appetite. She herself, after all, had spent time at the Warwick. But how deeply she was hurt by his infidelity is impossible to say, and there is no agreement among those who knew them. Gould insisted—as he would have to—that his peccadillos did not cause her disaffection and anger. Some who knew her agreed. "I don't think she cared about that part," Berger said. "Getting laid was sex. Sex and love have nothing to do with one another."

Johanna Fiedler, Arthur Fiedler's youngest child, made her career in music administration and public relations, and she put a particularly subtle eye on the Goulds' relationship, although she never met Shirley. Gould and Fiedler had known one another since long before Johanna was born, so she saw Morton as family friend and musician. "He was one of the very few people my mother and father would actually have come over to the house," she said.

Johanna Fiedler's own family life was profoundly affected by her father's infidelities, and she said of Morton, "I always had the sense he was somebody who on some level was very unhappy with his personal life. My family was not the happiest in the world, and you could pick up on that in other people pretty well. . . . He was always making these bitter remarks about how she didn't understand him or wasn't interested." And so, when Fiedler eventually learned through gossip that Gould had lovers outside his marriage: "I was a little surprised, but I wasn't."

Candy Gould observed that in all Shirley's bitterness, she never complained—to her, at least—about his women. But Morton once told Candy's parents that Shirley had slapped him without provocation and exclaimed, "That's for all the things that I don't know about." The suspicions must have bitten into a wife's deepest pride. And the pain must have become worse as they grew older, when she was no longer the beauty she had been while Morton still had that knowing little smile. Norma Perlman stated flatly, "I think that's why she left him." Matty Gould was also convinced that Morton's womanizing was the source of the anger.

Morton and Shirley had long ceased to be good companions for one another. Gould was very private; even Shirley Uzin had complained that he never shared what he was doing. "I didn't think it was important, or that anybody would be interested," he said in 1985. But he communicated freely with his lovers, many of whom maintained warm friendships long after their ardor had cooled. One, a New Yorker who met Gould in the mid-1960s, recalled for me in 1996, with great affection, the afternoons she and Morton had spent in hotels near Kennedy Airport:

> I would pack a picnic lunch—go to German delis and get some wonderful cheeses, some wonderful hunters' bread, and we'd have wonderful romantic afternoons. . . . He was a funny, very sweet man. He loved women. He appreciated women. A lot of men love women and don't care for them: it's chase and conquer, they don't really care about friendship. But he had a female side that was very warm and very affectionate. Women were an important part of his life, more than for most men. Morton craved female companionship. He really visited; we talked about everything. And I imagine he did with other women too. On the phone we would have long, long conversations.

And that, this compassionate lover supposed, was why the marriage ended: "Finally she couldn't stand the fact that he loved so many women—I couldn't think of any other reason."

Although Shirley was not ready to leave in the late 1960s, the economic foundation of Gould's musical life—his recordings—was disappearing, and he was worried once more. Rock had taken over; the generation coming of age actively despised music like Morton's. Anything connected with the immediate postwar years and the 1950s was banal, conformist, hopelessly square—counter-revolutionary to people who thought themselves the young rebels.

James Gould died in the fall of 1970 at the age of eighty-seven, in the Sands Point Nursing Home, where Morton placed him when the family could no longer find housekeepers willing to stay with a difficult old man. The family jokes about Pop had edges. He ordered a twenty-year subscription to *Sports Illustrated*—and, laughed Morton, "We were afraid he was going to be around for the whole thing." The nursing home staff had warned Morton his father would not last the night. Next day, Abby said, Morton got a call. "Suddenly he shouted, 'God damn it!'" Pop had rallied and lived for weeks longer. "The doctors have been saying he was going to die for sixty years now," Morton said. "Promises, promises."

Beneath Morton's sarcasm was a dense weave of love, hate, and fear. But Shirley did not have that history. Shortly before James passed away, he asked his daughter-in-law to visit. Reluctantly, she approached an old foe coming to the end of his road. James took her hands and said, "Shirley, please forgive me." Too bad, Pop. "I didn't forgive that fucking bastard," she boasted to Abby. "I wasn't going to let him get the best of me."

There was a hasty, minimal service at a Forest Hills funeral home to which not even the grandchildren were invited, a quick trip to the cemetery, and it was over. The Goulds were not observant, and there was no period of shiva or mourning. "There was absolutely no recognition of respect," Matty Gould said. "At that point there was extreme bitterness about his role in their lives, about the fact that he controlled Morton and used his money, that he interfered with the family, that they were in competition for Morton's attention and work." Not for years could Gould acknowledge that he missed his father.

CHAPTER 21

Bicentennial

★ ★ ★ ★

THE DISAPPEARANCE of James Gould from his son's life, along with other markers of age, had a liberating effect. For one thing, Morton's personality started to peep through. A columnist in *Film and Television Daily* remarked on his comments at a Grammy ceremony: "Morton Gould, hardly known as a comedian, got multiple laughs when he said, 'I was thinking of a lot of funny lines backstage, but I won't take up your time with them.'"

On the larger canvas, Morton was beginning to shift from pops lightweight to grand old man. In 1969 he was elected secretary of ASCAP. In 1970 he became a first vice chairman of the American Symphony Orchestra League, "a celebrity who was at the conferences all the time," said Catherine French, who started as a low-level administrator and became president of the ASOL. "At the conferences, he used to cruise the cocktail parties all the time; he was very funny. It was like a rolling party." Gould was now considered an expert on recording techniques; his experience was beginning to be seen as valuable, not a handicap. Also in 1970 he gave private guidance on conducting to pianist Leon Fleisher, whose solo career was destroyed by the crippling of his right hand. Most tellingly of all, Gould refused to appear in Howard Scott's Rochester pops concerts, demanding instead the subscription series. In December 1970, asked for advice by a young pops composer, he wrote, "My performances and recordings in the last number of years have been restricted to a different kind of repertory."

Late in 1970, shortly before his fifty-seventh birthday, Dorothy

Hite Claybourne, an English professor at St. Louis University, asked Gould, for her unpublished dissertation, whether he wanted his documents destroyed upon his death. His answer, in a letter to her, was emphatic: "I personally do not believe that personal papers and documents of creative people should be destroyed. I think that any aspect of human behavior and experience is, in a sense, the common property of all, and might serve a constructive and helpful purpose. I intend leaving my personal documents for whatever purpose they might have."

Ironically, a few months later, in February 1971, a researcher at the New York Public Library for the Performing Arts at Lincoln Center asked to house the Morton Gould archive. But Gould's unhappiness with Lincoln Center was strong. His response, couched diplomatically, was "Maybe." (Ultimately his papers went to the Library of Congress in Washington, D.C., rather than any organization in his home city.)

Morton guest-conducted extensively. From 1968 through 1972 he lead orchestras in Genoa, Turin, and Rome; in Venice he conducted at an American jazz festival and at La Fenice, the opera house. RCA supported those trips with the release of five Gould discs, which won surprised and respectful reviews. He visited Venezuela to conduct the Caracas Symphony (during that trip, Gould and a newfound female acquaintance were serenaded by a restaurant violinist as they dined; the musician was convinced he was serenading Duke Ellington, who was in town at the same time). He toured Canada and made several tours of the Netherlands, conducting Christmas and American-music concerts.

In the United States Gould's itinerary included St. Louis, Detroit, Phoenix, Hartford, Minneapolis, Washington, D.C., and a host of other locations, though often in summer programs, such as Cleveland's Blossom Music Festival. These engagements usually resulted in a trail of letters from women. Gould rarely told his family where he was going; they were constantly surprised to read of one performance or another, or to hear from friends, as David did, that his father had just spent a weekend with the governor of Colorado.

In 1971 the Philharmonic invited the Goulds to a concert marking Bernstein's thousandth appearance with the orchestra. By then, times had changed so much that Russell Lynes, on behalf of the Mac-

Dowell Colony in New Hampshire, asked Gould for a written contribution to help mark Thomson's seventy-fifth birthday. Tubist William Bell, who had played in several Gould recordings, died in August 1971. Harvey Philips, his protégé, commissioned several composers, including Gould, to write works in Bell's memory.

The resulting *Tuba Suite* for solo tuba and three French horns was completed that very month and recorded in the fall of 1971 by Philips on the Golden Crest label, along with David Baker's Sonata for tuba and string quartet. *Tuba Suite* is one of Gould's most attractive pieces, relaxed, full of respect and mourning, and without any showy musical jokes. He also began to quote himself, inserting reflections of *Showpiece*, for example. It is an understated, exquisite work with plenty of straightforward display for the solo instrument. Philips wrote Gould gratefully on 19 September 1972, saying, "I think *Tuba Suite* is a great addition to our meager repertoire of solo works. Major composers like yourself will after all in the final analysis be the determining factor as to general acceptance of the tuba as a solo voice."

Composers of a new generation noticed Gould. The young Englishman Oliver Knussen had met him in 1969 when the London Symphony, led by André Previn, performed in Florida. On 24 May 1973, after the Louisville Orchestra released *Soundings* and *Columbia*, Knussen wrote, "I am hereby nominating you as 'honest composer of the century.' It's so nice to hear some enjoyable, 'no shit' (pardon the crudity) music, in this age of program notes and combinatorial hexachords. Anyway, *Columbia* has made my day."

Knussen knew of *Soundings* in England, then, five months before Barbara Kolb in New York asked Gould to change its name. The concert that had concerned Kolb was a 17 December 1973 performance by the American Symphony Orchestra, a week after Gould's sixtieth birthday. The orchestra, founded in 1962 by Stokowski and revived after his retirement in 1972 as a semi-cooperative run by its musicians, had reorganized and begun performing again that fall. Gould, who donated his services, led the Ives Symphony No. 1, *Soundings*, Gershwin's Concerto in F with Lorin Hollander (also donating his services), and Copland's *El salon Mexico*.

Earlier in the day, Gould was interviewed by Robert Sherman for WQXR. Sherman had thought of him in terms of his lighter pieces: "Only later, when I started doing interviews myself and began knowing him, when I began talking about music with other musicians and other artists, I began to realize there was a lot more. . . . One began to get a sense that this was a man of just extraordinary depth of interest and knowledge, and fascination." *The New York Times* and *Newsday* also ran short interviews, by Raymond Ericson and Bob Micklin. In each Gould spoke about the state of American music after two decades of dominance by the "international style." The current scene, he told Ericson, was more open and accepting, and Gould praised the "humanistic" writing of George Crumb, for example, which he found "very expressive, very rhapsodic, and in a strange way very simple and direct."

Robert Kimball (*The New York Post*, 18 December 1973) gave Gould the sort of acknowledgment he had rarely received: "Morton Gould, a vital, inspiring, and multitalented mainstay of the American musical scene for almost forty years, conducted the orchestra with consummate authority in an excellent program. [He] has as great an affinity for and understanding of Gershwin's music as any conductor around." Kimball, eventually a prominent historian and documenter of the Gershwin legacy and Broadway, described the performance of the Gershwin as "so outstanding that it could serve as a model of how America's most-beloved piano concerto should be played—but seldom is."

In New York, Gould had developed a primary musical relationship with the American Symphony Orchestra. Gould turned to the American Symphony partly because he no longer had any connection with the Philharmonic. After a second set of Proms in 1966, he mounted the podium there only three more times, in somewhat humiliating circumstances. In January 1974, for example, he was a substitute for a substitute. Thomas Schippers was ill and Erich Leinsdorf replaced him. But Leinsdorf would miss the Saturday, 19 January, performance; he would lead instead the Metropolitan Opera in Wagner's *Tristan und Isolde*. So the Philharmonic called on Gould—who barely knew the music and got no rehearsals. He led that night and during a tour concert in Orlando, Florida.

"I remember it vividly," Gould said in 1985. "It was the Mozart *Jupiter*, the *Afternoon of a Faun* with [principal flute] Julie Baker, and the Brahms First." This emergency earned him some respect. *The New York Post* wrote, "The responsiveness of the orchestra to Gould's own interpretation of the works, as well as its sharpness and precision, so surprising under the circumstances, were another indication of the Philharmonic's ability to meet difficulty with 'grace under pressure.' Gould is a modest man, but he is one of the best, most underrated musicians we have." As if one concert with no rehearsal wasn't enough, the Orlando program was changed, with the Debussy replaced by Richard Strauss's *Till Eulenspiegels lustige Streiche* —again without a rehearsal.

It was around this time that Johanna Fiedler noticed how respectful musicians and management were of Gould. "They didn't treat him in the kind of patronizing way they treated, say, Kostelanetz. There was something about him; he was such a complete professional. And I don't think they treated him as badly as I've seen my father get treated. They loved him because he was straight with them. One thing musicians hate more than anything else in a conductor is someone who comes in and tells them a story or acts all pretentious." Morton was never anything like pretentious.

Others took note of Gould's longevity, too. In June 1974 the publishers of the *Schwann Tape and Record Guide*, marking the twenty-fifth anniversary of their monthly publication, congratulated him for having appeared in every one of the 298 issues since the very first, in 1949. His shift in focus was apparent from a comparison of Gould's listings in 1949 and 1974. Everything in the first edition, although in the "classical" section, was a symphonic arrangement of popular music: *After Dark*, *Rendezvous*, *A Morton Gould Showcase*, and so forth. The June 1974 listings were very different: *American Salute*, *Derivations*, *Fall River Legend*, *Interplay*, *Soundings*, *Spirituals for String Choir and Orchestra*, and *Tuba Suite*, among others.

Also in 1974, Gould got three commissions for the 1976 Bicentennial celebration—nothing from the major orchestras, but work that tapped three different parts of his creativity. In May the U.S. Department of Labor asked for "a cantata of American work songs and music," an NEA commission. In June the Queens, New York, Symphony (founded and led by David Katz, one of Stokowski's American Symphony assistants) commissioned a piece, with funding from the New York State Council on the Arts and the U.S. Historical Society; and in November the Detroit Symphony under Aldo Ceccato commissioned yet another Bicentennial work, another NEA commission. Gould was one of fourteen American composers, including Elliott Carter, Ned Rorem, Jacob Druckman, and David Del Tredici, who received NEA Bicentennial commissions for major orchestral works. But Gould's *American Ballads* for the Queens Symphony, the least original, got the most play and recording.

The most notable sign of Gould's migration into the concert world occurred in 1975, when G. Schirmer took his catalog from Chappell, first handling rentals and eventually becoming his publisher. Gould had lost his recording outlet when RCA let his contract lapse in 1970, and the relationship with Chappell was weakening, too. Max Dreyfus had died in 1964, and the company was acquired in 1968 by Philips, the Dutch recording firm. Their focus was on rock and country music, and the old writers were edged aside. By 1972 Gould had joined the music advisory panel of the National Endowment for the Arts—and was demanding of Philips to know when his newer works would be published. But once Philips realized that it owned only part of its writers, because of the way Dreyfus structured their contracts, Chappell sold its shares in G & C to the Goulds.

"After Max Dreyfus died, Philips couldn't give two hoots about Morton," said Louis Brunelli, his copyist and arranger after Phil Lang moved to Broadway. "I said to Morton, 'Look, you better get the hell out of here. They are promising you the world, and nobody's delivering.'" Brunelli left Chappell in 1971 and eventually became a dean at the Juilliard School.

Gould stayed with Chappell until 1975, when Ed Murphy became president of G. Schirmer, the largest American publisher of concert music. "I thought, in terms of 'serious' music, Morton would be able to fit in well," Murphy said. "I took him seriously." The move to Schirmer gave Gould the musical legitimacy he yearned for. At Mills, he was a popular composer with symphonic leanings; Chappell was known primarily for show music. But Schirmer was as Carnegie Hall as you could get. "We had a platform, a place that was in the serious music field, an area which he wanted to write in," Murphy said in 1995. "Whether the world out there saw him that way—." He trailed off.

Gould stayed with Schirmer for the rest of his career. Murphy thought him a great success: "I published whatever he gave me. . . .

Morton would write, and we would publish—and he was not a minimalist in what he would provide for me." Like composers from Haydn's day onward, Gould rarely considered that the way he wrote a work was the only way it could be done. "He would do extractions and variations of pieces if he found another use for them," said Murphy. His ability to compose and orchestrate in his head ("a gift, a true gift—he does what a MIDI keyboard can do today") was also important to a publisher seeking to maximize income.

The Bicentennial year was a time of triumph for Gould such as he had not experienced in decades, though the three commissions came to life with the usual fuss and bother. Gould put most of his heart into *Symphony of Spirituals*, for the Detroit Symphony. Over the years, Gould wrote several works which claimed inspiration from Negro spirituals; the most prominent were *Spirituals for String Choir and Orchestra* (1941); *Spirituals for Strings* (1959, published in 1961 as *Spirituals* "for harp and strings"); and this *Symphony of Spirituals*. Only *Spirituals for Strings* was a setting of recognized songs. In *Symphony of Spirituals*, the title is either camouflage or an attempt to distract the listener.

For the Louisville recording of *Symphony of Spirituals*, Gould wrote of his idea for a large-scale symphonic work rooted in and derived from the spiritual idiom, both black and white. But no listener would guess that the highly charged, melodic music of black churchgoers had anything to do with this score. Its four movements resemble the symphonic format: "Hallelujah," a strong, moderately paced opening; "Blues," a slow movement; "Rag," like a scherzo, and "Shout," a heaving finale. The only trace of African America in the opening is the use of a very strong four-note rhythmic element. Otherwise, its main musical source is Gould himself, and nothing from American folk music.

This is even more apparent in "Blues," which is slow, strained, grieving, and tender, but has no touch of the traditional blues. Gould wrote that "Rag" is "a highly stylized and diverse distillation of rag phrases and patterns—a dancing movement." You'd never know that by listening; there are touches of *Dance Variations*, and the overall structure is syncopated and contrapuntal. It dances, all right, but not to the drums Gould would have a listener think. The same goes for "Shout": massive, rhythmic, packed with blaring and wailing brass in the way only an American who knew big bands could have written, but utterly transformed.

The symphony was premiered by the Detroiters on 1 April 1976. It didn't receive many other performances until 1978, when Gerhardt Zimmermann led it with the St. Louis Symphony, and Gould brought it to New York with the American Symphony for two performances on 15 April 1978, one at West Point and the other at Carnegie Hall. (The night before Eliot Feld unveiled his *Santa Fe Saga* as a solo for Mikhail Baryshnikov.) None of the critics enjoyed it. Harold Schonberg (*The New York Times*) had not changed his opinion of Gould: "The harmonic idiom is lacking in originality, the tunes are nondescript, and the work ends up a labored exercise in music that starts nowhere and hence goes nowhere."

Yet Gould eventually considered *Symphony of Spirituals* one of his most important compositions, the distillation of years of on-the-job training combined with native genius. He might have been better off giving the music an abstract title. Without an identifying blaze, the listener would have a better chance to hear it plain. Only once—and to himself—did he speak of what the score really meant. In his diary, on 22 May 1988, Gould described listening to the Louisville recording. "I'm proud of that work," he said. "It's very knotty, though some of it is more complex than it should be." Far from referring to American spirituals and dance music, the piece is a reflection on his own unhappiness. Although she did recover, Deborah was ill when he was composing the work ("We were afraid she had stomach cancer"); the "Blues" movement "definitely is Deborah's." And his marriage was nearing total dissolution: "I knew I was losing Shirley, . . . I knew that everything was going to break up." It was a black time.

The second Bicentennial commission, premiered on 24 April 1976, followed a path of less resistance. *American Ballads*, for the Queens Symphony, was a patriotic compilation: "Star-Spangled Overture," variations on the National Anthem; "Amber Waves," based on "America the Beautiful"; then "Jubilo," "Memorials," "Saratoga Quick Step," and "Hymnal." After decades of Gouldian Americana, it could easily be heard as yet another clever pandering to popular taste. That's how John Rockwell (*The New York Times*, 8 January 1980) felt when Gould led the American Symphony in a program that included "Star-Spangled Overture" and Robert Starer's Piano Concerto No. 3. Rockwell, a champion of the American vernacular and one of the earliest critical proponents of minimalism, tried to blow Gould (and Starer) out of the water. Other than Stravinsky's *Petrushka,* he wrote, the program was "pretty useless." He didn't much like the Starer, though it was "at least a serious work." But the Gould? "Popsy trash of the worst order—'worst' because it's technically sophisticated but also pretentious and empty. The American Symphony could make a real mark if it attempted to become a home for really interesting American music. Instead, it (cynically, one hopes) accepts congratulations for this sort of middlebrow tokenism."

After Gould's death, during an ASCAP awards ceremony in 1997, Rockwell explained he was reacting to Gould's location in the pop tradition for which the critic, a scholarly follower of rock, felt contempt. Yet again, what may have been operating here was received wisdom. Rockwell knew little of Gould's writing other than the arrangements of the 1940s and 1950s; he did not know the complete *American Ballads*; and he may have had little sympathy for the orchestral forms in which Gould was at home.

In fact, "Star-Spangled Overture" is a continuation of the brilliant variation style epitomized by *American Salute*. It changes moods brashly and unpredictably, playing high-handed games with the tough old melody. It is real Americana, full of affectionate irreverence, Ivesian in impulse but more transparent. The rest of the *Ballads* are like that, too, dealing tenderly and inventively with classic American tunes using harmonies and structures that recall, in no particular order, Brahmsian chorale, swing band, and anything else the composer could think of. Gould, as usual, masked the depth of his feeling with wisecracks.

The remaining Bicentennial commission, the labor cantata *Something To Do,* suffered a fate similar to Gould's other theater-oriented works. There was a single performance marked by a grandstanding diva, a copyright battle with the lyricist, and the work's total disappearance. When Norman Corwin declined his invitation to collaborate, Gould turned to the Broadway lyricist Carolyn Leigh. "I had a ball working with her," Gould said in 1985. "She could be very aggravating on different levels—everybody could be peaceful and suddenly she would go off on a tear and get everyone polarized and antagonistic. But she was really a great lyricist. She was very adventuresome."

There were twelve songs, on subjects as somber as "With These Hands" and as lighthearted as "Twomblie's Thingamajig." The sole performance was on Labor Day, 6 September 1976, at the Kennedy Center. *Something To Do* was directed by Louis Johnson as a semi-staged musical; Pearl Bailey was the featured soloist; and the Robert De Cormier Singers provided the chorus. This was an important occasion for the Goulds; few in the younger generation had seen Morton at such an opening. Nearly all the family was there.

Bailey was a temperamental performer, and by 1976, after her Tony Award–winning run in an all-black production of *Hello, Dolly!*, she had become a powerful figure who threw her weight around. David Gould said that during rehearsals, Bailey got upset about a younger singer and flew into a rage. "She took off and ran her own ballgame with it," Morton said in 1985. "I got furious and had a terrible confrontation with her on the stage. She was a great artist, a great entertainer, but she was getting out of discipline. I said the equivalent of 'I don't care who she is or who anybody is. If they don't behave with discipline, as far as I was concerned they could leave.' I really let go. The whole cast was sort of in shock but very pleased to see me running the show."

After the premiere, Schirmer had the score set in type, ready to publish, but Leigh and Gould quarreled over royalties and copyright. So the music was never published nor performed again, and after Leigh died in 1981, Gould could not come to an agreement with her estate. *Something To Do* remains little more than a glowing memory in the minds of the Gould family.

Nevertheless, Morton felt pretty good during the Bicentennial. Six years after his father's death, he seemed to have established himself in the world he had always longed for: he was pleased with what he had written; he was published by G. Schirmer, the premier house in the nation, and felt welcomed into the artistic universe they represented; he was being given significant work to do; he was conducting constantly. Perhaps he had arrived.

CHAPTER 22

Revivals and Disasters

★ ★ ★ ★

THE GOULD CHILDREN seemed settled or on their way. Eric and Candy had two daughters, Jocelyn and Jessica; a son, Benjamin, was born in 1977. Eric's pediatric practice in Great Neck was thriving. David, an energetic attorney who worked with the federal and New York City governments, was attracted to politics. Abby, a teacher, worked with her mother for a while at Bellevue, and fell in love with and married a colleague, Stuart Burton. Deborah was earning a law degree at St. John's University. At home, though the couple were now essentially separated, Shirley made a major renovation to the kitchen and dining area to the tune of roughly $55,000. And although he was no longer under contract with RCA, Gould himself was also involved in a significant new recording project that may have contributed to the reconstruction of his musical reputation, and portions of the press were approaching him with a good deal more respect. "Everything looked so great, so glowing as a composer, as a recording artist," he recalled in a late 1987 diary entry. "I was recording, having things done. Lots of things were happening."

For example, despite their dispute over *Something To Do*, Gould and Leigh got along well enough that she asked him to join in a musical version of Federico Fellini's *Juliet of the Spirits*. She and producer Frank Dunlop had the rights to the film; writer Susan Silver was to handle the book, Dunlop was to direct, and Leigh recruited Gould to compose. The show was to open in the fall of 1978 originally but was postponed until the next spring. "The producers were young, they had stars in their eyes," Gould said in 1985. "The fact that they didn't have a second act or an ending seemed irrelevant." The project didn't jell. Eventually Leigh turned it into a one-woman show, *Enter Juliet;* nothing came of that either. Neither of Gould's works with Leigh were published, and except for that one Labor Day performance of *Something To Do,* neither was performed.

In 1978 Jerome Ruzicka, vice president and sales director for Bose, a high-end audio manufacturer, was looking for music to demonstrate the brand-new digital recording technology. He talked Bose into making several state-of-the-art recordings using Thomas J. Stockham Jr.'s cutting-edge Soundstream computer process, the top-rank British engineer Brian Culverhouse, and a good English orchestra such as the London Symphony. When the team was set, Ruzicka began considering who could conduct, and what should be recorded. He never considered Bernstein—too expensive and too far from the popular brands of music. Copland was noncommittal. Then he thought of Gould, whose music he had loved since he was a kid.

"Morton Gould really did bridge the gap over so many forms of music, from symphonic to pop and film," he said. "And film music also was one of the elements that struck me as kind of popular, and yet symphonic, and potentially really great demonstration material, sonically spectacular."

Ruzicka spent three days on Melbourne Road, discussing repertory, gorging on Chinese takeout, and meeting most of the family—except Shirley, whom he spoke to once on the phone but never saw. (When Ruzicka first called the Gould household, he had a pleasant conversation with Shirley—she refused to tell him where Morton was and declined to relay any messages.) Ruzicka, forty-three at the time, was a fan of the sixty-four-year-old composer; he regaled Morton with stories of broadcasts and sat at the piano and played the "Cresta Blanca Waltz." Ruzicka was attracted not only to Gould's experience but his willingness to try things for effect, to increase the impact of the listening experience—what Ruzicka called "the fun of listening."

He rummaged through Gould's files and turned up old recordings and scores. There was the "Quickstep" movement of the Symphony No. 2, *Philharmonic Waltzes, Festive Music.* Gould tried hard to interest him in *Showpiece,* but he didn't like the music. Eventually they settled on enough material for three discs: Gould conducting

Gould, film scores, and orchestral showpieces. The recordings were made over ten days in September 1978 with the London Symphony Orchestra, at Watford Town Hall and All Saints Church in Tooting, outside London. Gould described the work in *Audio* magazine (December 1981); when he told the percussionists they could play a full *fortissimo* or an actual *sforzando*, rather than the muted dynamics required for analog recordings, "They looked at me as if I had two heads." These were the first digital recordings ever made in the United Kingdom, and the first time Gould himself recorded the complete *Latin American Symphonette.*

During editing and production, Ruzicka left Bose, which sold the project to Varese Sarabande, which issued the discs. The audiophile reviews were ecstatic: "digital brilliance"; "three sonic tens"; "performance: stunning. recording: spectacular." "So it worked," Ruzicka concluded. "It was a spectacular recording with good material."

In October 1978 Gould returned to Watford Town Hall for another session with the London Philharmonic, this time to record *Foster Gallery* and *Spirituals for String Choir and Orchestra*, on the Crystal Clear label. The result was another very high-fidelity product, using the painstaking "direct to disc" method and the latest analog equipment. Suddenly Gould was again a significant presence on records and not on the mid- and low-level labels: these were high-priced, state-of-the-art discs bound to draw the attention of a discerning audience. Listeners who thought Morton Gould was just a middlebrow arranger were introduced to a senior musician who was new to them.

But this musical activity paled alongside the disaster that was finally happening on Melbourne Road. Morton's extensive touring was no help. In the spring and summer of 1977, for example, Gould made a seven-week tour of Australia for the Australian Broadcasting Corp, conducting most of the country's major orchestras. After the trip, he received several letters and a photograph from a violist who wrote, "I've been leading a very celibate life—no interesting men around—I told you that you spoilt me, so I am having to be content with beautiful memories."

The closest Morton came to expressing his feelings during this period was in a letter he wrote Shirley on 11 August 1978, after she had left on what Gould called "one of her trips" (by now Shirley was traveling alone to visit friends as far away as New Orleans; Morton suspected her of straying, too). It's a bleak, unsentimental missive which makes clear that Morton knew precisely what was happening: "Your departure this a.m. without even a verbal goodbye is the coda to your long, unrelenting, and shockingly cruel and destructive rampage against me." He calls her behavior "rude and arrogant," especially to someone who has been so long a part of her life—"distasteful as it has been to you—a point you made so abundantly and effectively clear privately and publicly . . . I literally do not exist for you, except to be exiled and condemned not only for my foibles and errors, but for all your other wounds and frustrations from others, and your own weaknesses."

Morton acknowledges that their life together is over: "There is comparatively little time left, and I finally accept and reconcile to your verdict. I will be sixty-five—and now I too have some scores to settle—and I too turn away and no longer wait. As there were no 'goodbyes,'—there will be no more 'hellos.' "

It is similar in tone to the letters Gould wrote to Shirley Uzin after she left him. But the envelope has a further note, dated 1 September 1978: "Never sent—couldn't spoil her vacation (?)—but an indication of what was in my head—and soul—and what I probably should have done—or still do—and follow the inevitable as charted by SBG."

Perhaps Shirley Bank Gould sensed his surrender, or perhaps she had finally reached the end of her own tether. Later that fall, she told their children she was going to leave their father on New Year's Day. "She said that she couldn't stand it, that she would move out; she would stay with him another couple of months, but by January 1 she was going," said Candy Gould.

Morton was shocked and hurt. Joan Peyser, by now editor of *The Musical Quarterly*, recalled how upset he was. "I do remember the day when he came to my office at *The Musical Quarterly*," Peyser told me in 1994, "in a state of absolute despair. He said that just before he had left for his trip to Japan, she appeared at the door and said, 'I won't be here when you get back. I'm leaving you.' And when he came back, she was gone—he said he was devastated, he didn't know if he could ever recover.

"I said to him, 'Morton, you're talking to me. I know you. You've been screwing around all of your married life.' He answered with absolute conviction, 'But I loved only her.'"

In January 1979 Gould went to Japan to lead the Yomiuri Nippon Symphony. He wrote Deborah, the only child still in the house, a letter from Tokyo on 5 January 1979 to be shown to everyone else. At the top he scrawled: "Do not destroy—keep or xerox for family (children only) to be read with expression—no wisecracks." After a gossipy, jokey opening, he turned serious:

> So far I am alone—how nice it would have been to be here with Mom—but she never wanted this, even when she could have, and I gave up asking a long time ago. . . . I know we all wish that she hadn't "cut out"—and done it the way she did—and I regret that you bear part of this pressure and discomfiture. I will try very hard to cope with discipline and courage, and avoid inflicting needless hardship on all of you. Be supportive, but contain her if at all possible—for her own sake, and well being. Despite the long barren years, and her obvious complete rejection of me and what I feel—I love her. The riches of my life—all of you—I owe to her. I hope she finds herself—but in the attempt doesn't lock herself out of what she has—and throw away the key.

There may be other letters from that period, but Shirley, in her wrath, destroyed all the correspondence she could find.

The separation came as a surprise to many people who thought they knew them well. "I was dumbfounded," said psychiatrist Richard Glavine. "I had absolutely no idea, other than a certain coldness that would come into her voice when she talked about Morton."

Danny Daniels and his wife, Bea, had been close friends of the Goulds until the Daniels moved to California in 1971. They had dined together frequently; Abby spent Christmases with them. "It came as a terrible blow to my wife and myself," Daniels said. "It never even occurred to us that it could possibly happen."

Even Shirley did not seem to believe it. She took years finding a place to live. For a while, she slept on a convertible sofa in Glavine's apartment; she spent time with the Bernbachs, in the UN Plaza complex just north of the United Nations. She sublet an apartment owned by Annette Nancarrow, wife of the composer Conlon Nancarrow and a friend of Morton's from Richmond Hill. She lived with Eric and Candy. She even moved back into the house, which led to scenes that would have been ludicrous had they not been so painful.

Meanwhile, Morton kept his feelings suppressed beneath that tight-lipped grin. One of his most important projects during the year before Shirley left was the score for the NBC film *Holocaust*. It is tempting to believe that beneath the sorrow in this score, Gould was also grieving for the end of his marriage.

Holocaust was a major television event in the spring of 1978. It was conceived as a mass-market attempt to do for the destruction of the Jews in Europe, in nine and half hours over four nights, what *Roots* had done for the history of slavery in the United States. The production was elaborate and the cast first-rate—Meryl Streep, Joseph Bottoms, Ian Holm, Rosemary Harris, Michael Moriarty, Fritz Weaver. The producers, Robert Berger and Herbert Brodkin, were friends of Morton's who had first approached him about the project in 1977, although it was not a subject he wanted to deal with. Even the children argued with him about it. Abby Gould Burton remembered her father musing, "I don't know why they called me. Word is out that the network would like Lenny to do it, but Bud and Herb would like me to take a look at it. Well, you know, Lenny is a very talented guy."

"Excuse me, so are you a very talented guy."

"Well, you know, Lenny is Jewish."

"Excuse me, you are too."

Gould went to a screening of the first two hours of the rough cut, and brought Abby along. Afterward, Morton leaned over to Berger and Brodkin and said, "You know what? I don't think you should put any music to this." Gould said he feared the impact would be diluted by the use of music. Nevertheless, they asked him to score the production, and he wrote his usual reams of music. But the final version used very little of it, as if the producers agreed with him, finally.

The reaction to *Holocaust* was harsh; it was criticized as too much like a soap opera, with its star-crossed lovers and sobbing patriarchs. After an initial burst of enthusiasm, *Holocaust* slowly sank, and two decades later Stephen Spielberg's *Schindler's List*, complete with John Williams's score, gave it the coup de grâce.

But Gould created a suite released by RCA that stands superbly on its own. If *World War I* was devoted to the European world that had been lost to his parents, *Holocaust* may fairly be considered a somber, gorgeously executed elegy to the impending end of his own married life.

Each movement is linked to episodes in the film; an opening theme recurs in various forms throughout. It's followed by a joyously macabre setting for Kristallnacht, when Nazi gangs set upon the Jews of Germany: a garish blend of Weill, Stravinsky, the "Horst Wessel" Song and "Die Lorelei." Other passages deal with the comfortable lives of assimilated Jews, the burning of synagogues, the death camps, and the Warsaw Ghetto uprising. The survivors mark their freedom in a touching movement that graciously blends the main theme with "Hatikvah," the anthem of the Israeli state just being born, and it ends with a quiet, flowing restatement of the theme. The impression is one of deep, controlled grief and sorrow, in an idiom that avoids the saccharine and sentimental.

Until this time, Gould had displayed no interest in the Jews of Europe. If important elements of *Symphony of Spirituals* related directly to his family, how much more likely that this mournful score contained his sadness over the end of his marriage?

As the years went by, Shirley alienated almost all her friends. The only person who claimed to have some understanding of her frustration and anger was Deborah, who found herself in her mother's very uncomfortable shoes. "He's a difficult man to live with, very difficult," she said.

Deborah got a look at Morton that none of the others had. For years Shirley had begged for a lawn sprinkler system, but Morton refused to pay although she was the one who moved the sprinklers from one part of the lawn to another. "Two days after she left, and he realized he would have to schlep that thing from the back to the front, guess who got a sprinkler system?" Deborah said. She would spend all day at school, then go food shopping. Eric would just drop over and begin to eat, which angered her. But Morton would shrug off his son's behavior: "Let him alone, he likes fruit."

"Or I would knock myself out to get a gift for someone, and they would say, 'Oh that's nice.' And all Dad would do would be to write a check—'Oooooh, isn't this wonderful!' He always got extra special treatment. All he had to do was blink, and everybody thought it was great. And I really started to understand why she resented him. The fact that it took him two years to realize he could take his own plate off the table, and that he could wash his own pot."

After Shirley's departure the legend of Incompetent Morton took hold once more. Each of the children has stories about his apparent befuddlement when confronted with domesticity. Trying to make an instant meal, he put a box into boiling water; it never occurred to him to open the package. He couldn't figure out how to use a coffeemaker: he put the water and coffee in it, but neglected to put the pot underneath, so that the liquid spread all over the counter. He once stood over the sink trying to squeeze the soap out of a Brillo pad. Gould had been brought up so completely the center of his family's fortunes and future that they and he always worked to shelter him from daily life.

Yet Gould fully understood recording technology, both as a musician and later as president of ASCAP. "He was technologically competent; he understood the process," Schirmer's Ed Murphy maintained. "Maybe he didn't want to fix the vacuum cleaner. He understood the digitalization issue—he testified in Congress about it."

Ironically, the year Shirley left him was also the first time Gould died, on page 211 of a coffee-table book called *The Music Makers*, published in 1979 by Harry N. Abrams. The respectful entry, headed "Gould, Morton (1913–1976)," noted that "many of Gould's orchestral works such as *Minstrel Show* and the *Symphonettes* were seen as bridging the gap between serious and light music with elegance and craftsmanship."

Gould lived another seventeen years, and this final period became a race between the forces that brought him position and honors, and those that tried to make him disappear. He knew of the judgment and fought the matter out wretchedly within his mind.

In 1980, approaching his sixty-seventh birthday, the public Gould was as busy as ever. He even conducted the Philharmonic, the first time since he substituted for Leinsdorf in 1974. This was a substitution also—and particularly ironic. André Kostelanetz, who still had a Saturday night concert series, died on 13 January 1980. Gould took his place twice thereafter: on 9 February 1980 for a performance in Kostelanetz's honor; and again on 8 March, in a program marking Barber's seventieth birthday. So it was Gould, whom Kostelanetz had not even mentioned in his memoirs, who led the orchestra in his memory. These were the last times Gould conducted the ensemble where he had once been so much at home.

Gould never stopped reaching—and he was generous to others who might want to stretch their hands, too. Gould may have been uncomfortable with academia, but he was recognized as a person with something to offer. On 12 October 1980, for example, he presented a detailed lecture-demonstration, "The Art of Arranging Popular Music" at the Peabody Conservatory in Baltimore. He declared, "All music is an arrangement," defined as "transference, transformation, using an already established melody, a setting of the familiar—either literal or a fantasy based on a melody." Bach arranged Vivaldi, Beethoven arranged Scottish folk songs, Liszt made transcriptions, Stokowski arranged Bach.

He was also composing at a sustained pace. On 11 September 1979 he had completed *Burchfield Gallery*, commissioned by the family of painter Charles E. Burchfield for the Cleveland Orchestra and premiered under Lorin Maazel in April 1981. That year the commissions arrived in earnest: for G. Schirmer an incidental piece, *Celebration '81* (later called *Celebration Strut*), for the NBC television series *Live from Studio 8H*; for L. Antony Fisher, a member of the New York Choral Society, the choral work *Quotations*; from the Library of Congress, Concerto Concertante, for violinist Elmar Oliveira; from the Chamber Music Society of Lincoln Center, *Cello Suite* for cellist Leslie Parnas and pianist Charles Wadsworth. Gould was also preparing *Housewarming*, to mark the opening of the Baltimore Symphony's new Meyerhoff Hall in 1982.

Many people in the concert world were now prepared to accept Gould. He seemed to be emerging as a bona-fide "serious" composer after all. Not that this was met with complete equanimity. A reviewer for *International Musician*, writing about a performance of "Elegy" from *Holocaust* at the 1981 Congress of Strings, said, "Its brevity, lack of artifice, and obvious sincerity came as a shock to those who knew Gould's 'Pavanne' and *American Salute*." Morton Gould sincere? I'm shocked, inspector, shocked!

Other publications also began treating Gould as a more significant figure. Pianist David Dubal wrote a wide-ranging interview, complete with exquisite childhood photos, for the January 1981 issue of *Keynote*, the magazine of New York classical music station WNCN-FM. The station broadcast nineteen of Gould's orchestral and band scores, as well as selections from his Chicago and other RCA recordings, most of the performances airing at prime time.

In 1982 Roy Hemming, a producer of the Philharmonic radio broadcasts, wrote "The Serious Side of Morton Gould" for *Ovation Magazine*. It began: "Morton Gould probably should be a bitter man. But he isn't. Disappointed, perhaps. And sometimes vexed and even deeply pained. For here he is, in his late sixties, one of the best-known names in music in America—but not for what *he* thinks is his most important or, he hopes, his most enduring work." In a tortured, funny, yet self-aware statement, Gould told Hemming: "As some of my pieces got more and more public acceptance, I almost felt like getting up and saying, 'Look, I'm terribly sorry. I wrote something that a lot of people like—and I'll try not to do it again.' In a number of instances, I *tried* not to do it again—perhaps successfully, which I sometimes regret."

He put a good face on things—it would be hard not to, since he was among the few Americans who'd been able to spend their lives composing and conducting, without accepting academic or administrative jobs. But by now Gould *was* a bitter man. He rehearsed all the rationalizations about how well he had done compared with colleagues. Nevertheless, as revealed in extraordinary detail in the taped diary he began on 29 October 1982, Gould was terribly unhappy about his place in the musical firmament.

On 7 March 1982, two years after his last appearance there, the Philharmonic had committed a sin of omission that Morton considered the crowning insult. Music director Zubin Mehta led the orchestra's ten-thousandth concert. The elaborate program book included an essay entitled "Contemporary Music and the New York Philharmonic," which chronicled the scope of first performances given by the Philharmonic and listed many Americans whose work had been premiered. From the 1940s and 1950s came Lukas Foss, William Grant Still, Marc Blitzstein, Deems Taylor, Leon Kirchner, Elie Siegmeister, and the like.

But not Morton Gould—an absence that hurt him deeply. The essay was written by a freelancer named Kenneth LaFave and passed by program annotator Phillip Ramey. When Gould called in anguish and anger, Ramey said his name was left out to save space. The incident grew in Gould's mind to seem part of a plot to write him out of the Philharmonic completely.

After Gould's death, LaFave, now arts critic for the *Arizona Republic*, wrote me on 25 August 1996 to apologize and set the record straight (though his apology confirms Morton's low standing at the time). LaFave said he'd been told to "include only the most important ones" and keep the essay short: "In my twenty-nine-year-old, just-out-of-graduate-school mentality, Gould didn't qualify, because he was a pops composer—wasn't he?" LaFave said he had been so embarrassed at the time that he "went out of [his] way to write about Morton whenever possible." He became a fan and a friend, and Gould encouraged him in his own composition. "There was no conspiracy against Morton at the Phil," LaFave wrote revealingly, "just the cultural conspiracy that pigeonholes composers in 'serious' and 'pops' categories and makes young idiots like the dunce I was think they understand something profound." The Philharmonic was not deliberately trying to eliminate Gould; the world had already done it.

Gould had begun working with Balanchine again on *Birds of America*. One afternoon during the spring of 1982, Robbins left a note for Gould on his seat at the theater: "If you get tired of *Birds*, I've got a ballet (new) I'd like you to do. Easy—and fun. Call. Love, Jerry." Morton added his own postscript right on the original: "Jerry left this note for me the day . . . I met with George Balanchine going over and discussing the *Birds—Audubon* ballet—for the coming season. He took very ill shortly after this session—was hospitalized—and after a long siege, died. This note was the beginning of *I'm Old Fashioned: Astaire Variations*."

Gould and Robbins began a difficult collaboration with a brilliant outcome. Robbins wanted to create a celebration of the dancing of Fred Astaire, with variations on Jerome Kern's *I'm Old Fashioned*. Gould sent the choreographer tapes of music. "I think we are hearing and seeing the same things," he wrote him on 7 July 1982. But by October the project was in trouble. Whereas Balanchine, Gould said in his diary in 1982, "comes in with the music in his head, and really knows where he is going, Jerry really starts to work when he gets the dancers up in the theater. He improvises and goes back and forth, gets dissatisfied, restless, antagonistic toward the music, toward himself, toward what he did." Gould had to be talked out of quitting at least three times, by Scott and Murphy at Schirmer, and City Ballet administrator Betty Cage.

Gould wanted to write more elaborate and complex music. He felt Jerry was telling him how to compose, which he considered an affront. And Gould was uncomfortable writing music to choreography rather than the other way around. Nevertheless, the piece was a hit of the 1982–83 season and has been frequently revived since. (In another Gouldian irony, they had planned to call it *Astaire Variations*, but shortly before opening night a Canadian company came to town with a piece called *Astaire*, so the title was changed to *I'm Old Fashioned: Variations on a Theme by Jerome Kern*).

While worrying about Balanchine, fighting with Robbins, conducting, and working on commissions, Gould was struck an intensely personal blow: Shirley developed bone cancer—the rare and nearly always fatal multiple myeloma. During the week of 16 September, while Morton was in Baltimore for the opening of Meyerhoff Hall, Shirley had a biopsy performed at New York Hospital that confirmed the diagnosis. "I know she's terrified," Gould said in his diary. "She's been amazingly brave. The week after she was in the hospital, she went back to school and taught, functioned the way she has. It's just unbelievable." Then Shirley fell during a trip to Washington, D.C., and shattered her kneecap—now she not only had cancer, but she was on crutches, too.

Morton's feelings were painfully convoluted. Time and again he spoke of his longing for her, how he dreamed of her, dreamed of making love, wished that she would return to him. "I'd give anything to have her come back here, so I can take care of her," he said to his diary, late in 1982, but added revealingly: "She couldn't be here and teach, it's physically difficult."At the same time he kept up his affairs. Whenever he saw a woman who attracted him, "my engine starts running," he said.

By this time, Morton was alone in the house on Melbourne, surrounded by memories (Eric and Candy had bought an apartment in Brooklyn Heights for Deborah, as a gift and an investment). "The clothes I wear, the great sweaters that she has gotten me over the years, the bathrobes, the antique cufflinks. I use all these things, this is all hers, all Shirley's. My children, my family, I cannot stop saying how fantastic they are—this is all because of Shirley, this is Shirley's doing."

As his seventieth birthday year approached, portions of the musical press were working to alter misconceptions, writing about Gould and his career with a respect that bordered on awe, and the people around Morton tried to prepare a proper birthday celebration. Walter Gould campaigned to get his brother the Kennedy Center Honors and formed a committee with Sylvia Craft, publicity director for G. Schirmer; American Symphony Orchestra general manager Arthur Aaron and his successor, executive director Benjamin Dunham; and publicist Alix Williamson. They solicited contributions for a $100,000 Morton Gould Fund for American Music, to endow new scores for the American Symphony. In addition, Peter Kermani, president of the Albany, New York, Symphony and the American Symphony Orchestra League, named him honorary chairman and awarded him the league's Gold Baton for contributions to American music. Yet he grew increasingly depressed.

Morton expressed his appreciation but felt a failure nonetheless. The Philharmonic omission continued to sting. On 16 November 1982, for example, he mentioned Kermani's ASOL invitation in his diary: "I think it's a very sweet gesture. I am flattered, and honored to accept, et cetera. But of course in a way, this is not what I want. I would like to feel for my seventieth birthday that a major orchestra would be recognizing me. Well, they're not. I think I'm being recognized by being ignored." He caught himself and remarked,

> I'm not an idiot, I know I'm relatively better off than a lot of other people, and have accomplished more. But that's irrelevant. The fact that the New York Philharmonic, my home orchestra, with which I've been associated as composer and conductor for so many years—I can't remember all of them who have done my works—Rodzinski, Stokowski, Mitropoulos, De Sabata, Golschmann—to completely sort of obliterate me, which is what they've been doing. Mehta, as far as he is concerned, I don't think I exist. Maybe he is right—I don't want to give any impression that I am in my own way snobbish or ungrateful to

> those who have been supportive and will play me. But I missed the ring. I thought I was reaching out, I thought I could grab it at least for a moment, but it was not to be.

Not even Sylvia Craft, "a most conscientious, wonderful woman," could get an article about him in the *Times*. "I'm sure it won't happen," he said. "I am just not important enough or not visible enough or not audible enough."

Meanwhile, Gould continued to meet sorrowfully with Balanchine, shamefacedly hoping for his recovery so they could finish the ballet. "He sounds so sad," he said in his diary, late in 1982. "It's sad for the world, for a person of unqualified, unique genius to deteriorate this way. It's certainly sad for me." The week of 12 November 1982, Gould spent time with three choreographers: he lunched with De Mille; he rehearsed with Robbins; he brought some chocolates to Balanchine at Roosevelt Hospital. "He just gobbled them up like a little kid," the composer reported. "To my amazement, we ended up in a work session for *Audubon*. He is determined to do that. He said that as soon as he gets better, he wants Peter Martins [who had succeeded him as ballet master at the City Ballet] to transmit what he wants, because he can't move around. But he also said a touching thing to me. He said, 'This will be my last ballet, my farewell ballet, and we must do it, we must do it!' "

Gould brought the now bedridden Balanchine a cassette of parts of *Apple Waltzes*, performed in open rehearsal by the National Orchestral Association. He put a set of earphones over the choreographer's head. "I'd see his face light up, his eyes would open when he heard parts of it," Gould said in his diary. "A few times he started to talk and make comments. He was doing the ballet, he was putting it together, he suddenly became alert. Then he got tired, his eyes closed, he would signal for me to take the earphones off. I came away from there quite depressed to see this man deteriorating this way. And the fact that we never got through the ballet together. It's something it seems that can only happen to me."

That final remark, self-interested and self-pitying, exemplifies the darkest side of Gould. He mourned for Balanchine but could not forget how big a loss it meant for him. Balanchine died 30 April 1983, and the Audubon ballet, *Birds of America*, was never staged.

Internally the struggle continued, between common sense, which told him he was loved and appreciated, and the demon that said he had failed. Nevertheless 1983 was an exceptional year. The Louisville Orchestra asked him to write a fanfare for their new concert hall, and the orchestra planned to perform and record the Viola Concerto, premiered in 1943 by Milton Katims on the radio and since forgotten. On 5 February, Gould conducted as Arthur Mitchell's Dance Theater of Harlem premiered its own staging of *Fall River Legend*, about which Anna Kisselgoff (*The New York Times*) wrote, "Rarely has it sounded more gripping." Four days later, Gould, Schirmer, and the Chicago Symphony made official his commission to write a concerto for Donald Peck, the orchestra's principal flutist (the money came from Katherine Lewis, an elderly Californian). Peck wanted "some real music, no experimentation." This was a challenge Gould could not denigrate in any way: a major orchestral work for one of the great ensembles, to be conducted by Georg Solti.

Not that Gould stopped complaining. In the spring, when Sylvia Craft suggested a celebratory broadcast on the public radio station WNYC-FM, Gould opposed it, according to publicist Alix Williamson, because the station didn't play enough of his music. But station spokesman Lloyd Trufelman sent Williamson a list of seven Gould performances between February and June 1983, including *West Point Symphony*, *Spirituals for String Choir and Orchestra* (four times), *Latin American Symphonette*, and *Fall River Legend*. All but two, though, were on the overnight program called "While the City Sleeps."

The Philharmonic at first was going to ignore his birthday entirely; the 1983–84 season announcement made no mention of any Gould. When the orchestra did add a piece, he considered it too little, too late. Zubin Mehta, who made no secret of his ignorance of most American music, asked Previn to approach Gould. André tactfully asked whether Morton had any scores that could be used as a concert opener by a big city orchestra.

"It's New York," Morton guessed.

"Well, yeah," replied Previn.

"I don't think Zubin is aware of the fact that I composed the 'Hatikvah' [Israel's national anthem]," Morton said.

"That's an absolutely glorious joke," Previn recalled in 1997. But it did not mask Gould's bitterness. Ultimately, Previn chose to give the New York premiere of *Festive Music*, composed in 1964 for the Tri-Cities Symphony in Iowa. But Previn had to undergo surgery, and the performance itself was conducted by Leonard Slatkin.

As summer turned to fall and the birthday approached, the pace of activities rose until Gould actually complained that there was *too much* birthday celebration. "Now I think this birthday thing has gotten out of hand," he told his diary in October 1983. "It's not such a big thing, the seventieth."

Morton Gould and Elliott Carter, considered in academic circles one of the century's most important American composers, were born five years and a day apart. The day after Gould's seventieth, Carter would mark his seventy-fifth. G. Schirmer distributed lists of activities for both men, and a comparison casts light on their differences in reception and perception.

For Gould, there were performances of *Jekyll and Hyde* by the American Composers Orchestra; *Tap Dance Concerto* at Avery Fisher Hall on 15 November; the premiere of the Louisville fanfare, *Flourishes and Galop*; *Fall River Legend* by Previn with the Pittsburgh; the New York premiere of *Cello Suite*, given by the Chamber Music Society of Lincoln Center; the birthday all-Gould program at Carnegie Hall, with himself conducting the American Symphony; *Festive Music* by the Philharmonic under Slatkin; and, on 28 January 1984, the premiere of *Quotations* by the New York Choral Society under Robert De Cormier at Carnegie Hall. In addition, the Cresta Blanca wine company sponsored a special broadcast 10 December 1983 over WNCN-FM and simulcast on WNYC-AM; and Chicago's WFMT-FM presented an hour-long Gould program over 155 stations the week of 5–11 December. Gould was on the cover of the December issue of *Musical America*. That should have been enough to satisfy anyone.

Compare it with Carter's programming. Performances by the BBC Philharmonic at the Huddersfield, England, Contemporary Music Festival; the London Sinfonietta at IRCAM in Paris; the Arditti String Quartet; the Fires of London and the Vega Wind Quintet. A program at Boston University, and a forum with pianist Claudia Stevens at Carnegie Recital Hall. All-Carter concerts by Speculum Musicae at the 92nd Street Y in Manhattan and in Washington, D.C.; the IRCAM Brass Quintet in Paris; the Boston Symphony (Carter's

Double Concerto); the Contemporary Music Ensemble in San Francisco; the St. Paul Chamber Orchestra in Minnesota; and at the Banff, Canada School of the Fine Arts and the Southeastern Center for Contemporary Art in Winston-Salem, North Carolina. Carter had already won two Pulitzer Prizes and a laundry list of international awards, including in 1983 the Edward MacDowell Medal. *The Music of Elliott Carter*, a thorough analysis by David Schiff, was published that year by Eulenburg Books.

Gould was honored by big, mainstream organizations, Carter by smaller groups of intelligentsia and academicians, which connoted prestige rather than popularity. Morton wanted both.

CHAPTER 23

"A Sort of Elder Statesman"

★ ★ ★ ★

NEWSDAY (13 DECEMBER 1983) published a review of Morton Gould's seventieth birthday concert with the American Symphony Orchestra, written by its music critic, Peter Goodman. After carefully noting the celebratory elements—the cake and greetings from the mayor, the governor, and the president, Goodman observed that the program presented a representative sample of Gould's orchestral writing, including *Apple Waltzes*, *Burchfield Gallery*, and *Spirituals for String Choir and Orchestra*.

Then I wrote: "It would be nice to say that neglected music was finally given its due. Unfortunately the works were generally gentle, diffuse, and bland. And the performance was not aided by the fact that the American Symphony, which ordinarily works at a high standard, sounded careless, sloppy, and uninterested." After dissecting and disliking virtually everything, and taking swipes at Gould's conducting, I concluded, "One heard music that was well constructed but avoided any great sense of direction or urgency."

My first professional encounter with the music of Morton Gould was not positive. We had already met at performances; *Newsday* paid relatively close attention to its local composers. But I was not impressed. Morton noticed.

His diary entry of 19 December 1983 included discussions of the birthday activities: Pittsburgh, *Cello Suite*, Slatkin's performance with the Philharmonic. "It's very hectic and tiring, and exhilarating, and depressing, up and down. I've been on the go. All the tributes have been great; there's been a tremendous amount of publicity about my seventieth birthday," he said. He acknowledged that the American Symphony was not in great shape—"It was difficult because they keep switching first chairs, a very typical situation with that orchestra." He went through the reviews, which were "really not too good. *The New York Times* was nice, nothing ecstatic but nice; at least they didn't kill me. . . . [Bill] Zakariasen [*Daily News*] was a nice write-up, *The Post* was nice. *Newsday*, a fellow named Peter Goodman, whom I know, gave me a bad write-up. Whether Peter is now trying to make waves, trying to enter the domain of *The New York Times*, sort of a super-critic idea, I don't know. I'm going to do a television show with him, ironically—some cablevision thing that probably three people look at. But I'll do it."

At that time *Newsday* operated a cable television channel with some live programming, and I had asked Gould to appear on an interview program. He was genial, a forthcoming and pleasant subject. At least one of his fans, James Donenfeld of Forest Hills, wrote to him directly criticizing my review; his response on 29 December 1983 was measured, reasonable—and false: "During a career one receives both positive and negative criticism and we have to survive both." He mentioned the television program, during which we had not discussed the matter, and said, in my defense, "He did not respond to that particular concert, which is his prerogative. Quite honestly, I don't think it important enough to lose sleep over, and, at any rate, I am too busy."

But Morton did lose sleep—not over that review in particular but over where he belonged in the musical spectrum. As he said in a late 1983 diary entry, "I'd hate to think that all these celebrations are because I'm a nice person. Unfortunately, a composer's objective is not to be a nice person, but to be a good composer, at least, if not a great one, if possible. I don't think I'm great. I think I'm good. But how important my works are, I just don't know. The artist, of course, is judged not by whether he is a nice person, but by his art."

He was seventy and doubting. The modesty of his public demeanor was an alloy of pride and insecurity—pride that would not let him demand attention, insecurity that made him crave unsolicited praise. Gould's perception was accurate. Alix Williamson, who had been hired to publicize his seventieth birthday, was aware of the patronizing attitude, especially at the *Times*. "If I'd gone to them with

Shostakovich or Carter, or something like that," she said, "their attitude was different. . . . Morton was a fairly popular name with the general public. But the serious music critics are very snobby." But by the end of 1983, it was clear that Williamson succeeded in what she was asked to do.

The commissions poured in: the Los Angeles Olympic Committee got *American Sing*, a song cycle for the Los Angeles Philharmonic under Michael Tilson Thomas, with soprano Benita Valente, mezzo-soprano Florence Quivar, tenor Placido Domingo, and bass-baritone Paul Plishka, to help open the 1984 Summer Olympics. The Second International Cello Congress wanted a piece for multiple cellos, to be conducted by Mstislav Rostropovich. The *Pittsburgh Post-Gazette*, to mark its own bicentennial, commissioned a work for the Pittsburgh Symphony.

He wants it, but he doesn't want it. He gets what he wants and is embarrassed. He cannot enjoy the congratulations, because to Morton his own talent has always been suspect. As for Peter Goodman, nascent "super-critic," he eventually became the third writer to work on a Morton Gould biography—but his doubts remained until after the writing began.

The first to attempt a biography was Andrew Kazdin, a former CBS engineer who impressed Gould during the Louisville Orchestra's recording of the Viola Concerto. Robert Glazer, who had resurrected the concerto, was a section player in the Chicago Symphony and not primarily a soloist. Gould felt Kazdin's deft editing made the release possible. "We did it in bits and pieces," Gould recalled in his diary early in 1988. "Andrew Kazdin did an amazing job of stitching it together."

Kazdin began to sort and document the composer's scores, rooting among papers and recordings in the third-floor studio while the composer was at work. He interviewed Gould, first on his own and then with the writer Roy Hemming. But the taping ended in March 1986 when Gould began discussions with Joan Peyser, who was looking for another subject after the succès de scandale of her Bernstein biography.

The end of the Kazdin project was painful, because the younger man had invested an enormous amount of his time and energy in the work and felt he was losing it to a writer with a higher profile. Peyser was an established author, an old friend, editor of *The Musical Quarterly*, and had strong connections with *The New York Times*, one of Gould's bêtes noires. She had written a respected book on twentieth-century music, a controversial biography of Pierre Boulez, and had just published her groundbreaking biography of Leonard Bernstein.

The Bernstein biography, with its sometimes salacious, uninhibited, and far-from-idolatrous portrait, became a scandalous best-seller. Looking for another project, Peyser turned to Gould. If Leonard Bernstein, with his flamboyant personality and often flagrant bisexuality, made a juicy topic, why not Morton Gould, at least as prolific and just as sexual—if hetero? In comparison, Andrew Kazdin—though thorough, musically knowledgeable, and devoted to Gould—was a recording engineer. He had not been able to find a publisher, while Peyser had a very long track record in print.

Gould was attracted by the idea, though in his usual reluctant way. "I don't know whether I should do it, or if I consider it do-able, or how much of my personal life I want on view," he said in an early 1987 diary entry. "I don't have anything to hide—I think the worst that can be said of me is that I was vulnerable to women." Peyser did some preliminary interviews with the children, partly to see how open they might be to her intense, psychoanalytically oriented, sexually charged approach.

Gould alarmed Kazdin by asking for copies of the interviews. Afraid that his own work would be used by another, Kazdin refused to hand them over, until David Gould wrote him a letter arguing the legal points of who actually owned the material. Although Kazdin asked the questions, the responses were the composer's, and Gould had the right to them. Reluctant and heartbroken, Kazdin made copies and gave them to Gould. Their relationship, once very close, was irrevocably severed.

Peyser was having difficulty finding a publisher. Gould, of course, proclaimed himself the difficulty in a late 1987 diary entry: "I don't see that there is a book about me. What's there to talk about? Lenny's book has built-in publicity and world-wide success. I come nowhere near him from any point of view." His prophecy was fulfilled. In June 1988 Peyser told him that she had not received sufficient interest from any publisher to pursue his life story. Peyser's biography was never written.

Gould's children said that he had expressed anxiety that Peyser would turn her psychoanalytic eye on his sexual life, as she had on Bernstein. That arena would indeed have been an important part of anything Peyser produced. "It is my belief," she told me in 1994, "that in addition to their talents and skill, artists possess two essential components: sexuality and aggression. It always surprises me that when I describe someone as fiercely active sexually, as Bernstein certainly was, it is viewed as a pejorative comment on the man. Every composer I have studied has this energy even if it is repressed. Morton had it, and it was not repressed. Unlike many composers of his generation in the United States, he was heterosexual and was always running around like mad."

But the travail over his biography was still in the future. In the summer of 1983 Gould had begun suffering from a painful and frightening illness. He experienced pains in his back and throat; eventually his joints swelled and he had difficulty walking. But he thought his aches were psychosomatic, brought on by depression, exhilaration, or both. Early in January 1984 he spent a painful ten days with the Chattanooga Symphony, with sore throat, glands, mouth, and tongue. Nevertheless, on 28 January, he attended the premiere of *Quotations*, performed by the New York Choral Society under Robert De Cormier.

The piece, which he had begun sketching in the 1950s, is one of his most successful and poignant. He himself took little notice at the time, but *Quotations* got positive reviews in *The New York Post* ("a terrific new choral piece," said Robert Kimball) and the *Daily News* ("Gould has written nothing finer," said Bill Zakariasen). Bernard Holland (*The New York Times*, 30 January 1984) was conciliatory: "There may have been nothing profound or arresting about [it]; but in its deft use of words, its bright colors, and its rhythmic variety, there was honest craftsmanship in the service of simple pleasures." *Quotations* is the composer's most heartfelt remembrance of childhood, love, aging, and death. He had first thought to call it, sardonically, *Platitudes*, but he had taken a string of cliches and made them sing.

Gould grew worse during February, with fatigue, crippling pain, and high fevers. Antibiotics and ibuprofin did not help. The climax began Friday, 2 March 1984. Gould was to lead the West Point Band at the military academy that night, and a car picked him up at eight in the morning. He was in such pain that it took him four hours to get ready. He spent the afternoon after rehearsal with chills and fever. As he described it shortly after in his diary, "My joints locked. I couldn't move them. I was in real agony."

Nevertheless, Gould conducted and attended the reception afterward. He ran a high fever the next day; Deborah dropped by, saw how bad he was, and stayed the night. On Sunday morning she called Eric, who took one look and called in a specialist friend, who had Morton taken immediately to the emergency room at North Shore University Hospital in Manhasset. The initial diagnosis was polymyalgic rheumatica, a muscle inflammation, and Gould was put on steroids. That didn't help, and he was admitted to the hospital. "They gave me all sorts of tests, many of which were torturous," he said in his diary. "My limbs were locked, I couldn't move. I was strapped down for x-rays; it was just terrible. I feared the night, feared going to sleep in the hospital."

On 20 March, after a biopsy, he was given huge doses of steroids and improved immediately. Candy took him home the next day. The children cared for him conscientiously. Morton gave special praise to Deborah in his diary—"If not for her, I don't know what I would have done"—and welcomed the attention of Abby and Candy.

Eventually the problem was diagnosed as rheumatoid arthritis and brought under control by medication. Nevertheless, for the rest of his life Gould endured long periods when his entire body ached, and the joints of his knuckles would become so swollen he could not hold a pen. Now his plaints were physical, not just in his head, and he was frustrated and frantic. "I have the Cello Congress piece, the L.A. thing with Michael Tilson Thomas, I've got to orchestrate the Flute Concerto and do some renovations on it, and I was paralyzed, physically and professionally," he exclaimed in a diary entry of 23 March 1984. (For the first time, his voice was high and weak; he sounded old.)

In addition, Shirley filed for divorce. She had moved back into Melbourne Road but refused even to speak to Morton.

But Gould would not submit. In April he conducted parts of programs at both the Great Neck and Queens Symphonies "because I promised them," attended a concert in his honor by the Nassau Symphony, and was the master of ceremonies at a dinner for the American Composers Orchestra. He composed through the night. In April and May, Gould researched, wrote, and orchestrated *American Sing;* finished *Cellos;* and rewrote the last movement of the Flute Concerto. On 28 May 1984 he completed a song for granddaughter Jessica's bas mitzvah ("The Girl with the Faraway Look") and wrote a few melodies for Benny Goodman to mark his successful open heart surgery (*Recovery Music: Greeting, Meditation, and Bounce*). "I still can't believe I got all this music done," he muttered in a diary entry that spring. "I just hope it's good."

This was one of the most frightening times of Gould's life. It was also one of the most productive, and he became depressed again almost as soon as the pressure lifted. "I am very aware intellectually when I come down from this work, come back to reality," he said in his diary in late May 1984. "For me, I don't know which is the reality: my work and the illusion that the kind of comfort writing always gives me, hearing sounds in my head, and then coming back to the reality—how important is it? does it make any difference?—the fact that I really never made it—maybe second or third, in the rear echelon."

After the illness and complaints, the Cello Congress in June 1984 was among the most enjoyable periods of Gould's life, highlighted by his first meeting with Rostropovich. Morton was beside himself with pleasure, as a contemporary diary entry makes clear: "We all know how great Rostropovich is, but to see him work, to see him rehearse my piece, and hearing the sound of those two hundred fifty or more cellos, and what he did with them—the musicality of his music-making was really one of the most stimulating and exciting things I've experienced in a long time. On parting, he said we would keep in contact with each other. I hope we do."

Morton even liked his own composition, *Cellos*, written for eight cellos or multiples thereof, arranged as a double quartet. "It all worked," he said in the same entry. "And I think it is an important piece of mine. I don't know how important it is in the musical world. But it represents me at this stage in a fairly authentic way."

Cellos is a different Gould. Its four movements ("Stringendo," "Sostenuto," "Pizzicato," and "Spiccato") plunge into the soul of the romantic cello: full, rich, passionate, yet not devoid of humor. The opening movements are impastos of sound. The third, with its sly glissandos, offers a slightly superior smile, while the finale is urgent and energetic. It is straight from the European tradition, with glances toward Tchaikovsky and Elgar, but with a confident, strong voice of its own, an unmistakable forerunner of *Stringmusic*.

This exhilaration was brief. Not only was Morton down from the high of composition, but his arthritis plagued him and he felt continually exhausted. The struggle with Shirley was worsening. Now that she had decided to divorce him, she attacked him mercilessly, both in and out of his presence. She horrified people by accusing Morton of having an affair with daughter Abby. (By this time, Abby hated her mother, bitterly.) Friend after friend dropped away; even her brothers felt they could only converse with Morton on the sly, or when she was not around. "She stays in her room like a caged animal," Morton noted in a diary entry that summer.

The divorce proceedings hit Morton very hard. Shirley would get a large portion of their property; they would have to sell the house, and he began to worry about money again. "Financially, I'm going to be absolutely decimated," he continued. "One of the things I've feared is financial insecurity. I've lived with that all my life, and that's like poking at a raw wound." Gould began to talk of doing away with himself if he became crippled.

The rest of 1984 was relatively unproductive. He wrote a short waltz for dancer Edward Villella. He traveled to Los Angeles for the Olympics, but the new work failed to raise his spirits, and the presence of many attractive women aroused, irritated, and depressed him. He struggled with the Pittsburgh commission, wishing for a burst of the energy like the one that had driven him after he got out of the hospital. He dreamed fervently of Shirley, even while calls and letters from others, including Shirley Uzin Quill, continued to arrive.

Yet, in a burst of Christmas introspection, Morton, at seventy-one, was almost content. He was alone for the holiday; Shirley had gone to Mexico with Eric and Candy and their three children. That day he dictated a cogent reflection on his life so far, in which he was able to find a large degree of satisfaction. The RCA recording of *Apple Waltzes* and *Burchfield Gallery* had been accepted by the critics; *Apple Waltzes* was even nominated for a Grammy. "I'm amazed," he said. "All over the place—twice in *The New York Times*—it's gotten all good write-ups." He was touched that the reviewers knew about his music and his life. "A few of them mentioned in glowing terms the wealth of music I've written and the variety of it, and they feel that I have a primary place in the pantheon of supposedly important American composers. It's all very pleasing and gratifying, considering the many years I had to fight off the business that I was just glib and superficial."

He admitted the attraction and warmth he had always felt for women. He no longer accepted all the blame for the failure of their marriage: "One hard fact is, that after Deborah's birth, she was never a woman to me—she managed to successfully avoid and evade me as a man." However much bitterness and pain the dissolution of his marriage caused him, he acknowledged the depth of his love for Shirley, who had provided him with this wonderful family and a magnificent home for many years.

He thought back to childhood, and his mother's many grand Christmas dinners. James and Frances would celebrate their anniversary on Christmas, and it was a family affair. "My mother would cook and bake up a storm. . . . I remember how eager I was for Christmas, and how bitterly disappointed I was when it didn't snow," he said. "I remember watching my relatives come off the elevated train on Jamaica Avenue. They would walk slowly, they were older, many of them sick, but they were wonderful human beings, the salt of the earth. Some of them were dolts, but many were very intelligent. They were good; they would bring presents of gifts and food. It was a wonderful family feeling."

It was as if the sentiments expressed in *Quotations*, with its idyllic pictures of Richmond Hill, had freed him to begin seeing his life with warmth and affection. He reminisced about Leo Fischer and Arnold Goldberg. He recalled his friendship and love affair with Jule Heuman—"one of the greatest human beings I have ever known"—who had died earlier in the year. For a brief Christmas moment, Gould seemed almost at peace with himself.

Despite that valedictory mood, 1985 began darkly. After the Pittsburgh score, and a few odds and ends, there were no more commissions and only one conducting date lined up. The official end of his marriage loomed, and with it the dissolution of the household. At the beginning of January, he put the house up for sale and, having put a binder down on a new house, talked of suicide again. He grew more and more agitated as the move continued; the impending departure from Melbourne was very upsetting to him. Shirley's cancer ate at her as she tongue-lashed him, and he reconciled himself to chronic arthritis.

Yet while he fretted, Gould's reputation was being polished as a result of recent compositions and the emergence of a new generation of critics and musicians who had not taken part in the earlier battles. In February he flew to Los Angeles for ASCAP, triggering another bout of nostalgia and a wave of calls from women. "I don't have the drive," he remarked in a diary entry early in 1985. "I'm not keepable." Shirley Uzin Quill (now a widow) continued to approach Morton. "Isn't there a little piece of you that I can share?" she had asked. ("That's sad," he reflected to himself in his diary that spring.) At the time, he was developing a relationship with Claire Speciner, a divorcée whom he had met while she was walking her dog.

Things looked a little better in March. After several miscarriages, daughter Abby gave birth to a son, Jeremy, and Morton was overjoyed. He completed the Pittsburgh piece, *Classical Variations on Colonial Themes*, months ahead of time. Music director André Previn had since gone to the Los Angeles Philharmonic, and the premiere would be led in 1986 by Lorin Maazel. This score was the last major work written in the beloved third-floor studio on Melbourne. He finished it at midnight on 10 March 1985 and stayed up until three proofreading, putting in markings, and writing a title page.

On 27 March, the National Arts Club honored Gould at its building on Gramercy Park. His friends Martin Segal, Benny Goodman, and Hal David (then president of ASCAP) spoke, and his portrait was hung in the society gallery. That didn't lift his depression, and he continued to speak of suicide. April was better. He visited Sioux Falls, South Dakota, where music director Kenneth Klein gave an all-Gould program. Upon his return on 14 April, he turned right around and flew to Chicago for the world premiere of the Flute Concerto, with Sir Georg Solti leading the Chicago Symphony. Here Gould had a wonderful time, meeting again with musicians he had known twenty years before, basking in the flattering program notes, and, especially, enjoying the performances and the positive receptions.

Donald Peck was pleased. "He gave me exactly what I asked for: a huge, big, four-movement piece of real music, not little ditties. It's quite modern but not avant-garde," the flutist said in an interview in 1996. Both Gould and Peck were gratified that Solti conducted. "The idea came up that Gould should conduct it," Peck recalled, "but Solti said, 'No, it's much better if I conduct it. A composer doing his own work would look as if he were pushing it. But if I conduct it, it will show we think it is a wonderful piece of music and think it should be performed.' "The Chicago critics—both John von Rhein (*Tribune*, 20 April 1985) and David Marsh (*Sun-Times*, 19 April 1985)—were pleased, too. Von Rhein called it "serious," "ambitious," "virtuosic"; Marsh judged it "a splendidly developed, lyrical work," music "destined to be played by many celebrated artists and heard, through the years to come, by many audiences." Not a "glib" nor "slick" in sight.

But darkness descended once more. Gould taped his last words in the house on Melbourne on 4 May 1985. He felt terrible. There were so many things to do—a symphony, a piano concerto, a violin concerto—and now, at seventy-one, he had hoped to relax, to write. But the divorce would destroy all that; it would even dissolve whatever financial security he had. "I am back practically where I started," he lamented. "I started off carrying a backbreaking financial burden, and now I'm doing it again. I made up my mind a long time ago that if I ever had to face that thing again I would destroy myself. I keep trying to talk myself into a situation where it becomes a natural thing to do."

As fortune would have it, writer Wendy Hanson had just asked Morton to contribute an essay on happiness for a book she was working on. His response, dated 7 May 1985, was the essence of Gould—funny, sad, and painfully accurate:

> Happiness spoils my depression. I am not too sad when depressed, but I am less sad when I am happy, and there are times when I'm happy being happy. Happiness is "a sometime thing," —a temporary state of well-being, of optimism, of gratification. . . . Happiness is a passing illusion of security and comfort that helps us survive and function.

In July 1985 Gould moved from 327 Melbourne Road to 231 Shoreward Drive, in the eastern portion of Great Neck. The new house was smaller and less elaborate, but Morton didn't need the space any more. He set up his drafting desks in a den opposite the master bedroom on the first floor. Eric and Candy bought him a queen-sized bed (he had always slept in a twin) and a state-of-the-art sound system. This new stereo was a joy: for the first time he could hear what his recordings actually sounded like. He was set.

Shirley stayed at Melbourne through August and distributed most of the furniture and antiques among their children. In his diary entry of 8 August 1985, after months of silence, Morton said, "I didn't tape anything because I didn't dare. It was one of the blackest periods of my life. I have been as close to suicide as I have ever been, and closer than I want to be." But now an entirely new life appeared: Gould mentioned for the first time the likelihood that he would be elected president of ASCAP when Hal David stepped down in April 1986, which would give him real financial security and raise his profile further.

At the time, ASCAP was the biggest of the three American performing rights societies in repertory and total revenue, more than $200 million annually. Broadcast Music Inc. had the largest share of the broadcast market and the largest membership; the Society of European State Authors and Composers, SESAC, was far smaller than either. ASCAP was still the venerable old boys club; its members, and especially its board, came from the old guard of Victor Herbert, John Philip Sousa, Irving Berlin, and the glory days of 1930s Broadway. It was the only one of the organizations actually operated by its members. BMI was managed by broadcasters, and SESAC was a private, family-run business.

When Gould joined the board in 1959, he became part of a cozy, almost arrogant operation. But by the mid-1980s, BMI, more open to all kinds of music, including rock, jazz, and country, was a serious threat. The development of new technologies, including compact discs, videocassette recorders, and digital recording, was having a serious effect on all their operations.

The ASCAP board comprised twenty-four elected members—twelve composers and twelve publishers. It was elected by the members, but voting was determined by revenue from the music. The society collected money from each broadcaster or outlet, which took a "blanket license" to use its work. That income was distributed by a formula based on frequency and type of performance (primary score, background music, live performance). The more performances, the more credit one got; the more credit, the more money; the more money, the more votes. As a result, composers with huge catalogs, such as Berlin, Kern, or Gould, had a lot of power, while many members with no performances to their credit had no vote at all.

There were other peculiarities: "standard" or concert music was over-represented. Six board members—three publishers, three composers—came from the concert world, and concert composers received more money per performance, since a symphony, no matter how popular, would get far fewer outings than a hit single. One more thing: the president was always a writer, never a publisher, though this was a matter of custom, not a bylaw.

The following account of Morton's ascension to the ASCAP presidency is based on conversations with board members, employees, and outside observers. Not all wished to be quoted by name, so I have written a narrative rather than attributing every statement.

Gould was considered an articulate, intelligent advocate for composers. His speeches to potential antagonists, such as school bandleaders, were models of clarity and reason. He attended monthly board meetings faithfully and was one of ASCAP's most popular and visible figures. He was regularly re-elected by exceptionally large numbers; in 1983, for example, Gould was the second-highest vote getter, with 6,578.16, after Hal David's 6,838.17. "He never had any problems winning elections," said Toni Winter, executive secretary to four ASCAP presidents. "He never campaigned, never wrote a letter in his behalf, but he had always done well."

There were no term limits, so the board—including Gould—tended to be self-perpetuating. For a long time there was great stability, even stagnation. The last twenty-seven years had seen only two presidents: Stanley Adams, from 1959 to 1980 (he also served from 1953 to 1956) and Hal David from 1980 until 1986.

Adams, a lawyer, was happy to run the organization, keeping track of the daily operations. But by the late 1970s, the rest of the board felt it was time for him to step down. Some supported David, the quiet partner of Burt Bacharach. Some backed Adams, who did not wish to retire. And some favored Gould. After a bit of politicking, Hal David was elected president in 1980, but within five years he and the board grew dissatisfied and he decided to step down.

David and Gould were friends, and Gould considered him a mentor within the organization. When the issue of a successor arose, Gould said he was reluctant—it would take up too much time, he didn't want to be tied to an office, he would not serve unless the election were unanimous.

The publishers resented the fact that this multi-million-dollar business, which controlled a great deal of their livelihood, had to be led by a writer who might be no businessman. Gould seemed a good choice to them precisely because of his lack of business experience: management could be left to the professionals, led by a managing director and a staff counsel.

If he won the post, Gould would have to visit an office daily and even spend some nights in the city (ASCAP arranged for an apartment for him in the headquarters building on Broadway directly opposite Lincoln Center, which he paid for from his salary).

Piously, he wished to serve well—"I hope I could do a good thing for the society; I would hopefully, if I am elected, be a good president and run a good ship," he said in that diary entry of August 1985. At the same time, in the world of Morton Gould there could be no silver lining without a cloud: "It's a little disconcerting, to put it mildly, that I should even be able to consider taking this position. I just don't know what happened to my career . . . . If I become president of ASCAP I'm not too sure I'm really giving up anything."

In a new will written in August 1985 he specified that he wanted to be cremated, and that there be no funeral service; as he reasoned aloud in his diary, "A service is needless torture. I was here, now I'm gone, that's it. There should be a celebration. I wish I had spent more time with my family." The rest of the summer and fall of 1985 were spent battling over the divorce, working with Kazdin and Hemming, and undertaking various odds and ends. But Gould was still plagued physically. His mouth became so dry he sometimes had trouble talking, and he had great difficulty at the piano. One day he worked through some Chopin Etudes and parts of Bach's *Goldberg Variations* and was dismayed at how much facility he had lost.

That fall, the Louisville Orchestra recorded *Symphony of Spirituals*, conducted by music director Lawrence Leighton Smith and produced by Kazdin. In October Gould was in a PBS documentary about Benny Goodman, with Teddy Wilson, Red Norvo, Slam Stewart, and

Rosemary Clooney. "I seem to have become a sort of elder statesman of music," he said in a late 1985 diary entry. "That's sort of nice. I get to the point where I can do no wrong, after apparently having done wrong most of my career."

In November he participated in the celebrations of Copland's eighty-fifth birthday; he led the American Symphony in three concerts at the 4500-seat Felt Forum, an arena within Madison Square Garden more comfortable for boxing matches. Walter Cronkite was the narrator and Ezio Flagello the tenor soloist. The acoustics were terrible. "It was sort of a thankless concert. No matter how well you played the sound was just horrible, there was no resonance," Morton commented in his diary. That month also brought him another glimpse of where he had been, when the choral director Gregg Smith, one of Walter's clients, conducted an excerpt from *Of Time and the River*. He confided his surprise in his diary: "It was very good, very moving, very virtuosic—goddamn it, I do know how to write for chorus!" The Musical Heritage Society planned to record Concerto Concertante in a performance by the Bronx Arts Ensemble, along with a chamber version of *Cellos*.

Morton spent Thanksgiving with Abby and Stuart in Plainview, southeast of Great Neck; Shirley had gone first to Europe and then to India (despite wearing a full leg cast, the result of an accident in Spain), to spend time with Kanti Rai's family. She and Morton were legally separated in December 1985, though she retained the right to call herself Mrs. Morton Gould. Despite the terrible blows they struck at one another—and the ferocity of their animosity—Morton and Shirley never divorced.

Judging by one of his last diary entries that year, Morton came to the end of 1985 feeling content, although he worried a bit about his children. He felt more comfortable financially, especially with the ASCAP presidency coming closer. Morton now enjoyed a sweet and comfortable relationship with Claire Speciner, though he "feared" that she was falling in love with him ("many of them do") and insisted that he would never marry again. What with advancing age, side effects from his medication, and trouble with his prostate, Gould was no longer as sexually active, though it didn't trouble him as much as it might have when he was younger. He even allowed himself to think aloud, with regret and pain, about the deaths of his parents—Frances alone in Creedmoor, James alone in Sands Point. "How tragic my mother's death was, in an asylum, an insane asylum—but it was an impossible situation, I was trapped. Even my father, dying alone in a nursing home. I visited him, but that is no way to die for anybody. I guess in a way we all die alone."

CHAPTER 24

ASCAP

GOULD'S RENAISSANCE started in 1986, with his election as president of ASCAP. The pace of activity increased even before the formal election in April, as word percolated through the arts community. Now the honors began to arrive, the recognition so deeply desired. He still plunged into depression, still worried that, as he put it, "I did little with much." But there was less time to brood, he was working so hard.

His musical activities continued—though at a slower pace, certainly. In late March he conducted the Brooklyn Philharmonic and pianist Leonard Pennario at Avery Fisher Hall, but to his dismay, the work was very painful and his legs nearly gave way. Shirley continued defiant and determined; when she returned from India she spent time at Eric's or with friends. Morton could not approach her; whenever she saw him, she railed at him. Fortunately, ASCAP occupied most of his attention.

The year began well, with Gould's election to the American Academy and Institute of Arts and Letters, headquartered on 155th Street near the City College of New York. This was the kind of organization to which Gould felt he could never belong. "To my mind," he said in his diary, upon learning of the nomination in January 1986, "it was an elitist, snobbish kind of setup." He always reacted with a prickly, sometimes self-defeating pride in confrontations with such institutions. But he accepted election with gratitude and grace; the membership became one of his proudest achievements, and he always wore the Institute lapel pin. At the induction on 21 May 1986,

Gould presented a "calling card in the form of an expurgated digest of a diary describing how I compose" that could serve as a template for one particularly tortuous form of the creation process.

Day 1: Sign commission agreement. Suspicious but optimistic; full of good intentions and ideas.
Day 2: Ideas gone, but still good intentions.
Day 3: No intentions, regret agreeing to commission.
Day 4: Force feeding—attempt sketches—nothing.
Day 5: A glimmer—one note!
Day 6: Glimmer and note dissolve.
Day 7 through Day 10: Suicidal.
Day 11: Read clipping re how facile I am.
Day 12: Moderately suicidal.
Day 13: Aha! Two notes! But no glimmer.
Day 14: Glimmer and three notes!
Day 15: Tentatively optimistic.
Day 16: Another clipping re my "facility"—allergic reaction.
Day 17: Depressed, but happily distracted by "head sounds."
Day 18: More head sounds. More notes—glimmers.
Day 19: Glimmers turn to light—head sounds to notes.
Day 20: Depression ruined! A gusher! More than needed!
Day 21 through 30: Pruning, deleting—save unused materials for another rainy day.
Days Into Nights: Around the clock until finished—Eureka! Euphoria!
The Day After: The bends—return to "reality" (?)
The Second Day After: Back to "normality" (?) (Depressed, paranoid, suicidal, but happy) until the next time!

Gould wrote this "digest" on 21 March 1986. That week he dreamed he was being executed: the whole family agreed that electrocution was the most efficient way for Morton to go. But it failed; he didn't die. "Oddly enough, it had worked before. I had actually died," he said in his diary that spring. "It was a weird thing. It felt so real. I can't figure out what the hell it means, if one accepts the fact that dreams reflect some of the things we actually feel. I don't want to interpret it, because I think of suicide."

It was barely a month before the ASCAP election; possibly Gould feared that taking on the responsibility of that fractious, embattled organization meant the death of his creative side. And considering how hard he had worked, how much of his own ambitions had not been achieved, and how much he had sacrificed for parents and children, it'd be no wonder that some deep part of Gould felt he had been killed by his own family, that for love or fear he had buried himself—and yet he would not die. Immediately after reporting this dream, he launched into yet another family encomium, rhapsodizing about the joy and pleasure of children and grandchildren, and how important they were to his own happiness.

If the American Academy was a place to which Morton was temperamentally "allergic," ASCAP was home. He was familiar with its organization and staff, the issues it faced, and the never-ending conflicts with everyone who did not want to pay—or wanted to pay less—for music. As winter brightened into spring, the outgoing president coached him weekly on the minutiae of operations.

Gould met individually with each board member. He knew the internal politics and he had his own ideas of what needed to be done. He knew that top management, particularly managing director Gloria Messinger and general counsel Bernard Korman, resented David's style, because he often bypassed them. "He tends to take the ball and run with it himself. I intend to give management more autonomy than Hal was giving them," Gould projected in a diary entry of 19 April 1986. At the same time he knew Messinger herself wanted to run the organization, with himself as figurehead rather than chief executive. "I think this can all be controlled," he said.

Of far more importance was a potentially disastrous bill in Congress being pushed by a group of local television broadcasters whose attempt to overturn the music payments system had been rejected in court. Now, working with the National Association of Broadcasters, they had gotten their changes incorporated into legislation introduced by Rep. Gene Boucher of Virginia.

For forty years, ASCAP and BMI sold "blanket licenses" giving broadcasters the right to play any of their music for an annual fee based on a percentage of gross advertising revenues. In 1986, ASCAP's fee was 1.2 percent; BMI got 65 percent of that. The fees cost the stations about $100 million a year in "performance royalties," the bulk of the income that the organizations then distributed to members. The broadcasters complained that they were forced to pay for music they never played, and wanted to pay only for what they put on the air, "pay for play" or "source-licensing."

The performing rights organizations feared that this would mean a loss of up to 30 percent in income for the people who actually wrote and published the music. In addition, source licensing would make it almost impossible to keep track of what was actually presented. "If they win," Gould told Kazdin and Hemming in March 1986, their last session, "it is the ultimate destruction, or dilution, or dissolution of ASCAP as we know it today. It would be a catastrophe."

While Gould looked to the heavy schedule that lay ahead, he was swept with nostalgia brought on by the deaths of colleagues and friends. He was hit particularly hard by the passing in February of Phil Lang, the gifted arranger and orchestrator who had been his WOR assistant. It was Lang who made the band arrangement for *American Salute* from Gould's radio-orchestra original, and his work with the composer on *Billion Dollar Baby* was Lang's first Broadway orchestration. They were great friends—Gould was best man at Lang's wedding—and remained so as Lang became the most important orchestrator of the postwar era, with dozens of credits including *Annie Get Your Gun*, *Applause*, *Mame*, *Hello, Dolly!*, *Camelot*, and *My Fair Lady*. They'd had a relationship of respect and affection, and Lang's death disturbed Gould greatly.

On 28 April 1986, just two days before assuming the presidency, he attended a service for Lucia Chase of New York City Ballet. The Bruno Walter Auditorium at Lincoln Center was filled with the great names of dance—Agnes De Mille, Jerome Robbins, Eliot Feld, Cynthia Gregory. In his diary, Gould remembered how much he had worked with them over the years, without feeling fully accepted. "In a professional sense I was part of that group," he mused aloud. He also mentioned that his prostate was bothering him—he hoped he wouldn't have to be hospitalized right after assuming the presidency. And family concerns were never far from his mind. Bachelor son David had married, and Deborah had become one of her father's frequent companions and, eventually, his unofficial amanuensis and bookkeeper. With his anticipated six-figure income, Gould planned to take over the mortgage for her Brooklyn Heights apartment, to relieve Eric and Candy and to guarantee that she would inherit it. At 1:30 in the morning on 30 April 1986, talking into his diary just before becoming president, he reflected on how strange it was to be beginning a new career at the age of seventy-two: "I'm behaving as if I'm in my twenties or thirties."

The changing of the guard took place at three that afternoon. Morton Gould was the first classical composer to hold the presidency since Deems Taylor in 1948, but the board felt it would be to their benefit to have someone of his background as head of the organization. "I do represent a certain kind of image," he said in March. "I do have crossover sympathy with people from both sides of the fence. And I also represent somebody who's done everything." Nevertheless, he did not expect to hold the post for more than a year or two.

Gould's new career was launched. He was touched and exhilarated by a profile written by Joan Peyser (*Sunday New York Times*, 25 May 1986). "A parallel can be found," she wrote, "in the careers of Mr. Gould, Robert Frost, and Edward Hopper. During their youth and middle years, they were dismissed by contemporary critics as naive, accessible craftsmen, and it was only in the later years that the genuine merit of the work was seen." By June he was reporting in his diary, "My life has been quite changed—it's now intriguing, challenging, exciting."

As if to take note of his accession, June 1986 saw performances of *Interplay* at City Ballet, and the Philharmonic resurrected the *Tap Dance Concerto* as part of its contemporary music series, "Horizons." Oliver Knussen conducted, and afterward Gould was tickled to be surrounded by a flock of young composers. "It turns out that they have been fans of mine since they were young," he said in his diary. He delighted in the letters and calls of congratulations. "I'm getting recognitions now, and an awareness on the part of colleagues whom I have admired and respected. I assumed they always looked at me as sort of a heathen, a philistine. I suppose that what it comes to is you gotta live long enough." Suspicious and cynical though he was, it did not occur to Gould that there might have been a strong element of sycophancy in all this—the flattery that comes to those in high places. He remained surprisingly naive and ingenuous.

The first months were a whirlwind. For the first time in decades he began each day at an office, where he had a staff of assistants and secretaries, and continuous meetings, discussions, and negotiations. Morton began traveling extensively. In May alone he went to Nashville, where BMI was gaining clear dominance; to Washington, D.C., to meet with lobbyists and legislators to fight source-licensing; and to Los Angeles, for ASCAP's annual pop music awards. For this last trip—for the first time—he accepted first-class tickets; in the past he had always turned them in for coach and contributed the difference to an ASCAP composers' fund.

But the next month he suffered a severe personal loss. On 12 June 1986 he dined with Benny Goodman and Carol Philips, Goodman's companion since his wife had died. The next morning Gould could not reach Goodman to thank him for the evening. That evening in Great Neck Morton learned that his old friend and comrade had died. "It was a shocking blow," he said that night in his diary. "He was a great artist and a good friend of mine—he was difficult and could be very strange at times, but he and I were so close. But one keeps in motion, and I am involved in so many things."

The schedule didn't let up: back to Los Angeles, and to Detroit for his last ASOL conference as a board member. He resigned to avoid a conflict with ASCAP, but the league gave him an honorary five-year appointment.

The ASCAP staff was beginning to get a full sense of Gould's female relationships. Among the incidents that passed into legend was the time he was wrestled out of a Los Angeles hotel elevator by a woman who begged him to marry her. Once, at a glittering dinner, another woman burst out and asked whether Gould was married. "Without missing a beat," publicity director Karen Sherry recalled, "he said he wasn't, but added, 'I'm permanently disabled.'"

"It's sort of amusing," Gould said in his diary, "but a little embarrassing, because it happens when there are other people around. I think the ASCAP management has a view of me that is not quite so."

"Oh, the ladies, the ladies," chuckled executive secretary Toni Winter. "Morton and I got along very well. I was married for a long time, I wasn't an old maid, I had no frustrations. So we used to have fun with these dames when they'd call. Morton would say to me, 'You don't know where I am.'" She screened his calls; sometimes he would take them, and tell Winter he would not be available that evening. "We would go to a party, and there's a dame monopolizing him, and he's delighted. And I circle around and I circle around, and if he doesn't look at me, I know he's happy. If he looks at me, it means, 'Interrupt me, I've gotta go somewhere.'"

And now it was Gould's turn to learn more about ASCAP's buried feuds and resentments, "certain hostilities between the board and management," as he termed them in his diary that spring of 1986. His manner was calm and conciliatory, his wit a definite asset. Lyricist Marilyn Bergman, the first female writer to serve on the board and Gould's eventual successor, said, "He was always witty. That was a given. If there was ever anything becoming too solemn, he would remedy that. He was extremely even-handed, and I understand that had not been the hallmark of the president before him. That was one thing the people on the board were always grateful to him for." Bergman also learned that beneath the non-confrontational surface was a surprising amount of strength. "There was steel there, real resolve there—I don't think this was somebody who was exactly what he seemed to be."

Winter considered Gould's personality a refreshing change from the dominating styles of his predecessors. "He was very fair in the board room," she said, "where the stronger personalities of the previous presidents might have influenced a lot of the wheeling and dealing. Morton was much more middle-of-the-road, and more fair. . . . Morton really believed in the roundtable discussion, in listening to all sides, in really voting on the issues. He also never bypassed a board member with a problem."

The value of his name and reputation were put to immediate use. Although Adams and David both were successful songwriters, they were not known to the general public. But Morton Gould was a famous man in the halls of Congress. Many legislators had grown up listening to his records; some didn't realize he was still alive. As Winter put it, "People would stand when he came into the room, not the other way around."

Gould asserted himself quickly. In July 1986 he took the board to Washington to speak with ASCAP's lobbyists and to meet with legislators about the source-licensing bill. The trip was meant to help educate the board about their problems; as Gould reported in his diary, "It turned out to be luckily a very successful experience for the board. It gave them a sense of what we are involved in." Other

ASCAP members—Cy Coleman, Sammy Cahn, Marvin Hamlisch—performed for the legislators. Gould was one of the negotiators; he spent time lobbying, developing relationships with such men as senators Edward M. Kennedy of Massachusetts and Orrin Hatch of Utah. "He knew the people who were influential and important in terms of getting things done," Murphy said.

At the end of July, he conducted a repeat of the Felt Forum Copland program in Philadelphia, this time with the Philadelphia Orchestra and Martin Bookspan as narrator. Later he returned to Washington to argue in favor of awarding Copland a Congressional Medal. In August he underwent prostate surgery. When he got back to the office in September, he was thrust again into the maelstrom. There were board meetings all week, yet he had to be in Pittsburgh for the premiere of *Classical Variations on Colonial Themes*. ASCAP business meant he could attend only one rehearsal; on Thursday, 11 September 1986, he spent the day in Manhattan, then flew to Pittsburgh for the opening performance, conducted by Lorin Maazel (who announced at that time that he would succeed Previn as music director). Gould was touched and gratified to spend time with old friends, and he relished the dinners and parties. But although he liked Maazel's performances, Gould wasn't very enthusiastic about the piece. "I think it works, but I don't think it's going to move the world," as he put it in his diary.

The battle with the broadcasters grew more intense. Gould tried an unusual move: he published an open letter asking for face-to-face negotiations. It worked. He and his negotiators sat down with the television industry committee on 2 October 1986 to begin to hash out a deal. At the same time, he was becoming more sensitive to the antagonisms within the organization. "I've been trying to unruffle ruffled feathers," he said in his diary, "to get all these egos sedated. . . . Hal David has been a very strong president, but he continues not to be what they call a team player." Yet now Morton understood why Hal acted the way he did, especially around upper management. ASCAP had not changed significantly for years, and the world outside was moving very fast. "Bit by bit I hope to get a more efficient apparatus going and to clean out a lot of old things that have been leftovers from different times," Gould said. Part of that efficiency meant bypassing people "who think they should be doing it but really are not as qualified as somebody else. It is a great management, a great staff, but I have to place them in what to me would be the best positions for them."

He was referring primarily to Messinger and Korman. Just five months after taking office, Gould knew he would have to spend a great deal of time not only fighting the outside interests, but his own staff as well. He and his staff continued their tense negotiations with the broadcasters; it took some years, but eventually the bill was beaten back and other issues arose, including such problems as how to treat digital tape recorders and copies made on home video recorders. Neither a lawyer, an engineer, nor a businessman, Gould held his own, helped by long experience in commercial radio and recording.

He traveled constantly—to London, Madrid, Nashville, Los Angeles, Australia. He threw himself into the work with as much energy as anything he had ever done. He butted heads continuously with Messinger and Korman.

A primary difficulty had to do with his own role. There were those on the board and in management who thought that Gould would not really take an active role in running the organization. They, and many of the publishers, had hoped Gould would be less active than Adams or David. "In the discussions the board had with management," said publisher Irwin Robinson of Famous Music Inc., "they [all] felt it was probably time to have somebody who would look at the job differently, who didn't see himself as a 'president' or chief executive in the business sense, but would leave that to the management of ASCAP."

Bergman was under the impression that, although he was nominally the chief executive officer, Gould actually worked "under Gloria Messinger." Bergman and others thought Gould was little more than a figurehead, a famous name to give speeches and go before the public. Even some good friends felt that way; Skitch Henderson thought Gould had no real power.

But many others, both within and without, realized that Gould had more skill than that. As Winter observed, "Morton was the one whose assignments were the more difficult. . . . Morton was a working president and a working composer at the same time, and he was much older than the others." Robert Sherman and Oscar Brand were also convinced that Gould was the true executive at ASCAP. "They didn't know what they were getting" when he was elected, said Brand, himself a member of BMI. "They thought they were getting a figurehead, but all the time he was there there was nobody pushing him around. Nobody pushed Morton around."

Ed Murphy said, "This is a man whose career was music writing, conducting, and performing, and you ask him to come in as president of an organization with a budget of $350 to $400 million and eight hundred workers—that's quite a responsibility, to be a CEO."

Few on the board had realized how quick a study he was, and how deep his experience with the business of music. As a musician, he had always been intellectually and professionally interested in the latest ideas and techniques; he was never afraid of the future; and he was determined to bring ASCAP fully in tune with the times. Morton knew what was going on.

"There is all kinds of trouble at ASCAP," he said in a late 1987 diary entry. "There are internal conflicts with management, basically with just two people, and a board that sort of wobbles back and forth." His complaints had become more detailed and exasperated; he spoke of Messinger and Korman as "an entrenched general manager and entrenched general counsel who have delusions of grandeur and power. I have to fight them every inch to achieve what I think I should achieve. I like them personally but I find it hard to be civil to them." Things had gotten rough: "I've been accused of being a dictator. . . . I thought I could go in and change things, but that's almost impossible. I am dealing with an entrenched senior management, who are really nice enough people, but they have limited assets with really no imagination. What they are doing is protecting their terrain. What should be done in one day can take one month." The politicking he characterized as "not even dirty, just inept and petty. There are vendettas and vindictiveness going back many years."

Gould turned to outside sources for advice, including his old friend Martin Segal, at one time chairman of the board of Lincoln Center and an experienced infighter. "When Morton became president, he consulted me regularly . . . about what was going on," Segal said. The financier assessed the situation bluntly: "Gloria simply wanted to replace Morton, and Morton didn't let it happen. To the contrary. She wanted to run the place herself. She wanted absolute control. And she really wanted to be the CEO, which she wasn't. She actually suggested it, that she become president and Morton become chairman.

"And Morton was the one who orchestrated her defeat," Segal asserted. "He would deny it, but there is no doubt in my mind about that. Morton just would not allow her to take over."

Segal did not accept Morton's habitual self-deprecation. "I learned that some of what he would say was completely self-serving and meant to elicit from you support for his views," he said. "And if you said something he didn't want to do, he would say, 'Well, you're absolutely right, and I wish I had the courage to do that,' and throw up his hands."

Gould was on the phone with Segal Sunday after Sunday, asking advice until Segal refused to give up his weekends in such a way. But the financier acknowledged the skill behind the cloud of jokes. "I loved him, but despite that I had absolutely no illusions about what he was like.... He stayed president for eight years, while all this turmoil was going on. He wasn't charismatic, or brilliant, or a leader people would automatically follow."

By 1988 the infighting was even more intense. Both Adams and various publishers tried what Gould called "end runs" around him. The struggles were so fierce that, starting in the spring of 1988, he carried a letter of resignation in his briefcase. Gould had been outmaneuvered by Messinger, Korman, and their allies. New rules were created that stripped the president of most of his powers and gave actual control to management. For a few years, Messinger was running the society.

Gould continued to appear, negotiate, speak, and work for ASCAP; he even developed a fairly close friendship with Messinger and her family. But then, in the early 1990s, ASCAP was further threatened by changes in technology and stronger competition from BMI. In 1992 a group of country music writers, who had discovered that BMI paid better than ASCAP, defected. Members from newer types of entertainment, including rock and jazz, grew restless over their lack of representation, and there was increasing unhappiness about the subsidy for classical composers.

Finally, in the spring of 1993, ASCAP hired the consulting firm of Booz-Allen & Hamilton Inc. to do a strategic review. As president,

Gould sat on the committee that coordinated its activities and was in close touch with Michael Wolf, chief of Booz-Allen's media and entertainment practice and the man who headed the study. "We were in contact with everyone on the committee"—which included Bergman, David, and Coleman—"but Morton was one of the people who was most concerned about ASCAP, about insuring its future," Wolf said. To Gould, the cigar-scented rooms and camaraderie of ASCAP was home. "He was very, very concerned about the future of the organization. As he described it, the patient needed a head-to-toe exam."

According to *Billboard* (25 September 1993), Messinger announced the start of the study because of the need to deal with "rapidly changing technologies, market fragmentation, shifting revenues, and the increasing complexity of monitoring usage, licensing, collecting and distributing royalties."

To Wolf, it appeared that Gould was the chief executive, while Messinger and Korman "were trying to wrestle power from the board. Management wanted to run the organization without the supervision of the board." From the consultant's perspective, Gould had been elected president because the board did not think he would make any major changes. Yet it was Gould who oversaw, in Wolf's words, "probably the most radical changes in the organization's history."

The reorganization was fast and brutal. On 9 September 1993, the board unanimously approved Booz-Allen's recommendations—which included a change in senior management. Gould made this diary entry shortly after:

> Friday morning, as president, I had to call in Gloria Messinger and Bernard Korman, people with whom I had established personal and friendly relations even though early on they had formed a coalition that was certainly not friendly to my presidency at the time, and up to the present moment they were running the show. The board gave them the power to do it, they did it, and it ended up unfortunately the way it did. I felt terrible to have to do what I did. I told them that as of noon they should start cleaning their offices, and we would accept their resignations—I do not enjoy that kind of thing. I had every reason to be

vindictive; I predicted this would happen in the third or fourth year of my presidency—I tried to protect them as much as I could. They played hardball with the board, and they lost.

This dramatic move shook the organization almost as much as the reorganization did. Messinger had been with ASCAP for twenty years, and Korman for forty. John LoFrumento, the chief financial officer, was named chief operating officer; Fred Koenigsberg, once Korman's protégé, was appointed special counsel. And a search was begun for an outsider for the newly created position of CEO–managing director. Gould would become chairman of the board, to whom the new chief executive would report.

Meanwhile, however, Gould found himself the actual CEO once again, meeting with LoFrumento and Koenigsberg constantly over day-to-day operations. The staff, which had been as large as 907 in 1992, was to shrink to about 730 by the end of 1994. LoFrumento was to preside over a massive "streamlining," as well as an updating of its operations. The board membership itself was to change drastically. No longer would the concert field be guaranteed half a dozen seats, although Gould and his allies managed to retain one seat each for classical composers and publishers. In addition, board service would have term and age limits, with the top being seventy-five years (Gould was about to turn eighty).

Now representatives of newer forms of music could have a voice. *Billboard* (25 September 1993) reported, "It appears, as one publisher puts it, that 'young turk' writers and publishers have won out—convincing the board, with likely backing from the study, that contemporary charted music was losing out in publisher and writer income to older copyrights." In addition, the formulas that distributed money to the estates of older writers were modified; the subsidy for classical music was reduced; and the society began working to increase the amount of money it collected.

This meant that under the leadership of Morton Gould, himself a classical composer, concert music lost almost all its power. Morton prevailed, but at some personal cost. Both Korman and Messinger cut off all relations with him. Korman was unwilling to provide his own interpretation of events, citing attorney-client privilege, and Messinger did not respond to a request for comment.

CHAPTER 25

The Sweet and the Bitter

★ ★ ★ ★

ASCAP PROVIDED financial relief for Gould, and an entirely new arena in which to focus his energy. But he never forgot that more than anything else he was a composer.

So in 1987, muttering about his reluctance and how he had disappeared and how much he had failed, Gould juggled commissions, conducting dates—even the revival of his City Ballet dances. The company, by now firmly in the hands of Peter Martins, planned a festival of American music for 1988. Martins hoped to reconstruct *Clarinade,* Balanchine's setting of *Derivations* that had opened the City Ballet's move to Lincoln Center. He also considered creating something for a few *Apple Waltzes,* as well as reviving *I'm Old-Fashioned.* Gould would conduct, and also perform in *Interplay.*

Morton's three new commissions—from the American Symphony Orchestra, a fanfare to open their 1987–88 season; for a consortium of choruses assembled by Gregg Smith, an a cappella piece for double chorus; and a two-piano piece for the brand-new Murray Dranoff Duo-Piano Competition in Florida—were all due in September 1987, and Gould had his usual hard time getting started. The fanfare, *Flares and Declamations,* was the least challenging. But he worried over the choral piece; he was still not comfortable with vocal music. And the two-piano work was personally disturbing for the memories it aroused (he did not enjoy being reminded of Gould and Shefter).

Smith asked for the choral piece to help fill out a recording of *Quotations* and *Of Time and the River.* The Dranoff had a longer history. Loretta and Murray Dranoff were a two-piano team in the 1950s and 1960s, and after the latter's death, his widow chose to memorialize him with a competition for that once-popular form. It would be biennial and require performance of a score composed for the occasion.

Characteristically, after accepting the assignments, Gould became frustrated and tried to withdraw. But the commissioners, who knew him, refused. By August he was "depressed" and "stalled," and—as he expressed it in his diary early in September, after he had finished—"frantic."

> But also deep into the process. At my age, at this stage in my life, I have an unbelievable schedule, working around the clock, writing between my ASCAP meetings. Very often when I was home I'd be cradling a phone on my shoulder while writing on score paper in front of me, trying to make an insertion, and having a consultation about ASCAP.

Unable to settle on a choral text—he named the piece simply *A Cappella*—he called its two movements "Tolling," after the line by John Donne, and "Solfegging," based on the singer's wordless solfeggio exercises. The Dranoff piece, about which he had been most reluctant, had finally caught his fancy. It became a five-movement, fifteen-and-a-half-minute composition entitled, naturally, *Two Pianos* —an undisguised remembrance of the early days. The movements ("Chords," "Blues," "Waltzes," "Echoes," and "Triplets") find the composer nostalgic for the era of *Interplay* and the Piano Concerto.

Despite the work he was doing, Gould took note that, though he would be turning seventy-five the following year, he wasn't getting the recognition he wanted. Early in September 1987 he remarked in his diary that, though the Pittsburgh Symphony was giving a full week of Gould concerts and symposia, there was nothing from New York, Boston, Philadelphia, Chicago. "I am so far away from what I thought I'd achieve that I have to face the fact that career-wise I have been a failure, I never made it."

Nevertheless, he was pleased with the premiere of *Flares and Declamations*, conducted by José Serebrier, that October. The Dranoff competition drew him to Miami in December. There had been a hundred and twenty applicants—"to everyone's amazement, particularly mine"—and the level of playing was high. The Canadian team of Dominique Morel and Douglas Nemish took first place, although Gould privately preferred the second-place team, Baltimoreans Thomas Hecht and Sandra Shapiro. James Roos (*Miami Herald*, 23 December 1987) was quite taken with the "flavorful" *Two Pianos*, calling it "a first-rate piece in [Gould's] best style" and "the unmistakable voice of an original mind in music."

Gould returned to Great Neck exhausted but pleased; as he reported in his diary, "I guess I'm not that bad, not that inept. I sort of like the piece, from what I heard. I really remembered none of it."

Unfortunately, though, Gould's perception of his place in music was continually being reinforced. When plans for the City Ballet's American music festival were announced in the fall of 1987, he was furious to discover that his name was not mentioned. Martins responded that the initial announcements concerned only newly commissioned scores. But in January 1988 Gould's name was once again left out of a program announcement, and he decided to withdraw from the festival. This time, Martins explained, the apparent oversight was the result of a fight between him and Robbins, who did not want Gould to conduct *I'm Old-Fashioned*. Robbins feared that the composer would not have enough time to rehearse the complex, multimedia score. "I can understand that," Gould said in his diary. "I thought, especially when I saw the tremendous number of new works, how could there be any rehearsal time?"

But Martins was too embarrassed to tell Gould. "Instead, Peter and Jerry got into a terrible fight," Gould said. He didn't mind if Robert Irving, a company conductor, led the performance. But the absence of his name? "That I do care about from any point of view. It's typical of my career. I've lived an illusion, that I was anybody important."

Worse was to follow. In a situation reminiscent of Ken LaFave's essay for the Philharmonic's ten thousandth concert, Mark Swed wrote about American music and its relationship with dance for the City Ballet program. Swed was a freelance journalist who wrote for *The Wall Street Journal*; he later wrote a biography of John Cage and succeeded Martin Bernheimer as chief music critic of *The Los Angeles Times*. His piece was thorough in its discussion of the relationship between American composers and dance. He mentioned John Adams, George Antheil, Samuel Barber, Irving Berlin, Leonard Bernstein, William Billings, William Bolcom, John Cage, John Coltrane, Aaron Copland, Henry Cowell, Lukas Foss, George Gershwin, Philip Glass, Charles Ives, Edward MacDowell, Glenn Miller, Harry Partch, Cole Porter, Steve Reich, Terry Riley, Michael Torke, Charles Wuorinen, La Monte Young, and Ellen Taaffe Zwilich.

Swed never mentioned Gould, despite his significant presence in the festival. Morton was hurt and angry, but did nothing. He was, however, pleased with the positive review by dance critic Anna Kisselgoff (*The New York Times*) and with his own work. Although he did not conduct *I'm Old-Fashioned*, he led *Apple Waltzes* and was the piano soloist in *Interplay* (the next day, he could barely move his hands).

That entire week was a busy one. On 4 May 1988, he had two ballet rehearsals, attended a seventieth birthday reception for Bernstein at ASCAP, changed into a tuxedo, and returned to Lincoln Center to conduct. "Lenny was in full form," Gould remarked in his diary. "He was exuberant, loved the reception, drank a great deal . . . . Despite all his aberrations he is such a unique genius. I have no idea how he survives." At the reception, Bernstein noted that he had once set to music a poem by his mother, Jennie. Gould immediately made her a member of ASCAP. "I told Lenny he would have to share the royalties with her. He was most pleased."

Jennie Bernstein replied with a card dated 22 May 1988: "Many thanks, Mr. Gould, for initiating me into this very prestigious society. I am indeed overjoyed that my lyrics of 'Little Smary' were joined with the great composer Leonard Bernstein."

Again Gould turned to his diary. "Seeing Lenny that day, I had such a warm feeling towards him. I know Lenny is for Lenny, basically—he's not particularly sympathetic to me or my music. My colleagues are basically egos; you have to live around them. However, in Lenny's case, he has every reason to be egotistical."

That day, 4 May 1988, was also Shirley's sixty-seventh birthday, and although Claire was his companion at the concerts and reception, Morton expressed his yearning for Shirley. She was now in continual pain, and Eric insisted she stay at his house during two weeks of testing and treatment.

In September 1988, after lobbying in Washington, Gould flew to Portland, Oregon, where James DePreist opened the Oregon Symphony season with *Soundings*, and then immediately to London for meetings with the British Performing Rights Society. In October the New York Choral Society revived *Quotations*, and Gould had a revelation. After attending a rehearsal under the chorus's new director, Jack Goodwin, he said in his diary, "I have written my own memorial piece—maybe in my old age, I'm getting more positive feelings about myself than I had when I was active."

But within weeks he was plunged into depression again. It didn't matter that the American Symphony, the American Composers Orchestra, and the Pittsburgh Symphony were playing his music, or that he had participated in a conference at *The New York Times* about "creativity in America." His recording career had disappeared, his back catalog wasn't being re-released, his publisher wasn't pushing his music, he still wasn't getting performed at the Philharmonic. "I should have been much bigger than I am. I should be turning down conducting engagements. I'm black black black black black"

Thanksgiving at Eric's with the clan, including a haggard Shirley, lifted his spirits a little. "It was wonderful, noisy, rambunctious, full of the atmosphere we always had on Melbourne Road," he said. Shirley's hostility had not abated, but her deterioration—he had not seen her in a year—was a shock. "She is an old, old lady; she's a dwarf; the cancer is in her bones, and they've collapsed. She's hunched over like a hunchback. It is pitiful when I think of what she was, the beautiful, elegant woman that she was."

Early in December 1988, the American Composers Orchestra premiered the Concerto Grosso for four violins in a program, led by Dennis Russell Davies, that included Elliott Carter's Piano Concerto, performed by Ursula Oppens. Bernard Holland (*The New York Times*) called the piece "a sophisticated hoedown [that] seems to lose itself in all the cross references, which mingle in a kind of amorphous uncertainty." "At least they put my name in the paper," Gould noted in his diary.

Although never satisfied in New York, Gould appreciated the week-long celebration of his seventy-fifth in Pittsburgh, held 6 through 11 December 1988. Claire and almost the entire family came down. Maazel conducted three concerts; Morton observed, demonstrated, and lectured at Carnegie-Mellon, Duquesne, and the University of Pittsburgh. The mayor declared Saturday to be "Morton Gould Day." "I didn't have one second to myself but I enjoyed every minute of it." (That Monday he was back in New York for a double root canal and ASCAP.)

The rest of the year was full of honors, ceremonies, and interviews: an association of impresarios gave him an award, the Conductors Guild hosted a luncheon for him, Joan Peyser threw him a surprise party at her Greenwich Village townhouse. And the new year opened with a surprise. The Louisville Orchestra played *Flourishes and Galop* at Carnegie Hall on 19 January 1989; Morton noted in his diary, "It was a wonderful performance, a great success. It even got good write-ups, and an excellent write-up in *The New York Times*—believe it or not." It was true: Holland (*The New York Times*, 22 January 1989), in a subtle comment about the newspaper's long hostility, wrote, "Long a cautious admirer of Morton Gould's music, I liked his new *Flourishes and Galop* unreservedly. . . . Its adaptation of outdoor brass-band flavor to the indoor symphonic medium is one of the most successful I have ever heard."

At the same time, there was little composing to do. The only significant commission in 1989 came when the saxophonist James Houlik asked him to write something for tenor sax. *Diversions* got its premiere at a Carnegie Hall program called the Absolut Concerto, sponsored by the Absolut vodka company. The most intriguing artistic endeavor was the production, in February 1989, of *Jerome Robbins' Broadway*, the Tony Award–winning revival of many of the choreographer's most important works for theater, including the Charleston sequence from *Billion Dollar Baby*.

When Gould did perform, the results were disturbing. During a set of concerts with the Houston Symphony, he got dizzy on the podium, and when Donald Peck brought him to Monterey, California, to conduct the Flute Concerto and *Spirituals for String Choir and Orchestra*, he tired quickly, lost his concentration, and brought the orchestra in wrong. Morton was alarmed: "My lacks as a conductor are getting worse. I don't have control; I'm making conducting mistakes," he said in his diary early in 1989.

The past and present were beginning to mingle incessantly. On 5 April, Morton had lunch with Shirley Uzin Quill, who brought him a sheaf of old love letters. He was incredulous, embarrassed, barely recognizing the teenager he had been. "They are really almost too hot to handle. I sound as if I was doing nothing but making love to her or thinking of making love to her, or discussing when we made love. I'm sure it was not that much," he said in his diary. She was still interested in him, but he? "I have compassion and consideration, but it's gone, done, finished."

He decided at last to identify Claire Speciner in his diary; up to that moment he had called her "Madame X" or "my lovely lady" (though everyone who knew him knew her). They had dinner on 12 April 1989 with Walter and Betty for Walter's birthday. Afterward, Gould confessed, "I don't know why I say 'my lovely lady.' Her name is Claire. Let's refer to her by her name from now on."

The battles at ASCAP escalated. The David and Adams factions fought each other; Messinger and a group of publishers mounted their own campaign—oh, and by the way, Morton Gould, resignation letter in reserve, was re-elected unanimously on 30 April. Shortly afterward, on 11 May 1989, he got another blast from the past during ceremonies for the Songwriters' Hall of Fame at Radio City Music Hall, as he noted in his diary. "I sat there, and I could see myself all over again coming up in that pit. I still get queasy in that place. When I was seventeen or eighteen, working there, I didn't think I would be sitting there as a seventy-five-year-old composer-conductor-president of ASCAP after a long, frustrating career." Later that month, he attended a reception for John Cage and Merce Cunningham, whose methods and philosophies could not have been more different from his. "I have respect for these peaceful people," he said in his diary. "There are a lot kookier people out there who have our destinies in their hands."

Mortality was all around him. William Schuman was dying, and Morton grieved to see him in a wheelchair. Ralph Black, a fixture at the ASOL and general manager of the National Symphony during the 1950s, had died in February, and the league commissioned Gould to write a commemorative piece, *Notes of Remembrance*—which, to Gould's pleasure, Rostropovich agreed, sight unseen, to perform with the National Symphony.

Early in 1990 Gould signed a contract to write a six- to-eight-minute piece for the Van Cliburn Foundation, led by Artur Rodzinski's son, Richard; this became *Ghost Waltzes*, performed at the 1993 competition. And in 1991 he was informed by a colleague, as he presided over an ASCAP board meeting, that he had "died" again, this time in the pages of *The Penguin Dictionary of Music*. He wrote a wry letter of protest to editor Arthur Jacobs at Oxford University: "I must tell you how singularly impressed [my colleagues] were (as was I) with my ability to still function against such odds." Jacobs responded immediately, "utterly abashed and apologetic." Gould's name had apparently been confused with that of pianist Glenn Gould. "I am deeply sorry," wrote Jacobs. "Long life to you!"

The grim sensation of mortality closing in was reinforced from the fall of 1991 through the summer of 1992, which brought the deaths in rapid succession of Shirley Uzin Quill, Alfred Gould, and Shirley Bank Gould. "When will I die? How will I die? At least I won't know it. . . . I am so aware of being in my final years. I've never been so depressed," Morton said in August 1991. Earlier that summer Shirley Bank Gould called to ask Morton for advice about a name for David and Laurie's new son; through the summer of 1991, as she grew more frail, she and Morton continued to talk civilly over the phone. Morton's brother Alfred, who had been sickly for years, was spending more time in the hospital than out.

On 26 September 1991, Shirley Uzin Quill died in the hospital after a stroke. Morton had visited her the week before she was taken off life support, as he recalled in a diary entry shortly thereafter. She had taken his hand and said, "It is so good to see you, dear Morton, it is so good to see you." Thus closed another door, although one that long had been nearly shut. He even felt a little guilty at the muted nature of his reaction. How terrified he had been when the young Shirley Uzin had a tonsillectomy! "I treated her as though she was Camille." There was none of that sensation now. He had "the strange feeling of being very aware of what one should feel," but without feeling it. He recalled standing with his young love on a elevated platform in Queens under a full moon. "I said to her, 'Every time I see that moon I will think of you.' And every time I've seen that moon I do think of her—but she was no longer part of me except in memory."

There was a more frightening blow barely a week later, on 4 November 1991. Shirley Bank Gould, who finally had settled into a duplex apartment in Manhattan, fell down the stairs and lay there, helpless, for half a day. The Bellevue staff contacted Eric; he alerted his daughter Jessica, a student at nearby NYU, who let herself in and discovered her grandmother on the floor. Shirley certainly had not lost her spirit. When an ambulance attendant asked her how she felt, she replied, "I feel like having a party! How the fuck do you think I feel?"

Shirley did not surrender to an ailment that would have destroyed almost anyone else. As she shuffled painfully down the hall at Bellevue, colleagues would hear her joke, "I just broke another bone." Physicians who saw her x-rays assumed that she was bedridden. But after weeks in and out of the hospital, Shirley returned to her apartment and to work, her pain relieved with massive doses of morphine. In her lucid moments, she continued to speak to Morton on the phone, but under no circumstances would she allow Morton to see her.

The grief continued. In early November 1991 Gould spoke, along with New York Mayor David Dinkins, at a memorial for Shirley Uzin Quill, who had herself been a much-honored labor, housing, and civil rights leader. Then he attended a memorial tribute for Agnes De Mille and another for Elie Siegmeister. "I'm spending a lot of time doing memorial tributes to people who were part of my life."

Gould's depression was now incessant. His latest royalty statement from BMG, which now owned RCA, indicated he had not earned one cent in 1991 from all those recordings. Even events that should not have affected him felt like the fates piling on. Claire's ex-husband, attorney Jules Speciner, pleaded guilty to tax evasion. Gould was among those who wrote letters to the judge supporting Speciner's good character. Speciner's fate—he was disbarred, declared bankruptcy, and was sentenced to prison—did not help Gould's mood.

Yet the new year brought with it an unexpected ray of joy. To his amazement and gratitude, as he noted early in 1992, Shirley "started to thaw out." In early January, he called to tell her of the death of Annette Nancarrow; one evening in mid-January, he called just to see how she was. Her speech was slurred and she seemed disoriented; "I'm going, this is the end," she said. Morton hurried to the apartment. Kanti Rai and Deborah were already there. Kanti determined that Shirley had been overmedicated and would be all right.

He left, and Deborah went out for food, leaving Morton and Shirley alone together for the first time in years. She broke down and began to cry like a frightened girl while Morton tried to comfort her. "Then she looked at me, and this is where the whole Berlin Wall came down. She said, 'Why did we muck it up?' She used an expletive. 'Why did we fuck it up? Why? Why?' Those are her exact words. She went on like that."

"For two smart people like us to fuck it up that way," Shirley said.

"The smarter the person, the more they fuck it up," replied Morton.

Deborah came back with dinner and laid it out. As they ate a pleasant dinner, all together, Deborah—who had never seen her parents at peace—said, "I've waited for this for thirty-five years." "That cut very deep," Gould admitted. "I realized then how badly Deborah had been hurt by all of this." Shirley was reluctant to see him return to Great Neck.

That night he hardly slept. "I felt like a yo-yo," Gould said in his diary. "I was going sideways and up and down." Shirley called early the next morning, her voice vibrant and strong, to apologize for her behavior. "And then we started to talk, about all the people we had known, the friends, the enemies, right down the line. There she was, calling the shots on all these people with her own interpretations—she was cutting to the bone again." He was euphoric. This was the old Shirley, tongue intact. "She did say, 'Don't ever marry Claire.' That, in a way, was symbolic: She's turning me out and turned me off, and yet she is jealous, she doesn't want anybody else in on what she feels is her turf." (Gould loved Claire, did not want to do anything to hurt her, and wanted her taken care of after his death. But he had decided long before that he would never re-marry.)

From then on, Shirley accepted Morton. In the next few days, he showed her his office (she complimented him for including one of son-in-law Stuart Burton's paintings on the wall), he took her to the theater. Finally one evening in late January, before he headed back to Shoreward Drive, where Claire was waiting for him, Morton kissed Shirley—"I really kissed her! I haven't done that in years and years and years, probably since before Deborah was born. This time I kissed her the way we used to kiss, like two people who feel warmly toward each other."

There was no question of a return. Gould no longer dreamed of Shirley as he had when he could not see her; his romantic feelings had faded; the cancer had made her a physical wreck; he was comfortable and happy with Claire. But this unexpected reconciliation buoyed Morton through the next few months, which included increasingly rancorous doings at ASCAP. On 21 April 1992, Gould flew to Los Angeles for the movie and television awards, and back to New York early the next morning. It was board week, and from Wednesday to Friday the schedule was full, but he still made time to visit with his brother Alfred, at the hospital, on Friday; that night he and Claire ate at Peyser's Greenwich Village home. The guests included composer Milton Babbitt and his wife; *New York* magazine theater critic John Simon, "very acerbic and bright"; Charles Wuorinen, "a wonderful composer but an independent spirit," and Edward Rothstein, chief music critic of *The New York Times*, "very young and very bright." Peyser was introducing Gould to the club he'd always been kept out of, and he wasn't sure he liked it. As he continued in his diary, "I was interested to be in the room with all these intellectual people, all of them sounding off their own agendas."

The next morning, 25 April, after years of illness, Alfred Gould died. Morton gave the eulogy at Alfred's memorial service; he said in his diary, "There was a minimum of ritual. . . . He suffered so much. It is a relief, after all the torment, that he died peacefully in his sleep. We live and see people die around us, and at one point we die." In May 1992 Gould was told that the ASOL had given him another honorary five-year term; as Catherine French recounted, he accepted—under one condition: "Subject only to my living five more years. And that not being the case, you can always cancel."

His mind occupied with thoughts of Shirley and mortality, Gould felt a little freer to cast a critical eye on the intelligentsia. In June 1992 a committee of composers, most members of the American Institute of Arts and Letters, met to discuss ways to contribute to the academy's centennial. Hugo Weisgall was the chairman; others in attendance included Gould, George Perle, Ellen Taaffe Zwilich, and Charles Wuorinen, with Ned Rorem sitting in by telephone. Gould—who knew more about commerce, politics, and the "real world" than any of the others—was "amazed at how insulated and introverted

[his] colleagues [were]." He continued in his diary, "Some of them have great hostility, and seem to be mad at everybody. They have a sort of contempt for the audience; they think it is full of philistines who have no understanding of what music is about. Some of them are purists, which is a strange thing to be in this day and age. . . . I respect them creatively," he said, chuckling, "but I am ambivalent about some of their other virtues."

Weisgall, Perle, Wuorinen—these represented the academic and serialist composers who dominated musical thought in the post–World War II era. Men such as these once scorned Gould for his determination to communicate directly with his listeners. Here he was, inside the ivory tower—and he was not impressed.

It did not help that by the middle of June it was apparent that Shirley could not live much longer. Reluctantly, she had left Manhattan and moved in with Eric and Candy again. "My golden girl—she's getting transfusions every couple of days, and she looks like a skeleton . . . . It is hard to witness her dying." The end came early in the morning of Sunday, 5 July 1992. Shirley Bank Gould died surrounded by her children and grandchildren. "It's done. It's gone," Morton reported in his diary that evening, in an entry marked by pauses and silences but no audible tears. "She was unbelievable and impossible, such a strange combination, as brave as they come. She was adored by her pupils, by her fellow teachers, and loved and admired by all of us. The ones she handled least effectively were the ones closest to her. I will always love her."

There was no funeral service; Shirley was cremated. The family, minus Abby, sat shiva at Eric's house, and he kept the ashes. Even at the end, Abby was so bitter that she refused to attend or participate in any of the planning.

"I have to get back to my life," said Morton in his diary. "I have to finish the children's piece. Isn't it ironic? I'm writing a children's piece." Gould threw himself into the work, which he had been pushed into doing by Marie Maazel and Frances DeBroff, chairman of the Pittsburgh Youth Symphony Orchestra. He called it *The Jogger and the Dinosaur*, a "concerto for rap singer and orchestra." What could be more appealing to children than a piece that included joggers, dinosaurs, and rap music? He wrote the libretto himself, in consultation with grandson Jeremy, who was now seven. Morton spent so much time on the phone with him that the boy complained to his mother, "He's the composer! Why is he calling *me* all the time?"

Plans were going ahead on another commission, involving Rostropovich and the National Symphony. A few years before, they had discussed a massive oratorio to mark the quincentennial of Columbus's first voyage, an ambitious project that got nowhere. But philanthropists John and Jane Hechinger were commissioning scores for the capital's orchestra. They had remarkable success with the first four, one of which—a trombone concerto by Christopher Rouse—won the Pulitzer Prize. Rouse and Rostropovich both knew Gould, the Russian beginning with 1984's Cello Congress, and Rouse as a musician and family acquaintance.

So by the end of 1992, Gould was preparing a major score for the National Symphony, intended as the orchestra's farewell to Rostropovich, their music director, who was leaving at the end of the season. Not that this cheered Morton up. Early in 1993 he had a long conversation with Susan Feder, the new vice president of G. Schirmer and a person he respected. He came away convinced that there was just no interest in works such as *Jekyll and Hyde Variations* or *Dance Variations*. "I don't exist," he said.

Even the academic world was losing its luster, just when it began showing an interest in Gould. In March 1993 he visited Yale University for three days of Gould seminars, organized by Ezra Laderman and Jacob Druckman. Gould enjoyed the hospitality and camaraderie; he liked the younger composers, though he was dismayed at the sparse attendance. "Sweet people, these academicians," he said. "But they live in another world."

Immediately afterward, Gould flew to Pittsburgh for *The Jogger and the Dinosaur*. No longer could his children complain that he never told them what he was doing: eleven members of the clan came along. Jeremy Burton got full credit for his contributions (the brochure even included illustrations he had drawn), and Morton brought the boy and his younger brother, Eli, up for bows after the performance on Sunday, 4 April 1993. It was a most successful premiere. The composition, with its timely subjects and style, and Gould's scenario, with its elaborate stage effects, drew a strong, positive response.

"I have a feeling it is going to get a lot of performances," said

Gould in his diary shortly after. He was right. Within the next two years, *The Jogger and the Dinosaur* got close to forty performances around the country, an extraordinary number for a contemporary orchestral piece. The Pittsburgh Youth Symphony immediately asked for another. Gould demurred; he suggested Philip Glass. But Maazel and DeBroff insisted on Gould.

Children's music wasn't the only project. On 21 May 1993 he and Claire flew to Fort Worth for the Van Cliburn Competition. This was an event he had looked forward to; he wanted to hear what the piece sounded like. (Not that anything could lift his depression, but that week he was even a clue in *The New York Times* crossword puzzle: "Morton Gould heads what organization?") Before they left, he commented again, in his diary, on how short a time he had left. "How will I die?" he asked. "How will I go?" Such musings became a litany as constant as the listing of his family and the recital of his failures.

He spent more than two weeks in Fort Worth (with a three-day ASCAP break in Los Angeles), soaking in the atmosphere of wealth, culture, and adoration. He gave one of his typical, extemporaneous speeches at the opening dinner 21 May 1993, as he noted in his diary: "I didn't know what to say, so I told them one of my stories, about how two books of music already have me dead. As soon as I mentioned the fact that I am really dead, the whole place broke up."

Ghost Waltzes was played by the dozen semi-finalists, and the very first performer experienced a true Gould moment. The assigned page-turner was sick, and the substitute left her glasses home; the pianist had to help turn the pages. (Ultimately, he was given a chance to play it again.) "I had great sympathy for him," said Morton.

Ghost Waltzes is another memorial piece. It recalls, in ways subtle and blatant, the waltzes from his parents' player piano; as the program notes indicated, "It evokes all the different kinds of waltz textures and rhythms: Viennese, Chopinesque, jazzlike, and so forth, in a wide spectrum that allows the pianist to indulge in a virtuoso fashion." The score has its moments of density and is difficult to play (Morton might not be able to practice, but he hadn't forgotten his immense hand-stretch). At the same time, it invites the listener in, rather than presenting a daunting facade.

"For those two and a half weeks I was in a different world," Gould said in his diary upon his return. "I felt important. . . . It really was a high point." But in practically the same breath he moaned about not being involved in the City Ballet's recent Balanchine festival, and what a great blow the loss of the Audubon ballet had been. His eightieth birthday was coming up, and the Philharmonic was doing nothing—although the Chicago Symphony planned to perform *Fall River Legend* a half dozen times. Gould hired publicist and manager Bette Snapp to try to get more performances and publicity, though he held out no great hope. "I am just not part of the groups, the clubs, the power structure," he lamented. "Why do I bother to pretend to participate?"

Never did Gould consider that, to the world at large, he *was* the establishment, and one of the most powerful composers in America. It didn't matter. No recognition, no honor could assuage the doubts that tore at his soul.

During the summer of 1993, tension mounted at ASCAP. The pressure at home increased when Deborah was hospitalized with symptoms of a stroke during the August break, which Gould had planned to use for music. It turned out she was just suffering from a severe migraine, but the incident only added another worry. "Poor Deborah," he said in his diary. "It was hair-raising."

In early September Gould spent long days in contact with all ASCAP's bureaus and officers. There was a trip to London on 14 September for the British Performing Rights Society's annual dinner, at which he presented awards to Elton John and Phil Collins. Then it was back to New York and the office, and nights spent working on the Rostropovich till the wee hours of the morning. "I have three big movements done, but I still have the shorter ones to go," he said on 30 September, shortly after returning from a meeting in Nashville (there was also a quick ASCAP trip to Washington).

By now he had accepted the fact that no writer could ever be the chief executive of ASCAP again. The work was too onerous and detailed; of all the people within the organization, writers and composers were the least qualified to be administrators. But Morton thrived under pressure. He finished the score for Rostropovich in early October 1993, just weeks after the reorganization blew ASCAP apart. "I'm curious to hear it," he said in his diary. "I wonder if it's a good piece. I hope it is." He called it *Stringmusic*.

If Gould could have been satisfied by a ceremony, it should

have been the program held on 17 October 1993 at Queens College. Organized by conductor and music historian Maurice Peress, "Mostly Morton" included a number of pieces that surprised and impressed the composer. Besides several of the more familiar works, including *American Symphonette* No. 2, *Vivaldi Gallery* (played by three student string quartets), and *Derivations*, Peress had uncovered some gems. One was an aircheck of Gould and Shefter playing "Tiger Rag." The other was the piano concerto written for Wallenstein's radio orchestra.

For once, it's possible to believe Gould when he said he had forgotten the concerto completely. Nobody had played it after 1938, and Peress found the score in Schirmer's files. "It's a blockbuster of a piece," Gould said in his diary, late in 1993. "It uses tone clusters and elbow playing. God, I really was sort of a wild guy in my own way at that age."

The program would not have been complete without its own difficulties. The soloist was pianist Randall Hodgkinson of Boston, the only person in the world who knew the music. But his wife, pianist Leslie Amper, was about to give birth. Hodgkinson left the labor room, hospital gown under his coat, to get to Logan Airport. The plane was almost fogged in, and he did not arrive at the concert hall until moments before the performance. His wife gave birth while Hodgkinson was in the air, and he was told about it when he finished—the arrival of his daughter was announced from the stage at intermission.

The only non-Gould in the program was a set of variations on "Happy Birthday" by John Corigliano, son of John Corigliano, longtime concertmaster of the Philharmonic and an old friend of Morton's. When the boy had showed interest in composition, his father took him to Gould, who said that little John had definite signs of talent. By 1993 Corigliano had had a great success with *The Ghosts of Versailles*, only the second opera commissioned by the Met in decades, and his Symphony No. 1 had won the Grawemeyer Prize.

The birthday variations were clever and original, without a trace of Stravinsky's classic set. "They are the best variations on "Happy Birthday" that I know of," Gould bubbled afterward in his diary. "I was so moved and touched by his doing this. He is a wonderful composer and a wonderful human being." (As his children loved to point out, anybody who said anything nice about Morton was a genius and a wonderful person.)

There was more to come. "To my amazement, I got two very good reviews in *Newsday* and *The New York Times*," he said, voice rising with excitement, in a diary entry shortly after the program. "This is going to be a wonderful memory for me. Why I forgot the piano concerto I have no idea. I think it is an important work of mine."

Now he had to fight to stay depressed. The Chicago Symphony was pulling out all the stops for *Fall River Legend*. There was a week-long residency at Iowa State University in Ames. Kenneth Schermerhorn conducted Gould with the Nashville Symphony, and performances were scheduled by the Los Angeles Choral Society and the Sacramento Symphony. In New York, the Little Orchestra Society under Dino Anagnost mounted *The Jogger and the Dinosaur* for its children's concert series. (Once again the family turned out; Gould had to buy more than thirty tickets.) Monique and Anne-Marie Mot played *Two Pianos* at Steinway Hall and recorded it. David Zinman led *Burchfield Gallery* in Pittsburgh. The Albany Symphony under David Alan Miller played the Flute Concerto, with Gary Shocker as soloist, and then it was back to Washington to attend the Kennedy Center Honors as president of ASCAP.

Before he left for Washington, though, on 1 December 1993, he was lured to the Museum of Radio and Broadcasting on the pretext of meeting Charles Osgood for dinner. "There was a whole mob of people! The first ones I see are Skitch Henderson, Betty Comden and Adolph Green, Ed Murphy, my board members. They yell out 'Surprise!' This is one of the great surprises of my life, I must say." The celebrants ran the gamut from André Previn to the actor Michael Moriarty, who had appeared in *Holocaust*, and Jane Powell, from *Delightfully Dangerous*. Al Hirschfeld did a caricature. Gould was given a framed photograph of the first Radio City Music Hall orchestra, with a circle around "young Mozart" at the piano. "I spoke. I was apparently very funny. I remember nothing. The first thing I said was 'I resign.'" But, as he was forced to admit in his diary, "It was a memorable evening. I am grateful beyond words to everybody who was a part of it."

Still, despite the plaudits, the performances, the seminars, Gould never took his eye off the fact that the "big orchestras" were not playing his music. "I have basically never gotten unreserved, unqualified acceptance," he said. "I'm beyond being bitter. I'm just frustrated that I didn't make it bigger; nothing in Cleveland, nothing in Boston . . . not in Philadelphia . . . . I am beating a dead horse. I am very aware of being eighty, and my time is running out."

He never mentioned that on 16 December 1993 he was named *Musical America*'s Composer of the Year. His predecessors had been John Corigliano and Elliott Carter. But he couldn't get the idea of death out of his head. "How will I die? Will I suddenly fall down somewhere, or will I suffer and deteriorate? Will I be a burden? I hope not."

On 31 December, as 1993 ran out, Gould sat in his studio and spoke mournfully into his diary: "I will never get the Kennedy Honors. I will never win a Pulitzer Prize."

CHAPTER 26

Triumph, and Curtain

★ ★ ★ ★

THE FINAL YEARS of Gould's life had been as rich with incident and creativity, accompanied by depression and talk of suicide, as any period since the peak of his fame. Morton had no idea what 1994 would bring. Of course, he wasn't hopeful, and the year started off roughly with a two-day engagement at the beginning of January with the Colorado Symphony, which had declared bankruptcy and been reorganized by its musicians. The weather was frigid, the flights were uncomfortable, the orchestra was not in very good condition, Morton was under the weather—"It was a waste of time for me," he said in his diary.

Morton was still preoccupied with ASCAP ("The situation is boiling," he said in a diary entry of 22 January 1994. "This will be my last year; it has to be.") and the continued losses brought by time. Stanley Adams, his mentor, colleague, neighbor, and friend, was diagnosed with lung cancer. Morton admired, respected, and liked Adams, even during their struggles over ASCAP. They dined almost weekly at Giovanni's, Gould's favorite Great Neck restaurant. "He was a bastion in the society, especially in these tumultuous times. He was a Rock of Gibraltar for knowledge, know-how, and a keen mind. I need him so badly," Gould said in an early 1994 diary entry. Adams was one of the few men now senior to Gould. He was eighty-seven; Morton was eighty ("it's drummed into me all the time").

But the schedule did not let up: he was off to Washington, then London and Cannes. He was correcting the parts for *Stringmusic* and making arrangements of older scores for a Delos recording by Gerard Schwarz, members of the Seattle Symphony, and trumpeter Jeffrey Silberschlag, Schwarz's brother-in-law. Adams died while Gould was in Europe. Depression, arthritis, travel, and loneliness were wearing him down. On 11 February, he announced in his diary that he intended to retire "very soon." He was supposed to head to California again for board week. "This is getting too much for me. It looks as if I will retire in April. . . . The last couple of months have been murderous," he said.

Gould worked to arrange a succession and announced his intention to retire, in California, on 18 February 1994. "I gave my resignation Friday to the board and left the room," he said. "They called me back in, accepted my resignation 'with deep regret,' and put Marilyn Bergman in place as president with my wholehearted support." His voice was brighter and stronger on the diary tape: "I'm a free man after eight years! What a burden to be lifted off my back. . . . I am so relieved. At long last I can get back to what I am supposed to be doing, making music." Gould was to be president emeritus for a year at full salary, but within a few months he gave up his office at ASCAP.

On 8 March, he and Claire flew to Washington for the premiere of *Stringmusic*. It is quintessential Gould, from the informality of the movement titles—"Prelude," "Tango," "Dirge," "Ballad," and "Strum"—to the challenges it poses for musicians. As Gould sat in on rehearsals, he began to think that perhaps he had written something special, as he reported in his diary:

> I listened to it as if somebody else had written it. I had very little recollection of it, and no idea of how I would react to it. I was much moved and touched by the way it sounded. When I heard the runthrough for the first time, it aroused so many turbulent feelings. I *do* have the ability to communicate, to make a piece of music. I'm beginning to sound like an egomaniac.

The family turned out again for the opening performances, appearing in shifts for one or another concert (except for David and Laurie, both ill). The premiere, on Friday, 10 March 1994, was a great success. "I got a standing ovation," he stated proudly in his diary. "Part of it was the fact of my eightieth birthday, but the work itself seemed to have moved a lot of people." Pianist Tedd Joselson, in the audience to listen to his friend Santiago Rodriguez, was impressed: "I was listening and listening, and I'm simply bowled over by it. The whole Kennedy Center audience was standing and cheering." Even the press had a good time. Paul Teare (*The Washington Post*, 11 March 1994) stated flatly: "To celebrate his eightieth birthday, Morton Gould composed a masterpiece called simply *Stringmusic*."

What exactly did he say with this music? The public and private records differ significantly. In the program notes, Gould spoke of Rostropovich. The overall work, he said, reflects "the many moods and many facets of a man and musician we have all come to know for the intensity and emotion of his commitment to music and life." The second movement in particular is a gift to Slava, Gould wrote, because Rostropovich had expressed his love for the tango after conducting *Latin American Symphonette* in 1990. Gould declared that the monumental "Dirge" was meant to reflect "not only the intensity but in particular the sense of sorrow, loss, and even anger that must be associated with so much that Slava has experienced in consequence of his ideals and loyalties. The cortege-like quality of this elegiac music, I feel, is in keeping with a prominent part of his personality."

But to his tape recorder (and, he hoped, to posterity) Gould told a different version. *Stringmusic*—and "Dirge" especially—was about him:

> I am proud of that piece. I think it is an important part of me. . . . When I'm gone, if one wants to know how I felt at this time, that's it. The "Dirge" is what I am all about now. I am getting close to death, and what I think about it, this dirge reflects it. It is basically about death, the act of living and the act of dying, and the activity of commemorating those who have died or gone before, the tragedy, the terror, the ice-cold sadness of it all. And along with that, the other movements reflect other aspects. The warmth of the movement after the dirge, a ballad, a love song: that's for all the people I've loved, all the family I've loved, all the women I've loved. The warmth and tenderness I've felt for these human beings.

"Tango" was sensuous. "The way Slava did it, I told him he was going to be raided for obscenity." And the opening, "Prelude," with all its musical evocations? "I probably sound like all composers who love their work," he said in a spring 1994 diary entry. "This is one piece I have a very, very warm feeling about, and apparently others have it, too."

He had no idea.

But the high of *Stringmusic* was brief. In the months that followed, his cloud was pierced only now and again. At the end of May he wrote a song for Previn, who had undergone heart surgery. Flutist Keith Brion planned to record the Flute Concerto, and Gould began collaborating with Joselson, who wanted to record some early piano music and was pushing him to complete the long-threatened piano concerto.

He felt no need to mention on his tapes a small commission from the public radio station WNYC, which asked the most prominent American composers to write scores, based on a poem by John Ashbery, for the station's fiftieth anniversary. Nor did he comment on a review of the 13 June premiere. Leighton Kerner (*Village Voice*, 28 June 1994), a knowledgeable and rigorous critic, termed Gould's contribution one of the two best works of the event (the other was by Milton Babbitt). Kerner called Gould's piece, *No Longer Very Clear*, "one of the neatest things he's ever written," and a second number, *The Anniversary Rag*, played by the composer, he found "a low-pressure gem."

The musical world was listening, but it was almost too late for him to hear.

Then, in the middle of August, came an announcement that Morton Gould "couldn't believe": he would receive the Kennedy Center Honors. These awards, given in Washington annually since 1978, are a peculiar mix of the popular and the highbrow, televised in prime time by CBS. They have commercial sponsorship, and they draw a national audience to "A National Celebration of the Performing Arts."

In keeping with the mongrel nation we are, the awards are highly political and amusingly eclectic, honoring as broad a spectrum—and one as "politically correct" in the best sense—as could be imagined. The first honorees were Richard Rodgers, from Broadway; George Balanchine, from dance; Marian Anderson, from music and civil rights; pianist Arthur Rubinstein; and Fred Astaire. The 1994 honorees, along with Gould, were soul singer Aretha Franklin; director Harold Prince; actor Kirk Douglas; and folksinger and activist Pete Seeger.

Although Gould was moved, there was no missing the fact that it had come to him only after a line of colleagues and competitors had gone ahead. Among the composers preceding him were Copland (1979), Bernstein (1980), Thomson (1983), and Schuman (1989). Other musicians included Isaac Stern, Rostropovich, Yehudi Menuhin, and Benny Goodman. Perhaps Morton was chosen, as ASCAP secretary Toni Winter whispered, "by elimination."

There had been no lack of effort on his behalf. Starting in 1983, Walter Gould mounted an active advocacy campaign. That year Frank Sinatra was among the honorees, and Walter asked him to plug for his brother; the singer returned a brief note agreeing that Morton might be a worthy addition but that he had no say in the matter. Sinatra passed Walter's note to Charles Wick of the United States Information Agency, and within a few weeks Morton was invited to the ceremony for the first time. ("It may just have been a coincidence," said Walter.)

Over the next decade Walter pulled all the strings, asking friends and colleagues to write in Morton's favor to Kennedy Center chairman James Wolfensohn and founder Roger Stevens. He even solicited a letter from the commandant of the United States Military Academy. When Gould became president of ASCAP in 1986, his staff —primarily publicist Karen Sherry and concert music director Fran Richard—joined the effort. Morton did not discourage them but would say little except, "You're wasting your time, you're wasting your time."

And, although ecstatic over being named, Morton thought little would come of it in the area he sought most eagerly: performance. He hired Ken Sunshine, a former ASCAP publicist, in a futile effort to get booked on television or radio as a result of the award.

Work continued. Choreographer David Parsons of the Pennsylvania Ballet had been commissioned by the Kennedy Center to create *Mood Swing*, to a combination of *Derivations* and *Benny's Gig*. Morton attended runthroughs and the performance in the fall.

The Kennedy Center weekend began on Friday, 2 December 1994, with a luncheon for the honorees. There was a State Department dinner Saturday night, and a reception Sunday afternoon at the White House, during which President Bill Clinton gave the honorees their medals, worn on ribbons around their necks.

This time even David made it, though Laurie did not—she had just given birth to the couple's second son. Walter and Betty were there, and Claire. I covered the event for *Newsday* (I had just begun work on this biography). The ceremony and glitter surrounding the event, as commonplace as they must be to the famous and the powerful, are nevertheless impressive. Spectators with cameras and autograph books line the building's lofty, marble corridors behind velvet-rope barricades, to sigh and applaud as the celebrities walk past.

Some make grand entrances in their gowns and jewels. Morton and Claire just walked quickly, almost with their heads down, along one side of the corridor. He was smiling uncomfortably, though he seemed genuinely surprised when I called to him from a spot behind the velvet ropes. "Peter, what are you doing here?" he said. What a question.

The evening was impressive yet paradoxical. Each honoree was given a biographical segment, including photographs, documents, and excerpts of their work. It turned out that several had strong left-wing political histories, and the Republicans under Newt Gingrich had just taken power in Congress.

Kirk Douglas had defied the Hollywood establishment when, during the filming of *Spartacus*, he demanded full credit for screenwriter Dalton Trumbo, who had been one of the "Hollywood Ten." Pete Seeger's long, active background, including a stretch on the blacklist, got a full airing, too. There was no mention of Gould's politics—he was, in fact, the source for much of the patriotic glue that held the show together.

Previn was host for Morton's portion, which kicked off after intermission with a parade down the aisles by a United States Army Band carrying banners and playing *American Salute*, accompanied by flashing lights and synthetic fireworks. There were clips from *Delightfully Dangerous*, old photographs, "Pavanne." When it was his turn in the spotlight, Morton rose, dour and tight-lipped as usual, and clasped his hands overhead like an awkward prizefighter. He looked as if he'd rather not be there.

There was some political flak afterward. Frank Rich, making his transition from *Times* theater critic to political columnist, criticized the program for being so relentlessly middlebrow. Instead of *American Salute*, why not *Interplay* or another more significant Gould work, for example? A letter writer in *The New York Times* complained about the dullness of the program; he remarked that Morton Gould must have been bored, because he didn't smile once!

And the show took place just as the bitter battles of the "Contract with America" Congress were about to begin, with government involvement in the arts a primary focus. The reactionary columnist John Podhoretz (*The New York Post*) took the show apart, deriding its very existence as "a PR stunt devised for the purpose of brownnosing and blackmailing the nation's legislators into continuing their support for the John F. Kennedy Center for the Performing Arts."

The awards were going to second-raters, Podhoretz asserted—Kirk Douglas, "a scenery-chomper with a second career as a dirty-book author." There was the outrageous selection of Seeger, "this song stylist of Stalinism, this troubador of tyranny, this Horace of Ho Chi Minh homiletics." How fortunate that Podhoretz didn't know of Gould's teenage dream of a Soviet America. Morton thought the fuss slightly ironic, since he had a longer entry in *Red Channels* than Seeger.

He shrugged off the criticism, both political and esthetic. He'd been weaned on blending the commercial with the artistic, and the need to provide entertainment if one wanted a large audience. He was overjoyed at the attention and the chance his family had to experience it. Personally, he was most moved by the appreciative essay by Leonard Slatkin, Rostropovich's successor at the National Symphony. The conductor, son of violinist and conductor Felix Slatkin, who had recorded *Latin American Symphonette* with the Hollywood Bowl Orchestra, wrote of how he grew up with Gould in his ears, from the arrangements to the radio classics to the more serious work. "Somehow, even if not consciously, virtually all American musicians have been touched by Morton and affected by him," Slatkin wrote. "Everything he did was guided by the sure hand of a master craftsman who brought his fine classical training to bear in every undertaking."

"To me," Morton said late in 1994, "that was one of the great highlights of that whole event."

The nationwide broadcast brought more pleasure, as he began hearing from old comrades. Robert Reed, director of the Major Bowes program, called and wrote with reminiscences. So did George Kimball Plochmann, who had known him at Woodstock.

But depression was never far away; barely a week later he complained in his diary, "Now it seems as if the Kennedy Honors never happened. I'm falling back to earth and reality." The small family celebration of his eighty-first birthday, on 10 December 1994, served only to remind him that now he was "living to die." Five days later, he sat for the first interview with me as biographer.

Not even the next round of honors cheered him. On 19 December he and Claire flew to Miami for a Murray Dranoff International Two-Piano Symposium, which this time focused almost exclusively on Gould's multiple-piano music. He was again the toast of the town and lapped it up, even with the knowledge that this pleasure was temporary. Now he worried not only about his place in history but the immediate financial future. It never occurred to him to live on even the diminished income from royalties and performances and his not-inconsiderable estate. The loss of the ASCAP salary frightened him; he began trying to think of ways to earn money again.

Depression continued into the new year, leavened only by birthday parties that February for Eric (his fiftieth) and Abby (her forty-fifth). It pleased Morton to give some keepsakes to his daughters: for Abby, a watercolor of a barn done at Woodstock that Deborah had found among his papers; for Deborah, a drawing of her when she was three or four years old, "watching television with that intense look she has." Sex seemed to be under control at last. He still had the eye and the desire, but, as he said in an early 1995 diary entry, at the age of eighty-one, "I am turning people down. I don't want to risk the relationship I have, I don't want to risk things like AIDS, I don't want to do things that are more destructive than before." Nor was there satisfaction in music, though he made this tautological argument: "I am performed more than composers who are not performed."

He found no enthusiasm for his second commission from the Pittsburgh Youth Symphony, which he'd decided would be about firefighters, in honor of grandson Benjamin, a volunteer in Great Neck. Even the work with Tedd Joselson irked him. He regretted having agreed to complete the piano concerto, which had no commission: "I am doing a major work for nothing, which makes me an amateur, not a professional. It is demeaning." On 30 March 1995, he groaned to his diary, "I feel so beaten. Nothing is happening in my career. There are no engagements, no really important commissions, my royalties are low. A lifetime of work, a catalog with Schirmer that is not moving at all—there is no place to go. Who do I turn to? Nobody."

Every year in mid-April, employees of ASCAP's concert music department call Columbia University, to see if one of their composers has won the Pulitzer. On Tuesday, 18 April 1995, Fran Richard asked her assistant, Chia Toscanini (the conductor's granddaughter), to check with the Pulitzer committee. Toscanini flew back down the stairs flushed with excitement. "My God! My God!" she cried. "Morton won the Pulitzer!"

"Are you sure? Are you kidding?" was Richard's immediate response.

"No, no! It's true. It's so wonderful. You've got to tell him."

"No, Chia," replied Richard. "You tell him."

First they notified the already assembled committee, and then Richard asked Gould to call Toscanini. He didn't believe it. He got brusque, even a little angry. "How come everybody knows but me?" he retorted, and hung up.

"I really was stunned," Gould said in his diary entry that night. "It was hard for me to react. I thought something was wrong. I was really moved. I didn't get too emotional about it, because I was in such shock. I never even dreamt of this at this time." The committee called for champagne. The rest of the day was a blur of calls, interviews, and congratulations. Gould went through the motions, but his head was elsewhere. He was frantic to get home to notify his children, "so they wouldn't accuse me of not telling them anything."

He returned to Great Neck to more congratulations. Of course the children all knew, they were crying with joy. "I was the last one to know this," Morton groused. "At ASCAP a lot of my colleagues are sort of teary-eyed about this."

Gould had been particularly grouchy that morning because he had finally made his breakthrough on the Pittsburgh piece. There was a "hemorrhage of ideas, more than I can keep up with." He'd been writing until four that morning and did not particularly want to attend the meeting. But John LoFrumento had insisted and sent a car to get him. "I just wanted to get the meeting over with," Gould said. And by his 11:30 p.m. diary entry on 18 April, despite what was only the beginning of the Pulitzer furor, Morton had begun tearing himself down again. He knew how absurd it sounded—"I've been talking the most negative things about myself"—but he couldn't help it. "It's wonderful to get these recognitions. I am very grateful to have lived long enough to see all this happen. . . . Obviously, I am in a more optimistic mood. It'll pass, like all my optimistic moods."

The congratulations poured in. He received letters from friends and colleagues, including Ted Kennedy and Orrin Hatch. "It just doesn't stop," he said a few days later in his diary. "It's wonderful, but it's eating up my time. . . . I still can't believe it happened, the Kennedy Honor and now the Pulitzer. I am grateful and elated. But I have to be writing. I have so many miles to go and not many years to go."

The Pulitzer was awarded for more than *Stringmusic*. It was also intended—and seen—as the overdue recognition of Morton Gould's significance to American music in the twentieth century. "I think there was the feeling on the committee that Morton had paid his dues, had been around for a long time and done a lot of things," said Christopher Rouse, a member of the committee. "He had written a very solid piece here, and I think there was some sentiment that it would be nice to show a little recognition of what he had done. . . . It was as much for a life's work as specifically for that piece."

There was also an acknowledgment that, prolific as Gould had been, the majority of his work from the 1950s onward had been accomplished away from the centers of musical power. Except for the Flute Concerto in Chicago, he did not get commissions from the rest of the Big Five of New York, Philadelphia, Boston, or Cleveland. "He didn't become a sort of homegrown star, the way Walter Piston did," as Rouse put it.

Nevertheless, Rouse, like Slatkin and generations of postwar composers and musicians, had grown up listening to Gould. The toppling of serialism opened the way once again for an acknowledgment of tonality and communication. Nothing Gould had written might have had a direct effect on the composers who came after, but the steadfast craftsmanship, quality, and sheer musicality of his life's work had come to impress many younger writers. Composer Libby Larsen, who knew Gould almost entirely by his reputation and work, said, "He was an extraordinary role model to me, because at graduate school I knew I did not want to teach. I wanted to be a composer making my way by commission in this country."

When *Stringmusic* won, Schirmer wanted to publish the score immediately, so Gould found himself once again in beloved overwork. Gould did have a vague sense of his stature, but nothing could permanently dispel the sorrow just beneath the surface. Only work could keep him anything like happy. And that spring he received another unusual commission, a work for wind ensemble for the dedication of the Thomas J. Dodd Research Center at the University of Connecticut at Storrs, which center would include an archive of documents from the Nuremberg War Crimes Tribunal. The opening ceremony in October would be an international event attended by President Bill Clinton and Holocaust chronicler Elie Wiesel.

He signed the contract for the UConn piece, which became *Remembrance Day: Soliloquy for a Passing Century*, on 9 May 1995 and finished the piano reduction for the Pittsburgh children's piece on 13 May. By late June he was working hard on both the Pittsburgh piece, now called (following a suggestion by Abby) *Hosedown*, and *Remembrance Day* ("I'm full of ideas," he said happily), and struggling with the piano concerto.

In addition, he was invited by Raymond Grant, a former American Symphony executive director who now was head of the performance program at the fledgling Disney Institute in Orlando, Florida, to be a featured guest when the unusual resort opened in February 1996.

Hosedown was completed 3 July; *Remembrance Day*, 8 August. Two days later Morton, along with Eric's and Abby's families, flew to Orlando to visit the yet-unopened facility. It was an odd venture for Disney, a sort of Chautauqua theme park with concerts and performances, short programs in photography, cartooning, dance, and the fine arts. The younger Goulds loved their trip, which included visits to Epcot Center and Disney World. But Morton left early, hot and tired. His physical deterioration infuriated him: "I resent being over eighty." And his pleasure at projected performances was diluted by fear that it would draw snickers. "I probably will be criticized for doing things for Disney," he said in his diary, "the way I was criticized for doing things for radio. But nobody else is calling me."

By late summer 1995 he dismissed the Kennedy Honors and the Pulitzer as "some fluke." All he could think of was time. "Whatever I do, I'd better get it done soon, because I'm going to be dead soon." Gould appeared healthy; the arthritis was under control, his vision and hearing were good, for eighty-one he was in fine shape. The pressure came from the sense that the sands were running out. But he was not sitting on a rocker waiting for the end. His date book was as full as ever.

The weekend of 15 October 1995 saw the opening of the Dodd Center, with ceremonies including speeches by President Clinton and two of the late senator's sons, Ambassador Thomas Dodd and Senator Christopher Dodd. Gould's *Remembrance Day* was performed in the university's Gampel Pavilion, a gymnasium, so the music itself was virtually inaudible. Morton enjoyed himself; he sat next to Wiesel at the dedication and managed to give Clinton two pieces he had written for him. Unfortunately, the president played tenor saxophone, and these were for alto.

Most of the Goulds traveled to Pittsburgh the first weekend of November for the premiere of *Hosedown*. The program included not only the Youth Symphony concert, led by associate conductor Arthur Post, but also a small firefighters' parade through two downtown blocks to Heinz Hall. Morton and grandchildren Benjamin, Jeremy, and Eli were seated in the back of an old horse-drawn fire engine. As it drew away from the curb, he turned to the family behind him and flashed a brief, broad smile in an instant of childlike glee. It was the happiest I'd ever seen him.

The performance included excerpts from Bartók's Concerto for Orchestra (Gould had been at the premiere), portions of Grofe's *Tabloid Suite* (Gould played it at Radio City), several movements from *The Jogger and the Dinosaur*, and *Hosedown*. The audience was raucous; the orchestra wore plastic fire helmets. There were a few stage effects, firefighters rushed across the stage, and the music was lost in an attempt to please the children. The composer thought the premiere went well, though his children were convulsed at a typographical error in the program which described Gould as "this year's Poutzer Prize winner in music."

The next day Gould flew to Portland, Oregon, where James DePreist led the Oregon Symphony in *Fall River Legend* and three pieces that had won the ASCAP Morton Gould Young Composers Prize. Then it was back to New York; on 10 November 1995, Gould met with Ellen Taaffe Zwilich, who occupied the Composer's Chair at Carnegie Hall, to be interviewed for the institution's video archives. He then addressed a young composer seminar at the Peabody Institute in Baltimore, and it was out to California again for an ASCAP board "retreat."

He spent the weekend of 10 December 1995, his eighty-second birthday, recording in Chicago with Joselson and producer Barry Faldner. Joselson had uncovered a slew of Gould's old piano music, and he was impressed with the pianist's virtuosity, particularly on the *Prelude and Toccata*. Morton sat at the keyboard for an arrangement of "Pavanne" for piano four-hands. Once again, young musicians were astounded at the old man's skill. When they realized that the arrangement was not working physically—the pianists kept bumping elbows—Morton sat down with the score and rearranged it in a matter of minutes. They were dumbfounded, Joselson recalled. "It was just such a beautiful picture. . . . He was hunched over this piece of paper, writing the corrections; he rewrote practically the whole page. . . . He was an old pro. He's been there before any of us." (BMG planned to issue the disc in 2000.)

Half-heartedly, Gould continued wrestling with the piano concerto. By the middle of January 1996, he wasn't getting anywhere. "I'm doing it with very little spirit," he said in his diary. "My mood has not improved." On 15 January, he addressed his family directly on the tape: "I've loved you all and appreciated you all. I have a feeling that I am just sitting and waiting to pass on, to get done with it." Again, on 30 January, he spoke full of sadness, going through a list of all the family he loved, naming every child and grandchild—and including both Claire and Norma Perlman—but in essence wishing he were dead.

"I feel that I have outlived myself," he said. "If I survive, I'll talk again into this thing. Once again, it's January 30, 1996." That was the last entry.

A few of those with him realized something was wrong. ASCAP's Fran Richard traveled with Gould to San Francisco on 5

February; his behavior there was unusual. He gave his after-dinner speech, meandering dangerously away from the subject as always. But this time he spoke at length about his father and about his youth. And Morton got lost during the speech, something he never did. Afterward, Richard remembered and wondered if he had already begun to wind down.

On Saturday, 17 February, I had dinner with Morton and Claire at Giovanni's. Two days later, he, Deborah and I flew to Orlando for the Disney Institute opening. (Gould had arranged for me to be included as master of ceremonies and interviewer.) On the plane, we spoke about composing for band and how he came to write *Prisms*. We spoke of the early days with Mills Music, and he lamented the "for-hire" contract, which meant that they owned his scores; he never gained the rights to his most popular pieces. The conversation ranged from an adventure in a train with a beautiful blonde German to the days he traveled with the NBC Orchestra to Washington. We talked at random, and we dozed.

In Orlando we were met by a pair of Disney employees, who were in constant radio contact with the Institute, reporting when we left the terminal and when we got onto the interstate. We were amused at the intrusive efficiency of all this (at one point, the driver announced that my parents and children, who planned to join us for three days, had just arrived). Gould spent that Monday night with Deborah and Ray Grant, while my family and I wandered through the nearby Treasure Island park.

They had planned two days of all-Gould performances in the brand-new, intimate concert hall. The programs featured the U.S. Military Academy Concert Band, to be conducted jointly by Gould and its director, Lt. Col. David Dietrick. On the second day, Wednesday, Morton was to give an hour-long discussion and demonstration.

Tuesday morning Morton mounted the podium to rehearse. He worked through *Fanfare for Freedom*, two movements from *Family Album*, and *West Point Symphony*. At first he seemed slightly uncomfortable, his movements stiff and cramped. He felt a little dizzy, and his knees locked, as they had in Houston years before. But as the work continued, Gould warmed up and appeared to relax.

After about an hour, they took a break. Morton came to the rear of the auditorium, where he was greeted unexpectedly by Stanley and sister-in-law Zara, who had driven to Orlando from their home nearby. Gould's face was flushed, and he seemed slightly out of breath.

As a precaution, Grant called for an ambulance. The paramedics arrived as Morton and I sat talking about music; they decided to take him to a nearby hospital for examination. After a few hours, Morton was released; the physicians had found nothing wrong and suggested that, if he wished, he could stay overnight for observation. Morton chose to return to Disney, though he would not conduct.

That evening I announced, Col. Dietrick conducted, and Morton sat in a box to the left of the stage. The Institute had been open for only two weeks, and this was the first full house. The program ended with Gould taking questions from the audience. The most striking exchange was with the only black person in the auditorium, a young man who asked whether there was a connection between Gould's music and jazz.

"There really is no connection," Gould said. "I've used some jazz elements, but my music has never been jazz." This from the man whose scores were called "swing symphonies" in the late 1930s. Later, as in San Francisco, he got lost in an anecdote, and I had to remind him how it went.

Afterward we sat in the green room as he signed autographs and chatted. My two sons asked for his autograph. He wrote a note for each but forgot to sign one. After about twenty minutes, looking tired, he returned to the villa. Deborah, Stanley, and a few others talked around the table, but Morton, drawn and white, sat quietly and then went to bed.

The next morning, Wednesday, 21 February 1996, he was late arising. Deborah heard a noise and looked into the room. He was not in bed, so she thought he was in the bathroom. A few minutes later, when he still had not appeared, she went into the room. Her father was on the floor leaning against the far side of the bed, with one sock on. One of the great arteries in his heart had ruptured. Death was apparently instantaneous.

Deborah was frantic with shock, grief, and fear. She thought immediately that her father's death was her fault, just as her mother had insisted it was her fault that Frances Gould fell down the stairs in Forest Hills. Grant, who had come to the villa to see where Morton was, called for help. Along with police and medical officials, Stanley and Zara rushed over. A Disney staff member notified me in the concert hall. "Ray Grant said to tell you that Morton is dead," he said.

My knees buckled and I knelt among the seats for a moment. Then I flung the news at Col. Dietrick as I passed him backstage, and together we rushed to the villa. It was typical Morton: the driver couldn't find his official car, and then we got lost. When we arrived, Stanley was seated on a golf cart outside the villa, head down, looking stricken. Inside, a nurse was trying to comfort Deborah, who was phoning her family up north, sobbing and shouting in sorrow and anger. A county social worker came into the room; she wore a Jewish star around her neck. Deborah screamed when she saw it: "Get out of here! That's the last thing Daddy would want!" Eventually she quieted. Just before the emergency workers took Morton's body, they asked if we wanted to see him one last time.

Morton was lying on a wheeled gurney, covered with a blanket. His face was waxen and his expression somber. Ray kissed his forehead and made the sign of the cross. Deborah leaned over and kissed his face tenderly. Feeling presumptuous merely for being in the room, I just watched.

Abby and Candy flew down that evening for a performance that was now a memorial concert. Afterward, the Goulds, Grant, the colonel and his assistant, and I ate in the Institute dining room. It was a strained meal. Ray sat moodily at one end of the table drinking vodka, while Abby regaled us with tales of her father's scandalous behavior. The next morning I flew home.

But a life like Morton Gould's does not just stop. He had one more work to go.

The previous spring, a young choral conductor named Francisco Nunez had heard *Quotations* in a performance by the New Amsterdam Singers. Nunez directed a choir affiliated with the Children's Aid Society, a charitable organization, and he wanted a new piece. Chorister Jesse Galdston was the son of pop songwriter Phil Galdston, whose "Save the Best for Last" had been a No. 1 hit in 1991 for Vanessa Williams. Phil Galdston had grown up in Great Neck and gone to school with Abby. In the fall of 1995 he asked Gould if he would write something for his son's chorus. To his surprise, Morton said yes.

As if in an afterthought, Gould asked Galdston whether he would write the lyrics, and the writer agreed. Galdston decided to write a lyric inspired by *There Are No Children Here*, a book by Alex Kotlowitz about the stunted lives of inner-city children in Chicago; on 16 January 1996, he faxed the lines to Morton (who never mentioned the commission in his diary).

The next day, Gould told Galdston he had completed a draft. "I thought, well, if he's got the first draft already, it must be pretty simple music," said Galdston. He was accustomed to working fast—"Save the Best for Last" took about half an hour—but he never expected the complexity of the work that resulted. Gould had written the music immediately on seeing the words.

When Morton played the score over the phone, Phil was taken aback. "I was totally unprepared for the range of it," he said. After all, he had sent Morton four relatively simple verses expressing despair and then hope. "I just never conceived this, never in the world." By the final movement—in Gould's hands, four verses had become four movements—Galdston was almost in tears. "It was one of the two or three most thrilling moments in my life doing this work: 'My God, Morton Gould is singing my lyrics to me over the phone, and he's just written this music!' It was overwhelming."

For the next two weeks, Galdston and Gould were in almost daily communication, visualizing how to stage, light, and present the work. Galdston worked out a bridge between the pessimistic first three verses and the sudden hope of the fourth. Galdston was surprised to find that Gould was as eager as he to give the piece exposure: "You have to be out there pushing it, because if you're not out there, no one is." Gladston felt completely comfortable working with this living legend, holder of the Pulitzer Prize. There seemed to be no distance between them. Gould mentioned almost offhandedly that he was going to the Disney Institute. They spoke several times even while he was in Orlando. In their last conversation, they agreed to get together in Great Neck that Friday—"to wrap up the piece, if possible," said Galdston.

When Phil got the first call from Abby Wednesday morning, he refused to believe it. Then Deborah called, hysterical, from Orlando. "You have to finish the piece! You have to finish the piece!" she begged.

"The news of his death was just totally incomprehensible and totally unthinkable," Galdston said. "Because I just didn't think of this guy as an old man."

There were two memorial concerts: the first, on Saturday, 24 February 1996, and largely arranged by his family, was at the 2200-seat Tilles Center for the Arts on Long Island University's C. W. Post Campus in Brookville. All four children spoke, as did grandchildren Benjamin and Jocelyn Gould; Carey Burton, Abby's stepson; Claire Speciner; Danny Daniels Giagni; David's wife, Laurie Murdoch; Sol Berkowitz; and myself. The West Point Band performed, led by associate conductor Maj. Tom Rotondo; Joselson and Faldner played; Eric found and played a tape of "Something To Do," a song from the eponymous cantata.

On Wednesday, 28 February 1996, ASCAP presented a memorial at Carnegie Hall. It was as eclectic as his life had been. The University of Connecticut Wind Ensemble played *Remembrance Day*; members of the New York Choral Society directed by John Daly Goodwin sang portions of *Quotations*; Van Cliburn medalist Christopher Taylor played *Ghost Waltzes*; Lane Alexander danced portions of *Tap Dance Concerto*; Cy Coleman sang "There Must Be Something Better Than Love" from *Arms and the Girl*; Betty Comden and Adolph Green sang "Bad Timing" from *Billion Dollar Baby*; Marvin Hamlisch and Tedd Joselson played *Boogie Woogie Etude*, and Joselson with drum and bass accompaniment played a movement from *Interplay*.

John Corigliano and choreographer Arthur Mitchell spoke; Michael Tilson Thomas sent a videotaped message. Finally, there was an excerpt from one of Morton's ASOL speeches, in which he recounted the time Deborah found one of the books that had listed him as dead. She had wailed at him: "Oh Daddy, you never tell us anything!"

The vision of him delivering that line, to roars of laughter, was the final image in the program.

This was the club Morton belonged in, not the rarified, insular world of concert music. This was an American place where anything went as long as it was good. He spent his life yearning for the ivory tower, while living fully in the bubbling cultural ferment that surrounded him.

Earlier that week the family had held a brief, private ceremony for their father. When he was buried in New Montefiore Cemetery in Farmingdale, New York, Eric brought Shirley's ashes up from the basement of his house, where he had stored them, and placed them in the plot next to Morton.

The Philharmonic did nothing in the weeks after Gould's death —not a moment of silence, not an unscheduled performance of "Pavanne," or *American Salute*, or *Interplay*. Finally, after staff consultations with the family, music director Kurt Masur, a German who had come to the orchestra years after any Gould connection, looked at the score and decided to play *Spirituals for String Choir and Orchestra*. It was substituted for another work in a subscription program the week of 23 May 1996, as part of an unusual concert featuring music by African-American composers Duke Ellington, Ulysses Kay, and Adolphus Hailstork and the German composer Karl-Heinz Popper.

Masur is a solid, middle-European musician, without flamboyance but musical and sure. His interpretation of *Spirituals* was Brahmsian in its strength, dignity, and fervor, a powerful and revealing performance. Reviewing the concert Bernard Holland (*The New York Times*, 25 May 1996), now the chief music critic, offered the praise Morton had longed for but never received in New York in his lifetime:

> Smart, concise, alternately shattering and soothing, always sincere: Gould's orchestral writing represents everything good and important in the American urban sensibility. Here the vernacular assimilates itself by dint of exceptional craftsmanship. Popular music does not drown in its symphonic setting; it is transformed.

Meanwhile, Phil Galdston completed *There Are No Children Here*. Gould had left the piano accompaniment and vocal score, with cues for percussion, sound effects, and a bit of choreography. *There Are No Children Here* was performed by the Children's Aid Society Chorus at the Ethical Culture Society on 10 June 1996.

Morton Gould's last work is an ingenious and touching blend, three-quarters darkness and despair ending with a great youthful shout of hope.

List of Interviewees

★ ★ ★ ★

All interviews were conducted by the author unless otherwise noted.

Lamar Alsop: 15 May 1996
Julius Baker: 16 May 1996
Helene Bank: 2 August 1996
James Bank: 2 August 1996
Stanley Baron: 30 May 1996
Betty Randolph Bean: 27 June 1996
Daniel Berger: 18 July 1996
Marilyn Bergman: 6 April 1996
Pearl Berkowitz: 4 June 1996
Sol Berkowitz: 12 December 1994; 5 June 1996
Martin Bernstein: 1 August 1996
Shannon Bolin: 27 December 1995
Oscar Brand: 14 June 1996
Arnold Broido: 29 July 1996
Louis Brunelli: 13 May 1996
Margaret Carson: 28 October 1996
Betty Comden: 14 February 1995
Hal David: 16 June 1996
David Diamond: 7 June 1996
Harold Diner: 13 August 1996
John Duffy: 5 June 1996
Silas Edman: 13 June 1996
Lee Evans: 24 February 1995
JoAnn Falletta: 23 July 1997
Johanna Fiedler: 31 July 1996
Lukas Foss: 27 July 1996
Catherine French: 21 June 1996
Geraldine Friedman: 2 July 1996
Philip Galdston: 11 June 1996
Stanley Gewirtz: 17 June 1996
Danny Daniels Giagni: 24 February 1996
Richard Glavine: 28 July 1996
Abby Gould Burton: 20 February 1995; 31 July 1996
Betty Gould: 28 December 1994
Candy Gould: 10 May 1996
David Gould: 13 February 1995
Deborah Gould: 9 August 1995
Eric Gould: 2 March 1995; 10 May 1996
Matty Gould: 20 February 1995
Morton Gould:
by Peter Goodman 15 and 29 December 1994; 1 and 8 January 1995; 16 March 1995; 19 and 24 April 1995; 7 and 24 May 1995; 29 December 1995; 1, 4, 17, and 19 February 1996
by David Gould December 1991
by Andrew Kazdin and Roy Hemming 1, 3, 13, 21, and 31 August 1985; 4, 14, 19, and 29

September 1985; 8, 21, and 28 October 1985; 18 and 26 November 1985; 5 February 1986; 11 March 1986
by Ellen Taaffe Zwilich 10 November 1995
Stanley Gould: 9 July 1995
Walter Gould: 28 December 1994; 9 May 1996; 17 July 1996; 26 January 1998
Roger Hall: 23 June 1996
Robert Helps: 29 September 1995
Skitch Henderson: 12 June 1996
Adolph Herseth: 8 May 1995
Gerhard Herz: 18 August 1996
Randall Hodgkinson: 18 June 1996
Barbara Horgan: 10 April 1995
Tedd Joselson: 27 February 1996
Sol Katz: 20 April 1995
Milton Kaye: 27 December 1995
Alan Kayes: 15 July 1996
Peter Kermani: 21 June 1996
Ken LaFave: 8 September 1996
Libby Larsen: 25 May 1995
Walter Levinsky: 14 February 1995
Martha Lomask: 1 July 1996
Milton Lomask: 1 July 1996
Bernard Lozea: 11 July 1996
Henry Martin: 28 July 1997
Alice Coltman Mayer: 5 May 1996
Norman Mellk: 28 July 1996
Homer Mensch: 24 May 1996
Jorge Mester: 16 August 1996
Frank Milburn: 19 August 1996
Mitch Miller: 5 June 1996
Richard Mohr: 31 July 1996
Carlos Moseley: 19 March 1995
R. Peter Munves: 18 May 1996
Ed Murphy: 18 April 1995
David Oppenheim: 31 May 1996
Donald Peck: 14 May 1996
Maurice Peress: 11 June 1996
Norma Perlman: 27 July 1995
Joan Peyser: 26 December 1994
George Kimball Plochmann: 2 March 1996
Jane Powell: 15 May 1996
André Previn: 14 July 1997
Jean Prostakoff: 9 July 1995
Kanti Rai: 14 July 1996
Susan Rai: 14 July 1996
Robert Reed: 9 January 1995; 6 January 1996
Fran Richard: 5 March 1996
Irwin Robinson: 31 July 1996
Richard Rodzinski: 19 August 1996
Seymour Rosen: 10 April 1997
Sophia Rosoff: 20 April 1995
Gerald Ross: 3 August 1996
Christopher Rouse: 9 March 1996
Jerome Ruzicka: 4 August 1996
Gerard Schwarz: 31 May 1996
Howard Scott: 18 April 1995
Martin Segal: 30 July 1996
Harvey Shapiro: 21 February 1995
Robert Sherman: 8 May 1996
Karen Sherry: 30 June 1997
Leonard Slatkin: 20 April 1995
Claire Speciner: 29 April 1995
Edith Stevens: 4 May 1996
Arthur Tracy: 20 May 1996
Dorothea Spreckles Wagner: 20 May 1996
David Walter: 24 February 1995
Alix Williamson: 11 July 1996
Toni Winter: 16 May 1995
Paul Wittke: 12 August 1996
Michael Wolf: 4 August 1996

Selected Discography

★ ★ ★ ★

All items are in compact-disc format.

As composer

American Ballads (1976)
London Philharmonic, Kenneth Klein, conductor. EMI CDC 7 49462 2; also Albany Records TROY202

American Salute (1942)
London Philharmonic, Kenneth Klein, conductor. EMI CDC 7 49462 2; also Albany Records TROY202
Cincinnati Wind Symphony, Eugene Corporon, conductor. Klavier KCD-11060

American Symphonette No. 2 (1938)
London Philharmonic, Kenneth Klein, conductor. EMI CDC 7 49462 2; also Albany Records TROY202

Benny's Gig for clarinet and double bass (1962)
Larry Combs, clarinet; Bradley Opland, bass; Deborah Sobol, piano. Summit DCD 172

Billion Dollar Baby (songs) (1945)
Helene Williams; Sheila Wormer; Craig Mason; Robert McCormick; Aldyn McKean; Leonard Lehrman, piano. Premier PRCD 1016

Cinerama Holiday ("Souvenirs of Paris," "On the Boulevard") (1955)
Seattle Symphony, Gerard Schwarz, conductor. Delos DC 3166

Concerto Grosso for four solo violins and orchestra (from *Audubon*) (1969)
Seattle Symphony, Gerard Schwarz, conductor. Delos DC 3166

"Cotillion" (from *Fall River Legend*) (1948)
London Symphony Orchestra, Morton Gould, conductor. Varese Sarabande VCD 47237

Dance Variations for two pianos and orchestra (1953)
Joshua Pierce and Anthony Jonas, pianos; Royal Philharmonic Orchestra, David Amos, conductor. Koch International Classics 3-7002-2

Declaration (1956)
National Symphony Orchestra, Howard Mitchell, conductor. BMG Classics 09026-61651-2

Enter Juliet (songs) (1977)
Helene Williams; Sheila Wormer; Craig Mason; Robert McCormick; Aldyn McKean; Leonard Lehrman, piano. Premier PRCD 1016

Fall River Legend (complete ballet) (1948)
National Philharmonic, Milton Rosenstock, conductor, Peter Brock, speaker for the jury. Albany Records TROY035

Fall River Legend (suite) (1948)
Morton Gould and his orchestra. BMG Classics 09026-61651-2
New Zealand Symphony Orchestra, James Sedaris, conductor. Koch International Classics 3-7380-2 H1

Fanfare for Freedom (1943)
London Symphony Orchestra, Morton Gould, conductor. Varese Sarabande VCD 47237

Festive Music (1964)
Maurice Murphy, trumpet; London Symphony Orchestra, Morton Gould, conductor. Varese Sarabande VCD 47237

Flute Concerto (1983–84)
Keith Brion, flute; Slovak Radio Symphony Orchestra, Bratislava, Zuohang Chen, conductor. Premier PRCD 1045

Formations (suite for marching band) (1964)
Seattle Symphony, Gerard Schwarz, conductor. Delos DC 3166

Foster Gallery (suite) (1939)
New Zealand Symphony Orchestra, JoAnn Falletta, conductor. Koch International Classics 3-7380-2 H1

"Guaracha" (*Latin American Symphonette* No. 4, third movement) (1941)
Morton Gould and his orchestra. BMG Classics 09026-61651-2

Holocaust (suite) (1978)
Krakow Philharmonic Orchestra, David Amos, conductor. Koch International Classics 3-7020-2 H1

Holocaust ("Theme," "Elegy") (1978)
Seattle Symphony, Gerard Schwarz, conductor. Delos DC 3166

Interplay (*American Concertette* No. 1) (1943)
Morton Gould, piano; Morton Gould and his orchestra. BMG Classics 09026-61651-2
William Tritt, piano; Cincinnati Pops Orchestra, Erich Kunzel, conductor. Telarc CD-80112

Latin American Symphonette No. 4 (1941)
London Symphony Orchestra, Morton Gould, conductor. Varese Sarabande VCD 47237
Hollywood Bowl Symphony Orchestra, Felix Slatkin, conductor. EMI CDM7 63738 2

Of Time and the River (1946)
The Gregg Smith Singers, Gregg Smith, director. Koch International Classics 3-7380-2-H1; also 3-7026-2 H1

"Pavanne" (*American Symphonette* No. 2, second movement) (1938)
Jeffrey Silberschlag, trumpet; Seattle Symphony, Gerard Schwarz, conductor. Delos DC 3166

Philharmonic Waltzes (1948)
London Symphony Orchestra, Morton Gould, conductor. Varese Sarabande VCD 47237

Piano Concerto (1938)
Randall Hodgkinson, piano; Albany Symphony Orchestra, David Alan Miller, conductor. Albany TROY300

Pieces of China (1985)
Miriam Conti, piano. Albany TROY299

"Quickstep" (Symphony No. 2 [*Symphony on Marching Tunes*], second movement) (1944)
London Symphony Orchestra, Morton Gould, conductor. Varese Sarabande VCD 47237

Quotations (1983)
New York Choral Society and Orchestra, John Daly Goodwin, conductor. Koch International Classics 3-7026-2 H1

Showpiece for orchestra (1954)
Albany Symphony Orchestra, David Alan Miller, conductor. Albany TROY300

"Solfegging" (from *A Cappella*) (1987)
Gregg Smith Singers, Gregg Smith, director. Koch International Classics 3-7026-2 H1

Something To Do (songs) (1976)
Helene Williams; Sheila Wormer; Craig Mason; Robert McCormick; Aldyn McKean; Leonard Lehrman, piano. Premier PRCD 1016

Spirituals for String Choir and Orchestra (1941)
London Symphony Orchestra, Walter Susskind, conductor. Bay Cities BCD 1016; also Everest EVC 9003

Spirituals for Strings (1959)
London Philharmonic, Kenneth Klein, conductor. EMI CDC 7 49462 2; also Albany TROY202

Stringmusic (1993)
Albany Symphony Orchestra, David Alan Miller, conductor. Albany TROY300

Symphony No. 4 (*West Point Symphony*) for band (1952)
Cincinnati Wind Symphony, Eugene Corporon, conductor. Klavier KCD-11042
Eastman Wind Ensemble, Frederick Fennell, conductor. Mercury Living Presence 434 320-2

"Tango" (*Latin American Symphonette* No. 4, second movement) (1941)
Morton Gould and his orchestra. BMG Classics 09026-61651-2

"Tolling" (from *A Cappella*) (1987)
Gregg Smith Singers, Gregg Smith, director. Koch International Classics 3-7026-2 H1

Two Pianos (1987)
Monique and Anne-Marie Mot, pianos. Rene Gailly International Productions CD 87 092

Windjammer (main title) (1958)
London Symphony Orchestra, Morton Gould, conductor. Varese Sarabande VCD 47237

World War I ("Prologue and Drum Waltz," "Sad Song," "Royal Hunt: Galop") (1964–65)
Seattle Symphony, Gerard Schwarz, conductor. Delos DC 3166

As arranger, orchestrator, pianist

Bizet: *Carmen* for orchestra
Morton Gould and his orchestra. BMG Classics 09026-68476-2

Gershwin: *Rhapsody in Blue*, Three Preludes, "Jazzbo Brown" piano solo from *Porgy and Bess*, suite from *Porgy and Bess*
Morton Gould, piano; Morton Gould and his orchestra. RCA Victor 09026 63276-2

Popular collections

A Musical Christmas Tree (various seasonal numbers arranged by Gould)
New Philharmonia, Chicago Symphony Orchestra, American Symphony Orchestra, Morton Gould and his orchestra. RCA Victor Gold Seal 7931-2-RG

Blues in the Night (blues arranged by Gould)
Morton Gould and his orchestra. RCA Victor 09026-68477-2

Brass and Percussion (American marches)
Morton Gould and his orchestra. RCA Victor 09026-61255-2

Digital Space (music from motion pictures)
London Symphony Orchestra, Morton Gould, conductor. Varese Sarabande VCD 47229

Jungle Drums (music of Lecuona, Ellington, Falla, Fernandez, and others, arranged by Gould)
Morton Gould and his orchestra. RCA Victor 09026-68173-2

Kern/Porter Favorites ("Night and Day," "I've Got You Under My Skin," and others, arranged by Gould)
Morton Gould and his orchestra. RCA Victor 09026-68478-2

Moon, Wind and Stars ("All Through the Night," "Stars in My Eyes," and others, arranged by Gould)
Morton Gould and his orchestra. RCA Victor 09026-68479-2

Morton Gould Conducts the London Symphony Orchestra (Ravel: *Bolero*; Shostakovich: *Festive Overture*; Weinberger: Polka and Fugue from *Schwanda the Bagpiper*; Turina: "Orgia"; Granados: "Intermezzo"; Ginastera: *Estancia Ballet Suite*)
London Symphony Orchestra, Morton Gould, conductor. Varese Sarabande VCD 47209

Selected Bibliography

★ ★ ★ ★

Anderson, David D. 1964. *Louis Bromfield*. New York: Twayne Publishers Inc.

Barnouw, Erik. 1966. *A History of Broadcasting in the United States*. Vol. 1, *A Tower in Babel*. New York: Oxford University Press.

———. 1968. *A History of Broadcasting in the United States*. Vol. 2, *The Golden Web*. New York: Oxford University Press.

Burton, Humphrey. 1994. *Leonard Bernstein*. New York: Doubleday.

Copland, Aaron, with Vivian Perlis. 1984. *Copland: 1900 through 1942*. New York: St. Martin's/Marek.

Daniel, Oliver. 1982. *Stokowski: A Counterpoint of View*. New York: Dodd, Mead and Co.

De Mille, Agnes. 1968. *Lizzie Borden: A Dance of Death*. Boston: Atlantic Monthly Press–Little, Brown and Co.

Evans, Lee. 1978. *Morton Gould: His Life and Music*. New York: Columbia University, Teachers College. Unpublished Ph.D. dissertation.

Evers, Alf. 1987. *Woodstock: History of an American Town*. Woodstock, N.Y.: The Overlook Press.

Ewen, David, 1952. *Complete Book of 20th Century Music*. New York: Prentice Hall.

Francisco, Charles. 1979. *The Radio City Music Hall: An Affectionate History of the World's Greatest Theater*. New York: E. P. Dutton.

Galkin, Elliott. 1988. *The History of Orchestral Conducting*. New York: Pendragon Press.

Gardner, Howard. 1993. *Creating Minds: An Anatomy of Creativity*. New York: Basic Books.

Gelb, Arthur, and Barbara Gelb. 1960. *O'Neill*. New York: Harper and Brothers.

Hart, Philip. 1994. *Fritz Reiner*. Evanston, Ill.: Northwestern University Press.

Kostelanetz, André, in collaboration with Gloria Hammond. 1981. *Echoes: Memoirs of André Kostelanetz*. New York: Harcourt Brace Jovanovich.

Lanza, Joseph. 1994. *Elevator Music: A Surreal History of Muzak, Easy-Listening, and Other Moodsong*. New York: Picador USA.

Lewis, Thomas S. W. 1991. *Empire of the Air: The Men Who Made Radio*. 1st ed. New York: HarperCollins.

Quill, Shirley. 1985. *Mike Quill: Himself*. Greenwich, Conn.: Devin-Adair.

Peyser, Joan. 1987. *Bernstein: A Biography*. New York: Beech Tree Books, William Morrow.

———. 1998. *The Memory of All That: The Life of George Gershwin*. New York: Billboard Books.

Ruttencutter, Helen Drees. 1985. *Previn*. New York: St. Martin's/Marek.

Secrest, Meryle. 1994. *Leonard Bernstein: A Life*. New York: Alfred A. Knopf.

Shostakovich, Dmitri. 1979. *Testimony: The Memoirs of Dmitri Shostakovich*. Solomon Volkov, ed. New York: Harper and Row.

Slonimsky, Nicolas. 1994. *Music Since 1900*. 5th ed. New York: Schirmer Books.

———, ed. 1994. *The Concise Baker's Biographical Dictionary of Musicians*. 8th ed. New York: Schirmer Books.

Smith, Anita M. 1959. *Woodstock: History and Hearsay*. Woodstock, N.Y.: Catskill Mountain Publishing Corp.

Struble, John Warthen. 1995. *The History of American Classical Music: MacDowell through Minimalism*. New York: Facts on File.

Trotter, William R. 1995. *Priest of Music: The Life of Dimitri Mitropoulos*. Portland, Oreg.: Amadeus Press.

Whiteside, Abby. 1997. *Abby Whiteside on Piano Playing*. Anthology reprint of *Indispensables of Piano Playing* and *Mastering the Chopin Etudes*. Portland, Oreg.: Amadeus Press.

Index

★ ★ ★ ★